Core Java® SE 9
for the Impatient

Second Edition

Core Java® SE 9
for the Impatient

Second Edition

Cay S. Horstmann

✦ Addison-Wesley

Boston • Columbus • Indianapolis • New York • San Francisco • Amsterdam • Cape Town
Dubai • London • Madrid • Milan • Munich • Paris • Montreal • Toronto • Delhi • Mexico City
São Paulo • Sydney • Hong Kong • Seoul • Singapore • Taipei • Tokyo

Library of Congress Control Number: 2017947587

ISBN-13: 978-0-13-469472-6
ISBN-10: 0-13-469472-4

1   17

To Chi—the most patient person in my life.

Contents

Preface

Java is now over twenty years old, and the classic book, *Core Java*, covers, in meticulous detail, not just the language but all core libraries and a multitude of changes between versions, spanning two volumes and well over 2,000 pages. However, if you just want to be productive with modern Java, there is a much faster, easier pathway for learning the language and core libraries. In this book, I don't retrace history and don't dwell on features of past versions. I show you the good parts of Java as it exists today, with Java 9, so you can put your knowledge to work quickly.

As with my previous "Impatient" books, I quickly cut to the chase, showing you what you need to know to solve a programming problem without lecturing about the superiority of one paradigm over another. I also present the information in small chunks, organized so that you can quickly retrieve it when needed.

Assuming you are proficient in some other programming language, such as C++, JavaScript, Objective C, PHP, or Ruby, with this book you will learn how to become a competent Java programmer. I cover all aspects of Java that a developer needs to know, including the powerful concepts of lambda expressions and streams. I tell you where to find out more about old-fashioned concepts that you might still see in legacy code, but I don't dwell on them.

A key reason to use Java is to tackle concurrent programming. With parallel algorithms and threadsafe data structures readily available in the Java library, the way application programmers should handle concurrent programming has completely changed. I provide fresh coverage, showing you how to use the powerful library features instead of error-prone low-level constructs.

Traditionally, books on Java have focused on user interface programming—but nowadays, few developers produce user interfaces on desktop computers. If you intend to use Java for server-side programming or Android programming, you will be able to use this book effectively without being distracted by desktop GUI code.

Finally, this book is written for application programmers, not for a college course and not for systems wizards. The book covers issues that application programmers need to wrestle with, such as logging and working with files—but you won't learn how to implement a linked list by hand or how to write a web server.

I hope you enjoy this rapid-fire introduction into modern Java, and I hope it will make your work with Java productive and enjoyable.

If you find errors or have suggestions for improvement, please visit http://horstmann.com/javaimpatient and leave a comment. On that page, you will also find a link to an archive file containing all code examples from the book.

Acknowledgments

My thanks go, as always, to my editor Greg Doench, who enthusiastically supported the vision of a short book that gives a fresh introduction to Java SE 9. Dmitry Kirsanov and Alina Kirsanova once again turned an XHTML manuscript into an attractive book with amazing speed and attention to detail. My special gratitude goes to the excellent team of reviewers for both editions who spotted many errors and gave thoughtful suggestions for improvement. They are: Andres Almiray, Gail Anderson, Paul Anderson, Marcus Biel, Brian Goetz, Marty Hall, Mark Lawrence, Doug Lea, Simon Ritter, Yoshiki Shibata, and Christian Ullenboom.

Cay Horstmann
San Francisco
July 2017

About the Author

Cay S. Horstmann is the author of *Java SE 8 for the Really Impatient* and *Scala for the Impatient* (both from Addison-Wesley), is principal author of *Core Java*™, *Volumes I and II, Tenth Edition* (Prentice Hall, 2016), and has written a dozen other books for professional programmers and computer science students. He is a professor of computer science at San Jose State University and is a Java Champion.

Fundamental Programming Structures

Topics in This Chapter

Chapter

In this chapter, you will learn about the basic data types and control structures of the Java language. I assume that you are an experienced programmer in some other language and that you are familiar with concepts such as variables, loops, function calls, and arrays, but perhaps with a different syntax. This chapter will get you up to speed on the Java way. I will also give you some tips on the most useful parts of the Java API for manipulating common data types.

The key points of this chapter are:

1. In Java, all methods are declared in a class. You invoke a nonstatic method on an object of the class to which the method belongs.

2. Static methods are not invoked on objects. Program execution starts with the static `main` method.

3. Java has eight primitive types: four signed integral types, two floating-point types, `char`, and `boolean`.

4. The Java operators and control structures are very similar to those of C or JavaScript.

5. The `Math` class provides common mathematical functions.

6. `String` objects are sequences of characters or, more precisely, Unicode code points in the UTF-16 encoding.

7. With the System.out object, you can display output in a terminal window. A Scanner tied to System.in lets you read terminal input.

8. Arrays and collections can be used to collect elements of the same type.

1.1 Our First Program

When learning any new programming language, it is traditional to start with a program that displays the message "Hello, World!". That is what we will do in the following sections.

1.1.1 Dissecting the "Hello, World" Program

Without further ado, here is the "Hello, World" program in Java.

```java
package ch01.sec01;

// Our first Java program

public class HelloWorld {
    public static void main(String[] args) {
        System.out.println("Hello, World!");
    }
}
```

Let's examine this program:

- Java is an object-oriented language. In your program, you manipulate (mostly) *objects* by having them do work. Each object that you manipulate belongs to a specific *class*, and we say that the object is an *instance* of that class. A class defines what an object's state can be and and what it can do. In Java, all code is defined inside classes. We will look at objects and classes in detail in Chapter 2. This program is made up of a single class HelloWorld.

- main is a *method*, that is, a function declared inside a class. The main method is the first method that is called when the program runs. It is declared as static to indicate that the method does not operate on any objects. (When main gets called, there are only a handful of predefined objects, and none of them are instances of the HelloWorld class.) The method is declared as void to indicate that it does not return any value. See Section 1.8.8, "Command-Line Arguments" (page 49) for the meaning of the parameter declaration String[] args.

- In Java, you can declare many features as public or private, and there are a couple of other visibility levels as well. Here, we declare the HelloWorld class and the `main` method as `public`, which is the most common arrangement for classes and methods.

- A *package* is a set of related classes. It is a good idea to place each class in a package so you can group related classes together and avoid conflicts when multiple classes have the same name. In this book, we'll use chapter and section numbers as package names. The full name of our class is `ch01.sec01.HelloWorld`. Chapter 2 has more to say about packages and package naming conventions.

- The line starting with `//` is a comment. All characters between `//` and the end of the line are ignored by the compiler and are meant for human readers only.

- Finally, we come to the body of the `main` method. In our example, it consists of a single line with a command to print a message to `System.out`, an object representing the "standard output" of the Java program.

As you can see, Java is not a scripting language that can be used to quickly dash off a few commands. It is squarely intended as a language for larger programs that benefit from being organized into classes, packages, and modules. (Modules are introduced in Chapter 15.)

Java is also quite simple and uniform. Some languages have global variables and functions as well as variables and methods inside classes. In Java, everything is declared inside a class. This uniformity can lead to somewhat verbose code, but it makes it easy to understand the meaning of a program.

 NOTE: You have just seen a `//` comment that extends to the end of the line. You can also have multiline comments between `/*` and `*/` delimiters, such as

```
/*
    This is the first sample program in Core Java for the Impatient.
    The program displays the traditional greeting "Hello, World!".
*/
```

There is a third comment style, called *documentation comment*, with `/**` and `*/` as delimiters, that you will see in the next chapter.

1.1.2 Compiling and Running a Java Program

To compile and run this program, you need to install the Java Development Kit (JDK) and, optionally, an integrated development environment (IDE). You should also download the sample code, which you will find at the companion website for this book, `http://horstmann.com/javaimpatient`. Since instructions for installing software don't make for interesting reading, I put them on the companion website as well.

Once you have installed the JDK, open a terminal window, change to the directory containing the ch01 directory, and run the commands

```
javac ch01/sec01/HelloWorld.java
java ch01.sec01.HelloWorld
```

The familiar greeting will appear in the terminal window (see Figure 1-1).

Note that two steps were involved to execute the program. The javac command *compiles* the Java source code into an intermediate machine-independent representation, called *byte codes*, and saves them in *class files*. The java command launches a *virtual machine* that loads the class files and executes the byte codes.

Once compiled, byte codes can run on any Java virtual machine, whether on your desktop computer or on a device in a galaxy far, far away. The promise of "write once, run anywhere" was an important design criterion for Java.

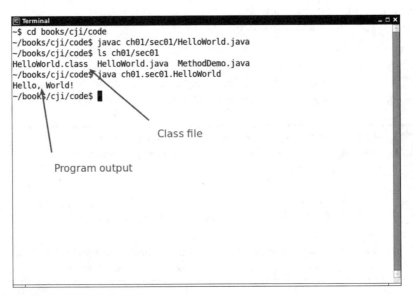

Figure 1-1 Running a Java program in a terminal window

NOTE: The `javac` compiler is invoked with the name of a *file*, with slashes separating the path segments, and an extension `.java`. The `java` virtual machine launcher is invoked with the name of a *class*, with dots separating the package segments, and no extension.

To run the program in an IDE, you need to first make a project, as described in the installation instructions. Then, select the `HelloWorld` class and tell the IDE to run it. Figure 1-2 shows how this looks in Eclipse. Eclipse is a popular IDE, but there are many other excellent choices. As you get more comfortable with Java programming, you should try out a few and pick one that you like.

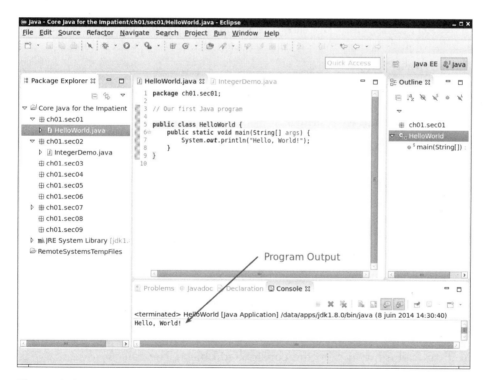

Figure 1-2 Running a Java program inside the Eclipse IDE

Congratulations! You have just followed the time-honored ritual of running the "Hello, World!" program in Java. Now we are ready to examine the basics of the Java language.

1.1.3 Method Calls

Let us have a closer look at the single statement of the `main` method:

```
System.out.println("Hello, World!");
```

`System.out` is an object. It is an *instance* of a class called `PrintStream`. The `PrintStream` class has methods `println`, `print`, and so on. These methods are called *instance methods* because they operate on objects, or instances, of the class.

To invoke an instance method on an object, you use the *dot notation*

   object.*methodName*(*arguments*)

In this case, there is just one argument, the string `"Hello, World!"`.

Let's try it with another example. Strings such as `"Hello, World!"` are instances of the `String` class. The `String` class has a method `length` that returns the length of a `String` object. To call the method, you again use the dot notation:

```
"Hello, World!".length()
```

The `length` method is invoked on the object `"Hello, World!"`, and it has no arguments. Unlike the `println` method, the `length` method returns a result. One way of using that result is to print it:

```
System.out.println("Hello, World!".length());
```

Give it a try. Make a Java program with this statement and run it to see how long the string is.

In Java, you need to *construct* most objects (unlike the `System.out` and `"Hello, World!"` objects, which are already there, ready for you to use). Here is a simple example.

An object of the `Random` class can generate random numbers. You construct a `Random` object with the `new` operator:

```
new Random()
```

After the class name is the list of construction arguments, which is empty in this example.

You can call a method on the constructed object. The call

```
new Random().nextInt()
```

yields the next integer that the newly constructed random number generator has to offer.

If you want to invoke more than one method on an object, store it in a variable (see Section 1.3, "Variables," page 14). Here we print two random numbers:

```
Random generator = new Random( );
System.out.println(generator.nextInt( ));
System.out.println(generator.nextInt( ));
```

 NOTE: The `Random` class is declared in the `java.util` package. To use it in your program, add an `import` statement, like this:

```
package ch01.sec01;

import java.util.Random;

public class MethodDemo {
    ...
}
```

We will look at packages and the `import` statement in more detail in Chapter 2.

1.1.4 JShell

In Section 1.1.2, "Compiling and Running a Java Program" (page 3), you saw how to compile and run a Java program. Java 9 introduces another way of working with Java. The JShell program provides a "read-evaluate-print loop" (REPL) where you type a Java expression, JShell evaluates your input, prints the result, and waits for your next input. To start JShell, simply type `jshell` in a terminal window (Figure 1-3).

JShell starts with a greeting, followed by a prompt:

```
|  Welcome to JShell -- Version 9-ea
|  For an introduction type: /help intro

jshell>
```

Now type any Java expression, such as

```
"Hello, World!".length( )
```

JShell responds with the result and another prompt.

```
$1 ==> 13

jshell>
```

Note that you do *not* type `System.out.println`. JShell automatically prints the value of every expression that you enter.

The $1 in the output indicates that the result is available in further calculations. For example, if you type

```
3 * $1 + 3
```

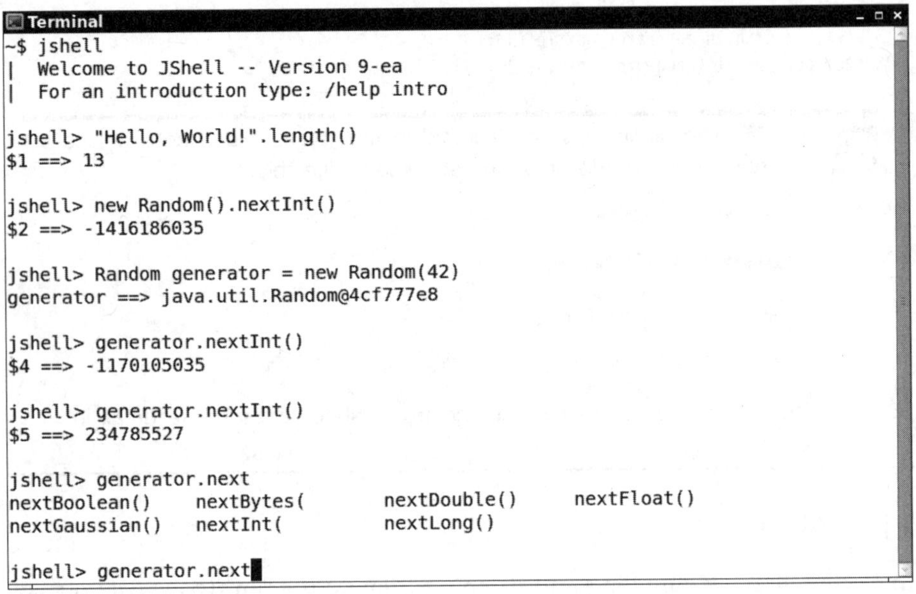

```
Terminal                                                              _ □ ×
~$ jshell
|  Welcome to JShell -- Version 9-ea
|  For an introduction type: /help intro

jshell> "Hello, World!".length()
$1 ==> 13

jshell> new Random().nextInt()
$2 ==> -1416186035

jshell> Random generator = new Random(42)
generator ==> java.util.Random@4cf777e8

jshell> generator.nextInt()
$4 ==> -1170105035

jshell> generator.nextInt()
$5 ==> 234785527

jshell> generator.next
nextBoolean()    nextBytes(       nextDouble()     nextFloat()
nextGaussian()   nextInt(         nextLong()

jshell> generator.next█
```

Figure 1-3 Running JShell

the response is

```
$2 ==> 42
```

If you need a variable many times, you can give it a more memorable name. You have to follow the Java syntax and specify both the type and the name (see Section 1.3, "Variables," page 14). For example,

```
jshell> int answer = 42
answer ==> 42
```

You can have JShell fill in the type for you. Type an expression and instead of hitting the Enter key, hit Shift+Tab and then the V key. For example, when you type

```
new Random()
```

followed by Shift+Tab and the V key, you get

```
jshell> Random  = new Random()
```

with the cursor positioned just before the = symbol. Now type a variable name and hit Enter:

```
jshell> Random generator = new Random()
generator ==> java.util.Random@3fee9989
```

Another useful feature is tab completion. Type

```
generator.
```

followed by the Tab key. You get a list of all methods that you can invoke on the `generator` variable:

```
jshell> generator.
doubles(       equals(        getClass()       hashCode()
ints(          longs(         nextBoolean()    nextBytes(
nextDouble()   nextFloat()    nextGaussian()   nextInt(
nextLong()     notify()       notifyAll()      setSeed(
toString()     wait(
```

Now type `ne` and hit the Tab key again. The method name is completed to `next`, and you get a shorter list:

```
jshell> generator.next
nextBoolean()    nextBytes(    nextDouble()    nextFloat()
nextGaussian()   nextInt(      nextLong()
```

Type a D and Tab again, and now the only completion, `nextDouble()`, is filled in. Hit Enter to accept it:

```
jshell> generator.nextDouble()
$8 ==> 0.9560346568377398
```

 NOTE: Note that in the autocompletion list, methods that require an argument are only followed by a left parenthesis, such as `nextInt(`, but methods without arguments have both parentheses, such as `nextBoolean()`.

To repeat a command, hit the ↑ key until you see the line that you want to reissue or edit. You can move the cursor in the line with the ← and → keys, and add or delete characters. Hit Enter when you are done. For example, hit ↑ and replace `Double` with `Int`, then hit Enter:

```
jshell> generator.nextInt()
$9 ==> -352355569
```

By default, JShell imports the following packages:

```
java.io
java.math
java.net
java.nio.file
java.util
java.util.concurrent
java.util.function
java.util.prefs
java.util.regex
java.util.stream
```

That's why you can use the `Random` class in JShell without any import statements. If you need to import another class, you can type the import statement at the JShell prompt. Or, more conveniently, you can have JShell search for it, by typing Shift+Tab and the I key. For example, type `Duration` followed by Shift+Tab and the I key. You get a list of potential actions:

```
jshell> Duration
0: Do nothing
1: import: java.time.Duration
2: import: javafx.util.Duration
3: import: javax.xml.datatype.Duration
Choice:
```

Type 1, and you receive a confirmation:

```
Imported: java.time.Duration
```

followed by

```
jshell> Duration
```

so that you can pick up where you left off, but with the import in place.

These commands are enough to get you started with JShell. To get help, type `/help` and Enter. To exit, type `/exit` and Enter, or simply Ctrl+D.

JShell makes it easy and fun to learn about the Java language and library, without having to launch a heavy-duty development environment, and without fussing with `public static void main`.

1.2 Primitive Types

Even though Java is an object-oriented programming language, not all Java values are objects. Instead, some values belong to *primitive types*. Four of these types are signed integer types, two are floating-point number types, one is the character type `char` that is used in the encoding for strings, and one is the `boolean` type for truth values. We will look at these types in the following sections.

1.2.1 Signed Integer Types

The signed integer types are for numbers without fractional parts. Negative values are allowed. Java provides the four signed integer types shown in Table 1-1.

Table 1-1 Java Signed Integer Types

Type	Storage requirement	Range (inclusive)
byte	1 byte	−128 to 127
short	2 bytes	−32,768 to 32,767
int	4 bytes	−2,147,483,648 to 2,147,483,647 (just over 2 billion)
long	8 bytes	−9,223,372,036,854,775,808 to 9,223,372,036,854,775,807

 NOTE: The constants `Integer.MIN_VALUE` and `Integer.MAX_VALUE` are the smallest and largest `int` values. The `Long`, `Short`, and `Byte` classes also have `MIN_VALUE` and `MAX_VALUE` constants.

In most situations, the `int` type is the most practical. If you want to represent the number of inhabitants of our planet, you'll need to resort to a `long`. The `byte` and `short` types are mainly intended for specialized applications, such as low-level file handling, or for large arrays when storage space is at a premium.

 NOTE: If the `long` type is not sufficient, use the `BigInteger` class. See Section 1.4.6, "Big Numbers" (page 23) for details.

In Java, the ranges of the integer types do not depend on the machine on which you will be running your program. After all, Java is designed as a "write once, run anywhere" language. In contrast, the integer types in C and C++ programs depend on the processor for which a program is compiled.

You write `long` integer literals with a suffix L (for example, `4000000000L`). There is no syntax for literals of type `byte` or `short`. Use the cast notation (see Section 1.4.4, "Number Type Conversions," page 20), for example, `(byte) 127`.

Hexadecimal literals have a prefix `0x` (for example, `0xCAFEBABE`). Binary values have a prefix `0b`. For example, `0b1001` is 9.

 CAUTION: Octal numbers have a prefix `0`. For example, `011` is 9. This can be confusing, so it seems best to stay away from octal literals and leading zeroes.

You can add underscores to number literals, such as `1_000_000` (or `0b1111_0100_0010_0100_0000`) to denote one million. The underscores are for human eyes only, the Java compiler simply removes them.

 NOTE: If you work with integer values that can never be negative and you really need an additional bit, you can, with some care, interpret signed integer values as unsigned. For example, a `byte` value b represents the range from −128 to 127. If you want a range from 0 to 255, you can still store it in a `byte`. Due to the nature of binary arithmetic, addition, subtraction, and multiplication will all work, provided they don't overflow. For other operations, call `Byte.toUnsignedInt(b)` to get an `int` value between 0 and 255, then process the integer value, and cast the result back to `byte`. The `Integer` and `Long` classes have methods for unsigned division and remainder.

1.2.2 Floating-Point Types

The floating-point types denote numbers with fractional parts. The two floating-point types are shown in Table 1-2.

Table 1-2 Floating-Point Types

Type	Storage requirement	Range
float	4 bytes	Approximately ±3.40282347E+38F (6–7 significant decimal digits)
double	8 bytes	Approximately ±1.79769313486231570E+308 (15 significant decimal digits)

Many years ago, when memory was a scarce resource, four-byte floating-point numbers were in common use. But seven decimal digits don't go very far, and nowadays, "double precision" numbers are the default. It only makes sense to use `float` when you need to store a large number of them.

Numbers of type `float` have a suffix F (for example, `3.14F`). Floating-point literals without an ⌐ suffix (such as `3.14`) have type `double`. You can optionally supply the D suffix (for example, `3.14D`).

NOTE: You can specify floating-point literals in hexadecimal. For example, 0.0009765625 = 2^{-10} can be written as `0x1.0p-10`. In hexadecimal notation, you use a `p`, not an `e`, to denote the exponent. (An `e` is a hexadecimal digit.) Note that, even though the digits are written in hexadecimal, the exponent (that is, the power of 2) is written in decimal.

There are special floating-point values `Double.POSITIVE_INFINITY` for ∞, `Double.NEGATIVE_INFINITY` for −∞, and `Double.NaN` for "not a number." For example, the result of computing `1.0 / 0.0` is positive infinity. Computing `0.0 / 0.0` or the square root of a negative number yields NaN.

 CAUTION: All "not a number" values are considered to be distinct from each other. Therefore, you cannot use the test `if (x == Double.NaN)` to check whether x is a NaN. Instead, call `if (Double.isNaN(x))`. There are also methods `Double.isInfinite` to test for ±∞, and `Double.isFinite` to check that a floating-point number is neither infinite nor a NaN.

Floating-point numbers are not suitable for financial calculations in which roundoff errors cannot be tolerated. For example, the command `System.out.println(2.0 - 1.1)` prints `0.8999999999999999`, not `0.9` as you would expect. Such roundoff errors are caused by the fact that floating-point numbers are represented in the binary number system. There is no precise binary representation of the fraction 1/10, just as there is no accurate representation of the fraction 1/3 in the decimal system. If you need precise numerical computations with arbitrary precision and without roundoff errors, use the `BigDecimal` class, introduced in Section 1.4.6, "Big Numbers" (page 23).

1.2.3 The char Type

The `char` type describes "code units" in the UTF-16 character encoding used by Java. The details are rather technical—see Section 1.5, "Strings" (page 24). You probably won't use the `char` type very much.

Occasionally, you may encounter character literals, enclosed in single quotes. For example, `'J'` is a character literal with value 74 (or hexadecimal 4A), the code unit for denoting the Unicode character "U+004A Latin Capital Letter J." A code unit can be expressed in hexadecimal, with the `\u` prefix. For example, `'\u004A'` is the same as `'J'`. A more exotic example is `'\u263A'`, the code unit for ☺, "U+263A White Smiling Face."

The special codes '\n', '\r', '\t', '\b' denote a line feed, carriage return, tab, and backspace.

Use a backslash to escape a single quote '\'' and a backslash '\\'.

1.2.4 The boolean Type

The boolean type has two values, false and true.

In Java, the boolean type is not a number type. There is no relationship between boolean values and the integers 0 and 1.

1.3 Variables

In the following sections, you will learn how to declare and initialize variables and constants.

1.3.1 Variable Declarations

Java is a strongly typed language. Each variable can only hold values of a specific type. When you declare a variable, you need to specify the type, the name, and an optional initial value. For example,

```
int total = 0;
```

You can declare multiple variables of the same type in a single statement:

```
int total = 0, count; // count is an uninitialized integer
```

Most Java programmers prefer to use separate declarations for each variable.

Consider this variable declation:

```
Random generator = new Random();
```

Here, the name of the object's class occurs twice. The first Random is the type of the variable generator. The second Random is a part of the new expression for constructing an object of that class.

1.3.2 Names

The name of a variable (as well as a method or class) must begin with a letter. It can consist of any letters, digits, and the symbols _ and $. However, the $ symbol is intended for automatically generated names, and you should not use it in your names. Finally, the _ by itself is not a valid variable name.

Here, letters and digits can be from *any* alphabet, not just the Latin alphabet. For example, π and élévation are valid variable names. Letter case is significant: count and Count are different names.

You cannot use spaces or symbols in a name. Finally, you cannot use a keyword such as double as a name.

By convention, names of variables and methods start with a lowercase letter, and names of classes start with an uppercase letter. Java programmers like "camel case," where uppercase letters are used when names consist of multiple words, like countOfInvalidInputs.

1.3.3 Initialization

When you declare a variable in a method, you must initialize it before you can use it. For example, the following code results in a compile-time error:

```
int count;
count++; // Error—uses an uninitialized variable
```

The compiler must be able to verify that a variable has been initialized before it has been used. For example, the following code is also an error:

```
int count;
if (total == 0) {
    count = 0;
} else {
    count++; // Error—count might not be initialized
}
```

You are allowed to declare a variable anywhere within a method. It is considered good style to declare a variable as late as possible, just before you need it for the first time. For example,

```
Scanner in = new Scanner(System.in); // See Section 1.6.1 for reading input
System.out.println("How old are you?");
int age = in.nextInt();
```

The variable is declared at the point at which its initial value is available.

1.3.4 Constants

The final keyword denotes a value that cannot be changed once it has been assigned. In other languages, one would call such a value a *constant*. For example,

```
final int DAYS_PER_WEEK = 7;
```

By convention, uppercase letters are used for names of constants.

You can also declare a constant outside a method, using the static keyword:

```
public class Calendar {
    public static final int DAYS_PER_WEEK = 7;
    ...
}
```

Then the constant can be used in multiple methods. Inside Calendar, you refer to the constant as DAYS_PER_WEEK. To use the constant in another class, prepend the class name: Calendar.DAYS_PER_WEEK.

 NOTE: The System class declares a constant

```
public static final PrintStream out
```

that you can use anywhere as System.out. This is one of the few examples of a constant that is not written in uppercase.

It is legal to defer the initialization of a final variable, provided it is initialized exactly once before it is used for the first time. For example, the following is legal:

```
final int DAYS_IN_FEBRUARY;
if (leapYear) {
    DAYS_IN_FEBRUARY = 29;
} else {
    DAYS_IN_FEBRUARY = 28;
}
```

That is the reason for calling them "final" variables. Once a value has been assigned, it is final and can never be changed.

 NOTE: Sometimes, you need a set of related constants, such as

```
public static final int MONDAY = 0;
public static final int TUESDAY = 1;
...
```

In this case, you can define an *enumerated type* like this:

```
enum Weekday { MONDAY, TUESDAY, WEDNESDAY, THURSDAY, FRIDAY,
    SATURDAY, SUNDAY };
```

Then, Weekday is a type with values Weekday.MONDAY and so on. Here is how you declare and initialize a Weekday variable:

```
Weekday startDay = Weekday.MONDAY;
```

We will discuss enumerated types in Chapter 4.

1.4 Arithmetic Operations

Java uses the familiar operators of any C-based language (see Table 1-3). We will review them in the following sections.

Table 1-3 Java Operators

Operators	Associativity
[] . () (method call)	Left
! ~ ++ -- + (unary) - (unary) () (cast) new	Right
* / % (modulus)	Left
+ -	Left
<< >> >>> (arithmetic shift)	Left
< > <= >= instanceof	Left
== !=	Left
& (bitwise and)	Left
^ (bitwise exclusive or)	Left
| (bitwise or)	Left
&& (logical and)	Left
|| (logical or)	Left
? : (conditional)	Left
= += -= *= /= %= <<= >>= >>>= &= ^= |=	Right

 NOTE: In this table, operators are listed by decreasing *precedence*. For example, since + has a higher precedence than <<, the value of 3 + 4 << 5 is (3 + 4) << 5. An operator is *left-associative* when it is grouped left to right. For example, 3 - 4 - 5 means (3 - 4) - 5. But -= is right-associative, and i -= j -= k means i -= (j -= k).

1.4.1 Assignment

The last row in Table 1-3 shows the assignment operators. The statement

```
x = expression;
```

sets x to the value of the right-hand side, replacing the previous value. When = is preceded by an operator, the operator combines the left- and right-hand sides and the result is assigned. For example,

```
amount -= 10;
```

is the same as

```
amount = amount - 10;
```

1.4.2 Basic Arithmetic

Addition, subtraction, multiplication, and division are denoted by + - * /. For example, 2 * n + 1 means to multiply 2 and n and add 1.

You need to be careful with the / operator. If both operands are integer types, it denotes integer division, discarding the remainder. For example, 17 / 5 is 3, whereas 17.0 / 5 is 3.4.

An integer division by zero gives rise to an exception which, if not caught, will terminate your program. (See Chapter 5 for more information on exception handling.) A floating-point division by zero yields an infinite value or NaN (see Section 1.2.2, "Floating-Point Types," page 12), without causing an exception.

The % operator yields the remainder. For example, 17 % 5 is 2, the amount that remains from 17 after subtracting 15 (the largest integer multiple of 5 that "fits" into 17). If the remainder of a % b is zero, then a is an integer multiple of b.

A common use is to test whether an integer is even. The expression n % 2 is 0 if n is even. What if n is odd? Then n % 2 is 1 if n is positive or -1 if n is negative. That handling of negative numbers is unfortunate in practice. Always be careful using % with potentially negative operands.

Consider this problem. You compute the position of the hour hand of a clock. An adjustment is applied, and you want to normalize to a number between 0 and 11. That is easy: (position + adjustment) % 12. But what if adjustment makes the position negative? Then you might get a negative number. So you have to introduce a branch, or use ((position + adjustment) % 12 + 12) % 12. Either way, it is a hassle.

TIP: In this case, it is easier to use the `Math.floorMod` method: `Math.floorMod(position + adjustment, 12)` always yields a value between 0 and 11.

Sadly, `floorMod` gives negative results for negative divisors, but that situation doesn't often occur in practice.

Java has increment and decrement operators:

```
n++; // Adds one to n
n--; // Subtracts one from n
```

As in other C-based languages, there is also a prefix form of these operators. Both `n++` and `++n` increment the variable `n`, but they have different values when they are used inside an expression. The first form yields the value before the increment, and the second the value after the increment. For example,

```
String arg = args[n++];
```

sets `arg` to `args[n]`, and *then* increments `n`. This made sense thirty years ago when compilers didn't do a good job optimizing code. Nowadays, there is no performance drawback in using two separate statements, and many programmers find the explicit form easier to read.

NOTE: One of the stated goals of the Java programming language is portability. A computation should yield the same results no matter which virtual machine executes it. However, many modern processors use floating-point registers with more than 64 bit to add precision and reduce the risk of overflow in intermediate steps of a computation. Java allows these optimizations, since otherwise floating-point operations would be slower and less accurate. For the small set of users who care about this issue, there is a `strictfp` modifier. When added to a method, all floating-point operations in the method are strictly portable.

1.4.3 Mathematical Methods

There is no operator for raising numbers to a power. Instead, call the `Math.pow` method: `Math.pow(x, y)` yields x^y. To compute the square root of x, call `Math.sqrt(x)`.

These are *static* methods that don't operate on objects. Like with `static` constants, you prepend the name of the class in which they are declared.

Also useful are `Math.min` and `Math.max` for computing the minimum and maximum of two values.

In addition, the `Math` class provides trigonometric and logarithmic functions as well as the constants `Math.PI` and `Math.E`.

 NOTE: The `Math` class provides several methods to make integer arithmetic safer. The mathematical operators quietly return wrong results when a computation overflows. For example, one billion times three (`1000000000 * 3`) evaluates to `-1294967296` because the largest `int` value is just over two billion. If you call `Math.multiplyExact(1000000000, 3)` instead, an exception is generated. You can catch that exception or let the program terminate rather than quietly continue with a wrong result. There are also methods `addExact`, `subtractExact`, `incrementExact`, `decrementExact`, `negateExact`, all with `int` and `long` parameters.

A few mathematical methods are in other classes. For example, there are methods `compareUnsigned`, `divideUnsigned`, and `remainderUnsigned` in the `Integer` and `Long` classes to work with unsigned values.

As discussed in the preceding section, some users require strictly reproducible floating-point computations even if they are less efficient. The `StrictMath` class provides strict implementations of mathematical methods.

1.4.4 Number Type Conversions

When an operator combines operands of different number types, the numbers are converted to a common type before they are combined. Conversion occurs in this order:

1. If either of the operands is of type `double`, the other one is converted to `double`.

2. If either of the operands is of type `float`, the other one is converted to `float`.

3. If either of the operands is of type `long`, the other one is converted to `long`.

4. Otherwise, both operands are converted to `int`.

For example, if you compute `3.14 + 42`, the second operand is converted to `42.0`, and then the sum is computed, yielding `45.14`.

If you compute `'J' + 1`, the char value `'J'` is converted to the `int` value `74`, and the result is the `int` value `75`. Read on to find out how to convert that value back to a `char`.

When you assign a value of a numeric type to a variable, or pass it as an argument to a method, and the types don't match, the value must be converted.

For example, in the assignment

```
double x = 42;
```

the value 42 is converted from int to double.

In Java, conversion is always legal if there is no loss of information:

- From byte to short, int, long, or double
- From short and char to int, long, or double
- From int to long or double

Conversion from an integer type to a floating-point type is always legal.

 CAUTION: The following conversions are legal, but they may lose information:

- From int to float
- From long to float or double

For example, consider the assignment

```
float f = 123456789;
```

Because a float only has about seven significant digits, f is actually 1.23456792E8.

To make a conversion that is not among these permitted ones, use a cast operator: the name of the target type in parentheses. For example,

```
double x = 3.75;
int n = (int) x;
```

In this case, the fractional part is discarded, and n is set to 3.

If you want to round to the nearest integer instead, use the Math.round method. That method returns a long. If you know the answer fits into an int, call

```
int n = (int) Math.round(x);
```

In our example, where x is 3.75, n is set to 4.

To convert an integer type to another one with fewer bytes, also use a cast:

```
int n = 1;
char next = (char)('J' + n); // Converts 75 to 'K'
```

In such a cast, only the last bytes are retained.

```
int n = (int) 3000000000L; // Sets n to -1294967296
```

 NOTE: If you worry that a cast can silently throw away important parts of a number, use the `Math.toIntExact` method instead. When it cannot convert a `long` to an `int`, an exception occurs.

1.4.5 Relational and Logical Operators

The `==` and `!=` operators test for equality. For example, `n != 0` is `true` when `n` is not zero.

There are also the usual `<` (less than), `>` (greater than), `<=` (less than or equal), and `>=` (greater than or equal) operators.

You can combine expressions of type `boolean` with the `&&` (and), `||` (or), and `!` (not) operators. For example,

```
0 <= n && n < length
```

is `true` if `n` lies between zero (inclusive) and `length` (exclusive).

If the first condition is `false`, the second condition is not evaluated. This "short circuit" evaluation is useful when the second condition could cause an error. Consider the condition

```
n != 0 && s + (100 - s) / n < 50
```

If `n` is zero, then the second condition, which contains a division by `n`, is never evaluated, and no error occurs.

Short circuit evaluation is also used for "or" operations, but then the evaluation stops as soon as an operand is `true`. For example, the computation of

```
n == 0 || s + (100 - s) / n >= 50
```

yields `true` if `n` is zero, again without evaluating the second condition.

Finally, the *conditional* operator takes three operands: a condition and two values. The result is the first of the values if the condition is `true`, the second otherwise. For example,

```
time < 12 ? "am" : "pm"
```

yields the string `"am"` if `time < 12` and the string `"pm"` otherwise.

NOTE: There are *bitwise* operators & (and), | (or), and ^ (xor) that are related to the logical operators. They operate on the bit patterns of integers. For example, since 0xF has binary digits 0...01111, n & 0xF yields the lowest four bits in n, n = n | 0xF sets the lowest four bits to 1, and n = n ^ 0xF flips them. The analog to the ! operator is ~, which flips all bits of its argument: ~0xF is 1...10000.

There are also operators which shift a bit pattern to left or right. For example, 0xF << 2 has binary digits 0...0111100. There are two right shift operators: >> extends the sign bit into the top bits, and >>> fills the top bits with zero. If you do bit-fiddling in your programs, you know what that means. If not, you won't need these operators.

CAUTION: The right-hand side argument of the shift operators is reduced modulo 32 if the left hand side is an int, or modulo 64 if the left hand side is a long. For example, the value of 1 << 35 is the same as 1 << 3 or 8.

TIP: The & (and) and | (or) operators, when applied to boolean values, force evaluation of both operands before combining the results. This usage is very uncommon. Provided that the right hand side doesn't have a side effect, they act just like && and ||, except they are less efficient. If you really need to force evaluation of the second operand, assign it to a boolean variable so that the flow of execution is plainly visible.

1.4.6 Big Numbers

If the precision of the primitive integer and floating-point types is not sufficient, you can turn to the BigInteger and BigDecimal classes in the java.math package. Objects of these classes represent numbers with an arbitrarily long sequence of digits. The BigInteger class implements arbitrary-precision integer arithmetic, and BigDecimal does the same for floating-point numbers.

The static valueOf method turns a long into a BigInteger:

```
BigInteger n = BigInteger.valueOf(876543210123456789L);
```

You can also construct a BigInteger from a string of digits:

```
BigInteger k = new BigInteger("9876543210123456789");
```

There are predefined constants BigInteger.ZERO, BigInteger.ONE, BigInteger.TWO, and BigInteger.TEN.

Java does not permit the use of operators with objects, so you must use method calls to work with big numbers.

```
BigInteger r = BigInteger.valueOf(5).multiply(n.add(k)); // r = 5 * (n + k)
```

In Section 1.2.2, "Floating-Point Types" (page 12), you saw that the result of the floating-point subtraction `2.0 - 1.1` is `0.8999999999999999`. The `BigDecimal` class can compute the result accurately.

The call `BigDecimal.valueOf(n, e)` returns a `BigDecimal` instance with value $n \times 10^{-e}$. The result of

```
BigDecimal.valueOf(2, 0).subtract(BigDecimal.valueOf(11, 1))
```

is exactly `0.9`.

1.5 Strings

A string is a sequence of characters. In Java, a string can contain any Unicode characters. For example, the string `"Java™"` or `"Java\u2122"` consists of the five characters J, a, v, a, and ™. The last character is "U+2122 Trade Mark Sign."

1.5.1 Concatenation

Use the `+` operator to concatenate two strings. For example,

```
String location = "Java";
String greeting = "Hello " + location;
```

sets greeting to the string `"Hello Java"`. (Note the space at the end of the first operand.)

When you concatenate a string with another value, that value is converted to a string.

```
int age = 42;
String output = age + " years";
```

Now output is `"42 years"`.

 CAUTION: If you mix concatenation and addition, then you may get unexpected results. For example,

```
"Next year, you will be " + age + 1 // Error
```

first concatenates age and then 1. The result is `"Next year, you will be 421"`. In such cases, use parentheses:

```
"Next year, you will be " + (age + 1) // OK
```

To combine several strings, separated with a delimiter, use the `join` method:

```
String names = String.join(", ", "Peter", "Paul", "Mary");
    // Sets names to "Peter, Paul, Mary"
```

The first argument is the separator string, followed by the strings you want to join. There can be any number of them, or you can supply an array of strings. (Arrays are covered in Section 1.8, "Arrays and Array Lists," page 43.)

It is somewhat inefficient to concatenate a large number of strings if all you need is the final result. In that case, use a `StringBuilder` instead:

```
StringBuilder builder = new StringBuilder();
while (more strings) {
    builder.append(next string);
}
String result = builder.toString();
```

1.5.2 Substrings

To take strings apart, use the `substring` method. For example,

```
String greeting = "Hello, World!";
String location = greeting.substring(7, 12); // Sets location to "World"
```

The first argument of the `substring` method is the starting position of the substring to extract. Positions start at `0`.

The second argument is the first position that should not be included in the substring. In our example, position `12` of `greeting` is the `!`, which we do not want. It may seem curious to specify an unwanted position, but there is an advantage: the difference `12 - 7` is the length of the substring.

Sometimes, you want to extract all substrings from a string that are separated by a delimiter. The `split` method carries out that task, returning an array of substrings.

```
String names = "Peter, Paul, Mary";
String[] result = names.split(", ");
    // An array of three strings ["Peter", "Paul", "Mary"]
```

The separator can be any regular expression (see Chapter 9). For example, `input.split("\\s+")` splits `input` at white space.

1.5.3 String Comparison

To check whether two strings are equal, use the `equals` method. For example,

```
location.equals("World")
```

yields `true` if `location` is in fact the string `"World"`.

CAUTION: Never use the `==` operator to compare strings. The comparison

```
location == "World" // Don't do that!
```

returns `true` only if `location` and `"World"` are *the same object in memory*. In the virtual machine, there is only one instance of each literal string, so `"World" == "World"` will be `true`. But if `location` was computed, for example, as

```
String location = greeting.substring(7, 12);
```

then the result is placed into a separate `String` object, and the comparison `location == "World"` will return `false`!

Like any object variable, a `String` variable can be `null`, which indicates that the variable does not refer to any object at all, not even an empty string.

```
String middleName = null;
```

To test whether an object is `null`, you do use the `==` operator:

```
if (middleName == null) ...
```

Note that `null` is not the same as an empty string `""`. An empty string is a string of length zero, whereas `null` isn't any string at all.

 CAUTION: Invoking any method on `null` causes a "null pointer exception." Like all exceptions, it terminates your program if you don't explicitly handle it.

 TIP: When comparing a string against a literal string, it is a good idea to put the literal string first:

```
if ("World".equals(location)) ...
```

This test works correctly even when `location` is `null`.

To compare two strings without regard to case, use the `equalsIgnoreCase` method. For example,

```
"world".equalsIgnoreCase(location);
```

returns `true` if `location` is `"World"`, `"world"`, `"WORLD"`, and so on.

Sometimes, one needs to put strings in order. The `compareTo` method tells you whether one string comes before another in dictionary order. The call

```
first.compareTo(second)
```

returns a negative integer (not necessarily -1) if `first` comes before `second`, a positive integer (not necessarily 1) if `first` comes after `second`, and 0 if they are equal.

The strings are compared a character at a time, until one of them runs out of characters or a mismatch is found. For example, when comparing `"word"` and `"world"`, the first three characters match. Since d has a Unicode value that is less than that of l, `"word"` comes first. The call `"word".compareTo("world")` returns -8, the difference between the Unicode values of d and l.

This comparison can be unintuitive to humans because it depends on the Unicode values of characters. `"blue/green"` comes before `"bluegreen"` because / happens to have a lower Unicode value than g.

 TIP: When sorting human-readable strings, use a `Collator` object that knows about language-specific sorting rules. See Chapter 13 for more information.

1.5.4 Converting Between Numbers and Strings

To turn an integer into a string, call the static `Integer.toString` method:

```
int n = 42;
String str = Integer.toString(n); // Sets str to "42"
```

A variant of this method has a second parameter, a radix (between 2 and 36):

```
String str2 = Integer.toString(n, 2); // Sets str2 to "101010"
```

 NOTE: An even simpler way of converting an integer to a string is to concatenate with the empty string: `"" + n`. Some people find this ugly, and it is slightly less efficient.

Conversely, to convert a string containing an integer to the number, use the `Integer.parseInt` method:

```
String str = "101010";
int n = Integer.parseInt(str); // Sets n to 101010
```

You can also specify a radix:

```
int n2 = Integer.parseInt(str, 2); // Sets n2 to 42
```

For floating-point numbers, use `Double.toString` and `Double.parseDouble`:

```
String str = Double.toString(3.14); // Sets str to "3.14"
double x = Double.parseDouble(str); // Sets x to 3.14
```

1.5.5 The String API

As you might expect, the String class has a large number of methods. Some of the more useful ones are shown in Table 1-4.

Table 1-4 Useful String Methods

Method	Purpose
boolean startsWith(String str) boolean endsWith(String str) boolean contains(CharSequence str)	Checks whether a string starts with, ends with, or contains a given string.
int indexOf(String str) int lastIndexOf(String str) int indexOf(String str, int fromIndex) int lastIndexOf(String str, int fromIndex)	Gets the position of the first or last occurrence of str, searching the entire string or the substring starting at fromIndex. Returns -1 if no match is found.
String replace(CharSequence oldString, CharSequence newString)	Returns a string that is obtained by replacing all occurrences of oldString with newString.
String toUpperCase() String toLowerCase()	Returns a string consisting of all characters of the original string converted to upper- or lowercase.
String trim()	Returns a string obtained by removing all leading and trailing white space.

Note that in Java, the String class is *immutable*. That is, none of the String methods modify the string on which they operate. For example,

```
greeting.toUpperCase()
```

returns a *new* string "HELLO, WORLD!" without changing greeting.

Also note that some methods have parameters of type CharSequence. This is a common supertype of String, StringBuilder, and other sequences of characters.

For a detailed description of each method, turn to the online Java API documentation at http://docs.oracle.com/javase/9/docs/api. Type the class name into the search box and select the matching type (in this case, java.lang.String), as shown in Figure 1-4.

Figure 1-4 Searching the API Documentation

You then get a page that documents each method (Figure 1-5). If you happen to know the name of a method, you can type its name into the search box.

In this book, I do not present the API in minute detail since it is easier to browse the API documentation. If you are not always connected to the Internet, you can download and unzip the documentation for offline browsing.

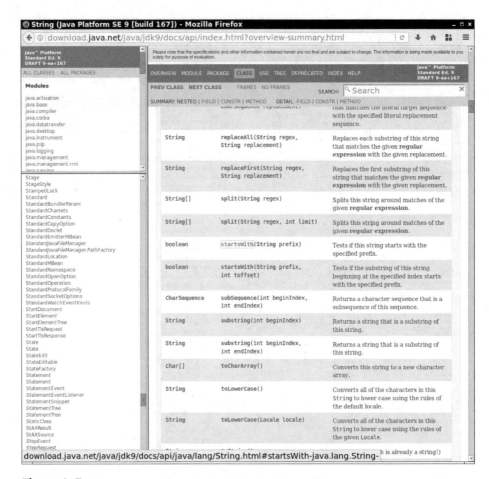

Figure 1–5 The String methods in the API Documentation

1.5.6 Code Points and Code Units

When Java was first created, it proudly embraced the Unicode standard that had been developed shortly before. The Unicode standard had been developed to solve a vexing issue of character encodings. Prior to Unicode, there were many incompatible character encodings. For English, there was near-universal agreement on the 7-bit ASCII standard that assigned codes between 0 and 127 to all English letters, the decimal digits, and many symbols. In Western Europe, ASCII was extended to an 8-bit code that contained accented characters such as ä and é. But in Russia, ASCII was extended to hold Cyrillic characters in the positions 128 to 255. In Japan, a variable-length encoding was used to encode English and Japanese characters. Every other country did something similar. Exchanging files with different encodings was a major problem.

Unicode set out to fix all that by assigning each character in all of the writing systems ever devised a unique 16-bit code between 0 and 65535. In 1991, Unicode 1.0 was released, using slightly less than half of the available 65536 code values. Java was designed from the ground up to use 16-bit Unicode characters, which was a major advance over other programming languages that used 8-bit characters. But then something awkward happened. There turned out to be many more characters than previously estimated—mostly Chinese ideographs. This pushed Unicode well beyond a 16-bit code.

Nowadays, Unicode requires 21 bits. Each valid Unicode value is called a *code point*. For example, the code point for the letter A is U+0041, and the mathematical symbol 𝕆 for the set of octonions (http://math.ucr.edu/home/baez/octonions) has code point U+1D546.

There is a variable-length backwards-compatible encoding, called UTF-16, that represents all "classic" Unicode characters with a single 16-bit value and the ones beyond U+FFFF as pairs of 16-bit values taken from a special region of the code space called "surrogate characters." In this encoding, the letter A is \u0041 and 𝕆 is \ud835\udd46.

Java suffers from having been born at the time between the transition from 16 to 21 bits. Instead of having strings that are pristine sequences of Unicode characters or code points, Java strings are sequences of *code units*, the 16-bit quantities of the UTF-16 encoding.

If you don't need to worry about Chinese ideographs and are willing to throw special characters such as 𝕆 under the bus, then you can live with the fiction that a String is a sequence of Unicode characters. In that case, you can get the ith character as

```
char ch = str.charAt(i);
```

and the length of a string as

```
int length = str.length();
```

But if you want to handle strings properly, you have to work harder.

To get the ith Unicode code point, call

```
int codePoint = str.codePointAt(str.offsetByCodePoints(0, i));
```

The total number of code points is

```
int length = str.codePointCount(0, str.length());
```

This loop extracts the code points sequentially:

```
int i = 0;
while (i < s.length()) {
    int j = s.offsetByCodePoints(i, 1);
    String codePoint = str.substring(i, j);
    ...
    i = j;
}
```

Alternatively, you can use the `codePoints` method that yields a *stream* of `int` values, one for each code point. We will discuss streams in Chapter 8. You can turn the stream into an array like this:

```
int[] codePoints = str.codePoints().toArray();
```

 NOTE: In the past, strings were always internally represented in the UTF-16 encoding, as arrays of `char` values. Nowadays, `String` objects use a `byte` array of ISO-8859-1 characters when possible. A future version of Java may switch to using UTF-8 internally.

1.6 Input and Output

To make our sample programs more interesting, they should be able to interact with the user. In the following sections, you will see how to read terminal input and how to produce formatted output.

1.6.1 Reading Input

When you call `System.out.println`, output is sent to the "standard output stream" and shows up in a terminal window. Reading from the "standard input stream" isn't quite as simple because the corresponding `System.in` object only has methods to read individual bytes. To read strings and numbers, construct a `Scanner` that is attached to `System.in`:

```
Scanner in = new Scanner(System.in);
```

The `nextLine` method reads a line of input.

```
System.out.println("What is your name?");
String name = in.nextLine();
```

Here, it makes sense to use the `nextLine` method because the input might contain spaces. To read a single word (delimited by whitespace), call

```
String firstName = in.next();
```

To read an integer, use the `nextInt` method.

```
System.out.println("How old are you?");
int age = in.nextInt();
```

Similarly, the nextDouble method reads the next floating-point number.

You can use the hasNextLine, hasNext, hasNextInt, and hasNextDouble methods to check that there is another line, word, integer, or floating-point number available.

```
if (in.hasNextInt()) {
    int age = in.nextInt();
    ...
}
```

The Scanner class is located in the java.util package. In order to use the class, add the line

```
import java.util.Scanner
```

to the top of your program file.

TIP: To read a password, you do not want to use the Scanner class since the input is visible in the terminal. Instead, use the Console class:

```
Console terminal = System.console();
String username = terminal.readLine("User name: ");
char[] passwd = terminal.readPassword("Password: ");
```

The password is returned in an array of characters. This is marginally more secure than storing the password in a String because you can overwrite the array when you are done.

TIP: If you want to read input from a file or write output to a file, you can use the redirection syntax of your shell:

```
java mypackage.MainClass < input.txt > output.txt
```

Now System.in reads from input.txt and System.out writes to output.txt. You will see in Chapter 9 how to carry out more general file input and output.

1.6.2 Formatted Output

You have already seen the println method of the System.out object for writing a line of output. There is also a print method that does not start a new line. That method is often used for input prompts:

```
System.out.print("Your age: "); // Not println
int age = in.nextInt();
```

Then the cursor rests after the prompt instead of the next line.

When you print a fractional number with `print` or `println`, all of its digits except trailing zeroes will be displayed. For example,

```
System.out.print(1000.0 / 3.0);
```

prints

```
333.3333333333333
```

That is a problem if you want to display, for example, dollars and cents. To limit the number of digits, use the `printf` method:

```
System.out.printf("%8.2f", 1000.0 / 3.0);
```

The *format string* `"%8.2f"` indicates that a floating-point number is printed with a *field width* of 8 and 2 digits of *precision*. That is, the printout contains two leading spaces and six characters:

```
333.33
```

You can supply multiple parameters to `printf`. For example:

```
System.out.printf("Hello, %s. Next year, you'll be %d.\n", name, age);
```

Each of the *format specifiers* that start with a % character is replaced with the corresponding argument. The *conversion character* that ends a format specifier indicates the type of the value to be formatted: `f` is a floating-point number, `s` a string, and `d` a decimal integer. Table 1-5 shows all conversion characters.

Table 1-5 Conversion Characters for Formatted Output

Conversion Character	Purpose	Example
d	Decimal integer	159
x or X	Hexadecimal integer	9f or 9F
o	Octal integer	237
f	Fixed floating-point	15.9
e or E	Exponential floating-point	1.59e+01 or 1.59E+01
g or G	General floating-point: e/E if the exponent is greater than the precision or < −4, f/F otherwise	15.9000 at the default precision of 6, 2e+01 at precision 1
a or A	Hexadecimal floating-point	0x1.fccdp3 or 0X1.FCCDP3
s or S	String	Java or JAVA
c or C	Character	j or J

(Continues)

Table 1-5 Conversion Characters for Formatted Output *(Continued)*

Conversion Character	Purpose	Example
b or B	boolean	false or FALSE
h or H	Hash code (see Chapter 4)	42628b2 or 42628B2
t or T	Date and time (obsolete; see Chapter 12 instead)	· —
%	The percent symbol	%
n	The platform-dependent line separator	—

In addition, you can specify flags to control the appearance of the formatted output. Table 1-6 shows all flags. For example, the comma flag adds grouping separators, and + yields a sign for positive numbers. The statement

```
System.out.printf("%,+.2f", 100000.0 / 3.0);
```

prints

```
+33,333.33
```

You can use the `String.format` method to create a formatted string without printing it:

```
String message = String.format("Hello, %s. Next year, you'll be %d.\n", name, age);
```

Table 1-6 Flags for Formatted Output

Flag	Purpose	Example
+	Prints sign for positive and negative numbers	+3333.33
space	Adds a space before positive numbers	_3333.33
-	Left-justifies field	3333.33___
0	Adds leading zeroes	003333.33
(	Encloses negative values in parentheses	(3333.33)
,	Uses group separators	3,333.33
# (for f format)	Always includes a decimal point	3333.
# (for x or o format)	Adds 0x or 0 prefix	0xcafe

(Continues)

Table 1-6 Flags for Formatted Output *(Continued)*

Flag	Purpose	Example
$	Specifies the index of the argument to be formatted; for example, %1$d %1$x prints the first argument in decimal and hexadecimal.	159 9f
<	Formats the same value as the previous specification; for example, %d %<x prints the same number in decimal and hexadecimal.	159 9f

1.7 Control Flow

In the following sections, you will see how to implement branches and loops. The Java syntax for control flow statements is very similar to that of other commonly used languages, in particular C/C++ and JavaScript.

1.7.1 Branches

The `if` statement has a condition in parentheses, followed by either one statement or a group of statements enclosed in braces.

```
if (count > 0) {
    double average = sum / count;
    System.out.println(average);
}
```

You can have an `else` branch that runs if the condition is not fulfilled.

```
if (count > 0) {
    double average = sum / count;
    System.out.println(average);
} else {
    System.out.println(0);
}
```

The statement in the `else` branch may be another `if` statement:

```
if (count > 0) {
    double average = sum / count;
    System.out.println(average);
} else if (count == 0) {
    System.out.println(0);
} else {
    System.out.println("Huh?");
}
```

When you need to test an expression against a finite number of constant values, use the `switch` statement.

```
switch (count) {
    case 0:
        output = "None";
        break;
    case 1:
        output = "One";
        break;
    case 2:
    case 3:
    case 4:
    case 5:
        output = Integer.toString(count);
        break;
    default:
        output = "Many";
        break;
}
```

Execution starts at the matching `case` label or, if there is no match, at the `default` label (if it is present). All statements are executed until a `break` or the end of the `switch` statement is reached.

CAUTION: It is a common error to forget a `break` at the end of an alternative. Then execution "falls through" to the next alternative. You can direct the compiler to be on the lookout for such bugs with a command-line option:

```
javac -Xlint:fallthrough mypackage/MainClass.java
```

With this option, the compiler will issue a warning message whenever an alternative does not end with a `break` or `return` statement.

If you actually want to use the fallthrough behavior, tag the surrounding method with the *annotation* `@SuppressWarnings("fallthrough")`. Then no warnings will be generated for that method. (An annotation supplies information to the compiler or another tool. You will learn all about annotations in Chapter 11.)

In the preceding example, the `case` labels were integers. You can use values of any of the following types:

- A constant expression of type `char`, `byte`, `short`, or `int` (or their corresponding wrapper classes `Character`, `Byte`, `Short`, and `Integer` that will be introduced in Section 1.8.3, "Array Lists," page 45)

- A string literal
- A value of an enumeration (see Chapter 4)

1.7.2 Loops

The `while` loop keeps executing its body while more work needs to be done, as determined by a condition.

For example, consider the task of summing up numbers until the sum has reached a target. For the source of numbers, we will use a random number generator, provided by the `Random` class in the `java.util` package.

```
Random generator = new Random();
```

This call gets a random integer between 0 and 9:

```
int next = generator.nextInt(10);
```

Here is the loop for forming the sum:

```
while (sum < target) {
    int next = generator.nextInt(10);
    sum += next;
    count++;
}
```

This is a typical use of a `while` loop. While the sum is less than the target, the loop keeps executing.

Sometimes, you need to execute the loop body before you can evaluate the condition. Suppose you want to find out how long it takes to get a particular value. Before you can test that condition, you need to enter the loop and get the value. In this case, use a `do/while` loop:

```
int next;
do {
    next = generator.nextInt(10);
    count++;
} while (next != target);
```

The loop body is entered, and `next` is set. Then the condition is evaluated. As long as it is fulfilled, the loop body is repeated.

In the preceding examples, the number of loop iterations was not known. However, in many loops that occur in practice, the number of iterations is fixed. In those situations, it is best to use the `for` loop.

This loop computes the sum of a fixed number of random values:

```
for (int i = 1; i <= 20; i++) {
    int next = generator.nextInt(10);
    sum += next;
}
```

This loop runs 20 times, with i set to 1, 2, ..., 20 in each loop iteration.

You can rewrite any for loop as a while loop. The loop above is equivalent to

```
int i = 1;
while (i <= 20) {
    int next = generator.nextInt(10);
    sum += next;
    i++;
}
```

However, with the while loop, the initialization, test, and update of the variable i are scattered in different places. With the for loop, they stay neatly together.

The initialization, test, and update can take on arbitrary forms. For example, you can double a value while it is less than the target:

```
for (int i = 1; i < target; i *= 2) {
    System.out.println(i);
}
```

Instead of declaring a variable in the header of the for loop, you can initialize an existing variable:

```
for (i = 1; i <= target; i++) // Uses existing variable i
```

You can declare or initialize multiple variables and provide multiple updates, separated by commas. For example,

```
for (int i = 0, j = n - 1; i < j; i++, j--)
```

If no initialization or update is required, leave them blank. If you omit the condition, it is deemed to always be true.

```
for (;;) // An infinite loop
```

You will see in the next section how you can break out of such a loop.

1.7.3 Breaking and Continuing

If you want to exit a loop in the middle, you can use the break statement. For example, suppose you want to process words until the user enters the letter Q. Here is a solution that uses a boolean variable to control the loop:

```
boolean done = false;
while (!done) {
    String input = in.next();
    if ("Q".equals(input)) {
        done = true;
    } else {
        Process input
    }
}
```

This loop carries out the same task with a `break` statement:

```
while (true) {
    String input = in.next();
    if (input.equals("Q")) break; // Exits loop
    Process input
}
// break jumps here
```

When the `break` statement is reached, the loop is exited immediately.

The `continue` statement is similar to `break`, but instead of jumping to the end of the loop, it jumps to the end of the current loop iteration. You might use it to skip unwanted inputs like this:

```
while (in.hasNextInt()) {
    int input = in.nextInt();
    if (input < 0) continue; // Jumps to test of in.hasNextInt()
    Process input
}
```

In a `for` loop, the `continue` statement jumps to the next update statement:

```
for (int i = 1; i <= target; i++) {
    int input = in.nextInt();
    if (n < 0) continue; // Jumps to i++
    Process input .
}
```

The `break` statement only breaks out of the immediately enclosing loop or `switch`. If you want to jump to the end of another enclosing statement, use a *labeled* `break` statement. Label the statement that should be exited, and provide the label with the `break` like this:

```
outer:
while (...) {
   ...
   while (...) {
      ...
      if (...) break outer;
      ...
   }
   ...
}
// Labeled break jumps here
```

The label can be any name.

 CAUTION: You label the top of the statement, but the break statement jumps to the *end*.

A regular break can only be used to exit a loop or switch, but a labeled break can transfer control to the end of any statement, even a block statement:

```
exit: {
   ...
   if (...) break exit;
   ...
}
// Labeled break jumps here
```

There is also a labeled continue statement that jumps to the next iteration of a labeled loop.

 TIP: Many programmers find the break and continue statements confusing. These statements are entirely optional—you can always express the same logic without them. In this book, I never use break or continue.

1.7.4 Local Variable Scope

Now that you have seen examples of nested blocks, it is a good idea to go over the rules for variable scope. A *local variable* is any variable that is declared in a method, including the method's parameter variables. The *scope* of a variable is the part of the program where you can access the variable. The scope of a local variable extends from the point where it is declared to the end of the enclosing block.

```
while (...) {
    System.out.println(...);
    String input = in.next(); // Scope of input starts here
    ...
    // Scope of input ends here
}
```

In other words, a new copy of input is created for each loop iteration, and the variable does not exist outside the loop.

The scope of a parameter variable is the entire method.

```
public static void main(String[] args) { // Scope of args starts here
    ...
    // Scope of args ends here
}
```

Here is a situation where you need to understand scope rules. This loop counts how many tries it takes to get a particular random digit:

```
int next;
do {
    next = generator.nextInt(10);
    count++;
} while (next != target);
```

The variable next had to be declared outside the loop so it is available in the condition. Had it been declared inside the loop, its scope would only reach to the end of the loop body.

When you declare a variable in a for loop, its scope extends to the end of the loop, including the test and update statements.

```
for (int i = 0; i < n; i++) { // i is in scope for the test and update
    ...
}
// i not defined here
```

If you need the value of i after the loop, declare the variable outside:

```
int i;
for (i = 0; !found && i < n; i++) {
    ...
}
// i still available
```

In Java, you cannot have local variables with the same name in overlapping scopes.

```
int i = 0;
while (...) {
    String i = in.next(); // Error to declare another variable i
    ...
}
```

However, if the scopes do not overlap, you can reuse the same variable name:

```
for (int i = 0; i < n / 2; i++) { ... }
for (int i = n / 2; i < n; i++) { ... } // OK to redefine i
```

1.8 Arrays and Array Lists

Arrays are a fundamental programming construct for collecting multiple items of the same type. Java has array types built into the language, and it also supplies an ArrayList class for arrays that grow and shrink on demand. The ArrayList class is a part of a larger collections framework that is covered in Chapter 7.

1.8.1 Working with Arrays

For every type, there is a corresponding array type. An array of integers has type int[], an array of String objects has type String[], and so on. Here is a variable that can hold an array of strings:

```
String[] names;
```

The variable isn't yet initialized. Let's initialize it with a new array. For that, we need the new operator:

```
names = new String[100];
```

Of course, you can combine these two statements:

```
String[] names = new String[100];
```

Now names refers to an array with 100 elements, which you can access as names[0] ... names[99].

 CAUTION: If you try to access an element that does not exist, such as names[-1] or names[100], an ArrayIndexOutOfBoundsException occurs.

The length of an array can be obtained as *array*.length. For example, this loop fills the array with empty strings:

```
for (int i = 0; i < names.length; i++) {
    names[i] = "";
}
```

NOTE: It is legal to use the C syntax for declaring an array variable, with the [] following the variable name:

```
int numbers[];
```

However, this syntax is unfortunate since it intertwines the name numbers and the type int[]. Few Java programmers use it.

1.8.2 Array Construction

When you construct an array with the new operator, it is filled with a default value.

- Arrays of numeric type (including char) are filled with zeroes.
- Arrays of boolean are filled with false.
- Arrays of objects are filled with null references.

CAUTION: Whenever you construct an array of objects, you need to fill it with objects. Consider this declaration:

```
BigInteger[] numbers = new BigInteger[100];
```

At this point, you do not have any BigInteger objects yet, just an array of 100 null references. You need to replace them with references to BigInteger objects:

```
for (int i = 0; i < 100; i++)
    numbers[i] = BigInteger.valueOf(i);
```

You can fill an array with values by writing a loop, as you saw in the preceding section. However, sometimes you know the values that you want, and you can just list them inside braces:

```
int[] primes = { 2, 3, 5, 7, 11, 13 };
```

You don't use the new operator, and you don't specify the array length. A trailing comma is allowed, which can be convenient for an array to which you keep adding values over time:

```
String[] authors = {
    "James Gosling",
    "Bill Joy",
    "Guy Steele",
    // Add more names here and put a comma after each name
};
```

Use a similar initialization syntax if you don't want to give the array a name—for example, to assign it to an existing array variable:

```
primes = new int[] { 17, 19, 23, 29, 31 };
```

 NOTE: It is legal to have arrays of length 0. You can construct such an array as `new int[0]` or `new int[] {}`. For example, if a method returns an array of matches, and there weren't any for a particular input, return an array of length 0. Note that this is not the same as `null`: If `a` is an array of length 0, then `a.length` is `0`; if `a` is `null`, then `a.length` causes a `NullPointerException`.

1.8.3 Array Lists

When you construct an array, you need to know its length. Once constructed, the length can never change. That is inconvenient in many practical applications. A remedy is to use the `ArrayList` class in the `java.util` package. An `ArrayList` object manages an array internally. When that array becomes too small or is insufficiently utilized, another internal array is automatically created, and the elements are moved into it. This process is invisible to the programmer using the array list.

The syntax for arrays and array lists is completely different. Arrays use a special syntax—the [] operator for accessing elements, the *Type*[] syntax for array types, and the `new` *Type*[*n*] syntax for constructing arrays. In contrast, array lists are classes, and you use the normal syntax for constructing instances and invoking methods.

However, unlike the classes that you have seen so far, the `ArrayList` class is a *generic class*—a class with a type parameter. Chapter 6 covers generic classes in detail.

To declare an array list variable, you use the syntax for generic classes and specify the type in angle brackets:

```
ArrayList<String> friends;
```

As with arrays, this only declares the variable. You now need to construct an array list:

```
friends = new ArrayList<>();
    // or new ArrayList<String>()
```

Note the empty <>. The compiler infers the type parameter from the type of the variable. (This shortcut is called the *diamond syntax* because the empty angle brackets have the shape of a diamond.)

There are no construction arguments in this call, but it is still necessary to supply the () at the end.

The result is an array list of size 0. You can add elements to the end with the add method:

```
friends.add("Peter");
friends.add("Paul");
```

Unfortunately, there is no initializer syntax for array lists. The best you can do is construct an array list like this:

```
ArrayList<String> friends = new ArrayList<>(List.of("Peter", "Paul"));
```

The List.of method yields an unmodifiable list of the given elements which you then use to construct an ArrayList.

You can add and remove elements anywhere in the ArrayList.

```
friends.remove(1);
friends.add(0, "Paul"); // Adds before index 0
```

To access elements, use method calls, not the [] syntax. The get method reads an element, and the set method replaces an element with another:

```
String first = friends.get(0);
friends.set(1, "Mary");
```

The size method yields the current size of the list. Use the following loop to traverse all elements:

```
for (int i = 0; i < friends.size(); i++) {
    System.out.println(friends.get(i));
}
```

1.8.4 Wrapper Classes for Primitive Types

There is one unfortunate limitation of generic classes: You cannot use primitive types as type parameters. For example, an ArrayList<int> is illegal. The remedy is to use a *wrapper class*. For each primitive type, there is a corresponding wrapper class: Integer, Byte, Short, Long, Character, Float, Double, and Boolean. To collect integers, use an ArrayList<Integer>:

```
ArrayList<Integer> numbers = new ArrayList<>();
numbers.add(42);
int first = numbers.get(0);
```

Conversion between primitive types and their corresponding wrapper types is automatic. In the call to add, an Integer object holding the value 42 was automatically constructed in a process called *autoboxing*.

In the last line of the code segment, the call to get returned an Integer object. Before assigning to the int variable, the object was *unboxed* to yield the int value inside.

 CAUTION: Conversion between primitive types and wrappers is almost completely transparent to programmers, with one exception. The == and != operators compare object references, not the contents of objects. A condition if (numbers.get(i) == numbers.get(j)) does not test whether the numbers at index i and j are the same. Just like with strings, you need to remember to call the equals method with wrapper objects.

1.8.5 The Enhanced for Loop

Very often, you want to visit all elements of an array. For example, here is how you compute the sum of all elements in an array of numbers:

```
int sum = 0;
for (int i = 0; i < numbers.length; i++) {
    sum += numbers[i];
}
```

As this loop is so common, there is a convenient shortcut, called the *enhanced* for loop:

```
int sum = 0;
for (int n : numbers) {
    sum += n;
}
```

The loop variable of the enhanced for loop traverses the elements of the array, not the index values. The variable n is assigned to numbers[0], numbers[1], and so on.

You can also use the enhanced for loop with array lists. If friends is an array list of strings, you can print them all with the loop

```
for (String name : friends) {
    System.out.println(name);
}
```

1.8.6 Copying Arrays and Array Lists

You can copy one array variable into another, but then both variables will refer to the same array, as shown in Figure 1-6.

```
int[] numbers = primes;
numbers[5] = 42; // Now primes[5] is also 42
```

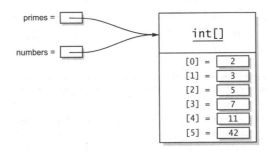

Figure 1-6 Two variables referencing the same array

If you don't want this sharing, you need to make a copy of the array. Use the static `Arrays.copyOf` method.

```
int[] copiedPrimes = Arrays.copyOf(primes, primes.length);
```

This method constructs a new array of the desired length and copies the elements of the original array into it.

Array list references work the same way:

```
ArrayList<String> people = friends;
people.set(0, "Mary"); // Now friends.get(0) is also "Mary"
```

To copy an array list, construct a new array list from the existing one:

```
ArrayList<String> copiedFriends = new ArrayList<>(friends);
```

That constructor can also be used to copy an array into an array list. Wrap the array into an immutable list, using the `List.of` method, and then construct an `ArrayList`:

```
String[] names = ...;
ArrayList<String> friends = new ArrayList<>(List.of(names));
```

You can also copy an array list into an array. For depressing reasons of backward compatibility that I will explain in Chapter 6, you must supply an array of the correct type.

```
String[] names = friends.toArray(new String[0]);
```

 NOTE: There is no easy way to convert between primitive type arrays and the corresponding array lists of wrapper classes. For example, to convert between an `int[]` and an `ArrayList<Integer>`, you need an explicit loop or an `IntStream` (see Chapter 8).

1.8.7 Array Algorithms

The `Arrays` and `Collections` classes provide implementations of common algorithms for arrays and array lists. Here is how to fill an array or an array list:

```
Arrays.fill(numbers, 0); // int[] array
Collections.fill(friends, ""); // ArrayList<String>
```

To sort an array or array list, use the `sort` method:

```
Arrays.sort(names);
Collections.sort(friends);
```

 NOTE: For arrays (but not array lists), you can use the `parallelSort` method that distributes the work over multiple processors if the array is large.

The `Arrays.toString` method yields a string representation of an array. This is particularly useful to print an array for debugging.

```
System.out.println(Arrays.toString(primes));
    // Prints [2, 3, 5, 7, 11, 13]
```

Array lists have a `toString` method that yields the same representation.

```
String elements = friends.toString();
    // Sets elements to "[Peter, Paul, Mary]"
```

For printing, you don't even need to call it—the `println` method takes care of that.

```
System.out.println(friends);
    // Calls friends.toString() and prints the result
```

There are a couple of useful algorithms for array lists that have no counterpart for arrays.

```
Collections.reverse(names); // Reverses the elements
Collections.shuffle(names); // Randomly shuffles the elements
```

1.8.8 Command–Line Arguments

As you have already seen, the `main` method of every Java program has a parameter that is a string array:

```
public static void main(String[] args)
```

When a program is executed, this parameter is set to the arguments specified on the command line.

For example, consider this program:

```
public class Greeting {
    public static void main(String[] args) {
        for (int i = 0; i < args.length; i++) {
            String arg = args[i];
            if (arg.equals("-h")) arg = "Hello";
            else if (arg.equals("-g")) arg = "Goodbye";
            System.out.println(arg);
        }
    }
}
```

If the program is called as

```
java Greeting -g cruel world
```

then `args[0]` is `"-g"`, `args[1]` is `"cruel"`, and `args[2]` is `"world"`.

Note that neither `"java"` nor `"Greeting"` are passed to the `main` method.

1.8.9 Multidimensional Arrays

Java does not have true multidimensional arrays. They are implemented as arrays of arrays. For example, here is how you declare and implement a two-dimensional array of integers:

```
int[][] square = {
    { 16, 3, 2, 13 },
    { 5, 10, 11, 8 },
    { 9, 6, 7, 12 },
    { 4, 15, 14, 1}
};
```

Technically, this is a one-dimensional array of `int[]` arrays—see Figure 1-7.

To access an element, use two bracket pairs:

```
int element = square[1][2]; // Sets element to 11
```

The first index selects the row array `square[1]`. The second index picks the element from that row.

You can even swap rows:

```
int[] temp = square[0];
square[0] = square[1];
square[1] = temp;
```

If you do not provide an initial value, you must use the `new` operator and specify the number of rows and columns.

```
int[][] square = new int[4][4]; // First rows, then columns
```

Behind the scenes, an array of rows is filled with an array for each row.

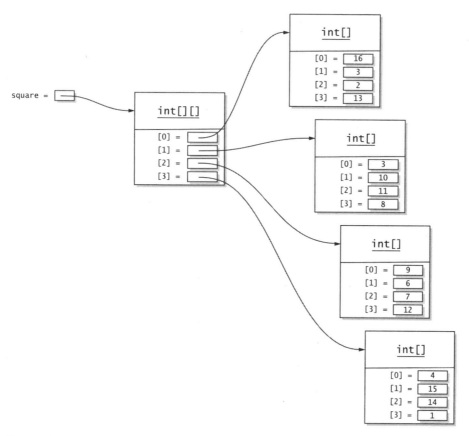

Figure 1-7 A two-dimensional array

There is no requirement that the row arrays have equal length. For example,
you can store the Pascal triangle:

```
1
1 1
1 2 1
1 3 3 1
1 4 6 4 1
...
```

First construct an array of n rows:

```
int[][] triangle = new int[n][];
```

Then construct each row in a loop and fill it.

```
for (int i = 0; i < n; i++) {
    triangle[i] = new int[i + 1];
    triangle[i][0] = 1;
    triangle[i][i] = 1;
    for (int j = 1; j < i; j++) {
        triangle[i][j] = triangle[i - 1][j - 1] + triangle[i - 1][j];
    }
}
```

To traverse a two-dimensional array, you need two loops, one for the rows and one for the columns:

```
for (int r = 0; r < triangle.length; r++) {
    for (int c = 0; c < triangle[r].length; c++) {
        System.out.printf("%4d", triangle[r][c]);
    }
    System.out.println();
}
```

You can also use two enhanced `for` loops:

```
for (int[] row : triangle) {
    for (int element : row) {
        System.out.printf("%4d", element);
    }
    System.out.println();
}
```

These loops work for square arrays as well as arrays with varying row lengths.

 TIP: To print out a list of the elements of a two-dimensional array for debugging, call

```
System.out.println(Arrays.deepToString(triangle));
    // Prints [[1], [1, 1], [1, 2, 1], [1, 3, 3, 1], [1, 4, 6, 4, 1], ...]
```

 NOTE: There are no two-dimensional array lists, but you can declare a variable of type `ArrayList<ArrayList<Integer>>` and build up the rows yourself.

1.9 Functional Decomposition

If your `main` method gets too long, you can decompose your program into multiple classes, as you will see in Chapter 2. However, for simple programs, you can place your program's code into separate methods in the same class. For reasons that will become clear in Chapter 2, these methods must be declared with the `static` modifier, just as the `main` method itself.

1.9.1 Declaring and Calling Static Methods

When you declare a method, provide the type of the return value (or `void` if the method doesn't return anything), the method name, and the types and names of the parameters in the *method header*. Then provide the implementation in the *method body*. Use a `return` statement to return the result.

```
public static double average(double x, double y) {
    double sum = x + y;
    return sum / 2;
}
```

Place the method in the same class as the `main` method. It doesn't matter if it's above or below `main`. Then, call it like this:

```
public static void main(String[] args) {
    double a = ...;
    double b = ...;
    double result = average(a, b);
    ...
}
```

1.9.2 Array Parameters and Return Values

You can pass arrays into methods. The method simply receives a reference to the array, through which it can modify it. This method swaps two elements in an array:

```
public static void swap(int[] values, int i, int j) {
    int temp = values[i];
    values[i] = values[j];
    values[j] = temp;
}
```

Methods can return arrays. This method returns an array consisting of the first and last values of a given array (which is not modified):

```
public static int[] firstLast(int[] values) {
    if (values.length == 0) return new int[0];
    else return new int[] { values[0], values[values.length - 1] };
}
```

1.9.3 Variable Arguments

Some methods allow the caller to supply a variable number of arguments. You have already seen such a method: `printf`. For example, the calls

```
System.out.printf("%d", n);
```

and

```
System.out.printf("%d %s", n, "widgets");
```

both call the same method, even though one call has two arguments and the other has three.

Let us define an `average` method that works the same way, so we can call `average` with as many arguments as we like, for example, `average(3, 4.5, -5, 0)`. Declare a "varargs" parameter with ... after the type:

```
public static double average(double... values)
```

The parameter is actually an array of type `double`. When the method is called, an array is created and filled with the arguments. In the method body, you use it as you would any other array.

```
public static double average(double... values) {
    double sum = 0;
    for (double v : values) sum += v;
    return values.length == 0 ? 0 : sum / values.length;
}
```

Now you can call

```
double avg = average(3, 4.5, -5, 0);
```

If you already have the arguments in an array, you don't have to unpack them. You can pass the array instead of the list of arguments:

```
double[] scores = { 3, 4.5, -5, 0 };
double avg = average(scores);
```

The variable parameter must be the *last* parameter of the method, but you can have other parameters before it. For example, this method ensures that there is at least one argument:

```
public static double max(double first, double... rest) {
    double result = first;
    for (double v : rest) result = Math.max(v, result);
    return result;
}
```

Exercises

1. Write a program that reads an integer and prints it in binary, octal, and hexadecimal. Print the reciprocal as a hexadecimal floating-point number.

2. Write a program that reads an integer angle (which may be positive or negative) and normalizes it to a value between 0 and 359 degrees. Try it first with the % operator, then with `floorMod`.

3. Using only the conditional operator, write a program that reads three integers and prints the largest. Repeat with `Math.max`.

4. Write a program that prints the smallest and largest positive `double` values. Hint: Look up `Math.nextUp` in the Java API.

5. What happens when you cast a `double` to an `int` that is larger than the largest possible `int` value? Try it out.

6. Write a program that computes the factorial $n! = 1 \times 2 \times \ldots \times n$, using `BigInteger`. Compute the factorial of 1000.

7. Write a program that reads in two integers between 0 and 4294967295, stores them in `int` variables, and computes and displays their unsigned sum, difference, product, quotient, and remainder. Do not convert them to `long` values.

8. Write a program that reads a string and prints all of its nonempty substrings.

9. Section 1.5.3, "String Comparison" (page 25) has an example of two strings s and t so that `s.equals(t)` but `s != t`. Come up with a different example that doesn't use `substring`).

10. Write a program that produces a random string of letters and digits by generating a random `long` value and printing it in base 36.

11. Write a program that reads a line of text and prints all characters that are not ASCII, together with their Unicode values.

12. The Java Development Kit includes a file `src.zip` with the source code of the Java library. Unzip and, with your favorite text search tool, find usages of the labeled `break` and `continue` sequences. Take one and rewrite it without a labeled statement.

13. Write a program that prints a lottery combination, picking six distinct numbers between 1 and 49. To pick six distinct numbers, start with an array list filled with 1...49. Pick a random index and remove the element. Repeat six times. Print the result in sorted order.

14. Write a program that reads a two-dimensional array of integers and determines whether it is a magic square (that is, whether the sum of all rows, all columns, and the diagonals is the same). Accept lines of input that you break up into individual integers, and stop when the user enters a blank line. For example, with the input

```
16  3  2 13
 5 10 11  8
 9  6  7 12
 4 15 14  1
(Blank line)
```

your program should respond affirmatively.

15. Write a program that stores Pascal's triangle up to a given n in an `ArrayList<ArrayList<Integer>>`.

16. Improve the `average` method so that it is called with at least one parameter.

Object-Oriented Programming

Topics in This Chapter

Chapter 2

In object-oriented programming, work is carried out by collaborating objects whose behavior is defined by the classes to which they belong. Java was one of the first mainstream programming languages to fully embrace object-oriented programming. As you have already seen, in Java every method is declared in a class and, except for a few primitive types, every value is an object. In this chapter, you will learn how to implement your own classes and methods.

The key points of this chapter are:

1. Mutator methods change the state of an object; accessor methods don't.

2. In Java, variables don't hold objects; they hold references to objects.

3. Instance variables and method implementations are declared inside the class declaration.

4. An instance method is invoked on an object, which is accessible through the this reference.

5. A constructor has the same name as the class. A class can have multiple (overloaded) constructors.

6. Static variables don't belong to any objects. Static methods are not invoked on objects.

7. Classes are organized into packages. Use import declarations so that you don't have to use the package name in your programs.

8. Classes can be nested in other classes.

9. An inner class is a nonstatic nested class. Its instances have a reference to the object of the enclosing class that constructed it.

10. The `javadoc` utility processes source files, producing HTML files with declarations and programmer-supplied comments.

2.1 Working with Objects

In ancient times, before objects were invented, you wrote programs by calling *functions*. When you call a function, it returns a result that you use without worrying how it was computed. Functions have an important benefit: they allow work to be shared. You can call a function that someone else wrote without having to know how it does its task.

Objects add another dimension. Each object can have its own *state*. The state affects the results that you get from calling a method. For example, if `in` is a `Scanner` object and you call `in.next()`, the object remembers what was read before and gives you the next input token.

When you use objects that someone else implemented and invoke methods on them, you do not need to know what goes on under the hood. This principle, called *encapsulation*, is a key concept of object-oriented programming.

At some point, you may want to make your work available for other programmers by providing them with objects they can use. In Java, you provide a *class*—a mechanism for creating and using objects with the same behavior.

Consider a common task: manipulation of calendar dates. Calendars are somewhat messy, with varying month lengths and leap years, not to mention leap seconds. It makes sense to have experts who figure out those messy details and who provide implementations that other programmers can use. In this situation, objects arise naturally. A date is an object whose methods can provide information such as "on what weekday does this date fall" and "what date is tomorrow."

In Java, experts who understand date computations provided classes for dates and other date-related concepts such as weekdays. If you want to do computations with dates, use one of those classes to create date objects and invoke methods on them, such as a method that yields the weekday or the next date.

Few of us want to ponder the details of date arithmetic, but you are probably an expert in some other area. To enable other programmers to leverage your knowledge, you can provide them with classes. And even if you are not enabling other programmers, you will find it useful in your own work to use classes so that your programs are structured in a coherent way.

Before learning how to declare your own classes, let us run through a nontrivial example of using objects.

The Unix program `cal` prints a calendar for a given month and year, in a format similar to the following:

```
Mon Tue Wed Thu Fri Sat Sun
                          1
  2   3   4   5   6   7   8
  9  10  11  12  13  14  15
 16  17  18  19  20  21  22
 23  24  25  26  27  28  29
 30
```

How can you implement such a program? With the standard Java library, you use the `LocalDate` class to express a date at some unspecified location. We need an object of that class representing the first of the month. Here is how you get one:

```
LocalDate date = LocalDate.of(year, month, 1);
```

To advance the date, you call `date.plusDays(1)`. The result is a newly constructed `LocalDate` object that is one day further. In our application, we simply reassign the result to the `date` variable:

```
date = date.plusDays(1);
```

You apply methods to obtain information about a date, such as the month on which it falls. We need that information so that we can keep printing while we are still in the same month.

```
while (date.getMonthValue() == month) {
    System.out.printf("%4d", date.getDayOfMonth());
    date = date.plusDays(1);
    ...
}
```

Another method yields the weekday on which a date falls.

```
DayOfWeek weekday = date.getDayOfWeek();
```

You get back an object of another class `DayOfWeek`. In order to compute the indentation of the first day of the month in the calendar, we need know the numerical value of the weekday. There is a method for that:

```
int value = weekday.getValue();
for (int i = 1; i < value; i++)
    System.out.print("    ");
```

The getValue method follows the international convention where the weekend comes at the end of the week, returning 1 for Monday, 2 for Tuesday, and so on. Sunday has value 7.

 NOTE: You can *chain* method calls, like this:

```
int value = date.getDayOfWeek().getValue();
```

The first method call is applied to the date object, and it returns a DayOfWeek object. The getValue method is then invoked on the returned object.

You will find the complete program in the book's companion code. It was easy to solve the problem of printing a calendar because the designers of the LocalDate class provided us with a useful set of methods. In this chapter, you will learn how to implement methods for your own classes.

2.1.1 Accessor and Mutator Methods

Consider again the method call date.plusDays(1). There are two ways in which the designers of the LocalDate class could have implemented the plusDays method. They could make it change the state of the date object and return no result. Or they could leave date unchanged and return a newly constructed LocalDate object. As you can see, they chose to do the latter.

We say that a method is a *mutator* if it changes the object on which it was invoked. It is an *accessor* if it leaves the object unchanged. The plusDays method of the LocalDate class is an accessor.

In fact, *all* methods of the LocalDate class are accessors. This situation is increasingly common because mutation can be risky, particularly if two computations mutate an object simultaneously. Nowadays, most computers have multiple processing units, and safe concurrent access is a serious issue. One way to address this issue is to make objects *immutable* by providing only accessor methods.

Still, there are many situations where mutation is desirable. The add method of the ArrayList class is an example of a mutator. After calling add, the array list object is changed.

```
ArrayList<String> friends = new ArrayList<>();
    // friends is empty
friends.add("Peter");
    // friends has size 1
```

2.1.2 Object References

In some programming languages (such as C++), a variable can actually hold the object—that is, the bits that make up the object's state. In Java, that is not the case. A variable can only hold a *reference* to an object. The actual object is elsewhere, and the reference is some implementation-dependent way of locating the object (see Figure 2-1).

 NOTE: References behave like pointers in C and C++, except that they are perfectly safe. In C and C++, you can modify pointers and use them to overwrite arbitrary memory locations. With a Java reference, you can only access a specific object.

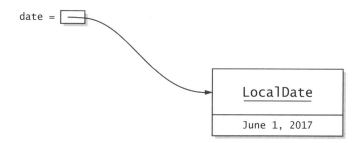

Figure 2-1 An object reference

When you assign a variable holding an object reference to another, you have two references to the same object.

```
ArrayList<String> people = friends;
    // Now people and friends refer to the same object
```

If you mutate the shared object, the mutation is observable through both references. Consider the call

```
people.add("Paul");
```

Now the array list `people` has size 2, and so does `friends` (see Figure 2-2). (Of course, it isn't technically true that `people` or `friends` "have" size 2. After all, `people` and `friends` are not objects. They are references to an object, namely an array list with size 2.)

Most of the time, this sharing of objects is efficient and convenient, but you have to be aware that it is possible to mutate a shared object through any of its references.

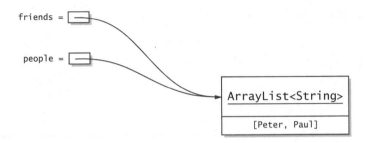

Figure 2-2 Two references to the same object

However, if a class has no mutator methods (such as String or LocalDate), you don't have to worry. Since nobody can change such an object, you can freely give out references to it.

It is possible for an object variable to refer to no object at all, by setting it to the special value null.

```
LocalDate date = null; // Now date doesn't refer to any object
```

This can be useful if you don't yet have an object for date to refer to, or if you want to indicate a special situation, such as an unknown date.

 CAUTION: Null values can be dangerous when they are not expected. Invoking a method on null causes a NullPointerException (which should really have been called a NullReferenceException). For that reason, it is not recommended to use null for optional values. Use the Optional type instead (see Chapter 8).

Finally, have another look at the assignments

```
date = LocalDate.of(year, month, 1);
date = date.plusDays(1);
```

After the first assignment, date refers to the first day of the month. The call to plusDays yields a new LocalDate object, and after the second assignment, the date variable refers to the new object. What happens to the first one?

There is no reference to the first object, so it is no longer needed. Eventually, the *garbage collector* will recycle the memory and make it available for reuse. In Java, this process is completely automatic, and programmers never need to worry about deallocating memory.

2.2 Implementing Classes

Now let us turn to implementing our own classes. To show the various language rules, I use the classic example of an `Employee` class. An employee has a name and a salary. In this example, the name can't change, but ever so often an employee can get a well-deserved raise.

2.2.1 Instance Variables

From the description of employee objects, you can see that the state of such an object is described by two values: name and salary. In Java, you use *instance variables* to describe the state of an object. They are declared in a class like this:

```
public class Employee {
    private String name;
    private double salary;
    ...
}
```

That means that every instance of the `Employee` class has these two variables.

In Java, instance variables are usually declared as `private`. That means that only methods of the same class can access them. There are a couple of reasons why this protection is desirable: You control which parts of your program can modify the variables, and you can decide at any point to change the internal representation. For example, you might store the employees in a database and only leave the primary key in the object. As long as you reimplement the methods so they work the same as before, the users of your class won't care.

2.2.2 Method Headers

Now let's turn to implementing the methods of the `Employee` class. When you declare a method, you provide its name, the types and names of its parameters, and the return type, like this:

```
public void raiseSalary(double byPercent)
```

This method receives a parameter of type `double` and doesn't return any value, as indicated by the return type `void`.

The `getName` method has a different signature:

```
public String getName()
```

The method has no parameters and returns a `String`.

NOTE: Most methods are declared as `public`, which means anyone can call such a method. Sometimes, a helper method is declared as `private`, which restricts it to being used only in other methods of the same class. You should do that for methods that are not relevant to class users, particularly if they depend on implementation details. You can safely change or remove private methods if the implementation changes.

2.2.3 Method Bodies

Following the method header, you provide the body:

```
public void raiseSalary(double byPercent) {
    double raise = salary * byPercent / 100;
    salary += raise;
}
```

Use the `return` keyword if the method yields a value:

```
public String getName() {
    return name;
}
```

Place the method declarations inside the class declaration:

```
public class Employee {
    private String name;
    private double salary;

    public void raiseSalary(double byPercent) {
        double raise = salary * byPercent / 100;
        salary += raise;
    }

    public String getName() {
        return name;
    }
    ...
}
```

2.2.4 Instance Method Invocations

Consider this example of a method call:

```
fred.raiseSalary(5);
```

In this call, the argument 5 is used to initialize the parameter variable `byPercent`, equivalent to the assignment

```
double byPercent = 5;
```

Then the following actions occur:

```
double raise = fred.salary * byPercent / 100;
fred.salary += raise;
```

Note that the salary instance variable is applied to the instance on which the method is invoked.

Unlike the methods that you have seen at the end of the preceding chapter, a method such as raiseSalary operates on an instance of a class. Therefore, such a method is called an *instance method*. In Java, all methods that are not declared as static are instance methods.

As you can see, two values are passed to the raiseSalary method: a reference to the object on which the method is invoked, and the argument of the call. Technically, both of these are parameters of the method, but in Java, as in other object-oriented languages, the first one takes on a special role. It is sometimes called the *receiver* of the method call.

2.2.5 The this Reference

When a method is called on an object, this is set to that object. If you like, you can use the this reference in the implementation:

```
public void raiseSalary(double byPercent) {
    double raise = this.salary * byPercent / 100;
    this.salary += raise;
}
```

Some programmers prefer that style because it clearly distinguishes between local and instance variables—it is now obvious that raise is a local variable and salary is an instance variable.

It is very common to use the this reference when you don't want to come up with different names for parameter variables. For example,

```
public void setSalary(double salary) {
    this.salary = salary;
}
```

When an instance variable and a local variable have the same name, the unqualified name (such as salary) denotes the local variable, and this.salary is the instance variable.

 NOTE: In some programming languages, instance variables are decorated in some way, for example _name and _salary. This is legal in Java but is not commonly done.

 NOTE: If you like, you can even declare this as a parameter of a method (but not a constructor):

```
public void setSalary(Employee this, double salary) {
    this.salary = salary;
}
```

However, this syntax is very rarely used. It exists so that you can annotate the receiver of the method—see Chapter 11.

2.2.6 Call by Value

When you pass an object to a method, the method obtains a copy of the object reference. Through this reference, it can access or mutate the parameter object. For example,

```
public class EvilManager {
    private Random generator;
    ...
    public void giveRandomRaise(Employee e) {
        double percentage = 10 * generator.nextGaussian();
        e.raiseSalary(percentage);
    }
}
```

Consider the call

```
boss.giveRandomRaise(fred);
```

The reference fred is copied into the parameter variable e (see Figure 2-3). The method mutates the object that is shared by the two references.

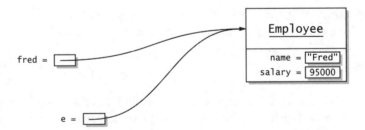

Figure 2-3 A parameter variable holding a copy of an object reference

In Java, you can never write a method that updates primitive type parameters. A method that tries to increase a double value won't work:

```
public void increaseRandomly(double x) { // Won't work
    double amount = x * generator.nextDouble();
    x += amount;
}
```

If you call

```
boss.increaseRandomly(sales);
```

then sales is copied into x. Then x is increased, but that doesn't change sales. The parameter variable then goes out of scope, and the increase leaves no useful effect.

For the same reason, it is not possible to write a method that changes an object reference to something different. For example, this method does not work as presumably intended:

```
public class EvilManager {
    ...
    public void replaceWithZombie(Employee e) {
        e = new Employee("", 0);
    }
}
```

In the call

```
boss.replaceWithZombie(fred);
```

the reference fred is copied into the variable e which is then set to a different reference. When the method exits, e goes out of scope. At no point was fred changed.

 NOTE: Some people say that Java uses "call by reference" for objects. As you can see from the second example, that is not true. In a language that supports call by reference, a method can replace the contents of variables passed to it. In Java, all parameters—object references as well as primitive type values—are passed by value.

2.3 Object Construction

One step remains to complete the Employee class: We need to provide a constructor, as detailed in the following sections.

2.3.1 Implementing Constructors

Declaring a constructor is similar to declaring a method. However, the name of the constructor is the same as the class name, and there is *no return type*.

```
public Employee(String name, double salary) {
    this.name = name;
    this.salary = salary;
}
```

NOTE: This constructor is public. It can also be useful to have private constructors. For example, the LocalDate class has no public constructors. Instead, users of the class obtain objects from "factory methods" such as now and of. These methods call a private constructor.

CAUTION: If you accidentally specify a return type, such as

```
public void Employee(String name, double salary)
```

then you declare a method named Employee, not a constructor!

A constructor executes when you use the new operator. For example, the expression

```
new Employee("James Bond", 500000)
```

allocates an object of the Employee class and invokes the constructor body, which sets the instance variables to the arguments supplied in the constructor.

The new operator returns a reference to the constructed object. You will normally want to save that reference in a variable:

```
Employee james = new Employee("James Bond", 500000);
```

or pass it to a method:

```
ArrayList<Employee> staff = new ArrayList<>();
staff.add(new Employee("James Bond", 500000));
```

2.3.2 Overloading

You can supply more than one version of a constructor. For example, if you want to make it easy to model nameless worker bees, supply a second constructor that only accepts a salary.

```
public Employee(double salary) {
    this.name = "";
    this.salary = salary;
}
```

Now the Employee class has two constructors. Which one is called depends on the arguments.

```
Employee james = new Employee("James Bond", 500000);
    // calls Employee(String, double) constructor
Employee anonymous = new Employee(40000);
    // calls Employee(double) constructor
```

In this case, we say that the constructor is *overloaded.*

 NOTE: A method is overloaded if there are multiple versions with the same name but different parameters. For example, there are overloaded versions of the `println` method with parameters `int`, `double`, `String`, and so on. Since you have no choice how to name a constructor, it is common to overload constructors.

2.3.3 Calling One Constructor from Another

When there are multiple constructors, they usually have some work in common, and it is best not to duplicate that code. It is often possible to put that common initialization into one constructor.

You can call one constructor from another, but only as the *first statement* of the constructor body. Somewhat surprisingly, you don't use the name of the constructor for the call but the keyword `this`:

```
public Employee(double salary) {
    this("", salary); // Calls Employee(String, double)
    // Other statements can follow
}
```

 NOTE: Here, `this` is *not* a reference to the object that is being constructed. Instead, it is a special syntax that is only used for invoking another constructor of the same class.

2.3.4 Default Initialization

If you don't set an instance variable explicitly in a constructor, it is automatically set to a default value: numbers to `0`, `boolean` values to `false`, and object references to `null`.

For example, you could supply a constructor for unpaid interns.

```
public Employee(String name) {
    // salary automatically set to zero
    this.name = name;
}
```

NOTE: In this regard, instance variables are very different from local variables. Recall that you must always explicitly initialize local variables.

For numbers, the initialization with zero is often convenient. But for object references, it is a common source of errors. Suppose we didn't set the name variable to the empty string in the Employee(double) constructor:

```
public Employee(double salary) {
    // name automatically set to null
    this.salary = salary;
}
```

If anyone called the getName method, they would get a null reference that they probably don't expect. A condition such as

```
if (e.getName().equals("James Bond"))
```

would then cause a null pointer exception.

2.3.5 Instance Variable Initialization

You can specify an initial value for any instance variables, like this:

```
public class Employee {
    private String name = "";
    ...
}
```

This initialization occurs after the object has been allocated and before a constructor runs. Therefore, the initial value is present in all constructors. Of course, some of them may choose to overwrite it.

In addition to initializing an instance variable when you declare it, you can include arbitrary *initialization blocks* in the class declaration.

```
public class Employee() {
    private String name = "";
    private int id;
    private double salary;

    { // An initialization block
        Random generator = new Random();
        id = 1 + generator.nextInt(1_000_000);
    }

    public Employee(String name, double salary) {
        ...
    }
}
```

NOTE: This is not a commonly used feature. Most programmers place lengthy initialization code into a helper method and invoke that method from the constructors.

Instance variable initializations and initialization blocks are executed in the order in which they appear in the class declaration, and before the body of the constructor.

2.3.6 Final Instance Variables

You can declare an instance variable as final. Such a variable must be initialized by the end of every constructor. Afterwards, the variable may not be modified again. For example, the name variable of the Employee class may be declared as final because it never changes after the object is constructed—there is no setName method.

```
public class Employee {
    private final String name;
    ...
}
```

 NOTE: When used with a reference to a mutable object, the final modifier merely states that the reference will never change. It is perfectly legal to mutate the object.

```
public class Person {
    private final ArrayList<Person> friends = new ArrayList<>();
        // OK to add elements to this array list
    ...
}
```

Methods may mutate the array list to which friends refers, but they can never replace it with another. In particular, it can never become null.

2.3.7 The Constructor with No Arguments

Many classes contain a constructor with no arguments that creates an object whose state is set to an appropriate default. For example, here is a constructor with no arguments for the Employee class:

```
public Employee() {
    name = "";
    salary = 0;
}
```

Just like an indigent defendant is provided with a public defender, a class with no constructors is automatically given a constructor with no arguments that does nothing at all. All instance variables stay at their default values (zero, false, or null) unless they have been explicitly initialized.

Thus, every class has at least one constructor.

 NOTE: If a class already has a constructor, it does *not* automatically get another constructor with no arguments. If you supply a constructor and also want a no-argument constructor, you have to write it yourself.

 NOTE: In the preceding sections, you saw what happens when an object is constructed. In some programming languages, notably C++, it is common to specify what happens when an object is destroyed. Java does have a mechanism for "finalizing" an object when it is reclaimed by the garbage collector. But this happens at unpredictable times, so you should not use it. However, as you will see in Chapter 5, there is a mechanism for closing resources such as files.

2.4 Static Variables and Methods

In all sample programs that you have seen, the main method is tagged with the static modifier. In the following sections, you will learn what this modifier means.

2.4.1 Static Variables

If you declare a variable in a class as static, then there is only one such variable per class. In contrast, each object has its own copy of an instance variable. For example, suppose we want to give each employee a distinct ID number. Then we can share the last ID that was given out.

```
public class Employee {
    private static int lastId = 0;
    private int id;
    ...
    public Employee() {
        lastId++;
        id = lastId;
    }
}
```

Every Employee object has its own instance variable id, but there is only one lastId variable that belongs to the class, not to any particular instance of the class.

When a new Employee object is constructed, the shared lastId variable is incremented and the id instance variable is set to that value. Thus, every employee gets a distinct id value.

 CAUTION: This code will not work if Employee objects can be constructed concurrently in multiple threads. Chapter 10 shows how to remedy that problem.

 NOTE: You may wonder why a variable that belongs to the class, and not to individual instances, is named "static." The term is a meaningless holdover from C++ which borrowed the keyword from an unrelated use in the C language instead of coming up with something more appropriate. A more descriptive term is "class variable."

2.4.2 Static Constants

Mutable static variables are rare, but static constants (that is, static final variables) are quite common. For example, the Math class declares a static constant:

```
public class Math {
    ...
    public static final double PI = 3.14159265358979323846;
    ...
}
```

You can access this constant in your programs as Math.PI.

Without the static keyword, PI would have been an instance variable of the Math class. That is, you would need an object of the class to access PI, and every Math object would have its own copy of PI.

Here is an example of a static final variable that is an object, not a number. It is both wasteful and insecure to construct a new random number generator each time you want a random number. You are better off sharing a single generator among all instances of a class.

```java
public class Employee {
    private static final Random generator = new Random();
    private int id;
    ...
    public Employee() {
        id = 1 + generator.nextInt(1_000_000);
    }
}
```

Another example of a static constant is System.out. It is declared in the System class like this:

```java
public class System {
    public static final PrintStream out;
    ...
}
```

> **CAUTION:** Even though out is declared as final in the System class, there is a method setOut that sets System.out to a different stream. This method is a "native" method, not implemented in Java, which can bypass the access control mechanisms of the Java language. This is a very unusual situation from the early days of Java, and not something you are likely to encounter elsewhere.

2.4.3 Static Initialization Blocks

In the preceding sections, static variables were initialized as they were declared. Sometimes, you need to do additional initialization work. You can put it into a *static initialization block*.

```java
public class CreditCardForm {
    private static final ArrayList<Integer> expirationYear = new ArrayList<>();
    static {
        // Add the next twenty years to the array list
        int year = LocalDate.now().getYear();
        for (int i = year; i <= year + 20; i++) {
            expirationYear.add(i);
        }
    }
    ...
}
```

Static initialization occurs when the class is first loaded. Like instance variables, static variables are 0, false, or null unless you explicitly set them to another value. All static variable initializations and static initialization blocks are executed in the order in which they occur in the class declaration.

2.4.4 Static Methods

Static methods are methods that do not operate on objects. For example, the pow method of the Math class is a static method. The expression

```
Math.pow(x, a)
```

computes the power x^a. It does not use any Math object to carry out its task.

As you have already seen in Chapter 1, a static method is declared with the static modifier:

```
public class Math {
    public static double pow(double base, double exponent) {
        ...
    }
}
```

Why not make pow into an instance method? It can't be an instance method of double since, in Java, primitive types are not classes. One could make it an instance method of the Math class, but then you would need to construct a Math object in order to call it.

Another common reason for static methods is to provide added functionality to classes that you don't own. For example, wouldn't it be nice to have a method that yields a random integer in a given range? You can't add a method to the Random class in the standard library. But you can provide a static method:

```
public class RandomNumbers {
    public static int nextInt(Random generator, int low, int high) {
        return low + generator.nextInt(high - low + 1);
    }
}
```

Call this method as

```
int dieToss = RandomNumbers.nextInt(gen, 1, 6);
```

 NOTE: It is legal to invoke a static method on an object. For example, instead of calling LocalDate.now() to get today's date, you can call date.now() on an object date of the LocalDate class. But that does not make a lot of sense. The now method doesn't look at the date object to compute the result. Most Java programmers would consider this poor style.

Since static methods don't operate on objects, you cannot access instance variables from a static method. However, static methods can access the static variables in their class. For example, in the RandomNumbers.nextInt method, we can make the random number generator into a static variable:

```
public class RandomNumbers {
    private static Random generator = new Random();
    public static int nextInt(int low, int high) {
        return low + generator.nextInt(high - low + 1);
            // OK to access the static generator variable
    }
}
```

2.4.5 Factory Methods

A common use for static methods is a *factory method*, a static method that returns new instances of the class. For example, the NumberFormat class uses factory methods that yield formatter objects for various styles.

```
NumberFormat currencyFormatter = NumberFormat.getCurrencyInstance();
NumberFormat percentFormatter = NumberFormat.getPercentInstance();
double x = 0.1;
System.out.println(currencyFormatter.format(x)); // Prints $0.10
System.out.println(percentFormatter.format(x)); // Prints 10%
```

Why not use a constructor instead? The only way to distinguish two constructors is by their parameter types. You cannot have two constructors with no arguments.

Moreover, a constructor new NumberFormat(...) yields a NumberFormat. A factory method can return an object of a subclass. In fact, these factory methods return instances of the DecimalFormat class. (See Chapter 4 for more information about subclasses.)

A factory method can also return a shared object, instead of unnecessarily constructing new ones. For example, the call Collections.emptyList() returns a shared immutable empty list.

2.5 Packages

In Java, you place related classes into a package. Packages are convenient for organizing your work and for separating it from code libraries provided by others. As you have seen, the standard Java library is distributed over a number of packages, including java.lang, java.util, java.math, and so on.

One reason for using packages is to guarantee the uniqueness of class names. Suppose two programmers come up with the bright idea of supplying an Element class. (In fact, at least five developers had that bright idea in the Java

API alone.) As long as all of them place their classes into different packages, there is no conflict.

In the following sections, you will learn how to work with packages.

2.5.1 Package Declarations

A package name is a dot-separated list of identifiers such as `java.util.regex`.

To guarantee unique package names, it is a good idea to use an Internet domain name (which is known to be unique) written in reverse. For example, I own the domain name `horstmann.com`. For my projects, I use package names such as `com.horstmann.corejava`. A major exception to this rule is the standard Java library whose package names start with `java` or `javax`.

 NOTE: In Java, packages do not nest. For example, the packages `java.util` and `java.util.regex` have nothing to do with each other. Each is its own independent collection of classes.

To place a class in a package, you add a `package` statement as the first statement of the source file:

```
package com.horstmann.corejava;

public class Employee {
    ...
}
```

Now the `Employee` class is in the `com.horstmann.corejava` package, and its *fully qualified name* is `com.horstmann.corejava.Employee`.

There is also a *default package* with no name that you can use for simple programs. To add a class to the default package, don't provide a `package` statement. However, the use of the default package is not recommended.

When class files are read from a file system, the path name needs to match the package name. For example, the file `Employee.class` must be in a subdirectory `com/horstmann/corejava`.

If you arrange the source files in the same way and compile from the directory that contains the initial package names, then the class files are automatically put in the correct place. Suppose the `EmployeeDemo` class makes use of `Employee` objects, and you compile it as

```
javac com/horstmann/corejava/EmployeeDemo.java
```

The compiler generates class files `com/horstmann/corejava/EmployeeDemo.class` and `com/horstmann/corejava/Employee.class`. You run the program by specifying the fully qualified class name:

```
java com.horstmann.corejava.EmployeeDemo
```

 CAUTION: If a source file is not in a subdirectory that matches its package name, the `javac` compiler will not complain and will generate a class file, but you will need to put the class file in the right place. This can be quite confusing—see Exercise 12.

 TIP: It is a good idea to run `javac` with the `-d` option. Then the class files are generated in a separate directory, without cluttering up the source tree, and they have the correct subdirectory structure.

2.5.2 The jar Command

Instead of storing class files in the file system, you can place them into one or more archive files called JAR files. You can make such an archive with the `jar` utility that is a part of the JDK. Its command-line options are similar to those of the Unix `tar` program.

```
jar --create --verbose --file library.jar com/mycompany/*.class
```

or, with short options,

```
jar -c -v -f library.jar com/mycompany/*.class
```

or, with tar-style options,

```
jar cvf library.jar com/mycompany/*.class
```

JAR files are commonly used to package libraries.

 TIP: You can use JAR files to package a program, not just a library. Generate the JAR file with

```
jar -c -f program.jar -e com.mycompany.MainClass com/mycompany/*.class
```

Then run the program as

```
java -jar program.jar
```

CAUTION: The options of commands in the Java development kit have traditionally used single dashes followed by multi-letter option names, such as `java -jar`. The exception was the `jar` command, which followed the classic option format of the `tar` command without dashes. Java 9 is moving towards the more common option format where multi-letter option names are preceded by double dashes, such as `--create`, with single-letter shortcuts for common options, such as `-c`.

This has created a muddle that will hopefully get cleaned up over time. Right now, `java -jar` works as always, but `java --jar` doesn't. You can combine some single-letter options but not others. For example, `jar -cvf` *filename* works, but `jar -cv -f` *filename* doesn't. Long argument options can follow a space or `=`, and short argument options can follow with or without a space. However, this is not fully implemented: `jar -c --file=`*filename* works, but `jar -c -f`*filename* doesn't.

2.5.3 The Class Path

When you use library JAR files in a project, you need to tell the compiler and the virtual machine where these files are by specifying the *class path*. A class path can contain

- Directories containing class files (in subdirectories that match their package names)
- JAR files
- Directories containing JAR files

The `javac` and `java` programs have an option `-cp` (with a verbose version `--class-path` or, for backwards compatibility, `-classpath`). For example,

```
java -cp .:../libs/lib1.jar:../libs/lib2.jar com.mycompany.MainClass
```

This class path has three elements: the current directory (.) and two JAR files in the directory `../libs`.

 NOTE: In Windows, use semicolons instead of colons to separate the path elements:

```
java -cp .;..\libs\lib1.jar;..\libs\lib2.jar com.mycompany.MainClass
```

If you have many JAR files, put them all in a directory and use a wildcard to include them all:

```
java -cp .:../libs/\* com.mycompany.MainClass
```

NOTE: In Unix, the * must be escaped to prevent shell expansion.

 CAUTION: The javac compiler always looks for files in the current directory, but the java program only looks into the current directory if the "." directory is on the class path. If you have no class path set, this is not a problem—the default class path consists of the "." directory. But if you have set the class path and forgot to include the "." directory, your programs will compile without error but won't run.

 CAUTION: The wildcard option for the class path is convenient, but it only works reliably if the JAR files are well structured. It is possible (but not a good idea) to have two versions of the same class in different JAR files. In such a situation, the first encountered class wins. The wildcard syntax does not guarantee the ordering in which the JAR files are processed, and you should not use it if you require a particular ordering of the JAR files. (Such "JAR file hell" is a problem that the Java platform module system aims to prevent—see Chapter 15.)

Using the -cp option is the preferred approach for setting the class path. An alternate approach is the CLASSPATH environment variable. The details depend on your shell. If you use bash, use a command such as

```
export CLASSPATH=.:/home/username/project/libs/\*
```

In Windows, it is

```
SET CLASSPATH=.;C:\Users\username\project\libs\*
```

 CAUTION: You can set the CLASSPATH environment variable globally (for example, in .bashrc or the Windows control panel). However, many programmers have regretted this when they forgot the global setting and were surprised that their classes were not found.

 NOTE: As you will see in Chapter 15, you can group packages together into *modules*. Modules provide strong encapsulation, hiding all packages except those that you make visible. You will see in Chapter 15 how to use the *module path* to specify the locations of the modules that your programs use.

2.5.4 Package Access

You have already encountered the access modifiers `public` and `private`. Features tagged as `public` can be used by any class. Private features can be used only by the class that declares them. If you don't specify either `public` or `private`, the feature (that is, the class, method, or variable) can be accessed by all methods in the same package.

Package access is useful for utility classes and methods that are needed by the methods of a package but are not of interest to the users of the package. Another common use case is for testing. You can place test classes in the same package, and then they can access internals of the classes being tested.

 NOTE: A source file can contain multiple classes, but at most one of them can be declared `public`. If a source file has a public class, its name must match the class name.

For variables, it is unfortunate that package access is the default. It is a common mistake to forget the `private` modifier and accidentally make an instance variable accessible to the entire package. Here is an example from the `Window` class in the `java.awt` package:

```
public class Window extends Container {
    String warningString;
    ...
}
```

Since the `warningString` variable is not private, the methods of all classes in the `java.awt` package can access it. Actually, no method other than those of the `Window` class itself does that, so it seems likely that the programmer simply forgot the `private` modifier.

This can be a security issue because packages are open ended. Any class can add itself to a package by providing the appropriate `package` statement.

If you are concerned about this openness of packages, you are not alone. A remedy is to place your package into a module—see Chapter 15. When a package is in a module, it is not possible to add classes to the package. All packages in the Java library are grouped into modules, so you cannot access the `Window.warningString` variable simply by crafting a class in the `java.awt` package.

2.5.5 Importing Classes

The `import` statement lets you use classes without the fully qualified name. For example, when you use

```
import java.util.Random;
```

then you can write `Random` instead of `java.util.Random` in your code.

 NOTE: Import declarations are a convenience, not a necessity. You could drop all import declarations and use fully qualified class names everywhere.

```
java.util.Random generator = new java.util.Random();
```

Place `import` statements above the first class declaration in the source file, but below the `package` statement.

You can import all classes from a package with a wildcard:

```
import java.util.*;
```

The wildcard can only import classes, not packages. You cannot use `import java.*;` to obtain all packages whose name starts with `java`.

When you import multiple packages, it is possible to have a name conflict. For example, the packages `java.util` and `java.sql` both contain a `Date` class. Suppose you import both packages:

```
import java.util.*;
import java.sql.*;
```

If your program doesn't use the `Date` class, this is not a problem. But if you refer to `Date`, without the package name, the compiler complains.

In that case, you can import the specific class that you want:

```
import java.util.*;
import java.sql.*;
import java.sql.Date;
```

If you really need both classes, you must use the fully qualified name for at least one of them.

 NOTE: The `import` statement is a convenience for programmers. Inside class files, all class names are fully qualified.

 NOTE: The `import` statement is very different from the `#include` directive in C and C++. That directive includes header files for compilation. Imports do not cause files to be recompiled. They just shorten names, like the C++ `using` statement.

2.5.6 Static Imports

A form of the `import` statement permits the importing of static methods and variables. For example, if you add the directive

```
import static java.lang.Math.*;
```

to the top of your source file, you can use the static methods and static variables of the `Math` class without the class name prefix:

```
r = sqrt(pow(x, 2) + pow(y, 2)); // i.e., Math.sqrt, Math.pow
```

You can also import a specific static method or variable:

```
import static java.lang.Math.sqrt;
import static java.lang.Math.PI;
```

 NOTE: As you will see in Chapters 3 and 8, it is common to use static import declarations with `java.util.Comparator` and `java.util.stream.Collectors`, which provide a large number of static methods.

2.6 Nested Classes

In the preceding section, you have seen how to organize classes into packages. Alternatively, you can place a class inside another class. Such a class is called a *nested class*. This can be useful to restrict visibility, or to avoid cluttering up a package with generic names such as `Element`, `Node`, or `Item`. Java has two kinds of nested classes, with somewhat different behavior. Let us examine both in the following sections.

2.6.1 Static Nested Classes

Consider an `Invoice` class that bills for items, each of which has a description, quantity, and unit price. We can make `Item` into a nested class:

```java
public class Invoice {
    private static class Item { // Item is nested inside Invoice
        String description;
        int quantity;
        double unitPrice;

        double price() { return quantity * unitPrice; }
    }

    private ArrayList<Item> items = new ArrayList<>();
    ...
}
```

It won't be clear until the next section why this inner class is declared `static`. For now, just accept it.

There is nothing special about the `Item` class, except for access control. The class is private in `Invoice`, so only `Invoice` methods can access it. For that reason, I did not bother making the instance variables of the inner class private.

Here is an example of a method that constructs an object of the inner class:

```
public class Invoice {
    ...
    public void addItem(String description, int quantity, double unitPrice) {
        Item newItem = new Item();
        newItem.description = description;
        newItem.quantity = quantity;
        newItem.unitPrice = unitPrice;
        items.add(newItem);
    }
}
```

A class can make a nested class public. In that case, one would want to use the usual encapsulation mechanism.

```
public class Invoice {
    public static class Item { // A public nested class
        private String description;
        private int quantity;
        private double unitPrice;

        public Item(String description, int quantity, double unitPrice) {
            this.description = description;
            this.quantity = quantity;
            this.unitPrice = unitPrice;
        }
        public double price() { return quantity * unitPrice; }
        ...
    }

    private ArrayList<Item> items = new ArrayList<>();

    public void add(Item item) { items.add(item); }
    ...
}
```

Now anyone can construct `Item` objects by using the qualified name `Invoice.Item`:

```
Invoice.Item newItem = new Invoice.Item("Blackwell Toaster", 2, 19.95);
myInvoice.add(newItem);
```

There is essentially no difference between this `Invoice.Item` class and a class `InvoiceItem` declared outside any other class. Nesting the class just makes it obvious that the `Item` class represents items in an invoice.

2.6.2 Inner Classes

In the preceding section, you saw a nested class that was declared as `static`. In this section, you will see what happens if you drop the `static` modifier. Such classes are called *inner classes*.

Consider a social network in which each member has friends that are also members.

```
public class Network {
    public class Member { // Member is an inner class of Network
        private String name;
        private ArrayList<Member> friends;

        public Member(String name) {
            this.name = name;
            friends = new ArrayList<>();
        }
        ...
    }

    private ArrayList<Member> members = new ArrayList<>();
    ...
}
```

With the `static` modifier dropped, there is an essential difference. A `Member` object knows to which network it belongs. Let's see how this works.

First, here is a method to add a member to the network:

```
public class Network {
    ...
    public Member enroll(String name) {
        Member newMember = new Member(name);
        members.add(newMember);
        return newMember;
    }
}
```

So far, nothing much seems to be happening. We can add a member and get a reference to it.

```
Network myFace = new Network();
Network.Member fred = myFace.enroll("Fred");
```

Now let's assume Fred feels this isn't the hottest social network anymore, so he wants to deactivate his membership.

```
fred.deactivate();
```

Here is the implementation of the `deactivate` method:

```
public class Network {
    public class Member {
        ...
        public void deactivate() {
            members.remove(this);
        }
    }

    private ArrayList<Member> members;
    ...
}
```

As you can see, a method of an inner class can access instance variables of its outer class. In this case, they are the instance variables of the outer class object that created it, the unpopular myFace network.

This is what makes an inner class different from a static nested class. Each inner class object has a reference to an object of the enclosing class. For example, the method

```
members.remove(this);
```

actually means

```
outer.members.remove(this);
```

where I use *outer* to denote the hidden reference to the enclosing class.

A static nested class does not have such a reference (just like a static method does not have the this reference). Use a static nested class when the instances of the nested class don't need to know to which instance of the enclosing class they belong. Use an inner class only if this information is important.

An inner class can also invoke methods of the outer class through its outer class instance. For example, suppose the outer class had a method to unenroll a member. Then the deactivate method can call it:

```
public class Network {
    public class Member {
        ...
        public void deactivate() {
            unenroll(this);
        }
    }

    private ArrayList<Member> members;

    public Member enroll(String name) { ... }
    public void unenroll(Member m) { ... }
    ...
}
```

In this case,

```
unenroll(this);
```

actually means

```
outer.unenroll(this);
```

2.6.3 Special Syntax Rules for Inner Classes

In the preceding section, I explained the outer class reference of an inner class object by calling it *outer*. The actual syntax for the outer reference is a bit more complex. The expression

```
OuterClass.this
```

denotes the outer class reference. For example, you can write the deactivate method of the Member inner class as

```
public void deactivate() {
    Network.this.members.remove(this);
}
```

In this case, the Network.this syntax was not necessary. Simply referring to members implicitly uses the outer class reference. But sometimes, you need the outer class reference explicitly. Here is a method to check whether a Member object belongs to a particular network:

```
public class Network {
    public class Member {
        ...
        public boolean belongsTo(Network n) {
            return Network.this == n;
        }
    }
}
```

When you construct an inner class object, it remembers the enclosing class object that constructed it. In the preceding section, a new member was created by this method:

```
public class Network {
    ...
    Member enroll(String name) {
        Member newMember = new Member(name);
        ...
    }
}
```

That is a shortcut for

```
Member newMember = this.new Member(name);
```

You can invoke an inner class constructor on any instance of an outer class:

```
Network.Member wilma = myFace.new Member("Wilma");
```

 NOTE: Inner classes cannot declare static members other than compile-time constants. There would be an ambiguity about the meaning of "static." Does it mean there is only one instance in the virtual machine? Or only one instance per outer object? The language designers decided not to tackle this issue.

 NOTE: By historical accident, inner classes were added to the Java language at a time when the virtual machine specification was considered complete, so they are translated into regular classes with a hidden instance variable referring to the enclosing instance. Exercise 14 invites you to explore this translation.

 NOTE: *Local classes* are another variant of inner classes that we will discuss in Chapter 3.

2.7 Documentation Comments

The JDK contains a very useful tool, called javadoc, that generates HTML documentation from your source files. In fact, the online API documentation that we described in Chapter 1 is simply the result of running javadoc on the source code of the standard Java library.

If you add comments that start with the special delimiter /** to your source code, you too can easily produce professional-looking documentation. This is a very nice approach because it lets you keep your code and documentation in one place. In the bad old days, programmers often put their documentation into a separate file, and it was just a question of time for the code and the comments to diverge. When documentation comments are in the same file as the source code, it is an easy matter to update both and run javadoc again.

2.7.1 Comment Insertion

The javadoc utility extracts information for the following items:

- Public classes and interfaces
- Public and protected constructors and methods

- Public and protected variables
- Packages and modules

Interfaces are introduced in Chapter 3 and protected features in Chapter 4.

You can (and should) supply a comment for each of these features. Each comment is placed immediately above the feature it describes. A comment starts with /** and ends with */.

Each /** ... */ documentation comment contains free-form text followed by tags. A tag starts with an @, such as @author or @param.

The *first sentence* of the free-form text should be a summary statement. The javadoc utility automatically generates summary pages that extract these sentences.

In the free-form text, you can use HTML modifiers such as ... for emphasis, <code>...</code> for a monospaced "typewriter" font, ... for boldface, and even <img ...> to include an image. You should, however, stay away from headings <h*n*> or rules <hr> because they can interfere with the formatting of the documentation.

 NOTE: If your comments contain links to other files such as images (for example, diagrams or images of user interface components), place those files into a subdirectory of the directory containing the source file, named doc-files. The javadoc utility will copy the doc-files directories and their contents from the source directory to the documentation directory. You need to specify the doc-files directory in your link, for example <img src="doc-files/uml.png" alt="UML diagram"/>.

2.7.2 Class Comments

The class comment must be placed directly before the class declaration. You may want to document the author and version of a class with the @author and @version tags. There can be multiple authors.

Here is an example of a class comment:

```
/**
 * An <code>Invoice</code> object represents an invoice with
 * line items for each part of the order.
 * @author Fred Flintstone
 * @author Barney Rubble
 * @version 1.1
 */
```

```
public class Invoice {
    ...
}
```

 NOTE: There is no need to put a * in front of every line. However, most IDEs supply the asterisks automatically, and some even rearrange them when the line breaks change.

2.7.3 Method Comments

Place each method comment immediately before its method. Document the following features:

- Each parameter, with a comment @param *variable description*

- The return value, if not void: @return *description*

- Any thrown exceptions (see Chapter 5): @throws *ExceptionClass description*

Here is an example of a method comment:

```
/**
 * Raises the salary of an employee.
 * @param byPercent the percentage by which to raise the salary (e.g., 10 means 10%)
 * @return the amount of the raise
 */
public double raiseSalary(double byPercent) {
    double raise = salary * byPercent / 100;
    salary += raise;
    return raise;
}
```

2.7.4 Variable Comments

You only need to document public variables—generally that means static constants. For example:

```
/**
 * The number of days per year on Earth (excepting leap years)
 */
public static final int DAYS_PER_YEAR = 365;
```

2.7.5 General Comments

In all documentation comments, you can use the @since tag to describe the version in which this feature became available:

```
@since version 1.7.1
```

The @deprecated tag adds a comment that the class, method, or variable should no longer be used. The text should suggest a replacement. For example,

```
@deprecated Use <code>setVisible(true)</code> instead
```

 NOTE: There is also a @Deprecated annotation that compilers use to issue warnings when deprecated items are used—see Chapter 11. The annotation does not have a mechanism for suggesting a replacement, so you should supply both the annotation and the Javadoc comment for deprecated items.

2.7.6 Links

You can add hyperlinks to other relevant parts of the javadoc documentation or to external documents with the @see and @link tags.

The tag @see *reference* adds a hyperlink in the "see also" section. It can be used with both classes and methods. Here, reference can be one of the following:

- *package.Class#feature label*
- <a href="...">*label*</a>
- "*text*"

The first case is the most useful. You supply the name of a class, method, or variable, and javadoc inserts a hyperlink to its documentation. For example,

```
@see com.horstmann.corejava.Employee#raiseSalary(double)
```

makes a link to the raiseSalary(double) method in the com.horstmann.corejava.Employee class. You can omit the name of the package, or both the package and class name. Then, the feature will be located in the current package or class.

Note that you must use a #, not a period, to separate the class from the method or variable name. The Java compiler itself is highly skilled in guessing the various meanings of the period character as a separator between packages, subpackages, classes, inner classes, and their methods and variables. But the javadoc utility isn't quite as clever, so you have to help it along.

If the @see tag is followed by a < character, you're specifying a hyperlink. You can link to any URL you like. For example: @see <a href="http://en.wikipedia.org/wiki/Leap_year">Leap years</a>.

In each of these cases, you can specify an optional label that will appear as the link anchor. If you omit the label, the user will see the target code name or URL as the anchor.

If the @see tag is followed by a " character, the text in quotes is displayed in the "see also" section. For example:

```
@see "Core Java for the Impatient"
```

You can add multiple @see tags for one feature but you must keep them all together.

If you like, you can place hyperlinks to other classes or methods anywhere in any of your documentation comments. Insert a tag of the form

```
{@link package.class#feature label}
```

anywhere in a comment. The feature description follows the same rules as for the @see tag.

2.7.7 Package, Module, and Overview Comments

The class, method, and variable comments are placed directly into the Java source files, delimited by /** ... */. However, to generate package comments, you need to add a separate file in each package directory.

Supply a Java file named package-info.java. The file must contain an initial javadoc comment, delimited with /** and */, followed by a package statement. It should contain no further code or comments.

To document a module, place your comments into module-info.java. You can include the @moduleGraph directive to include a module dependency graph. (See Chapter 15 about modules and the module-info.java file.)

You can also supply an overview comment for all source files. Place it in a file called overview.html, located in the parent directory that contains all the source files. All text between the tags <body>...</body> is extracted. This comment is displayed when the user selects "Overview" from the navigation bar.

2.7.8 Comment Extraction

Here, *docDirectory* is the name of the directory where you want the HTML files to go. Follow these steps:

1. Change to the directory that contains the source files you want to document. If you have nested packages to document, such as com.horstmann.corejava, you must be working in the directory that contains the subdirectory com. (This is the directory that contains the overview.html file, if you supplied one.)

2. Run the command

```
javadoc -d docDirectory package1 package2 ...
```

If you omit the -d *docDirectory* option, the HTML files are extracted to the current directory. That can get messy, so I don't recommend it.

The javadoc program can be fine-tuned by numerous command-line options. For example, you can use the -author and -version options to include the @author and @version tags in the documentation. (By default, they are omitted.)

Another useful option is -link to include hyperlinks to standard classes. For example, if you run the command

```
javadoc -link http://docs.oracle.com/javase/9/docs/api *.java
```

all standard library classes are automatically linked to the documentation on the Oracle website.

If you use the -linksource option, each source file is converted to HTML, and each class and method name turns into a hyperlink to the source.

Exercises

1. Change the calendar printing program so it starts the week on a Sunday. Also make it print a newline at the end (but only one).

2. Consider the nextInt method of the Scanner class. Is it an accessor or mutator? Why? What about the nextInt method of the Random class?

3. Can you ever have a mutator method return something other than void? Can you ever have an accessor method return void? Give examples when possible.

4. Why can't you implement a Java method that swaps the contents of two int variables? Instead, write a method that swaps the contents of two IntHolder objects. (Look up this rather obscure class in the API documentation.) Can you swap the contents of two Integer objects?

5. Implement an immutable class Point that describes a point in the plane. Provide a constructor to set it to a specific point, a no-arg constructor to set it to the origin, and methods getX, getY, translate, and scale. The translate method moves the point by a given amount in x- and y-direction. The scale method scales both coordinates by a given factor. Implement these methods so that they return new points with the results. For example,

```
Point p = new Point(3, 4).translate(1, 3).scale(0.5);
```

should set p to a point with coordinates (2, 3.5).

6. Repeat the preceding exercise, but now make translate and scale into mutators.

7. Add `javadoc` comments to both versions of the `Point` class from the preceding exercises.

8. In the preceding exercises, providing the constructors and getter methods of the `Point` class was rather repetitive. Most IDEs have shortcuts for writing the boilerplate code. What does your IDE offer?

9. Implement a class `Car` that models a car traveling along the *x*-axis, consuming gas as it moves. Provide methods to drive by a given number of miles, to add a given number of gallons to the gas tank, and to get the current distance from the origin and fuel level. Specify the fuel efficiency (in miles/gallons) in the constructor. Should this be an immutable class? Why or why not?

10. In the `RandomNumbers` class, provide two static methods `randomElement` that get a random element from an array or array list of integers. (Return zero if the array or array list is empty.) Why couldn't you make these methods into instance methods of `int[]` or `ArrayList<Integer>`?

11. Rewrite the `Cal` class to use static imports for the `System` and `LocalDate` classes.

12. Make a file `HelloWorld.java` that declares a class `HelloWorld` in a package `ch01.sec01`. Put it into some directory, but *not* in a `ch01/sec01` subdirectory. From that directory, run `javac HelloWorld.java`. Do you get a class file? Where? Then run `java HelloWorld`. What happens? Why? (Hint: Run `javap HelloWorld` and study the warning message.) Finally, try `javac -d . HelloWorld.java`. Why is that better?

13. Download the JAR file for OpenCSV from http://opencsv.sourceforge.net. Write a class with a `main` method that reads a CSV file of your choice and prints some of the content. There is sample code on the OpenCSV website. You haven't yet learned to deal with exceptions. Just use the following header for the `main` method:

    ```
    public static void main(String[] args) throws Exception
    ```

    The point of this exercise is not to do anything useful with CSV files, but to practice using a library that is delivered as a JAR file.

14. Compile the `Network` class. Note that the inner class file is named `Network$Member.class`. Use the `javap` program to spy on the generated code. The command

    ```
    javap -private Classname
    ```

displays the methods and instance variables. Where do you see the reference to the enclosing class? (In Linux/Mac OS, you need to put a \ before the $ symbol when running javap.)

15. Fully implement the Invoice class in Section 2.6.1, "Static Nested Classes" (page 85). Provide a method that prints the invoice and a demo program that constructs and prints a sample invoice.

16. Implement a class Queue, an unbounded queue of strings. Provide methods add, adding at the tail, and remove, removing at the head of the queue. Store elements as a linked list of nodes. Make Node a nested class. Should it be static or not?

17. Provide an *iterator*—an object that yields the elements of the queue in turn—for the queue of the preceding class. Make Iterator a nested class with methods next and hasNext. Provide a method iterator() of the Queue class that yields a Queue.Iterator. Should Iterator be static or not?

Interfaces and Lambda Expressions

Topics in This Chapter

Chapter 3

Java was designed as an object-oriented programming language in the 1990s when object-oriented programming was the principal paradigm for software development. Interfaces are a key feature of object-oriented programming: They let you specify what should be done, without having to provide an implementation.

Long before there was object-oriented programming, there were functional programming languages, such as Lisp, in which functions and not objects are the primary structuring mechanism. Recently, functional programming has risen in importance because it is well suited for concurrent and event-driven (or "reactive") programming. Java supports function expressions that provide a convenient bridge between object-oriented and functional programming. In this chapter, you will learn about interfaces and lambda expressions.

The key points of this chapter are:

1. An interface specifies a set of methods that an implementing class must provide.

2. An interface is a supertype of any class that implements it. Therefore, one can assign instances of the class to variables of the interface type.

3. An interface can contain static methods. All variables of an interface are automatically public, static, and final.

4. An interface can contain default methods that an implementing class can inherit or override.

5. An interface can contain private methods that cannot be called or overridden by implementing classes.

6. The `Comparable` and `Comparator` interfaces are used for comparing objects.

7. A functional interface is an interface with a single abstract method.

8. A lambda expression denotes a block of code that can be executed at a later point in time.

9. Lambda expressions are converted to functional interfaces.

10. Method and constructor references refer to methods or constructors without invoking them.

11. Lambda expressions and local classes can access effectively final variables from the enclosing scope.

3.1 Interfaces

An *interface* is a mechanism for spelling out a contract between two parties: the supplier of a service and the classes that want their objects to be usable with the service. In the following sections, you will see how to define and use interfaces in Java.

3.1.1 Declaring an Interface

Consider a service that works on sequences of integers, reporting the average of the first n values:

```
public static double average(IntSequence seq, int n)
```

Such sequences can take many forms. Here are some examples:

- A sequence of integers supplied by a user
- A sequence of random integers
- The sequence of prime numbers
- The sequence of elements in an integer array
- The sequence of code points in a string
- The sequence of digits in a number

We want to implement *a single mechanism* for dealing with all these kinds of sequences.

First, let us spell out what is common between integer sequences. At a minimum, one needs two methods for working with a sequence:

- Test whether there is a next element
- Get the next element

To declare an interface, you provide the method headers, like this:

```
public interface IntSequence {
    boolean hasNext();
    int next();
}
```

You need not implement these methods, but you can provide default implementations if you like—see Section 3.2.2, "Default Methods" (page 106). If no implementation is provided, we say that the method is *abstract*.

 NOTE: All methods of an interface are automatically `public`. Therefore, it is not necessary to declare `hasNext` and `next` as `public`. Some programmers do it anyway for greater clarity.

The methods in the interface suffice to implement the `average` method:

```
public static double average(IntSequence seq, int n) {
    int count = 0;
    double sum = 0;
    while (seq.hasNext() && count < n) {
        count++;
        sum += seq.next();
    }
    return count == 0 ? 0 : sum / count;
}
```

3.1.2 Implementing an Interface

Now let's look at the other side of the coin: the classes that want to be usable with the `average` method. They need to *implement* the `IntSequence` interface. Here is such a class:

```
public class SquareSequence implements IntSequence {
    private int i;

    public boolean hasNext() {
        return true;
    }
```

```
public int next() {
    i++;
    return i * i;
    }
}
```

There are infinitely many squares, and an object of this class delivers them all, one at a time. (To keep the example simple, we ignore integer overflow—see Exercise 6.)

The implements keyword indicates that the SquareSequence class intends to conform to the IntSequence interface.

 CAUTION: The implementing class must declare the methods of the interface as public. Otherwise, they would default to package access. Since the interface requires public access, the compiler would report an error.

This code gets the average of the first 100 squares:

```
SquareSequence squares = new SquareSequence();
double avg = average(squares, 100);
```

There are many classes that can implement the IntSequence interface. For example, this class yields a finite sequence, namely the digits of a positive integer starting with the least significant one:

```
public class DigitSequence implements IntSequence {
    private int number;

    public DigitSequence(int n) {
        number = n;
    }

    public boolean hasNext() {
        return number != 0;
    }

    public int next() {
        int result = number % 10;
        number /= 10;
        return result;
    }

    public int rest() {
        return number;
    }
}
```

An object new DigitSequence(1729) delivers the digits 9 2 7 1 before hasNext returns false.

 NOTE: The SquareSequence and DigitSequence classes implement all methods of the IntSequence interface. If a class only implements some of the methods, then it must be declared with the abstract modifier. See Chapter 4 for more information on abstract classes.

3.1.3 Converting to an Interface Type

This code fragment computes the average of the digit sequence values:

```
IntSequence digits = new DigitSequence(1729);
double avg = average(digits, 100);
    // Will only look at the first four sequence values
```

Look at the digits variable. Its type is IntSequence, not DigitSequence. A variable of type IntSequence refers to an object of some class that implements the IntSequence interface. You can always assign an object to a variable whose type is an implemented interface, or pass it to a method expecting such an interface.

Here is a bit of useful terminology. A type S is a *supertype* of the type T (the *subtype*) when any value of the subtype can be assigned to a variable of the supertype without a conversion. For example, the IntSequence interface is a supertype of the DigitSequence class.

 NOTE: Even though it is possible to declare variables of an interface type, you can never have an object whose type is an interface. All objects are instances of classes.

3.1.4 Casts and the `instanceof` Operator

Occasionally, you need the opposite conversion—from a supertype to a subtype. Then you use a *cast*. For example, if you happen to know that the object stored in an IntSequence is actually a DigitSequence, you can convert the type like this:

```
IntSequence sequence = ...;
DigitSequence digits = (DigitSequence) sequence;
System.out.println(digits.rest());
```

In this scenario, the cast was necessary because rest is a method of DigitSequence but not IntSequence.

See Exercise 2 for a more compelling example.

You can only cast an object to its actual class or one of its supertypes. If you are wrong, a compile-time error or class cast exception will occur:

```
String digitString = (String) sequence;
    // Cannot possibly work—IntSequence is not a supertype of String
RandomSequence randoms = (RandomSequence) sequence;
    // Could work, throws a class cast exception if not
```

To avoid the exception, you can first test whether the object is of the desired type, using the instanceof operator. The expression

object instanceof *Type*

returns true if *object* is an instance of a class that has *Type* as a supertype. It is a good idea to make this check before using a cast.

```
if (sequence instanceof DigitSequence) {
    DigitSequence digits = (DigitSequence) sequence;
    ...
}
```

 NOTE: The instanceof operator is null-safe: The expression obj instanceof *Type* is false if obj is null. After all, null cannot possibly be a reference to an object of any given type.

3.1.5 Extending Interfaces

An interface can *extend* another, requiring or providing additional methods on top of the original ones. For example, Closeable is an interface with a single method:

```
public interface Closeable {
    void close();
}
```

As you will see in Chapter 5, this is an important interface for closing resources when an exception occurs.

The Channel interface extends this interface:

```
public interface Channel extends Closeable {
    boolean isOpen();
}
```

A class that implements the Channel interface must provide both methods, and its objects can be converted to both interface types.

3.1.6 Implementing Multiple Interfaces

A class can implement any number of interfaces. For example, a FileSequence class that reads integers from a file can implement the Closeable interface in addition to IntSequence:

```
public class FileSequence implements IntSequence, Closeable {
    ...
}
```

Then the FileSequence class has both IntSequence and Closeable as supertypes.

3.1.7 Constants

Any variable defined in an interface is automatically public static final.

For example, the SwingConstants interface defines constants for compass directions:

```
public interface SwingConstants {
    int NORTH = 1;
    int NORTH_EAST = 2;
    int EAST = 3;
    ...
}
```

You can refer to them by their qualified name, SwingConstants.NORTH. If your class chooses to implement the SwingConstants interface, you can drop the SwingConstants qualifier and simply write NORTH. However, this is not a common idiom. It is far better to use enumerations for a set of constants; see Chapter 4.

 NOTE: You cannot have instance variables in an interface. An interface specifies behavior, not object state.

3.2 Static, Default, and Private Methods

In earlier versions of Java, all methods of an interface had to be abstract—that is, without a body. Nowadays you can add three kinds of methods with a concrete implementation: static, default, and private methods. The following sections describe these methods.

3.2.1 Static Methods

There was never a technical reason why an interface could not have static methods, but they did not fit into the view of interfaces as abstract specifications. That thinking has now evolved. In particular, factory methods make a lot of sense in interfaces. For example, the IntSequence interface can have a static method digitsOf that generates a sequence of digits of a given integer:

```
IntSequence digits = IntSequence.digitsOf(1729);
```

The method yields an instance of some class implementing the IntSequence interface, but the caller need not care which one it is.

```
public interface IntSequence {
    ...
    static IntSequence digitsOf(int n) {
        return new DigitSequence(n);
    }
}
```

 NOTE: In the past, it had been common to place static methods in a companion class. You find pairs of interfaces and utility classes, such as Collection/Collections or Path/Paths, in the Java API. This split is no longer necessary.

3.2.2 Default Methods

You can supply a *default* implementation for any interface method. You must tag such a method with the default modifier.

```
public interface IntSequence {
    default boolean hasNext() { return true; }
        // By default, sequences are infinite
    int next();
}
```

A class implementing this interface can choose to override the hasNext method or to inherit the default implementation.

 NOTE: Default methods put an end to the classic pattern of providing an interface and a companion class that implements most or all of its methods, such as Collection/AbstractCollection or WindowListener/WindowAdapter in the Java API. Nowadays you should just implement the methods in the interface.

An important use for default methods is *interface evolution*. Consider for example the Collection interface that has been a part of Java for many years. Suppose that way back when, you provided a class

```
public class Bag implements Collection
```

Later, in Java 8, a `stream` method was added to the interface.

Suppose the `stream` method was not a default method. Then the `Bag` class no longer compiles since it doesn't implement the new method. Adding a nondefault method to an interface is not *source-compatible*.

But suppose you don't recompile the class and simply use an old JAR file containing it. The class will still load, even with the missing method. Programs can still construct `Bag` instances, and nothing bad will happen. (Adding a method to an interface is *binary-compatible*.) However, if a program calls the `stream` method on a `Bag` instance, an `AbstractMethodError` occurs.

Making the method a `default` method solves both problems. The `Bag` class will again compile. And if the class is loaded without being recompiled and the `stream` method is invoked on a `Bag` instance, the `Collection.stream` method is called.

3.2.3 Resolving Default Method Conflicts

If a class implements two interfaces, one of which has a default method and the other a method (default or not) with the same name and parameter types, then you must resolve the conflict. This doesn't happen very often, and it is usually easy to deal with the situation.

Let's look at an example. Suppose we have an interface `Person` with a `getId` method:

```
public interface Person {
    String getName();
    default int getId() { return 0; }
}
```

And suppose there is an interface `Identified`, also with such a method.

```
public interface Identified {
    default int getId() { return Math.abs(hashCode()); }
}
```

You will see what the `hashCode` method does in Chapter 4. For now, all that matters is that it returns some integer that is derived from the object.

What happens if you form a class that implements both of them?

```
public class Employee implements Person, Identified {
    ...
}
```

The class inherits two `getId` methods provided by the `Person` and `Identified` interfaces. There is no way for the Java compiler to choose one over the other. The compiler reports an error and leaves it up to you to resolve the ambiguity.

Provide a `getId` method in the `Employee` class and either implement your own ID scheme, or delegate to one of the conflicting methods, like this:

```
public class Employee implements Person, Identified {
    public int getId() { return Identified.super.getId(); }
    ...
}
```

 NOTE: The `super` keyword lets you call a supertype method. In this case, we need to specify which supertype we want. The syntax may seem a bit odd, but it is consistent with the syntax for invoking a superclass method that you will see in Chapter 4.

Now assume that the `Identified` interface does not provide a default implementation for `getId`:

```
interface Identified {
    int getId();
}
```

Can the `Employee` class inherit the default method from the `Person` interface? At first glance, this might seem reasonable. But how does the compiler know whether the `Person.getId` method actually does what `Identified.getId` is expected to do? After all, it might return the level of the person's Freudian id, not an ID number.

The Java designers decided in favor of safety and uniformity. It doesn't matter how two interfaces conflict; if at least one interface provides an implementation, the compiler reports an error, and it is up to the programmer to resolve the ambiguity.

 NOTE: If neither interface provides a default for a shared method, then there Is no conflict. An implementing class has two choices: implement the method, or leave it unimplemented and declare the class as `abstract`.

 NOTE: If a class extends a superclass (see Chapter 4) and implements an interface, inheriting the same method from both, the rules are easier. In that case, only the superclass method matters, and any default method from the interface is simply ignored. This is actually a more common case than conflicting interfaces. See Chapter 4 for the details.

3.2.4 Private Methods

As of Java 9, methods in an interface can be private. A private method can be `static` or an instance method, but it cannot be a `default` method since that can be overridden. As private methods can only be used in the methods of the interface itself, their use is limited to being helper methods for the other methods of the interface.

For example, suppose the `IntSequence` class provides methods

```
static of(int a)
static of(int a, int b)
static of(int a, int b, int c)
```

Then each of these methods could call a helper method

```
private static IntSequence makeFiniteSequence(int... values) { ... }
```

3.3 Examples of Interfaces

At first glance, interfaces don't seem to do very much. An interface is just a set of methods that a class promises to implement. To make the importance of interfaces more tangible, the following sections show you four examples of commonly used interfaces from the Java API.

3.3.1 The Comparable Interface

Suppose you want to sort an array of objects. A sorting algorithm repeatedly compares elements and rearranges them if they are out of order. Of course, the rules for doing the comparison are different for each class, and the sorting algorithm should just call a method supplied by the class. As long as all classes can agree on what that method is called, the sorting algorithm can do its job. That is where interfaces come in.

If a class wants to enable sorting for its objects, it should implement the `Comparable` interface. There is a technical point about this interface. We want to compare strings against strings, employees against employees, and so on. For that reason, the `Comparable` interface has a type parameter.

```
public interface Comparable<T> {
    int compareTo(T other);
}
```

For example, the `String` class implements `Comparable<String>` so that its `compareTo` method has the signature

```
int compareTo(String other)
```

NOTE: A type with a type parameter such as `Comparable` or `ArrayList` is a *generic* type. You will learn all about generic types in Chapter 6.

When calling `x.compareTo(y)`, the `compareTo` method returns an integer value to indicate whether x or y should come first. A positive return value (not necessarily 1) indicates that x should come after y. A negative integer (not necessarily -1) is returned when x should come before y. If x and y are considered equal, the returned value is 0.

Note that the return value can be any integer. That flexibility is useful because it allows you to return a difference of integers. That is handy, provided the difference cannot produce integer overflow.

```
public class Employee implements Comparable<Employee> {
    ...
    public int compareTo(Employee other) {
        return getId() - other.getId(); // Ok if IDs always ≥ 0
    }
}
```

 CAUTION: Returning a difference of integers does not always work. The difference can overflow for large operands of opposite sign. In that case, use the `Integer.compare` method that works correctly for all integers. However, if you know that the integers are non-negative, or their absolute value is less than `Integer.MAX_VALUE / 2`, then the difference works fine.

When comparing floating-point values, you cannot just return the difference. Instead, use the static `Double.compare` method. It does the right thing, even for ±∞ and NaN.

Here is how the `Employee` class can implement the `Comparable` interface, ordering employees by salary:

```
public class Employee implements Comparable<Employee> {
    ...
    public int compareTo(Employee other) {
        return Double.compare(salary, other.salary);
    }
}
```

 NOTE: It is perfectly legal for the `compare` method to access `other.salary`. In Java, a method can access private features of *any* object of its class.

The String class, as well as over a hundred other classes in the Java library, implements the Comparable interface. You can use the Arrays.sort method to sort an array of Comparable objects:

```
String[] friends = { "Peter", "Paul", "Mary" };
Arrays.sort(friends); // friends is now ["Mary", "Paul", "Peter"]
```

 NOTE: Strangely, the Arrays.sort method does not check at compile time whether the argument is an array of Comparable objects. Instead, it throws an exception if it encounters an element of a class that doesn't implement the Comparable interface.

3.3.2 The Comparator Interface

Now suppose we want to sort strings by increasing length, not in dictionary order. We can't have the String class implement the compareTo method in two ways—and at any rate, the String class isn't ours to modify.

To deal with this situation, there is a second version of the Arrays.sort method whose parameters are an array and a *comparator*—an instance of a class that implements the Comparator interface.

```
public interface Comparator<T> {
    int compare(T first, T second);
}
```

To compare strings by length, define a class that implements Comparator<String>:

```
class LengthComparator implements Comparator<String> {
    public int compare(String first, String second) {
        return first.length() - second.length();
    }
}
```

To actually do the comparison, you need to make an instance:

```
Comparator<String> comp = new LengthComparator();
if (comp.compare(words[i], words[j]) > 0) ...
```

Contrast this call with words[i].compareTo(words[j]). The compare method is called on the comparator object, not the string itself.

 NOTE: Even though the LengthComparator object has no state, you still need to make an instance of it. You need the instance to call the compare method—it is not a static method.

To sort an array, pass a `LengthComparator` object to the `Arrays.sort` method:

```
String[] friends = { "Peter", "Paul", "Mary" };
Arrays.sort(friends, new LengthComparator());
```

Now the array is either `["Paul", "Mary", "Peter"]` or `["Mary", "Paul", "Peter"]`.

You will see in Section 3.4.2, "Functional Interfaces" (page 115) how to use a `Comparator` much more easily, using a lambda expression.

3.3.3 The Runnable Interface

At a time when just about every processor has multiple cores, you want to keep those cores busy. You may want to run certain tasks in a separate thread, or give them to a thread pool for execution. To define the task, you implement the `Runnable` interface. This interface has just one method.

```
class HelloTask implements Runnable {
    public void run() {
        for (int i = 0; i < 1000; i++) {
            System.out.println("Hello, World!");
        }
    }
}
```

If you want to execute this task in a new thread, create the thread from the `Runnable` and start it.

```
Runnable task = new HelloTask();
Thread thread = new Thread(task);
thread.start();
```

Now the `run` method executes in a separate thread, and the current thread can proceed with other work.

 NOTE: In Chapter 10, you will see other ways of executing a `Runnable`.

 NOTE: There is also a `Callable<T>` interface for tasks that return a result of type `T`.

3.3.4 User Interface Callbacks

In a graphical user interface, you have to specify actions to be carried out when the user clicks a button, selects a menu option, drags a slider, and so on. These actions are often called *callbacks* because some code gets called back when a user action occurs.

In Java-based GUI libraries, interfaces are used for callbacks. For example, in JavaFX, the following interface is used for reporting events:

```
public interface EventHandler<T> {
    void handle(T event);
}
```

This too is a generic interface where T is the type of event that is being reported, such as an ActionEvent for a button click.

To specify the action, implement the interface:

```
class CancelAction implements EventHandler<ActionEvent> {
    public void handle(ActionEvent event) {
        System.out.println("Oh noes!");
    }
}
```

Then, make an object of that class and add it to the button:

```
Button cancelButton = new Button("Cancel");
cancelButton.setOnAction(new CancelAction());
```

 NOTE: Since Oracle positions JavaFX as the successor to the Swing GUI toolkit, I use JavaFX in these examples. (Don't worry—you need not know any more about JavaFX than the couple of statements you just saw.) The details don't matter; in every user interface toolkit, be it Swing, JavaFX, or Android, you give a button some code that you want to run when the button is clicked.

Of course, this way of defining a button action is rather tedious. In other languages, you just give the button a function to execute, without going through the detour of making a class and instantiating it. The next section shows how you can do the same in Java.

3.4 Lambda Expressions

A *lambda expression* is a block of code that you can pass around so it can be executed later, once or multiple times. In the preceding sections, you have seen many situations where it is useful to specify such a block of code:

• To pass a comparison method to Arrays.sort

• To run a task in a separate thread

• To specify an action that should happen when a button is clicked

However, Java is an object-oriented language where (just about) everything is an object. There are no function types in Java. Instead, functions are expressed as objects, instances of classes that implement a particular interface. Lambda expressions give you a convenient syntax for creating such instances.

3.4.1 The Syntax of Lambda Expressions

Consider again the sorting example from Section 3.3.2, "The `Comparator` Interface" (page 111). We pass code that checks whether one string is shorter than another. We compute

```
first.length() - second.length()
```

What are `first` and `second`? They are both strings. Java is a strongly typed language, and we must specify that as well:

```
(String first, String second) -> first.length() - second.length()
```

You have just seen your first *lambda expression*. Such an expression is simply a block of code, together with the specification of any variables that must be passed to the code.

Why the name? Many years ago, before there were any computers, the logician Alonzo Church wanted to formalize what it means for a mathematical function to be effectively computable. (Curiously, there are functions that are known to exist, but nobody knows how to compute their values.) He used the Greek letter lambda (λ) to mark parameters, somewhat like

```
λfirst. λsecond. first.length() - second.length()
```

 NOTE: Why the letter λ? Did Church run out of letters of the alphabet? Actually, the venerable *Principia Mathematica* (see `http://plato.stanford.edu/entries/principia-mathematica`) used the ^ accent to denote function parameters, which inspired Church to use an uppercase lambda Λ. But in the end, he switched to the lowercase version. Ever since, an expression with parameter variables has been called a lambda expression.

If the body of a lambda expression carries out a computation that doesn't fit in a single expression, write it exactly like you would have written a method: enclosed in {} and with explicit `return` statements. For example,

```
(String first, String second) -> {
   int difference = first.length() < second.length();
   if (difference < 0) return -1;
   else if (difference > 0) return 1;
   else return 0;
}
```

If a lambda expression has no parameters, supply empty parentheses, just as with a parameterless method:

```
Runnable task = () -> { for (int i = 0; i < 1000; i++) doWork(); }
```

If the parameter types of a lambda expression can be inferred, you can omit them. For example,

```
Comparator<String> comp
    = (first, second) -> first.length() - second.length();
    // Same as (String first, String second)
```

Here, the compiler can deduce that `first` and `second` must be strings because the lambda expression is assigned to a string comparator. (We will have a closer look at this assignment in the next section.)

If a method has a single parameter with inferred type, you can even omit the parentheses:

```
EventHandler<ActionEvent> listener = event ->
    System.out.println("Oh noes!");
        // Instead of (event) -> or (ActionEvent event) ->
```

You never specify the result type of a lambda expression. However, the compiler infers it from the body and checks that it matches the expected type. For example, the expression

```
(String first, String second) -> first.length() - second.length()
```

can be used in a context where a result of type `int` is expected (or a compatible type such as `Integer`, `long`, or `double`).

3.4.2 Functional Interfaces

As you already saw, there are many interfaces in Java that express actions, such as `Runnable` or `Comparator`. Lambda expressions are compatible with these interfaces.

You can supply a lambda expression whenever an object of an interface with a *single abstract method* is expected. Such an interface is called a *functional interface*.

To demonstrate the conversion to a functional interface, consider the Arrays.sort method. Its second parameter requires an instance of Comparator, an interface with a single method. Simply supply a lambda:

```
Arrays.sort(words,
    (first, second) -> first.length() - second.length());
```

Behind the scenes, the second parameter variable of the Arrays.sort method receives an object of some class that implements Comparator<String>. Invoking the compare method on that object executes the body of the lambda expression. The management of these objects and classes is completely implementation-dependent and highly optimized.

In most programming languages that support function literals, you can declare function types such as (String, String) -> int, declare variables of those types, put functions into those variables, and invoke them. In Java, there is *only one thing* you can do with a lambda expression: put it in a variable whose type is a functional interface, so that it is converted to an instance of that interface.

 NOTE: You cannot assign a lambda expression to a variable of type Object, the common supertype of all classes in Java (see Chapter 4). Object is a class, not a functional interface.

The Java API provides a large number of functional interfaces (see Section 3.6.2, "Choosing a Functional Interface," page 120). One of them is

```
public interface Predicate<T> {
    boolean test(T t);
    // Additional default and static methods
}
```

The ArrayList class has a removeIf method whose parameter is a Predicate. It is specifically designed for receiving a lambda expression. For example, the following statement removes all null values from an array list:

```
list.removeIf(e -> e == null);
```

3.5 Method and Constructor References

Sometimes, there is already a method that carries out exactly the action that you'd like to pass on to some other code. There is special syntax for a *method reference* that is even shorter than a lambda expression calling the method. A similar shortcut exists for constructors. You will see both in the following sections.

3.5.1 Method References

Suppose you want to sort strings regardless of letter case. You could call

```
Arrays.sort(strings, (x, y) -> x.compareToIgnoreCase(y));
```

Instead, you can pass this method expression:

```
Arrays.sort(strings, String::compareToIgnoreCase);
```

The expression `String::compareToIgnoreCase` is a *method reference* that is equivalent to the lambda expression `(x, y) -> x.compareToIgnoreCase(y)`.

Here is another example. The `Objects` class defines a method `isNull`. The call `Objects.isNull(x)` simply returns the value of `x == null`. It seems hardly worth having a method for this case, but it was designed to be passed as a method expression. The call

```
list.removeIf(Objects::isNull);
```

removes all `null` values from a list.

As another example, suppose you want to print all elements of a list. The `ArrayList` class has a method `forEach` that applies a function to each element. You could call

```
list.forEach(x -> System.out.println(x));
```

It would be nicer, however, if you could just pass the `println` method to the `forEach` method. Here is how to do that:

```
list.forEach(System.out::println);
```

As you can see from these examples, the `::` operator separates the method name from the name of a class or object. There are three variations:

1. *Class*::*instanceMethod*

2. *Class*::*staticMethod*

3. *object*::*instanceMethod*

In the first case, the first parameter becomes the receiver of the method, and any other parameters are passed to the method. For example, `String::compareToIgnoreCase` is the same as `(x, y) -> x.compareToIgnoreCase(y)`.

In the second case, all parameters are passed to the static method. The method expression `Objects::isNull` is equivalent to `x -> Objects.isNull(x)`.

In the third case, the method is invoked on the given object, and the parameters are passed to the instance method. Therefore, `System.out::println` is equivalent to `x -> System.out.println(x)`.

NOTE: When there are multiple overloaded methods with the same name, the compiler will try to find from the context which one you mean. For example, there are multiple versions of the `println` method. When passed to the `forEach` method of an `ArrayList<String>`, the `println(String)` method is picked.

You can capture the `this` parameter in a method reference. For example, `this::equals` is the same as `x -> this.equals(x)`.

 NOTE: In an inner class, you can capture the `this` reference of an enclosing class as *EnclosingClass*.`this`::*method*. You can also capture `super`—see Chapter 4.

3.5.2 Constructor References

Constructor references are just like method references, except that the name of the method is `new`. For example, `Employee::new` is a reference to an `Employee` constructor. If the class has more than one constructor, then it depends on the context which constructor is chosen.

Here is an example for using such a constructor reference. Suppose you have a list of strings

```
List<String> names = ...;
```

You want a list of employees, one for each name. As you will see in Chapter 8, you can use streams to do this without a loop: Turn the list into a stream, and then call the `map` method. It applies a function and collects all results.

```
Stream<Employee> stream = names.stream().map(Employee::new);
```

Since `names.stream()` contains `String` objects, the compiler knows that `Employee::new` refers to the constructor `Employee(String)`.

You can form constructor references with array types. For example, `int[]::new` is a constructor reference with one parameter: the length of the array. It is equivalent to the lambda expression `n -> new int[n]`.

Array constructor references are useful to overcome a limitation of Java: It is not possible to construct an array of a generic type. (See Chapter 6 for details.) For that reason, methods such as `Stream.toArray` return an `Object` array, not an array of the element type:

```
Object[] employees = stream.toArray();
```

But that is unsatisfactory. The user wants an array of employees, not objects. To solve this problem, another version of toArray accepts a constructor reference:

```
Employee[] buttons = stream.toArray(Employee[]::new);
```

The toArray method invokes this constructor to obtain an array of the correct type. Then it fills and returns the array.

3.6 Processing Lambda Expressions

Up to now, you have seen how to produce lambda expressions and pass them to a method that expects a functional interface. In the following sections, you will see how to write your own methods that can consume lambda expressions.

3.6.1 Implementing Deferred Execution

The point of using lambdas is *deferred execution*. After all, if you wanted to execute some code right now, you'd do that, without wrapping it inside a lambda. There are many reasons for executing code later, such as:

- Running the code in a separate thread
- Running the code multiple times
- Running the code at the right point in an algorithm (for example, the comparison operation in sorting)
- Running the code when something happens (a button was clicked, data has arrived, and so on)
- Running the code only when necessary

Let's look at a simple example. Suppose you want to repeat an action n times. The action and the count are passed to a repeat method:

```
repeat(10, () -> System.out.println("Hello, World!"));
```

To accept the lambda, we need to pick (or, in rare cases, provide) a functional interface. In this case, we can just use Runnable:

```
public static void repeat(int n, Runnable action) {
    for (int i = 0; i < n; i++) action.run();
}
```

Note that the body of the lambda expression is executed when action.run() is called.

Now let's make this example a bit more sophisticated. We want to tell the action in which iteration it occurs. For that, we need to pick a functional interface that has a method with an `int` parameter and a `void` return. Instead of rolling your own, I strongly recommend that you use one of the standard ones described in the next section. The standard interface for processing `int` values is

```
public interface IntConsumer {
    void accept(int value);
}
```

Here is the improved version of the `repeat` method:

```
public static void repeat(int n, IntConsumer action) {
    for (int i = 0; i < n; i++) action.accept(i);
}
```

And here is how you call it:

```
repeat(10, i -> System.out.println("Countdown: " + (9 - i)));
```

3.6.2 Choosing a Functional Interface

In most functional programming languages, function types are *structural*. To specify a function that maps two strings to an integer, you use a type that looks something like `Function2<String, String, Integer>` or `(String, String) -> int`. In Java, you instead declare the intent of the function using a functional interface such as `Comparator<String>`. In the theory of programming languages this is called *nominal* typing.

Of course, there are many situations where you want to accept "any function" without particular semantics. There are a number of generic function types for that purpose (see Table 3-1), and it's a very good idea to use one of them when you can.

For example, suppose you write a method to process files that match a certain criterion. Should you use the descriptive `java.io.FileFilter` class or a `Predicate<File>`? I strongly recommend that you use the standard `Predicate<File>`. The only reason not to do so would be if you already have many useful methods producing `FileFilter` instances.

Table 3-1 Common Functional Interfaces

Functional Interface	Parameter types	Return type	Abstract method name	Description	Other methods
Runnable	none	void	run	Runs an action without arguments or return value	
Supplier<T>	none	T	get	Supplies a value of type T	
Consumer<T>	T	void	accept	Consumes a value of type T	andThen
BiConsumer<T, U>	T, U	void	accept	Consumes values of types T and U	andThen
Function<T, R>	T	R	apply	A function with argument of type T	compose, andThen, identity
BiFunction<T, U, R>	T, U	R	apply	A function with arguments of types T and U	andThen
UnaryOperator<T>	T	T	apply	A unary operator on the type T	compose, andThen, identity
BinaryOperator<T>	T, T	T	apply	A binary operator on the type T	andThen, maxBy, minBy
Predicate<T>	T	boolean	test	A boolean-valued function	and, or, negate, isEqual
BiPredicate<T, U>	T, U	boolean	test	A boolean-valued function with two arguments	and, or, negate

NOTE: Most of the standard functional interfaces have nonabstract methods for producing or combining functions. For example, `Predicate.isEqual(a)` is the same as `a::equals`, but it also works if `a` is `null`. There are default methods `and`, `or`, `negate` for combining predicates. For example,

```
Predicate.isEqual(a).or(Predicate.isEqual(b))
```

is the same as

```
x -> a.equals(x) || b.equals(x)
```

Table 3-2 lists the 34 available specializations for primitive types `int`, `long`, and `double`. It is a good idea to use these specializations to reduce autoboxing. For that reason, I used an `IntConsumer` instead of a `Consumer<Integer>` in the example of the preceding section.

Table 3-2 Functional Interfaces for Primitive Types
p, q is `int, long, double`; P, Q is `Int, Long, Double`

Functional Interface	Parameter types	Return type	Abstract method name
BooleanSupplier	none	boolean	getAsBoolean
PSupplier	none	p	getAsP
PConsumer	p	void	accept
Obj$P$Consumer<T>	T, p	void	accept
PFunction<T>	p	T	apply
PToQFunction	p	q	applyAsQ
ToPFunction<T>	T	p	applyAsP
ToPBiFunction<T, U>	T, U	p	applyAsP
PUnaryOperator	p	p	applyAsP
PBinaryOperator	p, p	p	applyAsP
PPredicate	p	boolean	test

3.6.3 Implementing Your Own Functional Interfaces

Ever so often, you will be in a situation where none of the standard functional interfaces work for you. Then you need to roll your own.

Suppose you want to fill an image with color patterns, where the user supplies a function yielding the color for each pixel. There is no standard type for a mapping (int, int) -> Color. You could use BiFunction<Integer, Integer, Color>, but that involves autoboxing.

In this case, it makes sense to define a new interface

```
@FunctionalInterface
public interface PixelFunction {
    Color apply(int x, int y);
}
```

 NOTE: It is a good idea to tag functional interfaces with the @FunctionalInterface annotation. This has two advantages. First, the compiler checks that the annotated entity is an interface with a single abstract method. Second, the javadoc page includes a statement that your interface is a functional interface.

Now you are ready to implement a method:

```
BufferedImage createImage(int width, int height, PixelFunction f) {
    BufferedImage image = new BufferedImage(width, height,
        BufferedImage.TYPE_INT_RGB);

    for (int x = 0; x < width; x++)
        for (int y = 0; y < height; y++) {
            Color color = f.apply(x, y);
            image.setRGB(x, y, color.getRGB());
        }
    return image;
}
```

To call it, supply a lambda expression that yields a color value for two integers:

```
BufferedImage frenchFlag = createImage(150, 100,
    (x, y) -> x < 50 ? Color.BLUE : x < 100 ? Color.WHITE : Color.RED);
```

3.7 Lambda Expressions and Variable Scope

In the following sections, you will learn how variables work inside lambda expressions. This information is somewhat technical but essential for working with lambda expressions.

3.7.1 Scope of a Lambda Expression

The body of a lambda expression has *the same scope as a nested block*. The same rules for name conflicts and shadowing apply. It is illegal to declare a parameter or a local variable in the lambda that has the same name as a local variable.

```
int first = 0;
Comparator<String> comp = (first, second) -> first.length() - second.length();
   // Error: Variable first already defined
```

Inside a method, you can't have two local variables with the same name, therefore you can't introduce such variables in a lambda expression either.

As another consequence of the "same scope" rule, the this keyword in a lambda expression denotes the this parameter of the method that creates the lambda. For example, consider

```
public class Application() {
    public void doWork() {
        Runnable runner = () -> { ...; System.out.println(this.toString()); ... };
        ...
    }
}
```

The expression this.toString() calls the toString method of the Application object, *not* the Runnable instance. There is nothing special about the use of this in a lambda expression. The scope of the lambda expression is nested inside the doWork method, and this has the same meaning anywhere in that method.

3.7.2 Accessing Variables from the Enclosing Scope

Often, you want to access variables from an enclosing method or class in a lambda expression. Consider this example:

```
public static void repeatMessage(String text, int count) {
    Runnable r = () -> {
        for (int i = 0; i < count; i++) {
            System.out.println(text);
        }
    };
    new Thread(r).start();
}
```

Note that the lambda expression accesses the parameter variables defined in the enclosing scope, not in the lambda expression itself.

Consider a call

```
repeatMessage("Hello", 1000); // Prints Hello 1000 times in a separate thread
```

Now look at the variables count and text inside the lambda expression. If you think about it, something nonobvious is going on here. The code of the lambda expression may run long after the call to repeatMessage has returned and the parameter variables are gone. How do the text and count variables stay around when the lambda expression is ready to execute?

To understand what is happening, we need to refine our understanding of a lambda expression. A lambda expression has three ingredients:

1. A block of code

2. Parameters

3. Values for the *free* variables—that is, the variables that are not parameters and not defined inside the code

In our example, the lambda expression has two free variables, text and count. The data structure representing the lambda expression must store the values for these variables—in our case, "Hello" and 1000. We say that these values have been *captured* by the lambda expression. (It's an implementation detail how that is done. For example, one can translate a lambda expression into an object with a single method, so that the values of the free variables are copied into instance variables of that object.)

 NOTE: The technical term for a block of code together with the values of free variables is a *closure*. In Java, lambda expressions are closures.

As you have seen, a lambda expression can capture the value of a variable in the enclosing scope. To ensure that the captured value is well defined, there is an important restriction. In a lambda expression, you can only reference variables whose value doesn't change. This is sometimes described by saying that lambda expressions capture values, not variables. For example, the following is a compile-time error:

```
for (int i = 0; i < n; i++) {
    new Thread(() -> System.out.println(i)).start();
        // Error—cannot capture i
}
```

The lambda expression tries to capture i, but this is not legal because i changes. There is no single value to capture. The rule is that a lambda expression can only access local variables from an enclosing scope that are *effectively final*. An effectively final variable is never modified—it either is or could be declared as `final`.

 NOTE: The same rule applies to variables captured by local classes (see Section 3.9, "Local and Anonymous Classes," page 129). In the past, the rule was more draconian and required captured variables to actually be declared `final`. This is no longer the case.

 NOTE: The variable of an enhanced `for` loop is effectively final since its scope is a single iteration. The following is perfectly legal:

```
for (String arg : args) {
    new Thread(() -> System.out.println(arg)).start();
        // OK to capture arg
}
```

A new variable `arg` is created in each iteration and assigned the next value from the `args` array. In contrast, the scope of the variable `i` in the preceding example was the entire loop.

As a consequence of the "effectively final" rule, a lambda expression cannot mutate any captured variables. For example,

```
public static void repeatMessage(String text, int count, int threads) {
    Runnable r = () -> {
        while (count > 0) {
            count--; // Error: Can't mutate captured variable
            System.out.println(text);
        }
    };
    for (int i = 0; i < threads; i++) new Thread(r).start();
}
```

This is actually a good thing. As you will see in Chapter 10, if two threads update `count` at the same time, its value is undefined.

 NOTE: Don't count on the compiler to catch all concurrent access errors. The prohibition against mutation only holds for local variables. If `count` is an instance variable or static variable of an enclosing class, then no error is reported even though the result is just as undefined.

CAUTION: One can circumvent the check for inappropriate mutations by using an array of length 1:

```
int[] counter = new int[1];
button.setOnAction(event -> counter[0]++);
```

The `counter` variable is effectively final—it is never changed since it always refers to the same array, so you can access it in the lambda expression.

Of course, code like this is not threadsafe. Except possibly for a callback in a single-threaded UI, this is a terrible idea. You will see how to implement a threadsafe shared counter in Chapter 10.

3.8 Higher-Order Functions

In a functional programming language, functions are first-class citizens. Just like you can pass numbers to methods and have methods that produce numbers, you can have arguments and return values that are functions. Functions that process or return functions are called *higher-order functions*. This sounds abstract, but it is very useful in practice. Java is not quite a functional language because it uses functional interfaces, but the principle is the same. In the following sections, we will look at some examples and examine the higher-order functions in the `Comparator` interface.

3.8.1 Methods that Return Functions

Suppose sometimes we want to sort an array of strings in ascending order and other times in descending order. We can make a method that produces the correct comparator:

```
public static Comparator<String> compareInDirecton(int direction) {
    return (x, y) -> direction * x.compareTo(y);
}
```

The call `compareInDirection(1)` yields an ascending comparator, and the call `compareInDirection(-1)` a descending comparator.

The result can be passed to another method (such as `Arrays.sort`) that expects such an interface.

```
Arrays.sort(friends, compareInDirection(-1));
```

In general, don't be shy to write methods that produce functions (or, technically, instances of classes that implement a functional interface). This is useful to generate custom functions that you pass to methods with functional interfaces.

3.8.2 Methods That Modify Functions

In the preceding section, you saw a method that yields an increasing or decreasing string comparator. We can generalize this idea by reversing any comparator:

```
public static Comparator<String> reverse(Comparator<String> comp) {
    return (x, y) -> comp.compare(y, x);
}
```

This method operates on functions. It receives a function and returns a modified function. To get case-insensitive descending order, use

```
reverse(String::compareToIgnoreCase)
```

 NOTE: The `Comparator` interface has a default method `reversed` that produces the reverse of a given comparator in just this way.

3.8.3 Comparator Methods

The `Comparator` interface has a number of useful static methods that are higher-order functions generating comparators.

The `comparing` method takes a "key extractor" function that maps a type `T` to a comparable type (such as `String`). The function is applied to the objects to be compared, and the comparison is then made on the returned keys. For example, suppose a `Person` class has a method `getLastName`. Then you can sort an array of `Person` objects by last name like this:

```
Arrays.sort(people, Comparator.comparing(Person::getLastName));
```

You can chain comparators with the `thenComparing` method to break ties. For example, sort an array of people by last name, then use the first name for people with the same last name:

```
Arrays.sort(people, Comparator
    .comparing(Person::getLastName)
    .thenComparing(Person::getFirstName));
```

There are a few variations of these methods. You can specify a comparator to be used for the keys that the `comparing` and `thenComparing` methods extract. For example, here we sort people by the length of their names:

```
Arrays.sort(people, Comparator.comparing(Person::getLastName,
    (s, t) -> s.length() - t.length()));
```

Moreover, both the `comparing` and `thenComparing` methods have variants that avoid boxing of `int`, `long`, or `double` values. An easier way of sorting by name length would be

```
Arrays.sort(people, Comparator.comparingInt(p -> p.getLastName().length()));
```

If your key function can return `null`, you will like the `nullsFirst` and `nullsLast` adapters. These static methods take an existing comparator and modify it so that it doesn't throw an exception when encountering `null` values but ranks them as smaller or larger than regular values. For example, suppose `getMiddleName` returns a `null` when a person has no middle name. Then you can use `Comparator.comparing(Person::getMiddleName(), Comparator.nullsFirst(...))`.

The `nullsFirst` method needs a comparator—in this case, one that compares two strings. The `naturalOrder` method makes a comparator for any class implementing `Comparable`. Here is the complete call for sorting by potentially null middle names. I use a static import of `java.util.Comparator.*` to make the expression more legible. Note that the type for `naturalOrder` is inferred.

```
Arrays.sort(people, comparing(Person::getMiddleName,
    nullsFirst(naturalOrder())));
```

The static `reverseOrder` method gives the reverse of the natural order.

3.9 Local and Anonymous Classes

Long before there were lambda expressions, Java had a mechanism for concisely defining classes that implement an interface (functional or not). For functional interfaces, you should definitely use lambda expressions, but once in a while, you may want a concise form for an interface that isn't functional. You will also encounter the classic constructs in legacy code.

3.9.1 Local Classes

You can define a class inside a method. Such a class is called a *local class*. You would do this for classes that are just tactical. This occurs often when a class implements an interface and the caller of the method only cares about the interface, not the class.

For example, consider a method

```
public static IntSequence randomInts(int low, int high)
```

that generates an infinite sequence of random integers with the given bounds.

Since `IntSequence` is an interface, the method must return an object of some class implementing that interface. The caller doesn't care about the class, so it can be declared inside the method:

```
private static Random generator = new Random();

public static IntSequence randomInts(int low, int high) {
    class RandomSequence implements IntSequence {
        public int next() { return low + generator.nextInt(high - low + 1); }
        public boolean hasNext() { return true; }
    }

    return new RandomSequence();
}
```

 NOTE: A local class is not declared as `public` or `private` since it is never accessible outside the method.

There are two advantages of making a class local. First, its name is hidden in the scope of the method. Second, the methods of the class can access variables from the enclosing scope, just like the variables of a lambda expression.

In our example, the `next` method captures three variables: `low`, `high`, and `generator`. If you turned `RandomInt` into a nested class, you would have to provide an explicit constructor that receives these values and stores them in instance variables (see Exercise 16).

3.9.2 Anonymous Classes

In the example of the preceding section, the name `RandomSequence` was used exactly once: to construct the return value. In this case, you can make the class *anonymous*:

```
public static IntSequence randomInts(int low, int high) {
    return new IntSequence() {
        public int next() { return low + generator.nextInt(high - low + 1); }
        public boolean hasNext() { return true; }
    };
}
```

The expression

```
new Interface() { methods }
```

means: Define a class implementing the interface that has the given methods, and construct one object of that class.

 NOTE: As always, the `()` in the `new` expression indicate the construction arguments. A default constructor of the anonymous class is invoked.

Before Java had lambda expressions, anonymous inner classes were the most concise syntax available for providing runnables, comparators, and other functional objects. You will often see them in legacy code.

Nowadays, they are only necessary when you need to provide two or more methods, as in the preceding example. If the IntSequence interface has a default hasNext method, as in Exercise 16, you can simply use a lambda expression:

```
public static IntSequence randomInts(int low, int high) {
    return () -> low + generator.nextInt(high - low + 1);
}
```

Exercises

1. Provide an interface Measurable with a method double getMeasure() that measures an object in some way. Make Employee implement Measurable. Provide a method double average(Measurable[] objects) that computes the average measure. Use it to compute the average salary of an array of employees.

2. Continue with the preceding exercise and provide a method Measurable largest(Measurable[] objects). Use it to find the name of the employee with the largest salary. Why do you need a cast?

3. What are all the supertypes of String? Of Scanner? Of ImageOutputStream? Note that each type is its own supertype. A class or interface without declared supertype has supertype Object.

4. Implement a static of method of the IntSequence class that yields a sequence with the arguments. For example, IntSequence.of(3, 1, 4, 1, 5, 9) yields a sequence with six values. Extra credit if you return an instance of an anonymous inner class.

5. Add a static method with the name constant of the IntSequence class that yields an infinite constant sequence. For example, IntSequence.constant(1) yields values 1 1 1..., ad infinitum. Extra credit if you do this with a lambda expression.

6. The SquareSequence class doesn't actually deliver an infinite sequence of squares due to integer overflow. Specifically, how does it behave? Fix the problem by defining a Sequence<T> interface and a SquareSequence class that implements Sequence<BigInteger>.

7. In this exercise, you will try out what happens when a method is added to an interface. In Java 7, implement a class DigitSequence that implements Iterator<Integer>, not IntSequence. Provide methods hasNext, next, and a do-nothing remove. Write a program that prints the elements of an instance.

In Java 8, the `Iterator` class gained another method, `forEachRemaining`. Does your code still compile when you switch to Java 8? If you put your Java 7 class in a JAR file and don't recompile, does it work in Java 8? What if you call the `forEachRemaining` method? Also, the `remove` method has become a default method in Java 8, throwing an `UnsupportedOperationException`. What happens when `remove` is called on an instance of your class?

8. Implement the method `void luckySort(ArrayList<String> strings, Comparator<String> comp)` that keeps calling `Collections.shuffle` on the array list until the elements are in increasing order, as determined by the comparator.

9. Implement a class `Greeter` that implements `Runnable` and whose `run` method prints n copies of `"Hello, "` + `target`, where `n` and `target` are set in the constructor. Construct two instances with different messages and execute them concurrently in two threads.

10. Implement methods

```
public static void runTogether(Runnable... tasks)
public static void runInOrder(Runnable... tasks)
```

The first method should run each task in a separate thread and then return. The second method should run all methods in the current thread and return when the last one has completed.

11. Using the `listFiles(FileFilter)` and `isDirectory` methods of the `java.io.File` class, write a method that returns all subdirectories of a given directory. Use a lambda expression instead of a `FileFilter` object. Repeat with a method expression and an anonymous inner class.

12. Using the `list(FilenameFilter)` method of the `java.io.File` class, write a method that returns all files in a given directory with a given extension. Use a lambda expression, not a `FilenameFilter`. Which variable from the enclosing scope does it capture?

13. Given an array of `File` objects, sort it so that directories come before files, and within each group, elements are sorted by path name. Use a lambda expression to specify the `Comparator`.

14. Write a method that takes an array of `Runnable` instances and returns a `Runnable` whose `run` method executes them in order. Return a lambda expression.

15. Write a call to `Arrays.sort` that sorts employees by salary, breaking ties by name. Use `Comparator.thenComparing`. Then do this in reverse order.

16. Implement the `RandomSequence` in Section 3.9.1, "Local Classes" (page 129) as a nested class, outside the `randomInts` method.

Inheritance and Reflection

Topics in This Chapter

Chapter 4

The preceding chapters introduced you to classes and interfaces. In this chapter, you will learn about another fundamental concept of object-oriented programming: inheritance. Inheritance is the process of creating new classes that are built on existing classes. When you inherit from an existing class, you reuse (or inherit) its methods, and you can add new methods and fields.

 NOTE: Instance variables and static variables are collectively called *fields*. The fields, methods, and nested classes/interfaces inside a class are collectively called its *members*.

This chapter also covers reflection, the ability to find out more about classes and their members in a running program. Reflection is a powerful feature, but it is undeniably complex. Since reflection is of greater interest to tool builders than to application programmers, you can probably glance over that part of the chapter upon first reading and come back to it later.

The key points of this chapter are:

1. A subclass can inherit or override methods from the superclass, provided they are not `private`.

2. Use the `super` keyword to invoke a superclass method or constructor.

3. A `final` method cannot be overridden; a `final` class cannot be extended.

4. An abstract method has no implementation; an abstract class cannot be instantiated.

5. A protected member of a superclass is accessible in a subclass method, but only when applied to objects of the same subclass. It is also accessible in its package.

6. Every class is a subclass of Object which provides the toString, equals, hashCode, and clone methods.

7. Each enumerated type is a subclass of Enum which provides instance methods toString and compareTo, and a static valueOf method.

8. The Class class provides information about a Java type, which can be a class, array, interface, primitive type, or void.

9. You can use a Class object to load resources that are placed alongside class files.

10. You can load classes from locations other than the class path by using a class loader.

11. The ServiceLoader class provides a mechanism for locating and selecting service implementations.

12. The reflection library enables programs to discover members of objects, access variables, and invoke methods.

13. Proxy objects dynamically implement arbitrary interfaces, routing all method invocations to a handler.

4.1 Extending a Class

Let's return to the Employee class that we discussed in Chapter 2. Suppose (alas) you work for a company at which managers are treated differently from other employees. Managers are, of course, just like employees in many respects. Both employees and managers are paid a salary. However, while employees are expected to complete their assigned tasks in return for their salary, managers get bonuses if they actually achieve what they are supposed to do. This is the kind of situation that can be modeled with inheritance.

4.1.1 Super- and Subclasses

Let's define a new class, Manager, retaining some functionality of the Employee class but specifying how managers are different.

```
public class Manager extends Employee {
    added fields
    added or overriding methods
}
```

The keyword `extends` indicates that you are making a new class that derives from an existing class. The existing class is called the *superclass* and the new class is called the *subclass*. In our example, the `Employee` class is the superclass and the `Manager` class is the subclass. Note that the superclass is not "superior" to its subclass. The opposite is true: Subclasses have more functionality than their superclasses. The super/sub terminology comes from set theory. The set of managers is a subset of the set of employees.

4.1.2 Defining and Inheriting Subclass Methods

Our `Manager` class has a new instance variable to store the bonus and a new method to set it:

```
public class Manager extends Employee {
    private double bonus;
    ...
    public void setBonus(double bonus) {
        this.bonus = bonus;
    }
}
```

When you have a `Manager` object, you can of course apply the `setBonus` method, as well as nonprivate methods from the `Employee` class. Those methods are *inherited*.

```
Manager boss = new Manager(...);
boss.setBonus(10000); // Defined in subclass
boss.raiseSalary(5); // Inherited from superclass
```

4.1.3 Method Overriding

Sometimes, a superclass method needs to be modified in a subclass. For example, suppose that the `getSalary` method is expected to report the total salary of an employee. Then the inherited method is not sufficient for the `Manager` class. Instead, you need to *override* the method so that it returns the sum of the base salary and the bonus.

```
public class Manager extends Employee {
    ...
    public double getSalary() { // Overrides superclass method
        return super.getSalary() + bonus;
    }
}
```

This method invokes the superclass method, which retrieves the base salary, and adds the bonus. Note that a subclass method cannot access the private instance variables of the superclass directly. That is why the Manager.getSalary method calls the public Employee.getSalary method. The super keyword is used for invoking a superclass method.

 NOTE: Unlike this, super is not a reference to an object, but a directive to bypass dynamic method lookup (see Section 4.1.5, "Superclass Assignments," page 139) and invoke a specific method instead.

It is not required to call the superclass method when overriding a method, but it is common to do so.

When you override a method, you must be careful to match the parameter types exactly. For example, suppose that the Employee class has a method

```
public boolean worksFor(Employee supervisor)
```

If you override this method in the Manager class, you cannot change the parameter type, even though surely no manager would report to a mere employee. Suppose you defined a method

```
public class Manager extends Employee {
    ...
    public boolean worksFor(Manager supervisor) {
        ...
    }
}
```

This is simply a new method, and now Manager has two separate worksFor methods. You can protect yourself against this type of error by tagging methods that are intended to override superclass methods with the @Override annotation:

```
@Override public boolean worksFor(Employee supervisor)
```

If you made a mistake and are defining a new method, the compiler reports an error.

You can change the return type to a subtype when overriding a method. (In technical terms, *covariant return types* are permitted.) For example, if the Employee class has a method

```
public Employee getSupervisor()
```

then the Manager class can override it with the method

```
@Override public Manager getSupervisor()
```

CAUTION: When you override a method, the subclass method must be *at least as accessible* as the superclass method. In particular, if the superclass method is public, then the subclass method must also be declared public. It is a common error to accidentally omit the `public` modifier for the subclass method. The compiler then complains about the weaker access privilege.

4.1.4 Subclass Construction

Let us supply a constructor for the `Manager` class. Since the `Manager` constructor cannot access the private instance variables of the `Employee` class, it must initialize them through a superclass constructor.

```
public Manager(String name, double salary) {
    super(name, salary);
    bonus = 0;
}
```

Here, the keyword `super` indicates a call to the constructor of the `Employee` superclass with `name` and `salary` as arguments. The superclass constructor call must be the *first statement* in the constructor for the subclass.

If the subclass does not explicitly call any superclass constructor, the superclass must have a no-argument constructor which is implicitly called.

4.1.5 Superclass Assignments

It is legal to assign an object from a subclass to a variable whose type is a superclass, for example:

```
Manager boss = new Manager(...);
Employee empl = boss; // OK to assign to superclass variable
```

Now consider what happens when one invokes a method on the superclass variable.

```
double salary = empl.getSalary();
```

Even though the type of `empl` is `Employee`, the `Manager.getSalary` method is invoked. When invoking a method, the virtual machine looks at the actual class of the object and locates its version of the method. This process is called *dynamic method lookup*.

Why would you want to assign a `Manager` object to an `Employee` variable? It allows you to write code that works for *all* employees, be they managers or janitors or instances of another `Employee` subclass.

```
Employee[] staff = new Employee[...];
staff[0] = new Employee(...);
staff[1] = new Manager(...); // OK to assign to superclass variable
staff[2] = new Janitor(...);
...
double sum = 0;
for (Employee empl : staff)
    sum += empl.getSalary();
```

Thanks to dynamic method lookup, the call `empl.getSalary()` invokes the `getSalary` method belonging to the object to which `empl` refers, which may be `Employee.getSalary`, `Manager.getSalary`, and so on.

 CAUTION: In Java, superclass assignment also works for arrays: You can assign a `Manager[]` array to an `Employee[]` variable. (The technical term is that Java arrays are *covariant*.) This is convenient, but it is also *unsound*—that is, a possible cause of type errors. Consider this example:

```
Manager[] bosses = new Manager[10];
Employee[] empls = bosses; // Legal in Java
empls[0] = new Employee(...); // Runtime error
```

The compiler accepts the last statement since it is generally legal to store an `Employee` in an `Employee[]` array. However, here `empls` and `bosses` reference the same `Manager[]` array, which cannot hold a lowly `Employee`. This mistake is only caught at runtime, when the virtual machine throws an `ArrayStoreException`.

4.1.6 Casts

In the preceding section, you saw how a variable `empl` of type `Employee` can refer to objects whose class is `Employee`, `Manager`, or another subclass of `Employee`. That is useful for code that deals with objects from multiple classes. There is just one drawback. You can only invoke methods that belong to the superclass. Consider, for example,

```
Employee empl = new Manager(...);
empl.setBonus(10000); // Compile-time error
```

Even though this call could succeed at runtime, it is a compile-time error. The compiler checks that you only invoke methods that exist for the receiver type. Here, `empl` is of type `Employee` and that class has no `setBonus` method.

As with interfaces, you can use the `instanceof` operator and a cast to turn a superclass reference to a subclass.

```
if (empl instanceof Manager) {
    Manager mgr = (Manager) empl;
    mgr.setBonus(10000);
}
```

4.1.7 Final Methods and Classes

When you declare a method as `final`, no subclass can override it.

```
public class Employee {
    ...
    public final String getName() {
        return name;
    }
}
```

A good example of a `final` method in the Java API is the `getClass` method of the `Object` class that you will see in Section 4.4.1, "The Class `Class`" (page 159). It does not seem wise to allow objects to lie about the class to which they belong, so this method can never be changed.

Some programmers believe that the `final` keyword is good for efficiency. This may have been true in the early days of Java, but it no longer is. Modern virtual machines will speculatively "inline" simple methods, such as the `getName` method above, even if they are not declared `final`. In the rare case when a subclass is loaded that overrides such a method, the inlining is undone.

Some programmers believe that most methods of a class should be declared `final`, and only methods specifically designed to be overridden should not be. Others find this too draconian since it prevents even harmless overriding, for example for logging or debugging purposes.

Occasionally, you may want to prevent someone from forming a subclass from one of your classes. Use the `final` modifier in the class definition to indicate this. For example, here is how to prevent others from subclassing the `Executive` class:

```
public final class Executive extends Manager {
    ...
}
```

There is a good number of final classes in the Java API, such as `String`, `LocalTime`, and `URL`.

4.1.8 Abstract Methods and Classes

A class can define a method without an implementation, forcing subclasses to implement it. Such a method, and the class containing it, are called *abstract* and must be tagged with the abstract modifier. This is commonly done for very general classes, for example:

```
public abstract class Person {
    private String name;

    public Person(String name) { this.name = name; }
    public final String getName() { return name; }

    public abstract int getId();
}
```

Any class extending Person must either supply an implementation of the getId method or be itself declared as abstract.

Note that an abstract class can have nonabstract methods, such as the getName method in the preceding example.

 NOTE: Unlike an interface, an abstract class can have instance variables and constructors.

It is not possible to construct an instance of an abstract class. For example, the call

```
Person p = new Person("Fred"); // Error
```

would be a compile-time error.

However, you can have a variable whose type is an abstract class, provided it contains a reference to an object of a concrete subclass. Suppose the class Student is declared as

```
public class Student extends Person {
    private int id;

    public Student(String name, int id) { super(name); this.id = id; }
    public int getId() { return id; }
}
```

Then you can construct a Student and assign it to a Person variable.

```
Person p = new Student("Fred", 1729); // OK, a concrete subclass
```

4.1.9 Protected Access

There are times when you want to restrict a method to subclasses only or, less commonly, to allow subclass methods to access an instance variable of a superclass. For that, declare a class feature as protected.

For example, suppose the superclass `Employee` declares the instance variable `salary` as `protected` instead of `private`.

```
package com.horstmann.employees;

public class Employee {
    protected double salary;
    ...
}
```

All classes in the same package as `Employee` can access this field. Now consider a subclass from a different package:

```
package com.horstmann.managers;

import com.horstmann.employees.Employee;

public class Manager extends Employee {
    ...
    public double getSalary() {
        return salary + bonus; // OK to access protected salary variable
    }
}
```

The `Manager` class methods can peek inside the `salary` variable of `Manager` objects only, not of other `Employee` objects. This restriction is made so that you can't abuse the protected mechanism by forming subclasses just to gain access to protected features.

Of course, protected fields should be used with caution. Once provided, you cannot take them away without breaking classes that are using them.

Protected methods and constructors are more common. For example, the `clone` method of the `Object` class is protected since it is somewhat tricky to use (see Section 4.2.4, "Cloning Objects," page 151).

 CAUTION: In Java, `protected` grants package-level access, and it only protects access from other packages.

4.1.10 Anonymous Subclasses

Just as you can have an anonymous class that implements an interface, you can have an anonymous class that extends a superclass. This can be handy for debugging:

```
ArrayList<String> names = new ArrayList<String>(100) {
    public void add(int index, String element) {
        super.add(index, element);
        System.out.printf("Adding %s at %d\n", element, index);
    }
};
```

The arguments in the parentheses following the superclass name are passed
to the superclass constructor. Here, we construct an anonymous subclass of
`ArrayList<String>` that overrides the `add` method. The instance is constructed with
an initial capacity of 100.

A trick called *double brace initialization* uses the inner class syntax in a rather
bizarre way. Suppose you want to construct an array list and pass it to a
method:

```
ArrayList<String> friends = new ArrayList<>();
friends.add("Harry");
friends.add("Sally");
invite(friends);
```

If you won't ever need the array list again, it would be nice to make it
anonymous. But then, how can you add the elements? Here is how:

```
invite(new ArrayList<String>() {{ add("Harry"); add("Sally"); }});
```

Note the double braces. The outer braces make an anonymous subclass of
`ArrayList<String>`. The inner braces are an initialization block (see Chapter 2).

I am not recommending that you use this trick outside of Java trivia contests.
There are several drawbacks beyond the confusing syntax. It is inefficient,
and the constructed object can behave strangely in equality tests, depending
on how the `equals` method is implemented.

4.1.11 Inheritance and Default Methods

Suppose a class extends a class and implements an interface, both of which
happen to have a method of the same name.

```
public interface Named {
    default String getName() { return ""; }
}

public class Person {
    ...
    public String getName() { return name; }
}

public class Student extends Person implements Named {
    ...
}
```

In this situation, the superclass implementation always wins over the interface implementation. There is no need for the subclass to resolve the conflict.

In contrast, as you saw in Chapter 3, you must resolve a conflict when the same default method is inherited from two interfaces.

The "classes win" rule ensures compatibility with Java 7. If you add default methods to an interface, it has no effect on code that worked before there were default methods.

4.1.12 Method Expressions with super

Recall from Chapter 3 that a method expression can have the form *object::instanceMethod*. It is also valid to use `super` instead of an object reference. The method expression

```
super::instanceMethod
```

uses `this` as the target and invokes the superclass version of the given method. Here is an artificial example that shows the mechanics:

```
public class Worker {
    public void work() {
        for (int i = 0; i < 100; i++) System.out.println("Working");
    }
}

public class ConcurrentWorker extends Worker {
    public void work() {
        Thread t = new Thread(super::work);
        t.start();
    }
}
```

The thread is constructed with a `Runnable` whose `run` method calls the `work` method of the superclass.

4.2 Object: The Cosmic Superclass

Every class in Java directly or indirectly extends the class `Object`. When a class has no explicit superclass, it implicitly extends `Object`. For example,

```
public class Employee { ... }
```

is equivalent to

```
public class Employee extends Object { ... }
```

The `Object` class defines methods that are applicable to any Java object (see Table 4-1). We will examine several of these methods in detail in the following sections.

 NOTE: Arrays are classes. Therefore, it is legal to convert an array, even a primitive type array, to a reference of type `Object`.

Table 4-1 The Methods of the `java.lang.Object` Class

Method	Description
`String toString()`	Yields a string representation of this object, by default the name of the class and the hash code.
`boolean equals(Object other)`	Returns `true` if this object should be considered equal to `other`, `false` if `other` is `null` or different from `other`. By default, two objects are equal if they are identical. Instead of `obj.equals(other)`, consider the null-safe alternative `Objects.equals(obj, other)`.
`int hashCode()`	Yields a hash code for this object. Equal objects must have the same hash code. Unless overridden, the hash code is assigned in some way by the virtual machine.
`Class<?> getClass()`	Yields the `Class` object describing the class to which this object belongs.
`protected Object clone()`	Makes a copy of this object. By default, the copy is shallow.
`protected void finalize()`	This method is called when this object is reclaimed by the garbage collector. Don't override it.
`wait, notify, notifyAll`	See Chapter 10.

4.2.1 The `toString` Method

An important method in the `Object` class is the `toString` method that returns a string description of an object. For example, the `toString` method of the `Point` class returns a string like this:

```
java.awt.Point[x=10,y=20]
```

Many `toString` methods follow this format: the name of the class, followed by the instance variables enclosed in square brackets. Here is such an implementation of the `toString` method of the `Employee` class:

```
public String toString() {
    return getClass().getName() + "[name=" + name
        + ",salary=" + salary + "]";
}
```

By calling `getClass().getName()` instead of hardwiring the string `"Employee"`, this method does the right thing for subclasses as well.

In a subclass, call `super.toString()` and add the instance variables of the subclass, in a separate pair of brackets:

```
public class Manager extends Employee {
    ...
    public String toString() {
        return super.toString() + "[bonus=" + bonus + "]";
    }
}
```

Whenever an object is concatenated with a string, the Java compiler automatically invokes the `toString` method on the object. For example:

```
Point p = new Point(10, 20);
String message = "The current position is " + p;
    // Concatenates with p.toString()
```

TIP: Instead of writing `x.toString()`, you can write `"" + x`. This expression even works if `x` is `null` or a primitive type value.

The `Object` class defines the `toString` method to print the class name and the hash code (see Section 4.2.3, "The `hashCode` Method," page 150). For example, the call

```
System.out.println(System.out)
```

produces an output that looks like `java.io.PrintStream@2f6684` since the implementor of the `PrintStream` class didn't bother to override the `toString` method.

CAUTION: Arrays inherit the `toString` method from `Object`, with the added twist that the array type is printed in an archaic format. For example, if you have the array

```
int[] primes = { 2, 3, 5, 7, 11, 13 };
```

then `primes.toString()` yields a string such as `"[I@1a46e30"`. The prefix `[I` denotes an array of integers.

The remedy is to call `Arrays.toString(primes)` instead, which yields the string `"[2, 3, 5, 7, 11, 13]"`. To correctly print multidimensional arrays (that is, arrays of arrays), use `Arrays.deepToString`.

4.2.2 The equals Method

The equals method tests whether one object is considered equal to another. The equals method, as implemented in the Object class, determines whether two object references are identical. This is a pretty reasonable default—if two objects are identical, they should certainly be equal. For quite a few classes, nothing else is required. For example, it makes little sense to compare two Scanner objects for equality.

Override the equals method only for state-based equality testing, in which two objects are considered equal when they have the same contents. For example, the String class overrides equals to check whether two strings consist of the same characters.

 CAUTION: Whenever you override the equals method, you *must* provide a compatible hashCode method as well—see Section 4.2.3, "The hashCode Method" (page 150).

Suppose we want to consider two objects of a class Item equal if their descriptions and prices match. Here is how you can implement the equals method:

```
public class Item {
    private String description;
    private double price;
    ...
    public boolean equals(Object otherObject) {
        // A quick test to see if the objects are identical
        if (this == otherObject) return true;

        // Must return false if the parameter is null
        if (otherObject == null) return false;
        // Check that otherObject is an Item
        if (getClass() != otherObject.getClass()) return false;
        // Test whether the instance variables have identical values
        Item other = (Item) otherObject;
        return Objects.equals(description, other.description)
            && price == other.price;
    }

    public int hashCode() { ... } // See Section 4.2.3
}
```

There are a number of routine steps that you need to go through in an equals method:

1. It is common for equal objects to be identical, and that test is very inexpensive.

2. Every `equals` method is required to return `false` when comparing against `null`.

3. Since the `equals` method overrides `Object.equals`, its parameter is of type `Object`, and you need to cast it to the actual type so you can look at its instance variables. Before doing that, make a type check, either with the `getClass` method or with the `instanceof` operator.

4. Finally, compare the instance variables. Use `==` for primitive types. However, for `double` values, if you are concerned about $\pm\infty$ or NaN, use `Double.equals`. For objects, use `Objects.equals`, a null-safe version of the `equals` method. The call `Objects.equals(x, y)` returns `false` if `x` is `null`, whereas `x.equals(y)` would throw an exception.

 TIP: If you have instance variables that are arrays, use the static `Arrays.equals` method to check that the arrays have equal length and the corresponding array elements are equal.

When you define the `equals` method for a subclass, first call `equals` on the superclass. If that test doesn't pass, the objects can't be equal. If the instance variables of the superclass are equal, then you are ready to compare the instance variables of the subclass.

```
public class DiscountedItem extends Item {
    private double discount;
    ...
    public boolean equals(Object otherObject) {
        if (!super.equals(otherObject)) return false;
        DiscountedItem other = (DiscountedItem) otherObject;
        return discount == other.discount;
    }

    public int hashCode() { ... }
}
```

Note that the `getClass` test in the superclass fails if `otherObject` is not a `DiscountedItem`.

How should the `equals` method behave when comparing values that belong to different classes? This has been an area of some controversy. In the preceding example, the `equals` method returns `false` if the classes don't match exactly. But many programmers use an `instanceof` test instead:

```
if (!(otherObject instanceof Item)) return false;
```

This leaves open the possibility that `otherObject` can belong to a subclass. For example, you can compare an `Item` with a `DiscountedItem`.

However, that kind of comparison doesn't usually work. One of the requirements of the equals method is that it is *symmetric*: For non-null x and y, the calls x.equals(y) and y.equals(x) need to return the same value.

Now suppose x is an Item and y a DiscountedItem. Since x.equals(y) doesn't consider discounts, neither can y.equals(x).

NOTE: The Java API contains over 150 implementations of equals methods, with a mixture of instanceof tests, calling getClass, catching a ClassCastException, or doing nothing at all. Check out the documentation of the java.sql.Timestamp class, where the implementors note with some embarrassment that the Timestamp class inherits from java.util.Date, whose equals method uses an instanceof test, and it is therefore impossible to override equals to be both symmetric and accurate.

There is one situation where the instanceof test makes sense: if the notion of equality is fixed in the superclass and never varies in a subclass. For example, this is the case if we compare employees by ID. In that case, make an instanceof test and declare the equals method as final.

```
public class Employee {
    private int id;
    ...
    public final boolean equals(Object otherObject) {
        if (this == otherObject) return true;
        if (!(otherObject instanceof Employee)) return false;
        Employee other = (Employee) otherObject;
        return id == other.id;
    }

    public int hashCode() { ... }
}
```

4.2.3 The hashCode Method

A *hash code* is an integer that is derived from an object. Hash codes should be scrambled—if x and y are two unequal objects, there should be a high probability that x.hashCode() and y.hashCode() are different. For example, "Mary".hashCode() is 2390779, and "Myra".hashCode() is 2413819.

The String class uses the following algorithm to compute the hash code:

```
int hash = 0;
for (int i = 0; i < length(); i++)
    hash = 31 * hash + charAt(i);
```

The hashCode and equals methods must be *compatible*: If x.equals(y), then it must be the case that x.hashCode() == y.hashCode(). As you can see, this is the case for the String class since strings with equal characters produce the same hash code.

The Object.hashCode method derives the hash code in some implementation-dependent way. It can be derived from the object's memory location, or a number (sequential or pseudorandom) that is cached with the object, or a combination of both. Since Object.equals tests for identical objects, the only thing that matters is that identical objects have the same hash code.

If you redefine the equals method, you will also need to redefine the hashCode method to be compatible with equals. If you don't, and users of your class insert objects into a hash set or hash map, they might get lost!

In your hashCode method, simply combine the hash codes of the instance variables. For example, here is a hashCode method for the Item class:

```
class Item {
    ...
    public int hashCode() {
        return Objects.hash(description, price);
    }
}
```

The Objects.hash varargs method computes the hash codes of its arguments and combines them. The method is null-safe.

If your class has instance variables that are arrays, compute their hash codes first with the static Arrays.hashCode method, which computes a hash code composed of the hash codes of the array elements. Pass the result to Objects.hash.

 CAUTION: In an interface, you can never make a default method that redefines one of the methods in the Object class. In particular, an interface can't define a default method for toString, equals, or hashCode. As a consequence of the "classes win" rule (see Section 4.1.11, "Inheritance and Default Methods," page 144), such a method could never win against Object.toString, Object.equals, or Object.hashCode.

4.2.4 Cloning Objects

You have just seen the "big three" methods of the Object class that are commonly overridden: toString, equals, and hashCode. In this section, you will learn how to override the clone method. As you will see, this is complex, and it is also rarely necessary. Don't override clone unless you have a good reason to do so. Less than five percent of the classes in the standard Java library implement clone.

The purpose of the `clone` method is to make a "clone" of an object—a distinct object with the same state of the original. If you mutate one of the objects, the other stays unchanged.

```
Employee cloneOfFred = fred.clone();
cloneOfFred.raiseSalary(10); // fred unchanged
```

The `clone` method is declared as `protected` in the `Object` class, so you must override it if you want users of your class to clone instances.

The `Object.clone` method makes a *shallow copy*. It simply copies all instance variables from the original to the cloned object. That is fine if the variables are primitive or immutable. But if they aren't, then the original and the clone share mutable state, which can be a problem.

Consider a class for email messages that has a list of recipients.

```
public final class Message {
    private String sender;
    private ArrayList<String> recipients;
    private String text;
    ...
    public void addRecipient(String recipient) { ... };
}
```

If you make a shallow copy of a `Message` object, both the original and the clone share the `recipients` list (see Figure 4-1):

```
Message specialOffer = ...;
Message cloneOfSpecialOffer = specialOffer.clone();
```

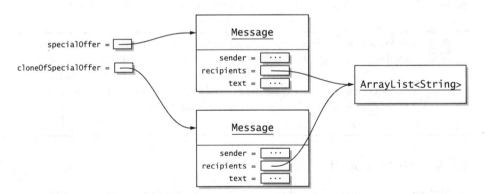

Figure 4-1 A shallow copy of an object

If either object changes the recipient list, the change is reflected in the other. Therefore, the Message class needs to override the clone method to make a *deep copy*.

It may also be that cloning is impossible or not worth the trouble. For example, it would be very challenging to clone a Scanner object.

In general, when you implement a class, you need to decide whether

1. You do not want to provide a clone method, or

2. The inherited clone method is acceptable, or

3. The clone method should make a deep copy.

For the first option, simply do nothing. Your class will inherit the clone method, but no user of your class will be able to call it since it is protected.

To choose the second option, your class must implement the Cloneable interface. This is an interface without any methods, called a *tagging* or *marker* interface. (Recall that the clone method is defined in the Object class.) The Object.clone method checks that this interface is implemented before making a shallow copy, and throws a CloneNotSupportedException otherwise.

You will also want to raise the scope of clone from protected to public, and change the return type.

Finally, you need to deal with the CloneNotSupportedException. This is a *checked* exception, and as you will see in Chapter 5, you must either declare or catch it. If your class is final, you can catch it. Otherwise, declare the exception since it is possible that a subclass might again want to throw it.

```java
public class Employee implements Cloneable {
    ...
    public Employee clone() throws CloneNotSupportedException {
        return (Employee) super.clone();
    }
}
```

The cast (Employee) is necessary since the return type of Object.clone is Object.

The third option for implementing the clone method, in which a class needs to make a deep copy, is the most complex case. You don't need to use the Object.clone method at all. Here is a simple implementation of Message.clone:

```java
public Message clone() {
    Message cloned = new Message(sender, text);
    cloned.recipients = new ArrayList<>(recipients);
    return cloned;
}
```

Alternatively, you can call clone on the superclass and the mutable instance variables.

The ArrayList class implements the clone method, yielding a shallow copy. That is, the original and cloned list share the element references. That is fine in our case since the elements are strings. If not, we would have had to clone each element as well.

However, for historical reasons, the ArrayList.clone method has return type Object. You need to use a cast.

```
cloned.recipients = (ArrayList<String>) recipients.clone(); // Warning
```

Unhappily, as you will see in Chapter 6, that cast cannot be fully checked at runtime, and you will get a warning. You can suppress the warning with an annotation, but that annotation can only be attached to a declaration (see Chapter 12). Here is the complete method implementation:

```
public Message clone() {
    try {
        Message cloned = (Message) super.clone();
        @SuppressWarnings("unchecked") ArrayList<String> clonedRecipients
            = (ArrayList<String>) recipients.clone();
        cloned.recipients = clonedRecipients;
        return cloned;
    } catch (CloneNotSupportedException ex) {
        return null; // Can't happen
    }
}
```

In this case, the CloneNotSupportedException cannot happen since the Message class is Cloneable and final, and ArrayList.clone does not throw the exception.

 NOTE: Arrays have a public clone method whose return type is the same as the type of the array. For example, if recipients had been an array, not an array list, you could have cloned it as

```
cloned.recipients = recipients.clone(); // No cast required
```

4.3 Enumerations

You saw in Chapter 1 how to define enumerated types. Here is a typical example, defining a type with exactly four instances:

```
public enum Size { SMALL, MEDIUM, LARGE, EXTRA_LARGE };
```

In the following sections, you will see how to work with enumerations.

4.3.1 Methods of Enumerations

Since each instance of an enumerated type is unique, you never need to use the equals method for values of enumerated types. Simply use == to compare them. (You can, if you like, call equals which makes the == test.)

You also don't need to provide a toString method. It is automatically provided to yield the name of the enumerated object—in our example, "SMALL", "MEDIUM", and so on.

The converse of toString is the static valueOf method that is synthesized for each enumerated type. For example, the statement

```
Size notMySize = Size.valueOf("SMALL");
```

sets notMySize to Size.SMALL. The valueOf method throws an exception if there is no instance with the given name.

Each enumerated type has a static values method that returns an array of all instances of the enumeration, in the order in which they were declared. The call

```
Size[] allValues = Size.values();
```

returns the array with elements Size.SMALL, Size.MEDIUM, and so on.

TIP: Use this method to traverse all instances of an enumerated type in an enhanced for loop:

```
for (Size s : Size.values()) { System.out.println(s); }
```

The ordinal method yields the position of an instance in the enum declaration, counting from zero. For example, Size.MEDIUM.ordinal() returns 1. Of course, you need to be careful with this method. The values shift if new constants are inserted.

Every enumerated type E automatically implements Comparable<E>, allowing comparisons only against its own objects. The comparison is by ordinal values.

NOTE: Technically, an enumerated type E extends the class Enum<E> from which it inherits the compareTo method as well as the other methods described in this section. Table 4-2 shows the methods of the Enum class.

Table 4-2 Methods of the `java.lang.Enum<E>` Class

Method	Description
`String toString()` `String name()`	The name of this instance, as provided in the `enum` declaration. The `name` method is final.
`int ordinal()`	The position of this instance in the `enum` declaration.
`int compareTo(Enum<E> other)`	Compares this instance against `other` by ordinal value.
`static T valueOf(Class<T> type, String name)`	Returns the instance for a given name. Consider using the synthesized `valueOf` or `values` method of the enumeration type instead.
`Class<E> getDeclaringClass()`	Gets the class in which this instance was defined. (This differs from `getClass()` if the instance has a body.)
`int hashCode()` `protected void finalize()`	These methods call the corresponding `Object` methods and are final.
`protected Object clone()`	Throws a `CloneNotSupportedException`.

4.3.2 Constructors, Methods, and Fields

You can, if you like, add constructors, methods, and fields to an enumerated type. Here is an example:

```
public enum Size {
    SMALL("S"), MEDIUM("M"), LARGE("L"), EXTRA_LARGE("XL");

    private String abbreviation;

    Size(String abbreviation) {
        this.abbreviation = abbreviation;
    }

    public String getAbbreviation() { return abbreviation; }
}
```

Each instance of the enumeration is guaranteed to be constructed exactly once.

NOTE: The constructor of an enumeration is always private. You can omit the `private` modifier, as in the preceding example. It is a syntax error to declare an enum constructor as `public` or `protected`.

4.3.3 Bodies of Instances

You can add methods to each individual `enum` instance, but they have to override methods defined in the enumeration. For example, to implement a calculator, you might do this:

```
public enum Operation {
    ADD {
        public int eval(int arg1, int arg2) { return arg1 + arg2; }
    },
    SUBTRACT {
        public int eval(int arg1, int arg2) { return arg1 - arg2; }
    },
    MULTIPLY {
        public int eval(int arg1, int arg2) { return arg1 * arg2; }
    },
    DIVIDE {
        public int eval(int arg1, int arg2) { return arg1 / arg2; }
    };

    public abstract int eval(int arg1, int arg2);
}
```

In the loop of a calculator program, one would set a variable to one of these values, depending on user input, and then invoke `eval`:

```
Operation op = ...;
int result = op.eval(first, second);
```

 NOTE: Technically, each of these constants belongs to an anonymous subclass of `Operation`. Anything that you could place into an anonymous subclass body you can also add into the body of a member.

4.3.4 Static Members

It is legal for an enumeration to have static members. However, you have to be careful with construction order. The enumerated constants are constructed *before* the static members, so you cannot refer to any static members in an enumeration constructor. For example, the following would be illegal:

```
public enum Modifier {
    PUBLIC, PRIVATE, PROTECTED, STATIC, FINAL, ABSTRACT;
    private static int maskBit = 1;
    private int mask;
    Modifier() {
        mask = maskBit; // Error—cannot access static variable in constructor
        maskBit *= 2;
    }
    ...
}
```

The remedy is to do the initialization in a static initializer:

```
public enum Modifier {
    PUBLIC, PRIVATE, PROTECTED, STATIC, FINAL, ABSTRACT;
    private int mask;

    static {
        int maskBit = 1;
        for (Modifier m : Modifier.values()) {
            m.mask = maskBit;
            maskBit *= 2;
        }
    }
    ...
}
```

Once the constants have been constructed, static variable initializations and static initializers run in the usual top-to-bottom fashion.

 NOTE: Enumerated types can be nested inside classes. Such nested enumerations are implicitly static nested classes—that is, their methods cannot reference instance variables of the enclosing class.

4.3.5 Switching on an Enumeration

You can use enumeration constants in a switch statement.

```
enum Operation { ADD, SUBTRACT, MULTIPLY, DIVIDE };

public static int eval(Operation op, int arg1, int arg2) {
    int result = 0;
    switch (op) {
        case ADD: result = arg1 + arg2; break;
        case SUBTRACT: result = arg1 - arg2; break;
        case MULTIPLY: result = arg1 * arg2; break;
        case DIVIDE: result = arg1 / arg2; break;
    }
    return result;
}
```

You use ADD, not Operation.ADD, inside the switch statement—the type is inferred from the type of the expression on which the switch is computed.

 NOTE: According to the language specification, compilers are encouraged to give a warning if a switch on an enumeration is not exhaustive—that is, if there aren't cases for all constants and no default clause. The Oracle compiler does not produce such a warning.

 TIP: If you want to refer to the instances of an enumeration by their simple name outside a switch, use a static import declaration. For example, with the declaration

```
import static com.horstmann.corejava.Size.*;
```

you can use SMALL instead of Size.SMALL.

4.4 Runtime Type Information and Resources

In Java, you can find out at runtime to which class a given object belongs. This is sometimes useful, for example in the implementation of the equals and toString methods. Moreover, you can find out how the class was loaded and load its associated data, called *resources*.

4.4.1 The Class Class

Suppose you have a variable of type Object, filled with some object reference, and you want to know more about the object, such as to which class it belongs.

The getClass method yields an object of a class called, not surprisingly, Class.

```
Object obj = ...;
Class<?> cl = obj.getClass();
```

 NOTE: See Chapter 6 for an explanation of the <?> suffix. For now, just ignore it. But don't omit it. If you do, not only does your IDE give you an unsightly warning, but you also turn off useful type checks in expressions involving the variable.

Once you have a Class object, you can find out the class name:

```
System.out.println("This object is an instance of " + cl.getName());
```

Alternatively, you can get a Class object by using the static Class.forName method:

```
String className = "java.util.Scanner";
Class<?> cl = Class.forName(className);
    // An object describing the java.util.Scanner class
```

 CAUTION: The Class.forName method, as well as many other methods used with reflection, throws checked exceptions when something goes wrong (for example, when there is no class with the given name). For now, tag the calling method with throws ReflectiveOperationException. You will see in Chapter 5 how to handle the exception.

The Class.forName method is intended for constructing Class objects for classes that may not be known at compile time. If you know in advance which class you want, use a *class literal* instead:

```
Class<?> cl = java.util.Scanner.class;
```

The .class suffix can be used to get information about other types as well:

```
Class<?> cl2 = String[].class; // Describes the array type String[]
Class<?> cl3 = Runnable.class; // Describes the Runnable interface
Class<?> cl4 = int.class; // Describes the int type
Class<?> cl5 = void.class; // Describes the void type
```

Arrays are classes in Java, but interfaces, primitive types, and void are not. The name Class is a bit unfortunate—Type would have been more accurate.

 CAUTION: The getName method returns strange names for array types:

- String[].class.getName() returns "[Ljava.lang.String;"

- int[].class.getName() returns "[I"

This notation has been used since archaic times in the virtual machine. Use getCanonicalName instead to get names such as "java.lang.String[]" and "int[]". You need to use the archaic notation with the Class.forName method if you want to generate Class objects for arrays.

The virtual machine manages a unique Class object for each type. Therefore, you can use the == operator to compare class objects. For example:

```
if (other.getClass() == Employee.class) ...
```

You have already seen this use of class objects in Section 4.2.2, "The equals Method" (page 148).

In the following sections, you will see what you can do with Class objects. See Table 4-3 for a summary of useful methods.

Table 4-3 Useful Methods of the `java.lang.Class<T>` Class

Method	Description
`static Class<?> forName(String className)`	Gets the `Class` object describing `className`.

`String getCanonicalName()`
`String getSimpleName()`
`String getTypeName()`
`String getName()`
`String toString()`
`String toGenericString()`
	Gets the name of this class, with various idiosyncrasies for arrays, inner classes, generic classes, and modifiers (see Exercise 8).

`Class<? super T> getSuperclass()`
`Class<?>[] getInterfaces()`
`Package getPackage()`
`int getModifiers()`
	Gets the superclass, the implemented interfaces, package, and modifiers of this class. Table 4-4 shows how to analyze the value returned by `getModifiers`.

`boolean isPrimitive()`
`boolean isArray()`
`boolean isEnum()`
`boolean isAnnotation()`
`boolean isMemberClass()`
`boolean isLocalClass()`
`boolean isAnonymousClass()`
`boolean isSynthetic()`
	Tests whether the represented type is primitive or void, an array, an enumeration, an annotation (see Chapter 12), nested in another class, local to a method or constructor, anonymous, or synthetic (see Section 4.5.7).

`Class<?> getComponentType()`
`Class<?> getDeclaringClass()`
`Class<?> getEnclosingClass()`
`Constructor getEnclosingConstructor()`
`Method getEnclosingMethod()`
	Gets the component type of an array, the class declaring a nested class, the class and constructor or method in which a local class is declared.

`boolean isAssignableFrom(Class<?> cls)` `boolean isInstance(Object obj)`	Tests whether the type `cls` or the class of `obj` is a subtype of this type.
`String getPackageName()`	Gets the fully qualified package name of this class or, if it is not a top-level class, its enclosing class.
`ClassLoader getClassLoader()`	Gets the class loader that loaded this class (see Section 4.4.3).
`InputStream getResourceAsStream(String path)` `URL getResource(String path)`	Loads the requested resource from the same location from which this class was loaded.

(Continues)

Table 4-3 Useful Methods of the `java.lang.Class<T>` Class *(Continued)*

Method	Description

`Field[] getFields()`
`Method[] getMethods()`
`Field getField(String name)`
`Method getMethod(String name,`
`    Class<?>... parameterTypes)`
	Gets all public fields or methods, or the specified field or method, from this class or a superclass.

`Field[] getDeclaredFields()`
`Method[] getDeclaredMethods()`
`Field getDeclaredField(String name)`
`Method getDeclaredMethod(String name,`
`    Class<?>... parameterTypes)`
	Gets all fields or methods, or the specified field or method, from this class.

`Constructor[] getConstructors()`
`Constructor[] getDeclaredConstructors()`
`Constructor getConstructor(Class<?>...`
`    parameterTypes)`
`Constructor getDeclaredConstructor(Class<?>...`
`    parameterTypes)`
	Gets all public constructors, or all constructors, or the specified public constructor, or the specified constructor, for this class.

Table 4-4 Methods of the `java.lang.reflect.Modifier` Class

Method	Description
`static String toString(int modifiers)`	Returns a string with the modifiers that correspond to the bits set in `modifiers`.

`static boolean is(Abstract|Interface|Native|`
`Private|Protected|Public|Static|Strict|`
`Synchronized|Volatile)(int modifiers)`
	Tests the bit in the `modifiers` argument that corresponds to the modifier in the method name.

4.4.2 Loading Resources

One useful service of the `Class` class is to locate resources that your program may need, such as configuration files or images. If you place a resource into the same directory as the class file, you can open an input stream to the file like this:

```
InputStream stream = MyClass.class.getResourceAsStream("config.txt");
Scanner in = new Scanner(stream);
```

NOTE: Some legacy methods such as `Applet.getAudioClip` and the `javax.swing.ImageIcon` constructor read data from a `URL` object. In that case, you can use the `getResource` method which returns a URL to the resource.

Resources can have subdirectories which can be relative or absolute. For example, `MyClass.class.getResourceAsStream("/config/menus.txt")` locates `config/menus.txt` in the directory that contains the root of the package to which `MyClass` belongs.

If you package classes into JAR files, zip up the resources together with the class files, and they will be located as well.

4.4.3 Class Loaders

Virtual machine instructions are stored in class files. Each class file contains the instructions for a single class or interface. A class file can be located on a file system, in a JAR file, at a remote location, or it can even be dynamically constructed in memory. A *class loader* is responsible for loading the bytes and turning them into a class or interface in the virtual machine.

The virtual machine loads class files on demand, starting with the class whose `main` method is to be invoked. That class will depend on other classes, such as `java.lang.System` and `java.util.Scanner`, which will be loaded together with the classes that they depend on.

When executing a Java program, at least three class loaders are involved.

The *bootstrap class loader* loads the most fundamental Java library classes. It is a part of the virtual machine.

The *platform class loader* loads other library classes. Unlike the classes loaded with the bootstrap class loader, platform class permissions can be configured with a security policy.

The *system class loader* loads the application classes. It locates classes in the directories and JAR files on the class path and module path.

 CAUTION: In previous releases of the Oracle JDK, the platform and system class loaders were instances of the `URLClassLoader` class. This is no longer the case. Some programmers used the `getURLs` method of the `URLClassLoader` to find the class path. Use `System.getProperty( "java.class.path")` instead.

You can load classes from a directory or JAR file that is not already on the class path, by creating your own `URLClassLoader` instance. This is commonly done to load plugins.

```
URL[] urls = {
    new URL("file:///path/to/directory/"),
    new URL("file:///path/to/jarfile.jar")
};
String className = "com.mycompany.plugins.Entry";
try (URLClassLoader loader = new URLClassLoader(urls)) {
    Class<?> cl = Class.forName(className, true, loader);
    // Now construct an instance of cl—see Section 4.5.4
    ...
}
```

 CAUTION: The second parameter in the call `Class.forName(className, true, loader)` ensures that the static initialization of the class happens after loading. You definitely want that to happen.

Do not use the `ClassLoader.loadClass` method. It does not run the static initializers.

 NOTE: The `URLClassLoader` loads classes from the file system. If you want to load a class from somewhere else, you need to write your own class loader. The only method you need to implement is `findClass`, like this:

```
public class MyClassLoader extends ClassLoader {
    ...
    @Override public Class<?> findClass(String name)
            throws ClassNotFoundException {
        byte[] bytes = the bytes of the class file
        return defineClass(name, bytes, 0, bytes.length);
    }
}
```

See Chapter 14 for an example in which classes are compiled into memory and then loaded.

4.4.4 The Context Class Loader

Most of the time you don't have to worry about the class loading process. Classes are transparently loaded as they are required by other classes. However, if a method loads classes dynamically, and that method is called from a class that itself was loaded with another class loader, then problems can arise. Here is a specific example.

1. You provide a utility class that is loaded by the system class loader, and it has a method

```
public class Util {
    Object createInstance(String className) {
        Class<?> cl = Class.forName(className);
        ...
    }
    ...
}
```

2. You load a plugin with another class loader that reads classes from a plugin JAR.

3. The plugin calls Util.createInstance("com.mycompany.plugins.MyClass") to instantiate a class in the plugin JAR.

The author of the plugin expects that class to be loaded. However, Util.createInstance uses its own class loader to execute Class.forName, and that class loader won't look into the plugin JAR. This phenomenon is called *classloader inversion*.

One remedy is to pass the class loader to the utility method and then to the forName method.

```
public class Util {
    public Object createInstance(String className, ClassLoader loader) {
        Class<?> cl = Class.forName(className, true, loader);
        ...
    }
    ...
}
```

Another strategy is to use the *context class loader* of the current thread. The main thread's context class loader is the system class loader. When a new thread is created, its context class loader is set to the creating thread's context class loader. Thus, if you don't do anything, all threads will have their context class loaders set to the system class loader. However, you can set any class loader by calling

```
Thread t = Thread.currentThread();
t.setContextClassLoader(loader);
```

The utility method can then retrieve the context class loader:

```
public class Util {
    public Object createInstance(String className) {
        Thread t = Thread.currentThread();
        ClassLoader loader = t.getContextClassLoader();
        Class<?> cl = Class.forName(className, true, loader);
        ...
    }
    ...
}
```

When invoking a method of a plugin class, the application should set the context class loader to the plugin class loader. Afterwards, it should restore the previous setting.

 TIP: If you write a method that loads a class by name, don't simply use the class loader of the method's class. It is a good idea to offer the caller the choice between passing an explicit class loader and using the context class loader.

4.4.5 Service Loaders

Certain services need to be configurable when a program is assembled or deployed. One way to do this is to make different implementations of a service available, and have the program choose the most appropriate one among them. The ServiceLoader class makes it easy to load service implementations that conform to a common interface.

Define an interface (or, if you prefer, a superclass) with the methods that each instance of the service should provide. For example, suppose your service provides encryption.

```
package com.corejava.crypt;

public interface Cipher {
    byte[] encrypt(byte[] source, byte[] key);
    byte[] decrypt(byte[] source, byte[] key);
    int strength();
}
```

The service provider supplies one or more classes that implement this service, for example

```
package com.corejava.crypt.impl;

public class CaesarCipher implements Cipher {
    public byte[] encrypt(byte[] source, byte[] key) {
        byte[] result = new byte[source.length];
        for (int i = 0; i < source.length; i++)
            result[i] = (byte)(source[i] + key[0]);
        return result;
    }
    public byte[] decrypt(byte[] source, byte[] key) {
        return encrypt(source, new byte[] { (byte) -key[0] });
    }
    public int strength() { return 1; }
}
```

The implementing classes can be in any package, not necessarily the same package as the service interface. Each of them must have a no-argument constructor.

Now add the names of the provider classes to a UTF-8 encoded text file in a META-INF/services directory that a class loader can find. In our example, the file META-INF/services/com.corejava.crypt.Cipher would contain the line

```
com.corejava.crypt.impl.CaesarCipher
```

With this preparation done, the program initializes a service loader as follows:

```
public static ServiceLoader<Cipher> cipherLoader = ServiceLoader.load(Cipher.class);
```

This should be done just once in the program.

The iterator method of the service loader provides an iterator through all provided implementations of the service. (See Chapter 7 for more information about iterators.) It is easiest to use an enhanced for loop to traverse them. In the loop, pick an appropriate object to carry out the service.

```
public static Cipher getCipher(int minStrength) {
    for (Cipher cipher : cipherLoader) // Implicitly calls iterator
        if (cipher.strength() >= minStrength) return cipher;
    return null;
}
```

Alternatively, you can use streams (see Chapter 8) to locate the desired service. The stream method yields a stream of ServiceLoader.Provider instances. That interface has methods type and get for getting the provider class and the provider instance. If you select a provider by type, then you just call type and no service instances are unnecessarily instantiated. In our example, we need to get the providers since we filter the stream for ciphers that have the required strength:

```
public static Optional<Cipher> getCipher2(int minStrength) {
    return cipherLoader.stream()
        .map(ServiceLoader.Provider::get)
        .filter(c -> c.strength() >= minStrength)
        .findFirst();
}
```

If you are willing to take any implementation, simply call `findFirst`:

```
Optional<Cipher> cipher = cipherLoader.findFirst();
```

The `Optional` class is explained in Chapter 8.

4.5 Reflection

Reflection allows a program to inspect the contents of objects at runtime and to invoke arbitrary methods on them. This capability is useful for implementing tools such as object-relational mappers or GUI builders.

Since reflection is of interest mainly to tool builders, application programmers can safely skip this section and return to it as needed.

4.5.1 Enumerating Class Members

The three classes `Field`, `Method`, and `Constructor` in the `java.lang.reflect` package describe the fields, methods, and constructors of a class. All three classes have a method called `getName` that returns the name of the member. The `Field` class has a method `getType` that returns an object, again of type `Class`, that describes the field type. The `Method` and `Constructor` classes have methods to report the types of the parameters, and the `Method` class also reports the return type.

All three of these classes also have a method called `getModifiers` that returns an integer, with various bits turned on and off, that describes the modifiers used (such as `public` or `static`). You can use static methods such as `Modifier.isPublic` and `Modifier.isStatic` to analyze the integer that `getModifiers` returns. The `Modifier.toString` returns a string of all modifiers.

The `getFields`, `getMethods`, and `getConstructors` methods of the `Class` class return arrays of the *public* fields, methods, and constructors that the class supports; this includes public inherited members. The `getDeclaredFields`, `getDeclaredMethods`, and `getDeclaredConstructors` methods return arrays consisting of all fields, methods, and constructors that are declared in the class. This includes private, package, and protected members, but not members of superclasses.

The getParameters method of the Executable class, the common superclass of Method and Constructor, returns an array of Parameter objects describing the method parameters.

 NOTE: The names of the parameters are only available at runtime if the class has been compiled with the -parameters flag.

For example, here is how you can print all methods of a class:

```
Class<?> cl = Class.forName(className);
while (cl != null) {
    for (Method m : cl.getDeclaredMethods()) {
        System.out.println(
            Modifier.toString(m.getModifiers()) + " " +
            m.getReturnType().getCanonicalName() + " " +
            m.getName() +
            Arrays.toString(m.getParameters()));
    }
    cl = cl.getSuperclass();
}
```

What is remarkable about this code is that it can analyze any class that the Java virtual machine can load—not just the classes that were available when the program was compiled.

 CAUTION: As you will see in Chapter 15, the Java platform module system imposes significant restrictions on reflective access. By default, only classes in the same module can be analyzed through reflection. If you don't declare modules, all your classes belong to a single module, and they can all be accessed through reflection. However, the Java library classes belong to different modules, and reflective access to their non-public members is restricted.

4.5.2 Inspecting Objects

As you saw in the preceding section, you can get Field objects that describe the types and names of an object's fields. These Field objects can do more: They can access field values in objects that have the given field.

For example, here is how to enumerate the contents of all fields of an object:

```
Object obj = ...;
for (Field f : obj.getClass().getDeclaredFields()) {
    f.setAccessible(true);
    Object value = f.get(obj);
    System.out.println(f.getName() + ":" + value);
}
```

The key is the get method that reads the field value. If the field value is a primitive type value, a wrapper object is returned; in that case you can also call one of the methods getInt, getDouble, and so on.

NOTE: You must make private Field and Method objects "accessible" before you can use them. Calling setAccessible(true) "unlocks" the field or method for reflection. However, the module system or a security manager can block the request and protect objects from being accessed in this way. In that case, the setAccessible method throws an InaccessibleObjectException or SecurityException. Alternatively, you can call the trySetAccessible method which simply returns false if the field or method is not accessible.

CAUTION: As you will see in Chapter 15, the Java platform packages are contained in modules and their classes are protected from reflection. For example, if you call

```
Field f = String.class.getDeclaredField("value");
f.setAccessible(true);
```

an InaccessibleObjectException is thrown.

Once a field is accessible, you can also set it. This code will give a raise to obj, no matter to which class it belongs, provided that it has an accessible salary field of type double or Double.

```
Field f = obj.getClass().getDeclaredField("salary");
f.setAccessible(true);
double value = f.getDouble(obj);
f.setDouble(obj, value * 1.1);
```

4.5.3 Invoking Methods

Just like a `Field` object can be used to read and write fields of an object, a `Method` object can invoke the given method on an object.

```
Method m = ...;
Object result = m.invoke(obj, arg1, arg2, ...);
```

If the method is static, supply `null` for the initial argument.

To obtain a method, you can search through the array returned by `getMethods` or `getDeclaredMethods` that you saw in Section 4.5.1, "Enumerating Class Members" (page 168). Or you can call `getMethod` and supply the parameter types. For example, to get the `setName(String)` method on a `Person` object:

```
Person p = ...;
Method m = p.getClass().getMethod("setName", String.class);
m.invoke(obj, "********");
```

 CAUTION: Even though `clone` is a public method of all array types, it is not reported by `getMethod` when invoked on a `Class` object describing an array.

4.5.4 Constructing Objects

To construct an object, first find the `Constructor` object and then call its `newInstance` method. For example, suppose you know that a class has a public constructor whose parameter is an `int`. Then you can construct a new instance like this:

```
Constructor constr = cl.getConstructor(int.class);
Object obj = constr.newInstance(42);
```

 CAUTION: The `Class` class has a `newInstance` method to construct an object of the given class with the no-argument constructor. That method is now deprecated because it has a curious flaw. If the no-argument constructor throws a checked exception, the `newInstance` method rethrows it *even though it isn't declared*, thereby completely defeating the compile-time checking of checked exceptions. Instead, you should call `cl.getConstructor().newInstance()`. Then any exception is wrapped inside an `InvocationTargetException`.

Table 4-5 summarizes the most important methods for working with `Field`, `Method`, and `Constructor` objects.

Table 4-5 Useful Classes and Methods in the `java.lang.reflect` Package

Class	Method	Notes
AccessibleObject	void setAccessible(boolean flag) static void setAccessible(　AccessibleObject[] 　array, boolean flag)	AccessibleObject is a superclass of Field, Method, and Constructor. The methods set the accessibility of this member, or the given members.
Field	String getName() int getModifiers() Object get(Object obj) p get$P$(Object obj) void set(Object obj, Object newValue) void set$P$(Object obj, p newValue)	There is a get and set method for each primitive type p.
Method	Object invoke(Object obj, 　Object... args)	Invokes the method described by this object, passing the given arguments and returning the value that the method returns. For static methods, pass null for obj. Primitive type arguments and return values are wrapped.
Constructor	Object newInstance(Object... args)	Invokes the constructor described by this object, passing the given arguments and returning the constructed object.
Executable	String getName() int getModifiers() Parameters[] getParameters()	Executable is the superclass of Method and Constructor.
Parameter	boolean isNamePresent() String getName() Class<?> getType()	The getName method gets the name or a synthesized name such as arg0 if the name is not present.

4.5.5 JavaBeans

Many object-oriented programming languages support *properties*, mapping the expression *object.propertyName* to a call of a getter or setter method, depending on whether the property is read or written. Java does not have this syntax, but it has a convention in which properties correspond to getter/setter pairs. A *JavaBean* is a class with a no-argument constructor, getter/setter pairs, and any number of other methods.

The getters and setters must follow the specific pattern

```
public Type getProperty()
public void setProperty(Type newValue)
```

It is possible to have read-only and write-only properties by omitting the setter or getter.

The name of the property is the *decapitalized* form of the suffix after get/set. For example, a getSalary/setSalary pair gives rise to a property named salary. However, if the first *two* letters of the suffix are uppercase, then it is taken verbatim. For example, getURL yields a read-only property named URL.

 NOTE: For Boolean properties, you may use either get*Property* or is*Property* for the getter, and the latter is preferred.

JavaBeans have their origin in GUI builders, and the JavaBeans specification has arcane rules that deal with property editors, property change events, and custom property discovery. These features are rarely used nowadays.

It is a good idea to use the standard classes for JavaBeans support whenever you need to work with arbitrary properties. Given a class, obtain a BeanInfo object like this:

```
Class<?> cl = ...;
BeanInfo info = Introspector.getBeanInfo(cl);
PropertyDescriptor[] props = info.getPropertyDescriptors();
```

For a given PropertyDescriptor, call getName and getPropertyType to get the name and type of the property. The getReadMethod and getWriteMethod yield Method objects for the getter and setter.

Unfortunately, there is no method to get the descriptor for a given property name, so you'll have to traverse the array of descriptors:

```
String propertyName = ...;
Object propertyValue = null;
for (PropertyDescriptor prop : props) {
    if (prop.getName().equals(propertyName))
        propertyValue = prop.getReadMethod().invoke(obj);
}
```

4.5.6 Working with Arrays

The isArray method checks whether a given Class object represents an array. If so, the getComponentType method yields the Class describing the type of the array elements. For further analysis, or to create arrays dynamically, use the Array class in the java.lang.reflect package. Table 4-6 shows its methods.

Table 4-6 Methods of the java.lang.reflect.Array Class

Method	Description
static Object get(Object array, int index) static *p* get*P*(Object array, int index) static void set(Object array, int index, Object newValue) static void set*P*(Object array, int index, *p* newValue)	Gets or sets an element of the array at the given index, where *p* is a primitive type.
static int getLength(Object array)	Gets the length of the given array.
static Object newInstance(Class<?> componentType, 　　int length) static Object newInstance(Class<?> componentType, 　　int[] lengths)	Returns a new array of the given component type with the given dimensions.

As an exercise, let us implement the copyOf method in the Arrays class. Recall how this method can be used to grow an array that has become full.

```
Person[] friends = new Person[100];
...
// Array is full
friends = Arrays.copyOf(friends, 2 * friends.length);
```

How can one write such a generic method? Here is a first attempt:

```
public static Object[] badCopyOf(Object[] array, int newLength) { // Not useful
    Object[] newArray = new Object[newLength];
    for (int i = 0; i < Math.min(array.length, newLength); i++)
        newArray[i] = array[i];
    return newArray;
}
```

However, there is a problem with actually using the resulting array. The type of array that this method returns is Object[]. An array of objects cannot be cast to a Person[] array. The point is, as we mentioned earlier, that a Java array remembers the type of its elements—that is, the type used in the new expression that created it. It is legal to cast a Person[] array temporarily to an Object[] array and then cast it back, but an array that started its life as an Object[] array can never be cast into a Person[] array.

In order to make a new array of the same type as the original array, you need the newInstance method of the Array class. Supply the component type and the desired length:

```
public static Object goodCopyOf(Object array, int newLength) {
    Class<?> cl = array.getClass();
    if (!cl.isArray()) return null;
    Class<?> componentType = cl.getComponentType();
    int length = Array.getLength(array);
    Object newArray = Array.newInstance(componentType, newLength);
    for (int i = 0; i < Math.min(length, newLength); i++)
        Array.set(newArray, i, Array.get(array, i));
    return newArray;
}
```

Note that this copyOf method can be used to grow arrays of any type, not just arrays of objects.

```
int[] primes = { 2, 3, 5, 7, 11 };
primes = (int[]) goodCopyOf(primes, 10);
```

The parameter type of goodCopyOf is Object, not Object[]. An int[] is an Object but not an array of objects.

4.5.7 Proxies

The Proxy class can create, at runtime, new classes that implement a given interface or set of interfaces. Such proxies are only necessary when you don't yet know at compile time which interfaces you need to implement.

A proxy class has all methods required by the specified interfaces, and all methods defined in the Object class (toString, equals, and so on). However, since you cannot define new code for these methods at runtime, you supply an *invocation handler*, an object of a class that implements the InvocationHandler interface. That interface has a single method:

```
Object invoke(Object proxy, Method method, Object[] args)
```

Whenever a method is called on the proxy object, the invoke method of the invocation handler gets called, with the Method object and parameters of the original call. The invocation handler must then figure out how to handle the call. There are many possible actions an invocation handler might take, such as routing calls to remote servers or tracing calls for debugging purposes.

To create a proxy object, use the newProxyInstance method of the Proxy class. The method has three parameters:

- A class loader (see Section 4.4.3, "Class Loaders," page 163), or null to use the default class loader

- An array of Class objects, one for each interface to be implemented

- The invocation handler

To show the mechanics of proxies, here is an example where an array is populated with proxies for Integer objects, forwarding calls to the original objects after printing trace messages:

```
Object[] values = new Object[1000];

for (int i = 0; i < values.length; i++) {
    Object value = new Integer(i);
    values[i] = Proxy.newProxyInstance(
        null,
        value.getClass().getInterfaces(),
        // Lambda expression for invocation handler
        (Object proxy, Method m, Object[] margs) -> {
            System.out.println(value + "." + m.getName() + Arrays.toString(margs));
            return m.invoke(value, margs);
        });
}
```

When calling

```
Arrays.binarySearch(values, new Integer(500));
```

the following output is produced:

```
499.compareTo[500]
749.compareTo[500]
624.compareTo[500]
561.compareTo[500]
530.compareTo[500]
514.compareTo[500]
506.compareTo[500]
502.compareTo[500]
500.compareTo[500]
```

You can see how the binary search algorithm homes in on the key by cutting the search interval in half in every step.

The point is that the compareTo method is invoked through the proxy, even though this was not explicitly mentioned in the code. All methods in any interfaces implemented by Integer are proxied.

 CAUTION: When the invocation handler is called with a method call that has no parameters, the argument array is null, not an Object[] array of length 0. That is utterly reprehensible and not something you should do in your own code.

Exercises

1. Define a class `Point` with a constructor `public Point(double x, double y)` and accessor methods `getX`, `getY`. Define a subclass `LabeledPoint` with a constructor `public LabeledPoint(String label, double x, double y)` and an accessor method `getLabel`.

2. Define `toString`, `equals`, and `hashCode` methods for the classes of the preceding exercise.

3. Make the instance variables `x` and `y` of the `Point` class in Exercise 1 `protected`. Show that the `LabeledPoint` class can access these variables only in `LabeledPoint` instances.

4. Define an abstract class `Shape` with an instance variable of class `Point`, a constructor, a concrete method `public void moveBy(double dx, double dy)` that moves the point by the given amount, and an abstract method `public Point getCenter()`. Provide concrete subclasses `Circle`, `Rectangle`, `Line` with constructors `public Circle(Point center, double radius)`, `public Rectangle(Point topLeft, double width, double height)`, and `public Line(Point from, Point to)`.

5. Define `clone` methods for the classes of the preceding exercise.

6. Suppose that in Section 4.2.2, "The `equals` Method" (page 148), the `Item.equals` method uses an `instanceof` test. Implement `DiscountedItem.equals` so that it compares only the superclass if `otherObject` is an `Item`, but also includes the discount if it is a `DiscountedItem`. Show that this method preserves symmetry but fails to be *transitive*—that is, find a combination of items and discounted items so that `x.equals(y)` and `y.equals(z)`, but not `x.equals(z)`.

7. Define an enumeration type for the eight combinations of primary colors `BLACK, RED, BLUE, GREEN, CYAN, MAGENTA, YELLOW, WHITE` with methods `getRed`, `getGreen`, and `getBlue`.

8. The `Class` class has six methods that yield a string representation of the type represented by the `Class` object. How do they differ when applied to arrays, generic types, inner classes, and primitive types?

9. Write a "universal" `toString` method that uses reflection to yield a string with all instance variables of an object. Extra credit if you can handle cyclic references.

10. Use the `MethodPrinter` program in Section 4.5.1, "Enumerating Class Members" (page 168) to enumerate all methods of the `int[]` class. Extra credit if you can identify the one method (discussed in this chapter) that is wrongly described.

11. Write the "Hello, World" program, using reflection to look up the out field of java.lang.System and using invoke to call the println method.

12. Measure the performance difference between a regular method call and a method call via reflection.

13. Write a method that prints a table of values for any Method representing a static method with a parameter of type double or Double. Besides the Method object, accept a lower bound, upper bound, and step size. Demonstrate your method by printing tables for Math.sqrt and Double.toHexString. Repeat, using a DoubleFunction<Object> instead of a Method (see Section 3.6.2, "Choosing a Functional Interface," page 120). Contrast the safety, efficiency, and convenience of both approaches.

Exceptions, Assertions, and Logging

Topics in This Chapter

Chapter 5

In many programs, dealing with the unexpected can be more complex than implementing the "happy day" scenarios. Like most modern programming languages, Java has a robust exception-handling mechanism for transferring control from the point of failure to a competent handler. In addition, the `assert` statement provides a structured and efficient way of expressing internal assumptions. Finally, you will see how to use the logging API to keep a record of the various events, be they routine or suspicious, in the execution of your programs.

The key points of this chapter are:

1. When you throw an exception, control is transferred to the nearest handler of the exception.

2. In Java, checked exceptions are tracked by the compiler.

3. Use the `try`/`catch` construct to handle exceptions.

4. The try-with-resources statement automatically closes resources after normal execution or when an exception occurred.

5. Use the `try`/`finally` construct to deal with other actions that must occur whether or not execution proceeded normally.

6. You can catch and rethrow an exception, or chain it to another exception.

7. A stack trace describes all method calls that are pending at a point of execution.

8. An assertion checks a condition, provided that assertion checking is enabled for the class, and throws an error if the condition is not fulfilled.

9. Loggers are arranged in a hierarchy, and they can receive logging messages with levels ranging from SEVERE to FINEST.

10. Log handlers can send logging messages to alternate destinations, and formatters control the message format.

11. You can control logging properties with a log configuration file.

5.1 Exception Handling

What should a method do when it encounters a situation in which it cannot fulfill its contract? The traditional answer was that the method should return some error code. But that is cumbersome for the programmer calling the method. The caller is obliged to check for errors, and if it can't handle them, return an error code to its own caller. Not unsurprisingly, programmers didn't always check and propagate return codes, and errors went undetected, causing havoc later.

Instead of having error codes bubble up the chain of method calls, Java supports *exception handling* where a method can signal a serious problem by "throwing" an exception. One of the methods in the call chain, but not necessarily the direct caller, is responsible for handling the exception by "catching" it. The fundamental advantage of exception handling is that it decouples the processes of detecting and handling errors. In the following sections, you will see how to work with exceptions in Java.

5.1.1 Throwing Exceptions

A method may find itself in a situation where it cannot carry out the task at hand. Perhaps a required resource is missing, or it was supplied with inconsistent parameters. In such a case, it is best to throw an exception.

Suppose you implement a method that yields a random integer between two bounds:

```
public static int randInt(int low, int high) {
    return low + (int) (Math.random() * (high - low + 1));
}
```

What should happen if someone calls randInt(10, 5)? Trying to fix this is probably not a good idea because the caller might have been confused in more than one way. Instead, throw an appropriate exception:

```
if (low > high)
    throw new IllegalArgumentException(
        String.format("low should be <= high but low is %d and high is %d",
            low, high));
```

As you can see, the `throw` statement is used to "throw" an object of a class—here, `IllegalArgumentException`. The object is constructed with a debugging message. You will see in the next section how to pick an appropriate exception class.

When a `throw` statement executes, the normal flow of execution is interrupted immediately. The `randInt` method stops executing and does not return a value to its caller. Instead, control is transferred to a handler, as you will see in Section 5.1.4, "Catching Exceptions" (page 186).

5.1.2 The Exception Hierarchy

Figure 5-1 shows the hierarchy of exceptions in Java. All exceptions are subclasses of the class `Throwable`. Subclasses of `Error` are exceptions that are thrown when something exceptional happens that the program cannot be expected to handle, such as memory exhaustion. There is not much you can do about errors other than giving a message to the user that things have gone very wrong.

Programmer-reported exceptions are subclasses of the class `Exception`. These exceptions fall into two categories:

- *Unchecked* exceptions are subclasses of `RuntimeException`.

- All other exceptions are *checked* exceptions.

As you will see in the next section, programmers must either catch checked exceptions or declare them in the method header. The compiler checks that these exceptions are handled properly.

 NOTE: The name `RuntimeException` is unfortunate. Of course, all exceptions occur at runtime. However, the exceptions that are subclasses of `RuntimeException` are not checked during compilation.

Checked exceptions are used in situations where failure should be anticipated. One common reason for failure is input and output. Files may be damaged, and network connections may fail. A number of exception classes extend `IOException`, and you should use an appropriate one to report any errors that you encounter. For example, when a file that should be there turns out not be, throw a `FileNotFoundException`.

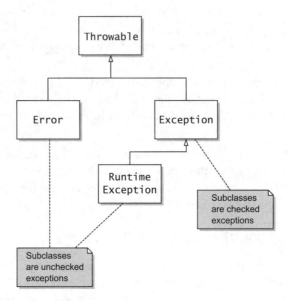

Figure 5-1 The exception hierarchy

Unchecked exceptions indicate logic errors caused by programmers, not by unavoidable external risks. For example, a NullPointerException is not checked. Just about any method might throw one, and programmers shouldn't spend time on catching them. Instead, they should make sure that no nulls are dereferenced in the first place.

Sometimes, implementors need to use their judgment to make a distinction between checked and unchecked exceptions. Consider the call Integer.parseInt(str). It throws an unchecked NumberFormatException when str doesn't contain a valid integer. On the other hand, Class.forName(str) throws a checked ClassNotFoundException when str doesn't contain a valid class name.

Why the difference? The reason is that it is possible to check whether a string is a valid integer before calling Integer.parseInt, but it is not possible to know whether a class can be loaded until you actually try to load it.

The Java API provides many exception classes, such as IOException, IllegalArgumentException, and so on. You should use these when appropriate. However, if none of the standard exception classes is suitable for your purpose, you can create your own by extending Exception, RuntimeException, or another existing exception class.

When you do so, it is a good idea to supply both a no-argument constructor and a constructor with a message string. For example,

```
public class FileFormatException extends IOException {
    public FileFormatException() {}
    public FileFormatException(String message) {
        super(message);
    }
    // Also add constructors for chained exceptions—see Section 5.1.7
}
```

5.1.3 Declaring Checked Exceptions

Any method that might give rise to a checked exception must declare it in the method header with a `throws` clause:

```
public void write(Object obj, String filename)
    throws IOException, ReflectiveOperationException
```

List the exceptions that the method might throw, either because of a `throw` statement or because it calls another method with a `throws` clause.

In the `throws` clause, you can combine exceptions into a common superclass. Whether or not that is a good idea depends on the exceptions. For example, if a method can throw multiple subclasses of `IOException`, it makes sense to cover them all in a clause `throws IOException`. But if the exceptions are unrelated, don't combine them into `throws Exception`—that would defeat the purpose of exception checking.

 TIP: Some programmers think it is shameful to admit that a method might throw an exception. Wouldn't it be better to handle it instead? Actually, the opposite is true. You should allow each exception to find its way to a competent handler. The golden rule of exceptions is, "Throw early, catch late."

When you override a method, it cannot throw more checked exceptions than those declared by the superclass method. For example, if you extend the `write` method from the beginning of this section, the overriding method can throw fewer exceptions:

```
public void write(Object obj, String filename)
    throws FileNotFoundException
```

But if the method tried to throw an unrelated checked exception, such as an `InterruptedException`, it would not compile.

CAUTION: If the superclass method has no `throws` clause, then no overriding method can throw a checked exception.

You can use the javadoc `@throws` tag to document when a method throws a (checked or unchecked) exception. Most programmers only do this when there is something meaningful to document. For example, there is little value in telling users that an `IOException` is thrown when there is a problem with input/output. But comments such as the following can be meaningful:

```
@throws NullPointerException if filename is null
@throws FileNotFoundException if there is no file with name filename
```

 NOTE: You never specify the exception type of a lambda expression. However, if a lambda expression can throw a checked exception, you can only pass it to a functional interface whose method declares that exception. For example, the call

```
list.forEach(obj -> write(obj, "output.dat"));
```

is an error. The parameter of the `forEach` method is the functional interface

```
public interface Consumer<T> {
    void accept(T t);
}
```

The `accept` method is declared not to throw any checked exception.

5.1.4 Catching Exceptions

To catch an exception, set up a `try` block. In its simplest form, it looks like this:

```
try {
    statements
} catch (ExceptionClass ex) {
    handler
}
```

If an exception of the given class occurs as the statements in the `try` block are executed, control transfers to the handler. The exception variable (`ex` in our example) refers to the exception object which the handler can inspect if desired.

There are two modifications that you can make to this basic structure. You can have multiple handlers for different exception classes:

```
try {
    statements
} catch (ExceptionClass₁ ex) {
    handler₁
} catch (ExceptionClass₂ ex) {
    handler₂
} catch (ExceptionClass₃ ex) {
    handler₃
}
```

The catch clauses are matched top to bottom, so the most specific exception classes must come first.

Alternatively, you can share one handler among multiple exception classes:

```
try {
    statements
} catch (ExceptionClass₁ | ExceptionClass₂ | ExceptionClass₃ ex) {
    handler
}
```

In that case, the handler can only call those methods on the exception variable that belong to all exception classes.

5.1.5 The Try-with-Resources Statement

One problem with exception handling is resource management. Suppose you write to a file and close it when you are done:

```
ArrayList<String> lines = ...;
PrintWriter out = new PrintWriter("output.txt");
for (String line : lines) {
    out.println(line.toLowerCase());
}
out.close();
```

This code has a hidden danger. If any method throws an exception, the call to out.close() never happens. That is bad. Output could be lost, or if the exception is triggered many times, the system could run out of file handles.

A special form of the try statement can solve this issue. You can specify *resources* in the header of the try statement. A resource must belong to a class implementing the AutoCloseable interface. You can declare variables in the try block header:

```
ArrayList<String> lines = ...;
try (PrintWriter out = new PrintWriter("output.txt")) { // Variable declaration
    for (String line : lines)
        out.println(line.toLowerCase());
}
```

Alternatively, you can provide previously declared effectively final variables in the header:

```
PrintWriter out = new PrintWriter("output.txt");
try (out) { // Effectively final variable
    for (String line : lines)
        out.println(line.toLowerCase());
}
```

The `AutoCloseable` interface has a single method

```
public void close() throws Exception
```

 NOTE: There is also a `Closeable` interface. It is a subinterface of `AutoCloseable`, also with a single `close` method. However, that method is declared to throw an `IOException`.

When the `try` block exits, either because its end is reached normally or because an exception is thrown, the `close` methods of the resource objects are invoked. For example:

```
try (PrintWriter out = new PrintWriter("output.txt")) {
    for (String line : lines) {
        out.println(line.toLowerCase());
    }
} // out.close() called here
```

You can declare multiple resources, separated by semicolons. Here is an example with two resource declarations:

```
try (Scanner in = new Scanner(Paths.get("/usr/share/dict/words"));
        PrintWriter out = new PrintWriter("output.txt")) {
    while (in.hasNext())
        out.println(in.next().toLowerCase());
}
```

The resources are closed in reverse order of their initialization—that is, `out.close()` is called before `in.close()`.

Suppose that the `PrintWriter` constructor throws an exception. Now `in` is already initialized but `out` is not. The `try` statement does the right thing: calls `in.close()` and propagates the exception.

Some `close` methods can throw exceptions. If that happens when the `try` block completed normally, the exception is thrown to the caller. However, if another exception had been thrown, causing the `close` methods of the resources to be called, and one of them throws an exception, that exception is likely to be of lesser importance than the original one.

In this situation, the original exception gets rethrown, and the exceptions from calling `close` are caught and attached as "suppressed" exceptions. This is a very useful mechanism that would be tedious to implement by hand (see Exercise 5). When you catch the primary exception, you can retrieve the secondary exceptions by calling the `getSuppressed` method:

```
try {
    ...
} catch (IOException ex) {
    Throwable[] secondaryExceptions = ex.getSuppressed();
    ...
}
```

If you want to implement such a mechanism yourself in a (hopefully rare) situation when you can't use the try-with-resources statement, call `ex.addSuppressed(secondaryException)`.

A try-with-resources statement can optionally have `catch` clauses that catch any exceptions in the statement.

5.1.6 The finally Clause

As you have seen, the try-with-resources statement automatically closes resources whether or not an exception occurs. Sometimes, you need to clean up something that isn't an `AutoCloseable`. In that case, use the `finally` clause:

```
try {
    Do work
} finally {
    Clean up
}
```

The `finally` clause is executed when the `try` block comes to an end, either normally or due to an exception.

This pattern occurs whenever you need to acquire and release a lock, or increment and decrement a counter, or push something on a stack and pop it off when you are done. You want to make sure that these actions happen regardless of what exceptions might be thrown.

You should avoid throwing an exception in the `finally` clause. If the body of the `try` block was terminated due to an exception, it is masked by an exception in the `finally` clause. The suppression mechanism that you saw in the preceding section only works for try-with-resources statements.

Similarly, a `finally` clause should not contain a `return` statement. If the body of the `try` block also has a `return` statement, the one in the `finally` clause replaces the return value.

It is possible to form `try` statements with `catch` clauses followed by a `finally` clause. But you have to be careful with exceptions in the `finally` clause. For example, have a look at this `try` block adapted from an online tutorial:

```
BufferedReader in = null;
try {
    in = Files.newBufferedReader(path, StandardCharsets.UTF_8);
    Read from in
} catch (IOException ex) {
    System.err.println("Caught IOException: " + ex.getMessage());
} finally {
    if (in != null) {
        in.close(); // Caution—might throw an exception
    }
}
```

The programmer clearly thought about the case when the `Files.newBufferedReader` method throws an exception. It appears as if this code would catch and print all I/O exceptions, but it actually misses one: the one that might be thrown by `in.close()`. It is often better to rewrite a complex `try`/`catch`/`finally` statement as a try-with-resources statement or by nesting a `try`/`finally` inside a `try`/`catch` statement—see Exercise 6.

5.1.7 Rethrowing and Chaining Exceptions

When an exception occurs, you may not know what to do about it, but you may want to log the failure. In that case, rethrow the exception so that a competent handler can deal with it:

```
try {
    Do work
}
catch (Exception ex) {
    logger.log(level, message, ex);
    throw ex;
}
```

 NOTE: Something subtle is going on when this code is inside a method that may throw a checked exception. Suppose the enclosing method is declared as

```
public void read(String filename) throws IOException
```

At first glance, it looks as if one would need to change the `throws` clause to `throws Exception`. However, the Java compiler carefully tracks the flow and realizes that `ex` could only have been an exception thrown by one of the statements in the `try` block, not an arbitrary `Exception`.

Sometimes, you want to change the class of a thrown exception. For example, you may need to report a failure of a subsystem with an exception class that makes sense to the user of the subsystem. Suppose you encounter a database error in a servlet. The code that executes the servlet may not want to know in detail what went wrong, but it definitely wants to know that the servlet is at fault. In this case, catch the original exception and chain it to a higher-level one:

```
try {
    Access the database
}
catch (SQLException ex) {
    throw new ServletException("database error", ex);
}
```

When the ServletException is caught, the original exception can be retrieved as follows:

```
Throwable cause = ex.getCause();
```

The ServletException class has a constructor that takes as a parameter the cause of the exception. Not all exception classes do that. In that case, you have to call the initCause method, like this:

```
try {
    Access the database
}
catch (SQLexception ex) {
    Throwable ex2 = new CruftyOldException("database error");
    ex2.initCause(ex);
    throw ex2;
}
```

If you provide your own exception class, you should provide, in addition to the two constructors described in Section 5.1.2, "The Exception Hierarchy" (page 183), the following constructors:

```
public class FileFormatException extends IOException {
    ...
    public FileFormatException(Throwable cause) { initCause(cause); }
    public FileFormatException(String message, Throwable cause) {
        super(message);
        initCause(cause);
    }
}
```

 TIP: The chaining technique is also useful if a checked exception occurs in a method that is not allowed to throw a checked exception. You can catch the checked exception and chain it to an unchecked one.

5.1.8 Uncaught Exceptions and the Stack Trace

If an exception is not caught anywhere, a *stack trace* is displayed—a listing of all pending method calls at the point where the exception was thrown. The stack trace is sent to System.err, the stream for error messages.

If you want to save the exception somewhere else, perhaps for inspection by your tech support staff, set the default uncaught exception handler:

```
Thread.setDefaultUncaughtExceptionHandler((thread, ex) -> {
    Record the exception
});
```

 NOTE: An uncaught exception terminates the thread in which it occurred. If your application only has one thread (which is the case for the programs that you have seen so far), the program exits after invoking the uncaught exception handler.

Sometimes, you are forced to catch an exception and don't really know what to do with it. For example, the Class.forName method throws a checked exception that you need to handle. Instead of ignoring the exception, at least print the stack trace:

```
try {
    Class<?> cl = Class.forName(className);
    ...
} catch (ClassNotFoundException ex) {
    ex.printStackTrace();
}
```

If you want to store the stack trace of an exception, you can put it into a string as follows:

```
ByteArrayOutputStream out = new ByteArrayOutputStream();
ex.printStackTrace(new PrintWriter(out));
String description = out.toString();
```

 NOTE: If you need to process the stack trace in more detail, use the StackWalker class. For example, the following prints all stack frames:

```
StackWalker walker = StackWalker.getInstance();
walker.forEach(frame -> System.err.println("Frame: " + frame));
```

You can also analyze the StackWalker.StackFrame instances in detail. See the API documentation for details.

5.1.9 The `Objects.requireNonNull` Method

The `Objects` class has a method for convenient null checks of parameters. Here is a sample usage:

```
public void process(String direction) {
    this.direction = Objects.requireNonNull(direction);
    ...
}
```

If `direction` is `null`, a `NullPointerException` is thrown—which doesn't seem like a huge improvement at first. But consider working back from a stack trace. When you see a call to `requireNonNull` as the culprit, you know right away what you did wrong.

You can also supply a message string for the exception:

```
this.direction = Objects.requireNonNull(direction, "direction must not be null");
```

A variant of this method allows you to supply an alternate value instead of throwing an exception:

```
this.direction = Objects.requireNonNullElse(direction, "North");
```

If the default is costly to compute, use yet another variant:

```
this.direction = Objects.requireNonNullElseGet(direction,
    () -> System.getProperty("com.horstmann.direction.default"));
```

The lambda expression is only evaluated if `direction` is `null`.

5.2 Assertions

Assertions are a commonly used idiom of defensive programming. Suppose you are convinced that a particular property is fulfilled, and you rely on that property in your code. For example, you may be computing

```
double y = Math.sqrt(x);
```

You are certain that `x` is not negative. Still, you want to double-check rather than have "not a number" floating-point values creep into your computation. You could, of course, throw an exception:

```
if (x < 0) throw new IllegalStateException(x + " < 0");
```

But this condition stays in the program, even after testing is complete, slowing it down. The assertion mechanism allows you to put in checks during testing and to have them automatically removed in the production code.

NOTE: In Java, assertions are intended as a debugging aid for validating internal assumptions, not as a mechanism for enforcing contracts. For example, if you want to report an inappropriate parameter of a public method, don't use an assertion but throw an `IllegalArgumentException`.

5.2.1 Using Assertions

There are two forms of the assertion statement in Java:

```
assert condition;
assert condition : expression;
```

The `assert` statement evaluates the condition and throws an `AssertionError` if it is false. In the second form, the expression is turned into a string that becomes the message of the error object.

 NOTE: If the expression is a `Throwable`, it is also set as the cause of the assertion error (see Section 5.1.7, "Rethrowing and Chaining Exceptions," page 190).

For example, to assert that x is non-negative, you can simply use the statement

```
assert x >= 0;
```

Or you can pass the actual value of x into the `AssertionError` object so it gets displayed later:

```
assert x >= 0 : x;
```

5.2.2 Enabling and Disabling Assertions

By default, assertions are disabled. Enable them by running the program with the `-enableassertions` or `-ea` option:

```
java -ea MainClass
```

You do not have to recompile your program because enabling or disabling assertions is handled by the class loader. When assertions are disabled, the class loader strips out the assertion code so that it won't slow execution. You can even enable assertions in specific classes or in entire packages, for example:

```
java -ea:MyClass -ea:com.mycompany.mylib... MainClass
```

This command turns on assertions for the class `MyClass` and all classes in the `com.mycompany.mylib` package *and its subpackages*. The option `-ea...` turns on assertions in all classes of the default package.

You can also disable assertions in certain classes and packages with the -disableassertions or -da option:

```
java -ea:... -da:MyClass MainClass
```

When you use the -ea and -da switches to enable or disable all assertions (and not just specific classes or packages), they do not apply to the "system classes" that are loaded without class loaders. Use the -enablesystemassertions/-esa switch to enable assertions in system classes.

It is also possible to programmatically control the assertion status of class loaders with the following methods:

```
void ClassLoader.setDefaultAssertionStatus(boolean enabled);
void ClassLoader.setClassAssertionStatus(String className, boolean enabled);
void ClassLoader.setPackageAssertionStatus(String packageName, boolean enabled);
```

As with the -enableassertions command-line option, the setPackageAssertionStatus method sets the assertion status for the given package and its subpackages.

5.3 Logging

Every Java programmer is familiar with the process of inserting System.out.println calls into troublesome code to gain insight into program behavior. Of course, once you have figured out the cause of trouble, you remove the print statements—only to put them back in when the next problem surfaces. The logging API is designed to overcome this problem.

5.3.1 Using Loggers

Let's get started with the simplest possible case. The logging system manages a default logger that you get by calling Logger.getGlobal(). Use the info method to log an information message:

```
Logger.getGlobal().info("Opening file " + filename);
```

The record is printed like this:

```
Aug 04, 2014 09:53:34 AM com.mycompany.MyClass read INFO: Opening file data.txt
```

Note that the time and the names of the calling class and method are automatically included.

However, if you call

```
Logger.getGlobal().setLevel(Level.OFF);
```

then calls to info have no effect.

NOTE: In the above example, the message `"Opening file "` + `filename` is created even if logging is disabled. If you are concerned about the cost of creating the message, you can use a lambda expression instead:

```
Logger.getGlobal().info(() -> "Opening file " + filename);
```

5.3.2 Loggers

In a professional application, you wouldn't want to log all records to a single global logger. Instead, you can define your own loggers.

When you request a logger with a given name for the first time, it is created.

```
Logger logger = Logger.getLogger("com.mycompany.myapp");
```

Subsequent calls to the same name yield the same logger object.

Similar to package names, logger names are hierarchical. In fact, they are more hierarchical than packages. There is no semantic relationship between a package and its parent, but logger parents and children share certain properties. For example, if you turn off messages to the logger `"com.mycompany"`, then the child loggers are also deactivated.

 NOTE: In this section, we introduce the `java.util.logging` framework that is a part of the JDK. This framework is not universally loved, and there are alternatives with better performance and more flexibility. Many projects use a logging façade such as SLF4J (`https://www.slf4j.org`) that lets users plug in the logging framework of their choice. Nevertheless, `java.util.logging` is fine for many use cases, and learning how it works will help you understand the alternatives.

 NOTE: Even the JVM doesn't love `java.util.logging`, but for an entirely different reason. In order to have a minimal footprint, the most basic JVM modules don't want to depend on the `java.logging` module that contains the `java.util.logging` package. There is a lightweight `System.Logger` interface that some JVM modules use for logging. On a full JVM, these logs are redirected to `java.util.logging`, but they can also be redirected elsewhere. This is not a facility that is intended for application programmers, so you should use `java.util.logging` or a logging façade.

5.3.3 Logging Levels

There are seven logging levels: SEVERE, WARNING, INFO, CONFIG, FINE, FINER, FINEST. By default, the top three levels are actually logged. You can set a different threshold, for example:

```
logger.setLevel(Level.FINE);
```

Now FINE and all levels above it are logged.

You can also use Level.ALL to turn on logging for all levels or Level.OFF to turn all logging off.

There are logging methods corresponding to each level, such as

```
logger.warning(message);
logger.fine(message);
```

and so on. Alternatively, if the level is variable, you can use the log method and supply the level:

```
Level level = ...;
logger.log(level, message);
```

 TIP: The default logging configuration logs all records with the level of INFO or higher. Therefore, you should use the levels CONFIG, FINE, FINER, and FINEST for debugging messages that are useful for diagnostics but meaningless to the user.

 CAUTION: If you set the logging level to a value finer than INFO, you also need to change the log handler configuration. The default log handler suppresses messages below INFO. See Section 5.3.6, "Log Handlers" (page 200) for details.

5.3.4 Other Logging Methods

There are convenience methods for tracing execution flow:

```
void entering(String className, String methodName)
void entering(String className, String methodName, Object param)
void entering(String className, String methodName, Object[] params)
void exiting(String className, String methodName)
void exiting(String className, String methodName, Object result)
```

For example:

```
public int read(String file, String pattern) {
    logger.entering("com.mycompany.mylib.Reader", "read",
        new Object[] { file, pattern });
    ...
    logger.exiting("com.mycompany.mylib.Reader", "read", count);
    return count;
}
```

These calls generate log records of level FINER that start with the strings ENTRY and RETURN.

 NOTE: Oddly enough, these methods have never been turned into methods with variable arguments.

A common use for logging is to log unexpected exceptions. Two convenience methods include a description of the exception in the log record.

```
void log(Level l, String message, Throwable t)
void throwing(String className, String methodName, Throwable t)
```

Typical uses are

```
try {
    ...
}
catch (IOException ex) {
    logger.log(Level.SEVERE, "Cannot read configuration", ex);
}
```

and

```
if (...) {
    IOException ex = new IOException("Cannot read configuration");
    logger.throwing("com.mycompany.mylib.Reader", "read", ex);
    throw ex;
}
```

The throwing call logs a record with level FINER and a message that starts with THROW.

 NOTE: The default log record shows the name of the class and method that contain the logging call, as inferred from the call stack. However, if the virtual machine optimizes execution, accurate call information may not be available. You can use the logp method to give the precise location of the calling class and method. The method signature is

```
void logp(Level l, String className, String methodName, String message)
```

NOTE: If you want the logging messages to be understood by users in multiple languages, you can localize them with the methods

```
void logrb(Level level, ResourceBundle bundle,
    String msg, Object... params)
void logrb(Level level, ResourceBundle bundle,
    String msg, Throwable thrown)
```

Resource bundles are described in Chapter 13.

5.3.5 Logging Configuration

You can change various properties of the logging system by editing a configuration file. The default configuration file is located at `jre/lib/logging.properties`. To use another file, set the `java.util.logging.config.file` property to the file location by starting your application with

```
java -Djava.util.logging.config.file=configFile MainClass
```

CAUTION: Calling `System.setProperty("java.util.logging.config.file", configFile)` in `main` has no effect because the log manager is initialized during VM startup, before `main` executes.

To change the default logging level, edit the configuration file and modify the line

```
.level=INFO
```

You can specify the logging levels for your own loggers by adding lines such as

```
com.mycompany.myapp.level=FINE
```

That is, append the `.level` suffix to the logger name.

As you will see in the next section, loggers don't actually send the messages to the console—that is the job of the handlers. Handlers also have levels. To see `FINE` messages on the console, you also need to set

```
java.util.logging.ConsoleHandler.level=FINE
```

CAUTION: The settings in the log manager configuration are not system properties. Starting a program with `-Dcom.mycompany.myapp.level=FINE` does not have any effect on the logger.

It is also possible to change logging levels in a running program by using the jconsole program. For details, see www.oracle.com/technetwork/articles/java/jconsole-1564139.html#LoggingControl for details.

5.3.6 Log Handlers

By default, loggers send records to a ConsoleHandler that prints them to the System.err stream. Specifically, the logger sends the record to the parent handler, and the ultimate ancestor (with name "") has a ConsoleHandler.

Like loggers, handlers have a logging level. For a record to be logged, its logging level must be above the threshold of both the logger and the handler. The log manager configuration file sets the logging level of the default console handler as

```
java.util.logging.ConsoleHandler.level=INFO
```

To log records with level FINE, change both the default logger level and the handler level in the configuration. Alternatively, you can bypass the configuration file altogether and install your own handler.

```
Logger logger = Logger.getLogger("com.mycompany.myapp");
logger.setLevel(Level.FINE);
logger.setUseParentHandlers(false);
Handler handler = new ConsoleHandler();
handler.setLevel(Level.FINE);
logger.addHandler(handler);
```

By default, a logger sends records both to its own handlers and the handlers of the parent. Our logger is a descendant of the ultimate ancestor "" that sends all records with level INFO and above to the console. We don't want to see those records twice, however, so we set the useParentHandlers property to false.

To send log records elsewhere, add another handler. The logging API provides two handlers for this purpose: a FileHandler and a SocketHandler. The SocketHandler sends records to a specified host and port. Of greater interest is the FileHandler that collects records in a file.

You can simply send records to a default file handler, like this:

```
FileHandler handler = new FileHandler();
logger.addHandler(handler);
```

The records are sent to a file javan.log in the user's home directory, where *n* is a number to make the file unique. By default, the records are formatted in XML. A typical log record has the form

```
<record>
    <date>2014-08-04T09:53:34</date>
    <millis>1407146014072</millis>
    <sequence>1</sequence>
    <logger>com.mycompany.myapp</logger>
    <level>INFO</level>
    <class>com.horstmann.corejava.Employee</class>
    <method>read</method>
    <thread>10</thread>
    <message>Opening file staff.txt</message>
</record>
```

You can modify the default behavior of the file handler by setting various parameters in the log manager configuration (see Table 5-1) or by using one of the following constructors:

```
FileHandler(String pattern)
FileHandler(String pattern, boolean append)
FileHandler(String pattern, int limit, int count)
FileHandler(String pattern, int limit, int count, boolean append)
```

See Table 5-1 for the meaning of the construction parameters.

You probably don't want to use the default log file name. Use a pattern such as `%h/myapp.log` (see Table 5-2 for an explanation of the pattern variables.)

If multiple applications (or multiple copies of the same application) use the same log file, you should turn the `append` flag on. Alternatively, use `%u` in the file name pattern so that each application creates a unique copy of the log.

It is also a good idea to turn file rotation on. Log files are kept in a rotation sequence, such as `myapp.log.0`, `myapp.log.1`, `myapp.log.2`, and so on. Whenever a file exceeds the size limit, the oldest log is deleted, the other files are renamed, and a new file with generation number `0` is created.

Table 5-1 File Handler Configuration Parameters

Configuration Property	Description	Default
`java.util.logging.FileHandler.level`	The handler level	`Level.ALL`
`java.util.logging.FileHandler.append`	When true, log records are appended to an existing file; otherwise, a new file is opened for each program run.	`false`

(Continues)

Table 5-1 File Handler Configuration Parameters *(Continued)*

Configuration Property	Description	Default
`java.util.logging.FileHandler.limit`	The approximate maximum number of bytes to write in a file before opening another (0 = no limit).	0 in the `FileHandler` class, `50000` in the default log manager configuration
`java.util.logging.FileHandler.pattern`	The file name pattern (see Table 5-2)	`%h/java%u.log`
`java.util.logging.FileHandler.count`	The number of logs in a rotation sequence	1 (no rotation)
`java.util.logging.FileHandler.filter`	The filter for filtering log records (see Section 5.3.7)	No filtering
`java.util.logging.FileHandler.encoding`	The character encoding	The platform character encoding
`java.util.logging.FileHandler.formatter`	The formatter for each log record	`java.util.logging.` `XMLFormatter`

Table 5-2 Log File Pattern Variables

Variable	Description
%h	The user's home directory (the `user.home` property)
%t	The system's temporary directory
%u	A unique number
%g	The generation number for rotated logs (a .%g suffix is used if rotation is specified and the pattern doesn't contain %g)
%%	The percent character

5.3.7 Filters and Formatters

Besides filtering by logging levels, each logger and handler can have an additional filter that implements the `Filter` interface, a functional interface with a method

```
boolean isLoggable(LogRecord record)
```

To install a filter into a logger or handler, call the `setFilter` method. Note that you can have at most one filter at a time.

The `ConsoleHandler` and `FileHandler` classes emit the log records in text and XML formats. However, you can define your own formats as well. Extend the `Formatter` class and override the method

```
String format(LogRecord record)
```

Format the record in any way you like and return the resulting string. In your format method, you may want to call the method

```
String formatMessage(LogRecord record)
```

That method formats the message part of the record, substituting parameters and applying localization.

Many file formats (such as XML) require head and tail parts that surround the formatted records. To achieve this, override the methods

```
String getHead(Handler h)
String getTail(Handler h)
```

Finally, call the `setFormatter` method to install the formatter into the handler.

Exercises

1. Write a method `public ArrayList<Double> readValues(String filename) throws ...` that reads a file containing floating-point numbers. Throw appropriate exceptions if the file could not be opened or if some of the inputs are not floating-point numbers.

2. Write a method `public double sumOfValues(String filename) throws ...` that calls the preceding method and returns the sum of the values in the file. Propagate any exceptions to the caller.

3. Write a program that calls the preceding method and prints the result. Catch the exceptions and provide feedback to the user about any error conditions.

4. Repeat the preceding exercise, but don't use exceptions. Instead, have `readValues` and `sumOfValues` return error codes of some kind.

5. Implement a method that contains the code with a `Scanner` and a `PrintWriter` in Section 5.1.5, "The Try-with-Resources Statement" (page 187). But don't use the try-with-resources statement. Instead, just use `catch` clauses. Be sure to close both objects, provided they have been properly constructed. You need to consider the following conditions:

- The `Scanner` constructor throws an exception.
- The `PrintWriter` constructor throws an exception.
- `hasNext`, `next`, or `println` throw an exception.
- `out.close()` throws an exception.
- `in.close()` throws an exception.

6. Section 5.1.6, "The `finally` Clause" (page 189) has an example of a broken `try` statement with `catch` and `finally` clauses. Fix the code with (a) catching the exception in the `finally` clause, (b) a `try`/`catch` statement containing a `try`/`finally` statement, and (c) a try-with-resources statement with a `catch` clause.

7. Explain why

```
try (Scanner in = new Scanner(Paths.get("/usr/share/dict/words"));
        PrintWriter out = new PrintWriter(outputFile)) {
    while (in.hasNext())
        out.println(in.next().toLowerCase());
}
```

is better than

```
Scanner in = new Scanner(Paths.get("/usr/share/dict/words"));
PrintWriter out = new PrintWriter(outputFile);
try (in; out) {
    while (in.hasNext())
        out.println(in.next().toLowerCase());
}
```

8. For this exercise, you'll need to read through the source code of the `java.util.Scanner` class. If input fails when using a `Scanner`, the `Scanner` class catches the input exception and closes the resource from which it consumes input. What happens if closing the resource throws an exception? How does this implementation interact with the handling of suppressed exceptions in the try-with-resources statement?

9. Design a helper method so that one can use a `ReentrantLock` in a try-with-resources statement. Call `lock` and return an `AutoCloseable` whose `close` method calls `unlock` and throws no exceptions.

10. The methods of the `Scanner` and `PrintWriter` classes do not throw checked exceptions to make them easier to use for beginning programmers. How do you find out whether errors occurred during reading or writing? Note that the constructors *can* throw checked exceptions. Why does that defeat the goal of making the classes easier to use for beginners?

11. Write a recursive `factorial` method in which you print all stack frames before you return the value. Construct (but don't throw) an exception object of any kind and get its stack trace, as described in Section 5.1.8, "Uncaught Exceptions and the Stack Trace" (page 192).

12. Compare the use of `Objects.requireNonNull(obj)` and `assert obj != null`. Give a compelling use for each.

13. Write a method `int min(int[] values)` that, just before returning the smallest value, asserts that it is indeed ≤ all values in the array. Use a private helper method or, if you already peeked into Chapter 8, `Stream.allMatch`. Call the method repeatedly on a large array and measure the runtime with assertions enabled, disabled, and removed.

14. Implement and test a log record filter that filters out log records containing bad words such as sex, drugs, and C++.

15. Implement and test a log record formatter that produces an HTML file.

Generic Programming

Topics in This Chapter

Chapter 6

You often need to implement classes and methods that work with multiple types. For example, an `ArrayList<T>` stores elements of an arbitrary class `T`. We say that the `ArrayList` class is *generic*, and `T` is a *type parameter*. The basic idea is very simple and incredibly useful. The first two sections of this chapter cover the simple part.

In any programming language with generic types, the details get tricky when you restrict or vary type parameters. For example, suppose you want to sort elements. Then you must specify that `T` provides an ordering. Furthermore, if the type parameter varies, what does that mean for the generic type? For example, what should be the relationship between `ArrayList<String>` to a method that expects an `ArrayList<Object>`? Sections 6.3, "Type Bounds" (page 210) and 6.4, "Type Variance and Wildcards" (page 211) show you how Java deals with these issues.

In Java, generic programming is more complex than it perhaps should be, because generics were added when Java had been around for a while, and they were designed to be backward-compatible. As a consequence, there are a number of unfortunate restrictions, some of which affect every Java programmer. Others are only of interest to implementors of generic classes. See Sections 6.5, "Generics in the Java Virtual Machine" (page 216) and 6.6, "Restrictions on Generics" (page 220) for the details. The final section covers generics and reflection, and you can safely skip it if you are not using reflection in your own programs.

The key points of this chapter are:

1. A generic class is a class with one or more type parameters.

2. A generic method is a method with type parameters.

3. You can require a type parameter to be a subtype of one or more types.

4. Generic types are invariant: When S is a subtype of T, there is no relationship between G<S> and G<T>.

5. By using wildcards G<? extends T> or G<? super T>, you can specify that a method can accept an instantiation of a generic type with a subclass or superclass argument.

6. Type parameters are erased when generic classes and methods are compiled.

7. Erasure puts many restrictions on generic types. In particular, you can't instantiate generic classes or arrays, cast to a generic type, or throw an object of a generic type.

8. The Class<T> class is generic, which is useful because methods such as cast are declared to produce a value of type T.

9. Even though generic classes and methods are erased in the virtual machine, you can find out at runtime how they were declared.

6.1 Generic Classes

A *generic class* is a class with one or more *type parameters*. As a simple example, consider this class for storing key/value pairs:

```
public class Entry<K, V> {
    private K key;
    private V value;

    public Entry(K key, V value) {
        this.key = key;
        this.value = value;
    }

    public K getKey() { return key; }
    public V getValue() { return value; }
}
```

As you can see, the type parameters K and V are specified inside angle brackets after the name of the class. In the definitions of class members, they are used as types for instance variables, method parameters, and return values.

You *instantiate* the generic class by substituting types for the type variables. For example, Entry<String, Integer> is an ordinary class with methods String getKey() and Integer getValue().

 CAUTION: Type parameters cannot be instantiated with primitive types. For example, Entry<String, int> is not valid in Java.

When you *construct* an object of a generic class, you can omit the type parameters from the constructor. For example,

```
Entry<String, Integer> entry = new Entry<>("Fred", 42);
    // Same as new Entry<String, Integer>("Fred", 42)
```

Note that you still provide an empty pair of angle brackets before the construction arguments. Some people call this empty bracket pair a *diamond*. When you use the diamond syntax, the type parameters for the constructor are inferred.

6.2 Generic Methods

Just like a generic class is a class with type parameters, a *generic method* is a method with type parameters. A generic method can be a method of a regular class or a generic class. Here is an example of a generic method in a class that is not generic:

```
public class Arrays {
    public static <T> void swap(T[] array, int i, int j) {
        T temp = array[i];
        array[i] = array[j];
        array[j] = temp;
    }
}
```

This swap method can be used to swap elements in an arbitrary array, as long as the array element type is not a primitive type.

```
String[] friends = ...;
Arrays.swap(friends, 0, 1);
```

When you declare a generic method, the type parameter is placed after the modifiers (such as `public` and `static`) and before the return type:

```
public static <T> void swap(T[] array, int i, int j)
```

When calling a generic method, you do not need to specify the type parameter. It is inferred from the method parameter and return types. For example, in the call `Arrays.swap(friends, 0, 1)`, the type of `friends` is `String[]`, and the compiler can infer that `T` should be `String`.

You can, if you like, supply the type explicitly, before the method name, like this:

```
Arrays.<String>swap(friends, 0, 1);
```

One reason why you might want to do this is to get better error messages when something goes wrong—see Exercise 5.

Before plunging into the morass of technical details in the sections that follow, it is worth contemplating the examples of the `Entry` class and the `swap` method and to admire how useful and natural generic types are. With the `Entry` class, the key and value types can be arbitrary. With the `swap` method, the array type can be arbitrary. That is plainly expressed with type variables.

6.3 Type Bounds

Sometimes, the type parameters of a generic class or method need to fulfill certain requirements. You can specify a *type bound* to require that the type extends certain classes or implements certain interfaces.

Suppose, for example, you have an `ArrayList` of objects of a class that implements the `AutoCloseable` interface, and you want to close them all:

```
public static <T extends AutoCloseable> void closeAll(ArrayList<T> elems)
        throws Exception {
    for (T elem : elems) elem.close();
}
```

The type bound `extends AutoCloseable` ensures that the element type is a subtype of `AutoCloseable`. Therefore, the call `elem.close()` is valid. You can pass an `ArrayList<PrintStream>` to this method, but not an `ArrayList<String>`. Note that the `extends` keyword in a type bound actually means "subtype"—the Java designers just used the existing `extends` keyword instead of coming up with another keyword or symbol.

Exercise 14 has a more interesting variant of this method.

NOTE: In this example, we need a type bound because the parameter is of type `ArrayList`. If the method accepted an array, you wouldn't need a generic method. You could simply use a regular method

```
public static void closeAll(AutoCloseable[] elems) throws Exception
```

This works because an array type such as `PrintStream[]` is a subtype of `AutoCloseable[]`. However, as you will see in the following section, an `ArrayList<PrintStream>` is *not* a subtype of `ArrayList<AutoCloseable>`. Using a bounded type parameter solves this problem.

A type parameter can have multiple bounds, such as

```
T extends Runnable & AutoCloseable
```

This syntax is similar to that for catching multiple exceptions, the only difference being that the types are combined with an "and" operator, whereas multiple exceptions are combined with an "or" operator.

You can have as many interface bounds as you like, but at most one of the bounds can be a class. If you have a class as a bound, it must be the first one in the bounds list.

6.4 Type Variance and Wildcards

Suppose you need to implement a method that processes an array of objects that are subclasses of the class `Employee`. You simply declare the parameter to have type `Employee[]`:

```
public static void process(Employee[] staff) { ... }
```

If `Manager` is a subclass of `Employee`, you can pass a `Manager[]` array to the method since `Manager[]` is a subtype of `Employee[]`. This behavior is called *covariance*. Arrays vary in the same way as the element types.

Now, suppose you want to process an array list instead. However, there is a problem: The type `ArrayList<Manager>` is *not* a subtype of `ArrayList<Employee>`.

There is a reason for this restriction. If it were legal to assign an `ArrayList<Manager>` to a variable of type `ArrayList<Employee>`, you could corrupt the array list by storing nonmanagerial employees:

```
ArrayList<Manager> bosses = new ArrayList<>();
ArrayList<Employee> empls = bosses; // Not legal, but suppose it is . . .
empls.add(new Employee(...)); // A nonmanager in bosses!
```

Since conversion from `ArrayList<Manager>` to `ArrayList<Employee>` is disallowed, this error cannot occur.

NOTE: Can you generate the same error with arrays, where the conversion from `Manager[]` to `Employee[]` is permitted? Sure you can, as you saw in Chapter 4. Java arrays are covariant, which is convenient but unsound. When you store a mere `Employee` in a `Manager[]` array, an `ArrayStoreException` is thrown. In contrast, all generic types in Java are *invariant*.

In Java, you use *wildcards* to specify how method parameter and return types should be allowed to vary. This mechanism is sometimes called *use-site variance*. You will see the details in the following sections.

6.4.1 Subtype Wildcards

In many situations it is perfectly safe to convert between different array lists. Suppose a method never writes to the array list, so it cannot corrupt its argument. Use a wildcard to express this fact:

```
public static void printNames(ArrayList<? extends Employee> staff) {
    for (int i = 0; i < staff.size(); i++) {
        Employee e = staff.get(i);
        System.out.println(e.getName());
    }
}
```

The wildcard type `? extends Employee` indicates some unknown subtype of `Employee`. You can call this method with an `ArrayList<Employee>` or an array list of a subtype, such as `ArrayList<Manager>`.

The `get` method of the class `ArrayList<? extends Employee>` has return type `? extends Employee`. The statement

```
Employee e = staff.get(i);
```

is perfectly legal. Whatever type `?` denotes, it is a subtype of `Employee`, and the result of `staff.get(i)` can be assigned to the `Employee` variable e. (I didn't use an enhanced `for` loop in this example to show exactly how the elements are fetched from the array list.)

What happens if you try to store an element into an `ArrayList<? extends Employee>`? That would not work. Consider a call

```
staff.add(x);
```

The `add` method has parameter type `? extends Employee`, and there is *no object* that you can pass to this method. If you pass, say, a `Manager` object, the compiler will refuse. After all, `?` could refer to *any* subclass, perhaps `Janitor`, and you can't add a `Manager` to an `ArrayList<Janitor>`.

NOTE: You can, of course, pass `null`, but that's not an object.

In summary, you can convert from `? extends Employee` to `Employee`, but you can never convert anything to `? extends Employee`. This explains why you can read from an `ArrayList<? extends Employee>` but cannot write to it.

6.4.2 Supertype Wildcards

The wildcard type `? extends Employee` denotes an arbitrary subtype of `Employee`. The converse is the wildcard type `? super Employee` which denotes a supertype of `Employee`. These wildcards are often useful as parameters in functional objects. Here is a typical example. The `Predicate` interface has a method for testing whether an object of type `T` has a particular property:

```
public interface Predicate<T> {
    boolean test(T arg);
    ...
}
```

This method prints the names of all employees with a given property:

```
public static void printAll(Employee[] staff, Predicate<Employee> filter) {
    for (Employee e : staff)
        if (filter.test(e))
            System.out.println(e.getName());
}
```

You can call this method with an object of type `Predicate<Employee>`. Since that is a functional interface, you can also pass a lambda expression:

```
printAll(employees, e -> e.getSalary() > 100000);
```

Now suppose you want to use a `Predicate<Object>` instead, for example

```
Predicate<Object> evenLength = e -> e.toString().length() % 2 == 0;
printAll(employees, evenLength);
```

This should not be a problem. After all, every `Employee` is an `Object` with a `toString` method. However, like all generic types, the `Predicate` interface is invariant, and there is no relationship between `Predicate<Employee>` and `Predicate<Object>`.

The remedy is to allow any `Predicate<? super Employee>`:

```
public static void printAll(Employee[] staff, Predicate<? super Employee> filter) {
    for (Employee e : staff)
        if (filter.test(e))
            System.out.println(e.getName());
}
```

Have a close look at the call `filter.test(e)`. Since the parameter of `test` has a type that is some supertype of `Employee`, it is safe to pass an `Employee` object.

This situation is typical. Functions are naturally *contravariant* in their parameter types. For example, when a function is expected that can process employees, it is OK to give one that is willing to process arbitrary objects.

In general, when you specify a generic functional interface as a method parameter, you should use a `super` wildcard.

 NOTE: Some programmers like the "PECS" mnemonic for wildcards: producer `extends`, consumer `super`. An `ArrayList` from which you read values is a producer, so you use an `extends` wildcard. A `Predicate` to which you give values for testing is a consumer, and you use `super`.

6.4.3 Wildcards with Type Variables

Consider a generalization of the method of the preceding section that prints arbitrary elements fulfilling a condition:

```
public static <T> void printAll(T[] elements, Predicate<T> filter) {
    for (T e : elements)
        if (filter.test(e))
            System.out.println(e.toString());
}
```

This is a generic method that works for arrays of any type. The type parameter is the type of the array that is being passed. However, it suffers from the limitation that you saw in the preceding section. The type parameter of `Predicate` must exactly match the type parameter of the method.

The solution is the same that you already saw—but this time, the bound of the wildcard is a type variable:

```
public static <T> void printAll(T[] elements, Predicate<? super T> filter)
```

This method takes a filter for elements of type `T` or any supertype of `T`.

Here is another example. The `Collection<E>` interface, which you will see in detail in the following chapter, describes a collection of elements of type `E`. It has a method

```
public boolean addAll(Collection<? extends E> c)
```

You can add all elements from another collection whose element type is also `E` or some subtype. With this method, you can add a collection of managers to a collection of employees, but not the other way around.

To see how complex type declarations can get, consider the definition of the `Collections.sort` method:

```
public static <T extends Comparable<? super T>> void sort(List<T> list)
```

The `List` interface, covered in detail in the next chapter, describes a sequence of elements, such as a linked list or `ArrayList`. The `sort` method is willing to sort any `List<T>`, provided `T` is a subtype of `Comparable`. But the `Comparable` interface is again generic:

```
public interface Comparable<T> {
    int compareTo(T other);
}
```

Its type parameter specifies the argument type of the `compareTo` method. So, it would seem that `Collections.sort` could be declared as

```
public static <T extends Comparable<T>> void sort(List<T> list)
```

But that is too restrictive. Suppose that the `Employee` class implements `Comparable<Employee>`, comparing employees by salary. And suppose that the `Manager` class extends `Employee`. Note that it implements `Comparable<Employee>`, and *not* `Comparable<Manager>`. Therefore, `Manager` is *not* a subtype of `Comparable<Manager>`, but it is a subtype of `Comparable<? super Manager>`.

 NOTE: In some programming languages (such as C# and Scala), you can declare type parameters to be covariant or contravariant. For example, by declaring the type parameter of `Comparable` to be contravariant, one doesn't have to use a wildcard for each `Comparable` parameter. This "declaration-site variance" is convenient, but it is less powerful than the "use-site variance" of Java wildcards.

6.4.4 Unbounded Wildcards

It is possible to have unbounded wildcards for situations where you only do very generic operations. For example, here is a method to check whether an `ArrayList` has any `null` elements:

```
public static boolean hasNulls(ArrayList<?> elements) {
    for (Object e : elements) {
        if (e == null) return true;
    }
    return false;
}
```

Since the type parameter of the `ArrayList` doesn't matter, it makes sense to use an `ArrayList<?>`. One could equally well have made `hasNulls` into a generic method:

```
public static <T> boolean hasNulls(ArrayList<T> elements)
```

But the wildcard is easy to understand, so that's the preferred approach.

6.4.5 Wildcard Capture

Let's try to define a swap method using wildcards:

```
public static void swap(ArrayList<?> elements, int i, int j) {
    ? temp = elements.get(i); // Won't work
    elements.set(i, elements.get(j));
    elements.set(j, temp);
}
```

That won't work. You can use ? as a type argument, but not as a type.

However, there is a workaround. Add a helper method, like this:

```
public static void swap(ArrayList<?> elements, int i, int j) {
    swapHelper(elements, i, j);
}

private static <T> void swapHelper(ArrayList<T> elements, int i, int j) {
    T temp = elements.get(i);
    elements.set(i, elements.get(j));
    elements.set(j, temp);
}
```

The call to swapHelper is valid because of a special rule called *wildcard capture*. The compiler doesn't know what ? is, but it stands for some type, so it is OK to call a generic method. The type parameter T of swapHelper "captures" the wildcard type. Since swapHelper is a generic method, not a method with wildcards in parameters, it can make use of the type variable T to declare variables.

What have we gained? The user of the API sees an easy-to-understand ArrayList<?> instead of a generic method.

6.5 Generics in the Java Virtual Machine

When generic types and methods were added to Java, the Java designers wanted the generic forms of classes to be compatible with their preexisting versions. For example, it should be possible to pass an ArrayList<String> to a method from pre-generic days that accepted the ArrayList class, which collects elements of type Object. The language designers decided on an implementation that "erases" the types in the virtual machine. This was very popular at the time since it enabled Java users to gradually migrate to using generics. As you can imagine, there are drawbacks to this scheme, and, as so often happens with compromises made in the interest of compatibility, the drawbacks remain long after the migration has successfully completed.

In this section, you will see what goes on in the virtual machine, and the next section examines the consequences.

6.5.1 Type Erasure

When you define a generic type, it is compiled into a *raw* type. For example, the Entry<K, V> class of Section 6.1, "Generic Classes" (page 208) turns into

```java
public class Entry {
    private Object key;
    private Object value;

    public Entry(Object key, Object value) {
        this.key = key;
        this.value = value;
    }

    public Object getKey() { return key; }
    public Object getValue() { return value; }
}
```

Every K and V is replaced by Object.

If a type variable has bounds, it is replaced with the first bound. Suppose we declare the Entry class as

```java
public class Entry<K extends Comparable<? super K> & Serializable,
                   V extends Serializable>
```

Then it is erased to a class

```java
public class Entry {
    private Comparable key;
    private Serializable value;
    ...
}
```

6.5.2 Cast Insertion

Erasure sounds somehow dangerous, but it is actually perfectly safe. Suppose for example, you used an Entry<String, Integer> object. When you construct the object, you must provide a key that is a String and a value that is an Integer or is converted to one. Otherwise, your program does not even compile. You are therefore guaranteed that the getKey method returns a String.

However, suppose your program compiled with "unchecked" warnings, perhaps because you used casts or mixed generic and raw `Entry` types. Then it is possible for an `Entry<String, Integer>` to have a key of a different type.

Therefore, it is also necessary to have safety checks at runtime. The compiler inserts a cast whenever one reads from an expression with erased type. Consider, for example,

```
Entry<String, Integer> entry = ...;
String key = entry.getKey();
```

Since the erased `getKey` method returns an `Object`, the compiler generates code equivalent to

```
String key = (String) entry.getKey();
```

6.5.3 Bridge Methods

In the preceding sections, you have seen the basics of what erasure does. It is simple and safe. Well, almost simple. When erasing method parameter and return types, it is sometimes necessary for the compiler to synthesize *bridge methods*. This is an implementation detail, and you don't need to know about it unless you want to know why such a method shows up in a stack trace, or you want an explanation for one of the more obscure limitations on Java generics (see Section 6.6.6, "Methods May Not Clash after Erasure," page 224).

Consider this example:

```
public class WordList extends ArrayList<String> {
    public boolean add(String e) {
        return isBadWord(e) ? false : super.add(e);
    }
    ...
}
```

Now consider this code fragment:

```
WordList words = ...;
ArrayList<String> strings = words; // OK—conversion to superclass
strings.add("C++");
```

The last method call invokes the (erased) `add(Object)` method of the `ArrayList` class.

One would reasonably expect dynamic method lookup to work in this case so that the `add` method of `WordList`, not the `add` method of `ArrayList`, is called when `add` is invoked on a `WordList` object.

To make this work, the compiler synthesizes a bridge method in the `WordList` class:

```
public boolean add(Object e) {
    return add((String) e);
}
```

In the call `strings.add("C++")`, the `add(Object)` method is called, and it calls the `add(String)` method of the `WordList` class.

Bridge methods can also be called when the return type varies. Consider this method:

```
public class WordList extends ArrayList<String> {
    public String get(int i) {
        return super.get(i).toLowerCase();
    }
    ...
}
```

In the `WordList` class, there are two `get` methods:

```
String get(int) // Defined in WordList
Object get(int) // Overrides the method defined in ArrayList
```

The second method is synthesized by the compiler, and it calls the first. This is again done to make dynamic method lookup work.

These methods have the same parameter types but different return types. In the Java language, you cannot implement such a pair of methods. But in the virtual machine, a method is specified by its name, the parameter types, *and* the return type, which allows the compiler to generate this method pair.

 NOTE: Bridge methods are not only used for generic types. They are also used to implement covariant return types. For example, in Chapter 4, you saw how you should declare a `clone` method with the appropriate return type:

```
public class Employee implements Cloneable {
    public Employee clone() throws CloneNotSupportedException { ... }
}
```

In this case, the `Employee` class has two `clone` methods:

```
Employee clone() // Defined above
Object clone() // Synthesized bridge method
```

The bridge method, again generated to make dynamic method lookup work, calls the first method.

6.6 Restrictions on Generics

There are several restrictions when using generic types and methods in Java—some merely surprising and others genuinely inconvenient. Most of them are consequences of type erasure. The following sections show you those that you will most likely encounter in practice.

6.6.1 No Primitive Type Arguments

A type parameter can never be a primitive type. For example, you cannot form an ArrayList<int>. As you have seen, in the virtual machine there is only one type, the raw ArrayList that stores elements of type Object. An int is not an object.

When generics were first introduced, this was not considered a big deal. After all, one can form an ArrayList<Integer> and rely on autoboxing. Now that generics are more commonly used, however, the pain is increasing. There is a profusion of functional interfaces such as IntFunction, LongFunction, DoubleFunction, ToIntFunction, ToLongFunction, ToDoubleFunction—and that only takes care of unary functions and three of the eight primitive types.

6.6.2 At Runtime, All Types Are Raw

In the virtual machine, there are only raw types. For example, you cannot inquire at runtime whether an ArrayList contains String objects. A condition such as

```
if (a instanceof ArrayList<String>)
```

is a compile-time error since no such check could ever be executed.

A cast to an instantiation of a generic type is equally ineffective, but it is legal.

```
Object result = ...;
ArrayList<String> list = (ArrayList<String>) result;
    // Warning—this only checks whether result is a raw ArrayList
```

Such a cast is allowed because there is sometimes no way to avoid it. If result is the outcome of a very general process (such as calling a method through reflection, see Chapter 4) and its exact type is not known to the compiler, the programmer must use a cast. A cast to ArrayList or ArrayList<?> would not suffice.

To make the warning go away, annotate the variable like this:

```
@SuppressWarnings("unchecked") ArrayList<String> list
    = (ArrayList<String>) result;
```

CAUTION: Abusing the @SuppressWarnings annotation can lead to *heap pollution*—objects that should belong to a particular generic type instantiation but actually belong to a different one. For example, you can assign an ArrayList<Employee> to an ArrayList<String> reference. The consequence is a ClassCastException when an element of the wrong type is retrieved.

 TIP: The trouble with heap pollution is that the reported runtime error is far from the source of the problem—the insertion of a wrong element. If you need to debug such a problem, you can use a "checked view." Where you constructed, say, an ArrayList<String>, instead use

```
List<String> strings
    = Collections.checkedList(new ArrayList<>(), String.class);
```

The view monitors all insertions into the list and throws an exception when an object of the wrong type is added.

The getClass method always returns a raw type. For example, if list is an ArrayList<String>, then list.getClass() returns ArrayList.class. In fact, there is no ArrayList<String>.class—such a class literal is a syntax error.

Also, you cannot have type variables in class literals. There is no T.class, T[].class, or ArrayList<T>.class.

6.6.3 You Cannot Instantiate Type Variables

You cannot use type variables in expressions such as new T(...) or new T[...]. These forms are outlawed because they would not do what the programmer intends when T is erased.

If you want to create a generic instance or array, you have to work harder. Suppose you want to provide a repeat method so that Arrays.repeat(n, obj) makes an array containing n copies of obj. Of course, you'd like the element type of the array to be the same as the type of obj. This attempt does not work:

```
public static <T> T[] repeat(int n, T obj) {
    T[] result = new T[n]; // Error—cannot construct an array new T[...]
    for (int i = 0; i < n; i++) result[i] = obj;
    return result;
}
```

To solve this problem, ask the caller to provide the array constructor as a method reference:

```
String[] greetings = Arrays.repeat(10, "Hi", String[]::new);
```

Here is the implementation of the method:

```
public static <T> T[] repeat(int n, T obj, IntFunction<T[]> constr) {
    T[] result = constr.apply(n);
    for (int i = 0; i < n; i++) result[i] = obj;
    return result;
}
```

Alternatively, you can ask the user to supply a class object, and use reflection.

```
public static <T> T[] repeat(int n, T obj, Class<T> cl) {
    @SuppressWarnings("unchecked") T[] result
        = (T[]) java.lang.reflect.Array.newInstance(cl, n);
    for (int i = 0; i < n; i++) result[i] = obj;
    return result;
}
```

This method is called as follows:

```
String[] greetings = Arrays.repeat(10, "Hi", String.class);
```

Another option is to ask the caller to allocate the array. Usually, the caller is allowed to supply an array of any length, even zero. If the supplied array is too short, the method makes a new one, using reflection.

```
public static <T> T[] repeat(int n, T obj, T[] array) {
    T[] result;
    if (array.length >= n)
        result = array;
    else {
        @SuppressWarnings("unchecked") T[] newArray
            = (T[]) java.lang.reflect.Array.newInstance(
                array.getClass().getComponentType(), n);
        result = newArray;
    }
    for (int i = 0; i < n; i++) result[i] = obj;
    return result;
}
```

 TIP: You *can* instantiate an ArrayList with a type variable. For example, the following is entirely legal:

```
public static <T> ArrayList<T> repeat(int n, T obj) {
    ArrayList<T> result = new ArrayList<>(); // OK
    for (int i = 0; i < n; i++) result.add(obj);
    return result;
}
```

This is much simpler than the workarounds you just saw, and I recommend it whenever you don't have a compelling reason for producing an array.

NOTE: If a generic class needs a generic array that is a private part of the implementation, you can get away with just constructing an `Object[]` array. This is what the `ArrayList` class does:

```
public class ArrayList<E> {
    private Object[] elementData;

    public E get(int index) {
        return (E) elementData[index];
    }
    ...
}
```

6.6.4 You Cannot Construct Arrays of Parameterized Types

Suppose you want to create an array of `Entry` objects:

```
Entry<String, Integer>[] entries = new Entry<String, Integer>[100];
    // Error—cannot construct an array with generic component type
```

This is a syntax error. The construction is outlawed because, after erasure, the array constructor would create a raw `Entry` array. It would then be possible to add `Entry` objects of any type (such as `Entry<Employee, Manager>`) without an `ArrayStoreException`.

Note that the *type* `Entry<String, Integer>[]` is perfectly legal. You can declare a variable of that type. If you really want to initialize it, you can, like this:

```
@SuppressWarnings("unchecked") Entry<String, Integer>[] entries
    = (Entry<String, Integer>[]) new Entry<?, ?>[100];
```

But it is simpler to use an array list:

```
ArrayList<Entry<String, Integer>> entries = new ArrayList<>(100);
```

Recall that a varargs parameter is an array in disguise. If such a parameter is generic, you can bypass the restriction against generic array creation. Consider this method:

```
public static <T> ArrayList<T> asList(T... elements) {
    ArrayList<T> result = new ArrayList<>();
    for (T e : elements) result.add(e);
    return result;
}
```

Now consider this call:

```
Entry<String, Integer> entry1 = ...;
Entry<String, Integer> entry2 = ...;
ArrayList<Entry<String, Integer>> entries = Lists.asList(entry1, entry2);
```

The inferred type for T is the generic type Entry<String, Integer>, and therefore elements is an array of type Entry<String, Integer>. That is just the kind of array creation that you cannot do yourself!

In this case, the compiler reports a warning, not an error. If your method only reads elements from the parameter array, it should use the @SafeVarargs annotation to suppress the warning:

```
@SafeVarargs public static <T> ArrayList<T> asList(T... elements)
```

This annotation can be applied to methods that are static, final, or private, or to constructors. Any other methods might be overridden and are not eligible for the annotation.

6.6.5 Class Type Variables Are Not Valid in Static Contexts

Consider a generic class with type variables, such as Entry<K, V>. You cannot use the type variables K and V with static variables or methods. For example, the following does not work:

```
public class Entry<K, V> {
    private static V defaultValue;
        // Error—V in static context
    public static void setDefault(V value) { defaultValue = value; }
        // Error—V in static context
    ...
}
```

After all, type erasure means there is only one such variable or method in the erased Entry class, and not one for each K and V.

6.6.6 Methods May Not Clash after Erasure

You may not declare methods that would cause clashes after erasure. For example, the following would be an error:

```
public interface Ordered<T> extends Comparable<T> {
    public default boolean equals(T value) {
        // Error—erasure clashes with Object.equals
        return compareTo(value) == 0;
    }
    ...
}
```

The equals(T value) method erases to equals(Object value), which clashes with the same method from Object.

Sometimes the cause for a clash is more subtle. Here is a nasty situation:

```
public class Employee implements Comparable<Employee> {
    ...
    public int compareTo(Employee other) {
        return name.compareTo(other.name);
    }
}

public class Manager extends Employee implements Comparable<Manager> {
    // Error—cannot have two instantiations of Comparable as supertypes
    ...
    public int compareTo(Manager other) {
        return Double.compare(salary, other.salary);
    }
}
```

The class Manager extends Employee and therefore picks up the supertype Comparable<Employee>. Naturally, managers want to compare each other by salary, not by name. And why not? There is no erasure. Just two methods

```
public int compareTo(Employee other)
public int compareTo(Manager other)
```

The problem is that *the bridge methods clash*. Recall from Section 6.5.3, "Bridge Methods" (page 218) that both of these methods yield a bridge method

```
public int compareTo(Object other)
```

6.6.7 Exceptions and Generics

You cannot throw or catch objects of a generic class. In fact, you cannot even form a generic subclass of Throwable:

```
public class Problem<T> extends Exception
    // Error—a generic class can't be a subtype of Throwable
```

You cannot use a type variable in a catch clause:

```
public static <T extends Throwable> void doWork(Runnable r, Class<T> cl) {
    try {
        r.run();
    } catch (T ex) { // Error—can't catch type variable
        Logger.getGlobal().log(..., ..., ex);
    }
}
```

However, you *can* have a type variable in the throws declaration:

```
public static <V, T extends Throwable> V doWork(Callable<V> c, T ex) throws T {
    try {
        return c.call();
    } catch (Throwable realEx) {
        ex.initCause(realEx);
        throw ex;
    }
}
```

 CAUTION: You can use generics to remove the distinction between checked and unchecked exceptions. The key ingredient is this pair of methods:

```
public class Exceptions {
    @SuppressWarnings("unchecked")
    private static <T extends Throwable>
            void throwAs(Throwable e) throws T {
        throw (T) e; // The cast is erased to (Throwable) e
    }
    public static <V> V doWork(Callable<V> c) {
        try {
            return c.call();
        } catch (Throwable ex) {
            Exceptions.<RuntimeException>throwAs(ex);
            return null;
        }
    }
}
```

Now consider this method:

```
public static String readAll(Path path) {
    return doWork(() -> new String(Files.readAllBytes(path)));
}
```

Even though `Files.readAllBytes` throws a checked exception when the path is not found, that exception is neither declared nor caught in the `readAll` method!

6.7 Reflection and Generics

In the following sections, you will see what you can do with the generic classes in the reflection package and how you can find out the small amount of generic type information in the virtual machine that survives the erasure process.

6.7.1 The Class<T> Class

The `Class` class has a type parameter, namely the class that the `Class` object describes. Huh? Let's do this slowly.

Consider the `String` class. In the virtual machine, there is a `Class` object for this class, which you can obtain as `"Fred".getClass()` or, more directly, as the class literal `String.class`. You can use that object to find out what methods the class has, or to construct an instance.

The type parameter helps write typesafe code. Consider for example the `getConstructor` method of `Class<T>`. It is declared to return a `Constructor<T>`. And the `newInstance` method of `Constructor<T>` is declared to returns an object of type `T`. That's why `String.class` has type `Class<String>`: Its `getConstructor` method yields a `Constructor<String>`, whose `newInstance` method returns a `String`.

That information can save you a cast. Consider this method:

```
public static <T> ArrayList<T> repeat(int n, Class<T> cl)
      throws ReflectiveOperationException {
   ArrayList<T> result = new ArrayList<>();
   for (int i = 0; i < n; i++)
      result.add(cl.getConstructor().newInstance());
   return result;
}
```

The method compiles since `cl.getConstructor().newInstance()` returns a result of type `T`.

Suppose you call this method as `repeat(10, Employee.class)`. Then `T` is inferred to be the type `Employee` since `Employee.class` has type `Class<Employee>`. Therefore, the return type is `ArrayList<Employee>`.

In addition to the `getConstructor` method, there are several other methods of the `Class` class that use the type parameter. They are:

```
Class<? super T> getSuperclass()
<U> Class<? extends U> asSubclass(Class<U> clazz)
T cast(Object obj)
Constructor<T> getDeclaredConstructor(Class<?>... parameterTypes)
T[] getEnumConstants()
```

As you have seen in Chapter 4, there are many situations where you know nothing about the class that a `Class` object describes. Then, you can simply use the wildcard type `Class<?>`.

6.7.2 Generic Type Information in the Virtual Machine

Erasure only affects instantiated type parameters. Complete information about the *declaration* of generic classes and methods is available at runtime.

For example, suppose a call `obj.getClass()` yields `ArrayList.class`. You cannot tell whether `obj` was constructed as an `ArrayList<String>` or `ArrayList<Employee>`. But you can tell that the class `ArrayList` is a generic class with a type parameter `E` that has no bounds.

Similarly, consider the method

```
static <T extends Comparable<? super T>> void sort(List<T> list)
```

of the `Collections` class. As you saw in Chapter 4, you can get the corresponding `Method` object as

```
Method m = Collections.class.getMethod("sort", List.class);
```

From this `Method` object, you can recover the entire method signature.

The interface `Type` in the `java.lang.reflect` package represents generic type declarations. The interface has the following subtypes:

1. The `Class` class, describing concrete types

2. The `TypeVariable` interface, describing type variables (such as `T extends Comparable<? super T>`)

3. The `WildcardType` interface, describing wildcards (such as `? super T`)

4. The `ParameterizedType` interface, describing generic class or interface types (such as `Comparable<? super T>`)

5. The `GenericArrayType` interface, describing generic arrays (such as `T[]`)

Note that the last four subtypes are interfaces—the virtual machine instantiates suitable classes that implement these interfaces.

Both classes and methods can have type variables. Technically speaking, constructors are not methods, and they are represented by a separate class in the reflection library. They too can be generic. To find out whether a `Class`, `Method`, or `Constructor` object comes from a generic declaration, call the `getTypeParameters` method. You get an array of `TypeVariable` instances, one for each type variable in the declaration, or an array of length 0 if the declaration was not generic.

The `TypeVariable<D>` interface is generic. The type parameter is `Class<T>`, `Method`, or `Constructor<T>`, depending on where the type variable was declared. For example, here is how you get the type variable of the `ArrayList` class:

```
TypeVariable<Class<ArrayList>>[] vars = ArrayList.class.getTypeParameters();
String name = vars[0].getName(); // "E"
```

And here is the type variable of the `Collections.sort` method:

```
Method m = Collections.class.getMethod("sort", List.class);
TypeVariable<Method>[] vars = m.getTypeParameters();
String name = vars[0].getName(); // "T"
```

The latter variable has a bound, which you can process like this:

```
Type[] bounds = vars[0].getBounds();
if (bounds[0] instanceof ParameterizedType) { // Comparable<? super T>
    ParameterizedType p = (ParameterizedType) bounds[0];
    Type[] typeArguments = p.getActualTypeArguments();
    if (typeArguments[0] instanceof WildcardType) { // ? super T
        WildcardType t = (WildCardType) typeArguments[0];
        Type[] upper = t.getUpperBounds(); // ? extends ... & ...
        Type[] lower = t.getLowerBounds(); // ? super ... & ...
        if (lower.length > 0) {
            String description = lower[0].getTypeName(); // "T"
            ...
        }
    }
}
```

This gives you a flavor of how you can analyze generic declarations. I won't dwell on the details since this is not something that commonly comes up in practice. The key point is that the declarations of generic classes and methods are not erased and you have access to them through reflection.

Exercises

1. Implement a class `Stack<E>` that manages an array list of elements of type `E`. Provide methods `push`, `pop`, and `isEmpty`.

2. Reimplement the `Stack<E>` class, using an array to hold the elements. If necessary, grow the array in the `push` method. Provide two solutions, one with an `E[]` array and one with an `Object[]` array. Both solutions should compile without warnings. Which do you prefer, and why?

3. Implement a class `Table<K, V>` that manages an array list of `Entry<K, V>` elements. Supply methods to get the value associated with a key, to put a value for a key, and to remove a key.

4. In the previous exercise, make `Entry` into a nested class. Should that class be generic?

5. Consider this variant of the `swap` method where the array can be supplied with varargs:

```
public static <T> T[] swap(int i, int j, T... values) {
    T temp = values[i];
    values[i] = values[j];
    values[j] = temp;
    return values;
}
```

Now have a look at the call

```
Double[] result = Arrays.swap(0, 1, 1.5, 2, 3);
```

What error message do you get? Now call

```
Double[] result = Arrays.<Double>swap(0, 1, 1.5, 2, 3);
```

Has the error message improved? What do you do to fix the problem?

6. Implement a generic method that appends all elements from one array list to another. Use a wildcard for one of the type arguments. Provide two equivalent solutions, one with a `? extends E` wildcard and one with `? super E`.

7. Implement a class `Pair<E>` that stores a pair of elements of type `E`. Provide accessors to get the first and second element.

8. Modify the class of the preceding exercise by adding methods `max` and `min`, getting the larger or smaller of the two elements. Supply an appropriate type bound for `E`.

9. In a utility class `Arrays`, supply a method

    ```
    public static <E> Pair<E> firstLast(ArrayList<___> a)
    ```

    that returns a pair consisting of the first and last element of `a`. Supply an appropriate type argument.

10. Provide generic methods `min` and `max` in an `Arrays` utility class that yield the smallest and largest element in an array.

11. Continue the preceding exercise and provide a method `minMax` that yields a `Pair` with the minimum and maximum.

12. Implement the following method that stores the smallest and largest element in `elements` in the `result` list:

    ```
    public static <T> void minmax(List<T> elements,
        Comparator<? super T> comp, List<? super T> result)
    ```

    Note the wildcard in the last parameter—any supertype of `T` will do to hold the result.

13. Given the method from the preceding exercise, consider this method:

```
public static <T> void maxmin(List<T> elements,
      Comparator<? super T> comp, List<? super T> result) {
    minmax(elements, comp, result);
    Lists.swapHelper(result, 0, 1);
}
```

Why would this method not compile without wildcard capture? Hint: Try to supply an explicit type `Lists.<___>swapHelper(result, 0, 1)`.

14. Implement an improved version of the `closeAll` method in Section 6.3, "Type Bounds" (page 210). Close all elements even if some of them throw an exception. In that case, throw an exception afterwards. If two or more calls throw an exception, chain them together.

15. Implement a method `map` that receives an array list and a `Function<T, R>` object (see Chapter 3), and that returns an array list consisting of the results of applying the function to the given elements.

16. What is the erasure of the following methods in the `Collection` class?

```
public static <T extends Comparable<? super T>>
    void sort(List<T> list)
public static <T extends Object & Comparable<? super T>>
    T max(Collection<? extends T> coll)
```

17. Define a class `Employee` that implements `Comparable<Employee>`. Using the `javap` utility, demonstrate that a bridge method has been synthesized. What does it do?

18. Consider the method

```
public static <T> T[] repeat(int n, T obj, IntFunction<T[]> constr)
```

in Section 6.6.3, "You Cannot Instantiate Type Variables" (page 221). The call `Arrays.repeat(10, 42, int[]::new)` will fail. Why? How can you fix that? What do you need to do for the other primitive types?

19. Consider the method

```
public static <T> ArrayList<T> repeat(int n, T obj)
```

in Section 6.6.3, "You Cannot Instantiate Type Variables" (page 221). This method had no trouble constructing an `ArrayList<T>` which contains an array of `T` values. Can you produce a `T[]` array from that array list without using a `Class` value or a constructor reference? If not, why not?

20. Implement the method

    ```
    @SafeVarargs public static final <T> T[] repeat(int n,  T... objs)
    ```

    Return an array with n copies of the given objects. Note that no Class value or constructor reference is required since you can reflectively increase objs.

21. Using the @SafeVarargs annotation, write a method that can construct arrays of generic types. For example,

    ```
    List<String>[] result = Arrays.<List<String>>construct(10);
        // Sets result to a List<String>[] of size 10
    ```

22. Improve the method public static <V, T extends Throwable> V doWork(Callable<V> c, T ex) throws T of Section 6.6.7, "Exceptions and Generics" (page 225) so that one doesn't have to pass an exception object, which may never get used. Instead, accept a constructor reference for the exception class.

23. In the cautionary note at the end of Section 6.6.7, "Exceptions and Generics" (page 225), the throwAs helper method is used to "cast" ex into a RuntimeException and rethrow it. Why can't you use a regular cast, i.e. throw (RuntimeException) ex?

24. Which methods can you call on a variable of type Class<?> without using casts?

25. Write a method public static String genericDeclaration(Method m) that returns the declaration of the method m listing the type parameters with their bounds and the types of the method parameters, including their type arguments if they are generic types.

Collections

Topics in This Chapter

Chapter 7

Many data structures have been developed so programmers can store and retrieve values efficiently. The Java API provides implementations of common data structures and algorithms, as well as a framework to organize them. In this chapter, you will learn how to work with lists, sets, maps, and other collections.

The key points of this chapter are:

1. The `Collection` interface provides common methods for all collections, except for maps which are described by the `Map` interface.

2. A list is a sequential collection in which each element has an integer index.

3. A set is optimized for efficient containment testing. Java provides `HashSet` and `TreeSet` implementations.

4. For maps, you have the choice between `HashMap` and `TreeMap` implementations. A `LinkedHashMap` retains insertion order.

5. The `Collection` interface and `Collections` class provide many useful algorithms: set operations, searching, sorting, shuffling, and more.

6. Views provide access to data stored elsewhere using the standard collection interfaces.

7.1 An Overview of the Collections Framework

The Java collections framework provides implementations of common data structures. To make it easy to write code that is independent of the choice of data structures, the collections framework provides a number of common interfaces, shown in Figure 7-1. The fundamental interface is Collection whose methods are shown in Table 7-1.

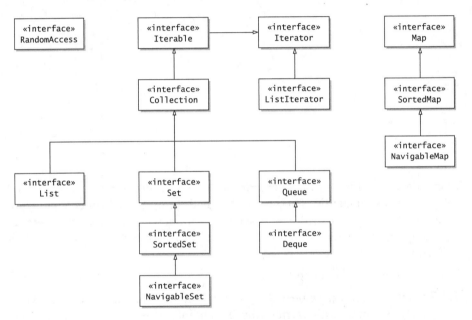

Figure 7-1 Interfaces in the Java collections framework

Table 7-1 The Methods of the Collection<E> Interface

Method	Description
boolean add(E e) boolean addAll(Collection<? extends E> c)	Adds e, or the elements in c. Returns true if the collection changed.
boolean remove(Object o) boolean removeAll(Collection<?> c) boolean retainAll(Collection<?> c) boolean removeIf(Predicate<? super E> filter) void clear()	Removes o, or the elements in c, or the elements not in c, or matching elements, or all elements. The first four methods return true if the collection changed.

(Continues)

Table 7-1 The Methods of the `Collection<E>` Interface *(Continued)*

Method	Description
`int size()`	Returns the number of elements in this collection.

`boolean isEmpty()`
`boolean contains(Object o)`
`boolean containsAll(Collection<?> c)`
	Returns `true` if this collection is empty, or contains `o`, or contains all elements in `c`.

`Iterator<E> iterator()`
`Stream<E> stream()`
`Stream<E> parallelStream()`
`Spliterator<E> spliterator()`
	Yields an iterator, or a stream, or a possibly parallel stream, or a spliterator for visiting the elements of this collection. See Section 7.2 for iterators and Chapter 8 for streams. Spliterators are only of interest to implementors of streams.

`Object[] toArray()` `T[] toArray(T[] a)`	Returns an array with the elements of this collection. The second method returns `a` if it has sufficient length.

A `List` is a sequential collection: Elements have position 0, 1, 2, and so on. Table 7-2 shows the methods of that interface.

The `List` interface is implemented both by the `ArrayList` class, which you have seen throughout this book, and the `LinkedList` class. If you took a course on data structures, you probably remember a linked list—a sequence of linked nodes, each carrying an element. Insertion in the middle of a linked list is speedy—you just splice in a node. But to get to the middle, you have to follow all the links from the beginning, which is slow. There are applications for linked lists, but most application programmers will probably stick with array lists when they need a sequential collection. Still, the `List` interface is useful. For example, the method `Collections.nCopies(n, o)` returns a `List` object with `n` copies of the object `o`. That object "cheats" in that it doesn't actually store `n` copies but, when you ask about any one of them, returns `o`.

 CAUTION: The `List` interface provides methods to access the nth element of a list, even though such an access may not be efficient. To indicate that it is, a collection class should implement the `RandomAccess` interface. This is a tagging interface without methods. For example, `ArrayList` implements `List` and `RandomAccess`, but `LinkedList` implements only the `List` interface.

Table 7-2 The List Interface

Method	Description

`boolean add(int index, E e)`
`boolean addAll(int index,`
`    Collection<? extends E> c)`
`boolean add(E e)`
`boolean addAll(Collection<? extends E> c)`
	Adds e, or the elements in c, before index or to the end. Returns true if the list changed.

`E get(int index)`
`E set(int index, E element)`
`E remove(int index)`
	Gets, sets, or removes the element at the given index. The last two methods return the element at the index before the call.

`int indexOf(Object o)` `int lastIndexOf(Object o)`	Returns the index of the first or last element equal to o, or -1 if there is no match.
`ListIterator<E> listIterator()` `ListIterator<E> listIterator(int index)`	Yields a list iterator for all elements or the elements starting at index.
`void replaceAll(UnaryOperator<E> operator)`	Replaces each element with the result of applying the operator to it.
`void sort(Comparator<? super E> c)`	Sorts this list, using the ordering given by c.
`static List<E> of(E... elements)`	Yields an unmodifiable list containing the given elements.
`List<E> subList(int fromIndex, int toIndex)`	Yields a view (Section 7.6) of the sublist starting at fromIndex and ending before toIndex.

In a Set, elements are not inserted at a particular position, and duplicate elements are not allowed. A SortedSet allows iteration in sort order, and a NavigableSet has methods for finding neighbors of elements. You will learn more about sets in Section 7.3, "Sets" (page 242).

A Queue retains insertion order, but you can only insert elements at the tail and remove them from the head (just like a queue of people). A Deque is a double-ended queue with insertion and removal at both ends.

All collection interfaces are generic, with a type parameter for the element type (Collection<E>, List<E>, and so on). The Map<K, V> interface has a type parameter K for the key type and V for the value type.

You are encouraged to use the interfaces as much as possible in your code. For example, after constructing an `ArrayList`, store the reference in a variable of type `List`:

```
List<String> words = new ArrayList<>();
```

Whenever you implement a method that processes a collection, use the least restrictive interface as parameter type. Usually, a `Collection`, `List`, or `Map` will suffice.

One advantage of a collections framework is that you don't have to reinvent the wheel when it comes to common algorithms. Some basic algorithms (such as `addAll` and `removeIf`) are methods of the `Collection` interface. The `Collections` utility class contains many additional algorithms that operate on various kinds of collections. You can sort, shuffle, rotate, and reverse lists, find the maximum or minimum, or the position of an arbitrary element in a collection, and generate collections with no elements, one element, or `n` copies of the same element. Table 7-3 provides a summary.

Table 7-3 Useful Methods of the `Collections` Class

Method (all are static)	Description
`boolean disjoint(Collection<?> c1, Collection<?> c2)`	Returns `true` if the collections have no elements in common.
`boolean addAll(Collection<? super T> c, T... elements)`	Adds all elements to `c`.
`void copy(List<? super T> dest, List<? extends T> src)`	Copies all elements from `src` to the same indexes in `dest` (which must be at least as long as `src`).
`boolean replaceAll(List<T> list, T oldVal, T newVal)`	Replaces all `oldVal` elements with `newVal`, either of which may be `null`. Returns `true` if at least one match was found.
`void fill(List<? super T> list, T obj)`	Sets all elements of the list to `obj`.
`List<T> nCopies(int n, T o)`	Yields an immutable list with `n` copies of `o`.
`int frequency(Collection<?> c, Object o)`	Returns the number of elements in `c` equal to `o`.

(Continues)

Table 7-3 Useful Methods of the `Collections` Class *(Continued)*

Method (all are static)	Description
`int indexOfSubList(List<?> source, List<?> target)` `int lastIndexOfSubList(List<?> source, List<?> target)`	Returns the start of the first or last occurrence of the target list within the source list, or -1 if there is none.

`int binarySearch(List<? extends`
`    Comparable<? super T>> list, T key)`
`int binarySearch(List<? extends T> list, T key,`
`    Comparator<? super T> c)`
	Returns the position of the key, assuming that the list is sorted by the natural element order or c. If the key is not present, returns -i - 1 where i is the location at which the key should be inserted.

`sort(List<T> list)` `sort(List<T> list, Comparator<? super T> c)`	Sorts the list, using the natural element order or c.
`void swap(List<?> list, int i, int j)`	Swaps the elements at the given position.
`void rotate(List<?> list, int distance)`	Rotates the list, moving the element with index i to (i + distance) % list.size().

`void reverse(List<?> list)`
`void shuffle(List<?> list)`
`void shuffle(List<?> list, Random rnd)`
	Reverses or randomly shuffles the list.

`synchronized(Collection|List|Set|SortedSet|` `    NavigableSet|Map|SortedMap|NavigableMap)()`	Yields a synchronized view (see Section 7.6).
`unmodifiable(Collection|List|Set|SortedSet|` `    NavigableSet|Map|SortedMap|NavigableMap)()`	Yields an unmodifiable view (see Section 7.6).
`checked(Collection|List|Set|SortedSet|` `    NavigableSet|Map|SortedMap|NavigableMap|Queue)()`	Yields a checked view (see Section 7.6).

7.2 Iterators

Each collection provides a way to iterate through its elements in some order. The `Iterable<T>` superinterface of `Collection` defines a method

```
Iterator<T> iterator()
```

It yields an iterator that you can use to visit all elements.

```
Collection<String> coll = ...;
Iterator<String> iter = coll.iterator();
while (iter.hasNext()) {
    String element = iter.next();
    Process element
}
```

In this case, you can simply use the enhanced `for` loop:

```
for (String element : coll) {
    Process element
}
```

NOTE: For *any* object `c` of a class that implements the `Iterable<E>` interface, the enhanced `for` loop is translated to the preceding form.

The `Iterator` interface also has a `remove` method which removes the previously visited element. This loop removes all elements that fulfill a condition:

```
while (iter.hasNext()) {
    String element = iter.next();
    if (element fulfills the condition)
        iter.remove();
}
```

However, it is easier to use the `removeIf` method:

```
coll.removeIf(e -> e fulfills the condition);
```

CAUTION: The `remove` method removes the last element that the iterator has returned, not the element to which the iterator points. You can't call `remove` twice without an intervening call to `next` or `previous`.

The `ListIterator` interface is a subinterface of `Iterator` with methods for adding an element before the iterator, setting the visited element to a different value, and for navigating backwards. It is mainly useful for working with linked lists.

```
List<String> friends = new LinkedList<>();
ListIterator<String> iter = friends.listIterator();
iter.add("Fred"); // Fred |
iter.add("Wilma"); // Fred Wilma |
iter.previous(); // Fred | Wilma
iter.set("Barney"); // Fred | Barney
```

CAUTION: If you have multiple iterators visiting a data structure and one of them mutates it, the other ones can become invalid. An invalid iterator may throw a `ConcurrentModificationException` if you continue using it.

7.3 Sets

A set can efficiently test whether a value is an element, but it gives up something in return: It doesn't remember in which order elements were added. Sets are useful whenever the order doesn't matter. For example, if you want to disallow a set of bad words as usernames, their order doesn't matter. You just want to know whether a proposed username is in the set or not.

The `Set` interface is implemented by the `HashSet` and `TreeSet` classes. Internally, these classes use very different implementations. If you have taken a course in data structures, you may know how to implement hash tables and binary trees—but you can use these classes without knowing their internals.

Generally, hash sets are a bit more efficient, provided you have a good *hash function* for your elements. Library classes such as `String` or `Path` have good hash functions. You learned how to write hash function for your own classes in Chapter 4.

For example, that set of bad words can be implemented simply as

```
Set<String> badWords = new HashSet<>();
badWords.add("sex");
badWords.add("drugs");
badWords.add("c++");
if (badWords.contains(username.toLowerCase()))
    System.out.println("Please choose a different user name");
```

You use a `TreeSet` if you want to traverse the set in sorted order. One reason you might want to do this is to present users a sorted list of choices.

The element type of the set must implement the `Comparable` interface, or you need to supply a `Comparator` in the constructor.

```
TreeSet<String> countries = new TreeSet<>(); // Visits added countries in sorted order
countries = new TreeSet<>((u, v) ->
    u.equals(v) ? 0
    : u.equals("USA") ? -1
    : v.equals("USA") ? 1
    : u.compareTo(v));
    // USA always comes first
```

The `TreeSet` class implements the `SortedSet` and `NavigableSet` interfaces, whose methods are shown in Tables 7-4 and 7-5.

Table 7-4 `SortedSet<E>` Methods

Method	Description
`E first()` `E last()`	The first and last element in this set.

`SortedSet<E> headSet(E toElement)`
`SortedSet<E> subSet(E fromElement, E toElement)`
`SortedSet<E> tailSet(E fromElement)`
	Returns a view of the elements starting at `fromElement` and ending before `toElement`.

Table 7-5 `NavigableSet<E>` Methods

Method	Description

`E higher(E e)`
`E ceiling(E e)`
`E floor(E e)`
`E lower(E e)`
	Returns the closest element $> \mid \geq \mid \leq \mid <$ e.

`E pollFirst()` `E pollLast()`	Removes and returns the first or last element, or returns `null` if the set is empty.

`NavigableSet<E> headSet(E toElement, boolean inclusive)`
`NavigableSet<E> subSet(E fromElement, boolean fromInclusive,`
`    E toElement, boolean toExclusive)`
`NavigableSet<E> tailSet(E fromElement, boolean inclusive)`
	Returns a view of the elements from `fromElement` to `toElement` (inclusive or exclusive).

7.4 Maps

Maps store associations between keys and values. Call `put` to add a new association, or change the value of an existing key:

```
Map<String, Integer> counts = new HashMap<>();
counts.put("Alice", 1); // Adds the key/value pair to the map
counts.put("Alice", 2); // Updates the value for the key
```

This example uses a hash map which, as for sets, is usually the better choice if you don't need to visit the keys in sorted order. If you do, use a `TreeMap` instead.

Here is how you can get the value associated with a key:

```
int count = counts.get("Alice");
```

If the key isn't present, the `get` method returns `null`. In this example, that would cause a `NullPointerException` when the value is unboxed. A better alternative is

```
int count = counts.getOrDefault("Alice", 0);
```

Then a count of `0` is returned if the key isn't present.

When you update a counter in a map, you first need to check whether the counter is present, and if so, add 1 to the existing value. The `merge` method simplifies that common operation. The call

```
counts.merge(word, 1, Integer::sum);
```

associates `word` with 1 if the key wasn't previously present, and otherwise combines the previous value and 1, using the `Integer::sum` function.

Table 7-6 summarizes the map operations.

You can get *views* of the keys, values, and entries of a map by calling these methods:

```
Set<K> keySet()
Set<Map.Entry<K, V>> entrySet()
Collection<V> values()
```

The collections that are returned are not copies of the map data, but they are connected to the map. If you remove a key or entry from the view, then the entry is also removed from the underlying map.

To iterate through all keys and values of a map, you can iterate over the set returned by the `entrySet` method:

```
for (Map.Entry<String, Integer> entry : counts.entrySet()) {
    String k = entry.getKey();
    Integer v = entry.getValue();
    Process k, v
}
```

Or simply use the `forEach` method:

```
counts.forEach((k, v) -> {
    Process k, v
});
```

 CAUTION: Some map implementations (for example, `ConcurrentHashMap`) disallow `null` for keys or values. And with those that allow it (such as `HashMap`), you need to be very careful if you do use `null` values. A number of map methods interpret a `null` value as an indication that an entry is absent, or should be removed.

Table 7-6 Map<K, V> Methods

Method	Description

`V get(Object key)`
`V getOrDefault(Object key,`
`    V defaultValue)`
	If key is associated with a non-null value v, returns v. Otherwise, returns null or defaultValue.

`V put(K key, V value)`	If key is associated with a non-null value v, associates key with value and returns v. Otherwise, adds entry and returns null.
`V putIfAbsent(K key, V value)`	If key is associated with a non-null value v, ignores value and returns v. Otherwise, adds entry and returns null.

`V merge(K key, V value, BiFunction<`
`    ? super V,? super V,? extends V>`
`    remappingFunction)`
	If key is associated with a non-null value v, applies the function to v and value and either associates key with the result or, if the result is null, removes the key. Otherwise, associates key with value. Returns get(key).

`V compute(K key, BiFunction<`
`    ? super K,? super V,? extends V>`
`    remappingFunction)`
	Applies the function to key and get(key). Either associates key with the result or, if the result is null, removes the key. Returns get(key).

`V computeIfPresent(K key, BiFunction<`
`    ? super K,? super V,? extends V>`
`    remappingFunction)`
	If key is associated with a non-null value v, applies the function to key and v and either associates key with the result or, if the result is null, removes the key. Returns get(key).

`V computeIfAbsent(K key, Function<`
`    ? super K,? extends V>`
`    mappingFunction)`
	Applies the function to key unless key is associated with a non-null value. Either associates key with the result or, if the result is null, removes the key. Returns get(key).

`void putAll(Map<? extends K,` `    ? extends V> m)`	Adds all entries from m.
`V remove(Object key)` `V replace(K key, V newValue)`	Removes the key and its associated value, or replaces the old value. Returns the old value, or null if none existed.

(Continues)

Table 7-6 Map<K, V> Methods *(Continued)*

Method	Description
`boolean remove(Object key, Object value)` `boolean replace(K key, V value, V newValue)`	Provided that key was associated with value, removes the entry or replaces the old value and returns true. Otherwise, does nothing and returns false. These methods are mainly of interest when the map is accessed concurrently.
`int size()`	Returns the number of entries.
`boolean isEmpty()`	Checks if this map is empty.
`void clear()`	Removes all entries.
`void forEach(BiConsumer<? super K, ? super V> action)`	Applies the action to all entries.
`void replaceAll(BiFunction<? super K, ? super V,? extends V> function)`	Calls the function on all entries. Associates keys with non-null results and removes keys with null results.
`boolean containsKey(Object key)` `boolean containsValue(Object value)`	Checks whether the map contains the given key or value.

`Set<K> keySet()`
`Collection<V> values()`
`Set<Map.Entry<K, V>> entrySet()`
	Returns views of the keys, values, and entries.

`static Map<K, V> of()`
`static Map<K, V> of(K k1, V v1)`
`static Map<K, V> of(K k1, V v1, K k2, V v2)`
`...`
	Yields an unmodifiable map containing up to ten keys and values.

 TIP: Sometimes, you need to present map keys in an order that is different from the sort order. For example, in the JavaServer Faces framework, you specify labels and values of a selection box with a map. Users would be surprised if the choices were sorted alphabetically (Friday, Monday, Saturday, Sunday, Thursday, Tuesday, Wednesday) or in the hash code order. In that case, use a LinkedHashMap that remembers the order in which entries were added and iterates through them in that order.

7.5 Other Collections

In the following sections, I briefly discuss some collection classes that you may find useful in practice.

7.5.1 Properties

The Properties class implements a map that can be easily saved and loaded using a plain text format. Such maps are commonly used for storing configuration options for programs. For example:

```
Properties settings = new Properties();
settings.put("width", "200");
settings.put("title", "Hello, World!");
try (OutputStream out = Files.newOutputStream(path)) {
    settings.store(out, "Program Properties");
}
```

The result is the following file:

```
#Program Properties
#Mon Nov 03 20:52:33 CET 2014
width=200
title=Hello, World\!
```

 NOTE: As of Java 9, property files are encoded in UTF-8. (Previously, they were encoded in ASCII, with characters greater than '\u007e' written as Unicode escapes \u*nnnn*.) Comments start with # or !. A newline in a key or value is written as \n. The characters \, #, ! are escaped as \\, \#, \!.

To load properties from a file, call

```
try (InputStream in = Files.newInputStream(path)) {
    settings.load(in);
}
```

Then use the getProperty method to get a value for a key. You can specify a default value used when the key isn't present:

```
String title = settings.getProperty("title", "New Document");
```

 NOTE: For historical reasons, the Properties class implements Map<Object, Object> even though the values are always strings. Therefore, don't use the get method—it returns the value as an Object.

The System.getProperties method yields a Properties object with system properties. Table 7-7 describes the most useful ones.

Table 7-7 Useful System Properties

Property Key	Description
user.dir	The "current working directory" of this virtual machine
user.home	The user's home directory
user.name	The user's account name
java.version	The Java runtime version of this virtual machine
java.home	The home directory of the Java installation
java.class.path	The class path with which this VM was launched
java.io.tmpdir	A directory suitable for temporary files (such as /tmp)
os.name	The name of the operating system (such as Linux)
os.arch	The architecture of the operating system (such as amd64)
os.version	The version of the operating system (such as 3.13.0-34-generic)
file.separator	The file separator (/ on Unix, \ on Windows)
path.separator	The path separator (: on Unix, ; on Windows)
line.separator	The newline separator (\n on Unix, \r\n on Windows)

7.5.2 Bit Sets

The BitSet class stores a sequence of bits. A bit set packs bits into an array of long values, so it is more efficient to use a bit set than an array of boolean values. Bit sets are useful for sequences of flag bits or to represent sets of non-negative integers, where the ith bit is 1 to indicate that i is contained in the set.

The BitSet class gives you convenient methods for getting and setting individual bits. This is much simpler than the bit-fiddling necessary to store bits in int or long variables. There are also methods that operate on all bits together for set operations, such as union and intersection. See Table 7-8 for a complete list. Note that the BitSet class is not a collection class—it does not implement Collection<Integer>.

Table 7-8 Methods of the `BitSet` Class

Method	Description
`BitSet()` `BitSet(int nbits)`	Constructs a bit set that can initially hold 64, or `nbits`, bits.

`void set(int bitIndex)`
`void set(int fromIndex, int toIndex)`
`void set(int bitIndex, boolean value)`
`void set(int fromIndex, int toIndex,`
   `boolean value)`
	Sets the bit at the given index, or from `fromIndex` (inclusive) to `toIndex` (exclusive), to 1 or to the given value.

`void clear(int bitIndex)`
`void clear(int fromIndex, int toIndex)`
`void clear()`
	Sets the bit at the given index, or from `fromIndex` (inclusive) to `toIndex` (exclusive), or all bits to 0.

`void flip(int bitIndex)` `void flip(int fromIndex, int toIndex)`	Flips the bit at the given index, or from `fromIndex` (inclusive) to `toIndex` (exclusive).
`boolean get(int bitIndex)` `BitSet get(int fromIndex, int toIndex)`	Gets the bit at the given index, or from `fromIndex` (inclusive) to `toIndex` (exclusive).

`int nextSetBit(int fromIndex)`
`int previousSetBit(int fromIndex)`
`int nextClearBit(int fromIndex)`
`int previousClearBit(int fromIndex)`
	Returns the index of the next/previous 1/0 bit, or -1 if none exists.

`void and(BitSet set)`
`void andNot(BitSet set)`
`void or(BitSet set)`
`void xor(BitSet set)`
	Forms the intersection|difference|union|symmetric difference with set.

`int cardinality()`	Returns the number of 1 bits in this bit set. **Caution:** The `size` method returns the current size of the bit vector, not the size of the set.
`byte[] toByteArray[]` `long[] toLongArray[]`	Packs the bits of this bit set into an array.
`IntStream stream()` `String toString()`	Returns a stream or string of the integers (that is, indexes of 1 bits) in this bit set.

`static BitSet valueOf(byte[] bytes)`
`static BitSet valueOf(long[] longs)`
`static BitSet valueOf(ByteBuffer bb)`
`static BitSet valueOf(LongBuffer lb)`
	Yields a bit set containing the supplied bits.

`boolean isEmpty()` `boolean intersects(BitSet set)`	Checks whether this bit set is empty, or has an element in common with set.

7.5.3 Enumeration Sets and Maps

If you collect sets of enumerated values, use the EnumSet class instead of BitSet. The EnumSet class has no public constructors. Use a static factory method to construct the set:

```
enum Weekday { MONDAY, TUESDAY, WEDNESDAY, THURSDAY, FRIDAY, SATURDAY, SUNDAY };
Set<Weekday> always = EnumSet.allOf(Weekday.class);
Set<Weekday> never = EnumSet.noneOf(Weekday.class);
Set<Weekday> workday = EnumSet.range(Weekday.MONDAY, Weekday.FRIDAY);
Set<Weekday> mwf = EnumSet.of(Weekday.MONDAY, Weekday.WEDNESDAY, Weekday.FRIDAY);
```

You can use the methods of the Set interface to work with an EnumSet.

An EnumMap is a map with keys that belong to an enumerated type. It is implemented as an array of values. You specify the key type in the constructor:

```
EnumMap<Weekday, String> personInCharge = new EnumMap<>(Weekday.class);
personInCharge.put(Weekday.MONDAY, "Fred");
```

7.5.4 Stacks, Queues, Deques, and Priority Queues

A stack is a data structure for adding and removing elements at one end (the "top" of the stack). A queue lets you efficiently add elements at one end (the "tail") and remove them from the other end (the "head"). A double-ended queue, or deque, supports insertion and removal at both ends. With all these data structures, adding elements in the middle is not supported.

The Queue and Deque interfaces define the methods for these data structures. There is no Stack interface in the Java collections framework, just a legacy Stack class from the earliest days of Java that you should avoid. If you need a stack, queue, or deque and are not concerned about thread safety, use an ArrayDeque.

With a stack, use the push and pop methods.

```
ArrayDeque<String> stack = new ArrayDeque<>();
stack.push("Peter");
stack.push("Paul");
stack.push("Mary");
while (!stack.isEmpty())
    System.out.println(stack.pop());
```

With a queue, use add and remove.

```
Queue<String> queue = new ArrayDeque<>();
queue.add("Peter");
queue.add("Paul");
queue.add("Mary");
while (!queue.isEmpty())
    System.out.println(queue.remove());
```

Threadsafe queues are commonly used in concurrent programs. You will find more information about them in Chapter 10.

A *priority queue* retrieves elements in sorted order after they were inserted in arbitrary order. That is, whenever you call the remove method, you get the smallest element currently in the priority queue.

A typical use for a priority queue is job scheduling. Each job has a priority. Jobs are added in random order. Whenever a new job can be started, the highest priority job is removed from the queue. (Since it is traditional for priority 1 to be the "highest" priority, the remove operation yields the minimum element.)

```
public class Job implements Comparable<Job> { ... }
...
PriorityQueue<Job> jobs = new PriorityQueue<>();
jobs.add(new Job(4, "Collect garbage"));
jobs.add(new Job(9, "Match braces"));
jobs.add(new Job(1, "Fix memory leak"));
...
while (jobs.size() > 0) {
    Job job = jobs.remove(); // The most urgent jobs are removed first
    execute(job);
}
```

Just like a TreeSet, a priority queue can hold elements of a class that implements the Comparable interface, or you can supply a Comparator in the constructor. However, unlike a TreeSet, iterating over the elements does not necessarily yield them in sorted order. The priority queue uses algorithms for adding and removing elements that cause the smallest element to gravitate to the root, without wasting time on sorting all elements.

7.5.5 Weak Hash Maps

The WeakHashMap class was designed to solve an interesting problem. What happens with a value whose key is no longer used anywhere in your program? If the last reference to a key has gone away, there is no longer any way to refer to the value object so it should be removed by the garbage collector.

It isn't quite so simple. The garbage collector traces live objects. As long as the map object is live, all entries in it are live and won't be reclaimed—and neither will be the values that are referenced by the entries.

This is the problem that the WeakHashMap class solves. This data structure cooperates with the garbage collector to remove key/value pairs when the only reference to the key is the one from the hash table entry.

Technically, the WeakHashMap uses *weak references* to hold keys. A WeakReference object holds a reference to another object—in our case, a hash table key. Objects of this type are treated in a special way by the garbage collector. If an object is reachable *only* by a weak reference, the garbage collector reclaims the object and places the weak reference into a queue associated with the WeakReference object. Whenever a method is invoked on it, a WeakHashMap checks its queue of weak references for new arrivals and removes the associated entries.

7.6 Views

A collection *view* is a lightweight object that implements a collection interface, but doesn't store elements. For example, the keySet and values methods of a map yield views into the map.

In the following sections, you will see some views that are provided by the Java collections framework.

7.6.1 Small Collections

The List, Set, and Map interfaces provide static methods yielding a set or list with given elements, and a map with given key/value pairs.

For example,

```
List<String> names = List.of("Peter", "Paul", "Mary");
Set<Integer> numbers = Set.of(2, 3, 5);
```

yield a list and a set with three elements. For a map, specify the keys and values like this:

```
Map<String, Integer> scores = Map.of("Peter", 2, "Paul", 3, "Mary", 5);
```

The elements, keys, or values may not be null.

The List and Set interfaces have 11 of methods with zero to ten arguments, and an of method with a variable number of arguments. The specializations are provided for efficiency.

For the Map interface, it is not possible to provide a version with variable arguments since the argument types alternate between the key and value types. There is a static method ofEntries that accepts an arbitrary number of Map.Entry<K, V> objects, which you can create with the static entry method. For example,

```
import static java.util.Map.*;
...
Map<String, Integer> scores = ofEntries(
    entry("Peter", 2),
    entry("Paul", 3),
    entry("Mary", 5));
```

The of and ofEntries methods produce objects of classes that have an instance variable for each element, or that are backed by an array.

These collection objects are *unmodifiable*. Any attempt to change their contents results in an UnsupportedOperationException.

If you want a mutable collection, you can pass the unmodifiable collection to the constructor:

```
List<String> names = new ArrayList<>(List.of("Peter", "Paul", "Mary"));
```

 NOTE: There is also a static Arrays.asList method that is similar to List.of. It returns a mutable list that is not resizable. That is, you can call set but not add or remove on the list.

7.6.2 Ranges

You can form a sublist view of a list. For example,

```
List<String> sentence = ...;
List<String> nextFive = sentence.subList(5, 10);
```

This view accesses the elements with index 5 through 9. Any mutations of the sublist (such as setting, adding, or removing elements) affect the original.

For sorted sets and maps, you specify a range by the lower and upper bound:

```
TreeSet<String> words = ...;
SortedSet<String> asOnly = words.subSet("a", "b");
```

As with subList, the first bound is inclusive, and the second exclusive.

The headSet and tailSet methods yield a subrange with no lower or upper bound.

```
NavigableSet<String> nAndBeyond = words.tailSet("n");
```

With the NavigableSet interface, you can choose for each bound whether it should be inclusive or exclusive—see Table 7-5.

For a sorted map, there are equivalent methods subMap, headMap, and tailMap.

7.6.3 Unmodifiable Views

Sometimes, you want to share the contents of a collection but you don't want it to be modified. Of course, you could copy the values into a new collection, but that is potentially expensive. An unmodifiable view is a better choice. Here is a typical situation. A `Person` object maintains a list of friends. If the `getFriends` gave out a reference to that list, a caller could mutate it. But it is safe to provide an unmodifiable list view:

```java
public class Person {
    private ArrayList<Person> friends;

    public List<Person> getFriends() {
        return Collections.unmodifiableList(friends);
    }
    ...
}
```

All mutator methods throw an exception when they are invoked on an unmodifiable view.

As you can see from Table 7-3, you can get unmodifiable views as collections, lists, sets, sorted sets, navigable sets, maps, sorted maps, and navigable maps.

 NOTE: In Chapter 6, you saw how it is possible to smuggle the wrong kind of elements into a generic collection (a phenomenon called "heap pollution"), and that a runtime error is reported when the inappropriate element is retrieved, not when it is inserted. If you need to debug such a problem, use a *checked view*. Where you constructed, say, an `ArrayList<String>`, instead use

```java
List<String> strings
    = Collections.checkedList(new ArrayList<>(), String.class);
```

The view monitors all insertions into the list and throws an exception when an object of the wrong type is added.

 NOTE: The `Collections` class produces *synchronized* views that ensure safe concurrent access to data structures. In practice, these views are not as useful as the data structures in the `java.util.concurrent` package that were explicitly designed for concurrent access. I suggest you use those classes and stay away from synchronized views.

Exercises

1. Implement the "Sieve of Erathostenes" algorithm to determine all prime numbers $\leq n$. Add all numbers from 2 to n to a set. Then repeatedly find the smallest element s in the set, and remove s^2, $s \cdot (s + 1)$, $s \cdot (s + 2)$, and so on. You are done when $s^2 > n$. Do this with both a HashSet<Integer> and a BitSet.

2. In an array list of strings, make each string uppercase. Do this with (a) an iterator, (b) a loop over the index values, and (c) the replaceAll method.

3. How do you compute the union, intersection, and difference of two sets, using just the methods of the Set interface and without using loops?

4. Produce a situation that yields a ConcurrentModificationException. What can you do to avoid it?

5. Implement a method public static void swap(List<?> list, int i, int j) that swaps elements in the usual way when the type of list implements the RandomAccess interface, and that minimizes the cost of visiting the positions at index i and j if it is not.

6. I encouraged you to use interfaces instead of concrete data structures—for example, a Map instead of a TreeMap. Unfortunately, that advice goes only so far. Suppose you have a method parameter of type Map<String, Set<Integer>>, and someone calls your method with a HashMap<String, HashSet<Integer>>. What happens? What parameter type can you use instead?

7. Write a program that reads all words in a file and prints out how often each word occurred. Use a TreeMap<String, Integer>.

8. Write a program that reads all words in a file and prints out on which line(s) each of them occurred. Use a map from strings to sets.

9. You can update the counter in a map of counters as

   ```
   counts.merge(word, 1, Integer::sum);
   ```

   Do the same without the merge method, (a) by using contains, (b) by using get and a null check, (c) by using getOrDefault, (d) by using putIfAbsent.

10. Implement Dijkstra's algorithm to find the shortest paths in a network of cities, some of which are connected by roads. (For a description, check out your favorite book on algorithms or the Wikipedia article.) Use a helper class Neighbor that stores the name of a neighboring city and the distance. Represent the graph as a map from cities to sets of neighbors. Use a PriorityQueue<Neighbor> in the algorithm.

11. Write a program that reads a sentence into an array list. Then, using `Collections.shuffle`, shuffle all but the first and last word, without copying the words into another collection.

12. Using `Collections.shuffle`, write a program that reads a sentence, shuffles the words, and prints the result. Fix the capitalization of the initial word and the punctuation of the last word (before and after the shuffle). Hint: Don't shuffle the words.

13. The `LinkedHashMap` calls the method `removeEldestEntry` whenever a new element is inserted. Implement a subclass `Cache` that limits the map to a given size provided in the constructor.

14. Write a method that produces an immutable list view of the numbers from 0 to `n`, without actually storing the numbers.

15. Generalize the preceding exercise to an arbitrary `IntFunction`. Note that the result is an infinite collection, so certain methods (such as `size` and `toArray`) should throw an `UnsupportedOperationException`.

16. Improve the implementation of the preceding exercise by caching the last 100 computed function values.

17. Demonstrate how a checked view can give an accurate error report for a cause of heap pollution.

18. The `Collections` class has static variables `EMPTY_LIST`, `EMPTY_MAP`, and `EMPTY_SET`. Why are they not as useful as the `emptyList`, `emptyMap`, and `emptySet` methods?

Streams

Topics in This Chapter

Chapter 8

Streams provide a view of data that lets you specify computations at a higher conceptual level than with collections. With a stream, you specify what you want to have done, not how to do it. You leave the scheduling of operations to the implementation. For example, suppose you want to compute the average of a certain property. You specify the source of data and the property, and the stream library can then optimize the computation, for example by using multiple threads for computing sums and counts and combining the results.

The key points of this chapter are:

1. Iterators imply a specific traversal strategy and prohibit efficient concurrent execution.

2. You can create streams from collections, arrays, generators, or iterators.

3. Use `filter` to select elements and `map` to transform elements.

4. Other operations for transforming streams include `limit`, `distinct`, and `sorted`.

5. To obtain a result from a stream, use a reduction operator such as `count`, `max`, `min`, `findFirst`, or `findAny`. Some of these methods return an `Optional` value.

6. The `Optional` type is intended as a safe alternative to working with `null` values. To use it safely, take advantage of the `ifPresent` and `orElse` methods.

7. You can collect stream results in collections, arrays, strings, or maps.

8. The `groupingBy` and `partitioningBy` methods of the `Collectors` class allow you to split the contents of a stream into groups, and to obtain a result for each group.

9. There are specialized streams for the primitive types `int`, `long`, and `double`.

10. Parallel streams automatically parallelize stream operations.

8.1 From Iterating to Stream Operations

When you process a collection, you usually iterate over its elements and do some work with each of them. For example, suppose we want to count all long words in a book. First, let's put them into a list:

```
String contents = new String(Files.readAllBytes(
    Paths.get("alice.txt")), StandardCharsets.UTF_8); // Read file into string
List<String> words = List.of(contents.split("\\PL+"));
    // Split into words; nonletters are delimiters
```

Now we are ready to iterate:

```
int count = 0;
for (String w : words) {
    if (w.length() > 12) count++;
}
```

With streams, the same operation looks like this:

```
long count = words.stream()
    .filter(w -> w.length() > 12)
    .count();
```

Now you don't have to scan the loop for evidence of filtering and counting. The method names tell you right away what the code intends to do. Moreover, where the loop prescribes the order of operations in complete detail, a stream is able to schedule the operations any way it wants, as long as the result is correct.

Simply changing `stream` into `parallelStream` allows the stream library to do the filtering and counting in parallel.

```
long count = words.parallelStream()
    .filter(w -> w.length() > 12)
    .count();
```

Streams follow the "what, not how" principle. In our stream example, we describe what needs to be done: get the long words and count them. We don't specify in which order, or in which thread, this should happen. In contrast, the loop at the beginning of this section specifies exactly how the computation should work, and thereby forgoes any chances of optimization.

A stream seems superficially similar to a collection, allowing you to transform and retrieve data. But there are significant differences:

1. A stream does not store its elements. They may be stored in an underlying collection or generated on demand.

2. Stream operations don't mutate their source. For example, the `filter` method does not remove elements from a stream, but it yields a new stream in which they are not present.

3. Stream operations are *lazy* when possible. This means they are not executed until their result is needed. For example, if you only ask for the first five long words instead of all, the `filter` method will stop filtering after the fifth match. As a consequence, you can even have infinite streams!

Let us have another look at the example. The `stream` and `parallelStream` methods yield a *stream* for the `words` list. The `filter` method returns another stream that contains only the words of length greater than twelve. The `count` method reduces that stream to a result.

This workflow is typical when you work with streams. You set up a pipeline of operations in three stages:

1. Create a stream.

2. Specify *intermediate operations* for transforming the initial stream into others, possibly in multiple steps.

3. Apply a *terminal operation* to produce a result. This operation forces the execution of the lazy operations that precede it. Afterwards, the stream can no longer be used.

In our example, the stream was created with the `stream` or `parallelStream` method. The `filter` method transformed it, and `count` was the terminal operation.

In the next section, you will see how to create a stream. The subsequent three sections deal with stream transformations. They are followed by five sections on terminal operations.

8.2 Stream Creation

You have already seen that you can turn any collection into a stream with the `stream` method of the `Collection` interface. If you have an array, use the static `Stream.of` method instead.

```
Stream<String> words = Stream.of(contents.split("\\PL+"));
    // split returns a String[] array
```

The `of` method has a varargs parameter, so you can construct a stream from any number of arguments:

```
Stream<String> song = Stream.of("gently", "down", "the", "stream");
```

Use `Arrays.stream(array, from, to)` to make a stream from a part of an array.

To make a stream with no elements, use the static `Stream.empty` method:

```
Stream<String> silence = Stream.empty();
    // Generic type <String> is inferred; same as Stream.<String>empty()
```

The `Stream` interface has two static methods for making infinite streams. The `generate` method takes a function with no arguments (or, technically, an object of the `Supplier<T>` interface—see Section 3.6.2, "Choosing a Functional Interface," page 120). Whenever a stream value is needed, that function is called to produce a value. You can get a stream of constant values as

```
Stream<String> echos = Stream.generate(() -> "Echo");
```

or a stream of random numbers as

```
Stream<Double> randoms = Stream.generate(Math::random);
```

To produce sequences such as 0 1 2 3 ..., use the `iterate` method instead. It takes a "seed" value and a function (technically, a `UnaryOperator<T>`) and repeatedly applies the function to the previous result. For example,

```
Stream<BigInteger> integers
    = Stream.iterate(BigInteger.ZERO, n -> n.add(BigInteger.ONE));
```

The first element in the sequence is the seed `BigInteger.ZERO`. The second element is `f(seed)`, or 1 (as a big integer). The next element is `f(f(seed))`, or 2, and so on.

To produce a finite stream instead, add a predicate that specifies when the iteration should finish:

```
BigInteger limit = new BigInteger("10000000");
Stream<BigInteger> integers
    = Stream.iterate(BigInteger.ZERO,
        n -> n.compareTo(limit) < 0,
        n -> n.add(BigInteger.ONE));
```

As soon as the predicate rejects an iteratively generated value, the stream ends.

NOTE: A number of methods in the Java API yield streams. For example, the `Pattern` class has a method `splitAsStream` that splits a `CharSequence` by a regular expression. You can use the following statement to split a string into words:

```
Stream<String> words = Pattern.compile("\\PL+").splitAsStream(contents);
```

The `Scanner.tokens` method yields a stream of tokens of a scanner. Another way to get a stream of words from a string is

```
Stream<String> words = new Scanner(contents).tokens();
```

The static `Files.lines` method returns a `Stream` of all lines in a file:

```
try (Stream<String> lines = Files.lines(path)) {
    Process lines
}
```

8.3 The filter, map, and flatMap Methods

A stream transformation produces a stream whose elements are derived from those of another stream. You have already seen the `filter` transformation that yields a new stream with those elements that match a certain condition. Here, we transform a stream of strings into another stream containing only long words:

```
List<String> words = ...;
Stream<String> longWords = words.stream().filter(w -> w.length() > 12);
```

The argument of `filter` is a `Predicate<T>`—that is, a function from `T` to `boolean`.

Often, you want to transform the values in a stream in some way. Use the `map` method and pass the function that carries out the transformation. For example, you can transform all words to lowercase like this:

```
Stream<String> lowercaseWords = words.stream().map(String::toLowerCase);
```

Here, we used `map` with a method reference. Often, you will use a lambda expression instead:

```
Stream<String> firstLetters = words.stream().map(s -> s.substring(0, 1));
```

The resulting stream contains the first letter of each word.

When you use `map`, a function is applied to each element, and the result is a new stream with the results. Now, suppose you have a function that returns not just one value but a stream of values. Here is an example—a method that turns a string into a stream of strings, namely the individual code points:

```
public static Stream<String> codePoints(String s) {
    List<String> result = new ArrayList<>();
    int i = 0;
    while (i < s.length()) {
        int j = s.offsetByCodePoints(i, 1);
        result.add(s.substring(i, j));
        i = j;
    }
    return result.stream();
}
```

This method correctly handles Unicode characters that require two `char` values because that's the right thing to do. But you don't have to dwell on that.

For example, `codePoints("boat")` is the stream `["b", "o", "a", "t"]`.

Now let's map the `codePoints` method on a stream of strings:

```
Stream<Stream<String>> result = words.stream().map(w -> codePoints(w));
```

You will get a stream of streams, like `[... ["y", "o", "u", "r"], ["b", "o", "a", "t"], ...]`. To flatten it out to a single stream `[... "y", "o", "u", "r", "b", "o", "a", "t", ...]`, use the `flatMap` method instead of `map`:

```
Stream<String> flatResult = words.stream().flatMap(w -> codePoints(w))
    // Calls codePoints on each word and flattens the results
```

 NOTE: You will find a `flatMap` method in classes other than streams. It is a general concept in computer science. Suppose you have a generic type G (such as `Stream`) and functions f from some type T to G<U> and g from U to G<V>. Then you can compose them—that is, first apply f and then g, by using `flatMap`. This is a key idea in the theory of *monads*. But don't worry—you can use `flatMap` without knowing anything about monads.

8.4 Extracting Substreams and Combining Streams

The call *stream*.limit(n) returns a new stream that ends after n elements (or when the original stream ends if it is shorter). This method is particularly useful for cutting infinite streams down to size. For example,

```
Stream<Double> randoms = Stream.generate(Math::random).limit(100);
```

yields a stream with 100 random numbers.

The call *stream*.skip(n) does the exact opposite. It discards the first n elements. This is handy in our book reading example where, due to the way the `split` method works, the first element is an unwanted empty string. We can make it go away by calling `skip`:

```
Stream<String> words = Stream.of(contents.split("\\PL+")).skip(1);
```

The *stream*.takeWhile(*predicate*) call takes all elements from the stream while the predicate is true, and then stops.

For example, suppose we use the codePoints method of the preceding section to split a string into characters, and we want to collect all initial digits. The takeWhile method can do this:

```
Stream<String> initialDigits = codePoints(str).takeWhile(
    s -> "0123456789".contains(s));
```

The dropWhile method does the opposite, dropping elements while a condition is true and yielding a stream of all elements starting with the first one for which the condition was false. For example,

```
Stream<String> withoutInitialWhiteSpace = codePoints(str).dropWhile(
    s -> s.trim().length() == 0);
```

You can concatenate two streams with the static concat method of the Stream class:

```
Stream<String> combined = Stream.concat(
    codePoints("Hello"), codePoints("World"));
    // Yields the stream ["H", "e", "l", "l", "o", "W", "o", "r", "l", "d"]
```

Of course, the first stream should not be infinite—otherwise the second wouldn't ever get a chance.

8.5 Other Stream Transformations

The distinct method returns a stream that yields elements from the original stream, in the same order, except that duplicates are suppressed. The duplicates need not be adjacent.

```
Stream<String> uniqueWords
    = Stream.of("merrily", "merrily", "merrily", "gently").distinct();
    // Only one "merrily" is retained
```

For sorting a stream, there are several variations of the sorted method. One works for streams of Comparable elements, and another accepts a Comparator. Here, we sort strings so that the longest ones come first:

```
Stream<String> longestFirst
    = words.stream().sorted(Comparator.comparing(String::length).reversed());
```

As with all stream transformations, the sorted method yields a new stream whose elements are the elements of the original stream in sorted order.

Of course, you can sort a collection without using streams. The sorted method is useful when the sorting process is part of a stream pipeline.

Finally, the peek method yields another stream with the same elements as the original, but a function is invoked every time an element is retrieved. That is handy for debugging:

```
Object[] powers = Stream.iterate(1.0, p -> p * 2)
    .peek(e -> System.out.println("Fetching " + e))
    .limit(20).toArray();
```

When an element is actually accessed, a message is printed. This way you can verify that the infinite stream returned by iterate is processed lazily.

 TIP: When you use a debugger to debug a stream computation, you can set a breakpoint in a method that is called from one of the transformations. With most IDEs, you can also set breakpoints in lambda expressions. If you just want to know what happens at a particular point in the stream pipeline, add

```
.peek(x -> {
    return; })
```

and set a breakpoint on the second line.

8.6 Simple Reductions

Now that you have seen how to create and transform streams, we will finally get to the most important point—getting answers from the stream data. The methods that we cover in this section are called *reductions*. Reductions are *terminal operations*. They reduce the stream to a nonstream value that can be used in your program.

You have already seen a simple reduction: the count method that returns the number of elements of a stream.

Other simple reductions are max and min that return the largest or smallest value. There is a twist—these methods return an Optional<T> value that either wraps the answer or indicates that there is none (because the stream happened to be empty). In the olden days, it was common to return null in such a situation. But that can lead to null pointer exceptions when it happens in an incompletely tested program. The Optional type is a better way of indicating a missing return value. We discuss the Optional type in detail in the next section. Here is how you can get the maximum of a stream:

```
Optional<String> largest = words.max(String::compareToIgnoreCase);
System.out.println("largest: " + largest.orElse(""));
```

The `findFirst` returns the first value in a nonempty collection. It is often useful when combined with `filter`. For example, here we find the first word that starts with the letter Q, if it exists:

```
Optional<String> startsWithQ
    = words.filter(s -> s.startsWith("Q")).findFirst();
```

If you are OK with any match, not just the first one, use the `findAny` method. This is effective when you parallelize the stream, since the stream can report any match that it finds instead of being constrained to the first one.

```
Optional<String> startsWithQ
    = words.parallel().filter(s -> s.startsWith("Q")).findAny();
```

If you just want to know if there is a match, use `anyMatch`. That method takes a predicate argument, so you won't need to use `filter`.

```
boolean aWordStartsWithQ
    = words.parallel().anyMatch(s -> s.startsWith("Q"));
```

There are methods `allMatch` and `noneMatch` that return `true` if all or no elements match a predicate. These methods also benefit from being run in parallel.

8.7 The Optional Type

An `Optional<T>` object is a wrapper for either an object of type `T` or no object. In the former case, we say that the value is *present*. The `Optional<T>` type is intended as a safer alternative for a reference of type `T` that either refers to an object or is `null`. But it is only safer if you use it right. The next section shows you how.

8.7.1 How to Work with Optional Values

The key to using `Optional` effectively is to use a method that either *produces an alternative* if the value is not present, or *consumes the value* only if it is present.

Let us look at the first strategy. Often, there is a default that you want to use when there was no match, perhaps the empty string:

```
String result = optionalString.orElse("");
    // The wrapped string, or "" if none
```

You can also invoke code to compute the default:

```
String result = optionalString.orElseGet(() -> System.getProperty("myapp.default"));
    // The function is only called when needed
```

Or you can throw an exception if there is no value:

```
String result = optionalString.orElseThrow(IllegalStateException::new);
    // Supply a method that yields an exception object
```

The orElseGet method assumes that the alternative computation always succeeds. If that computation can fail, use the or method:

```
Optional<String> result = optionalString.or(() ->
    Optional.ofNullable(System.getProperty("myapp.default")));
```

If optionalString has a value, then result is optionalString. If not, and System.getProperty("myapp.default") returns a non-null value, then that value, wrapped in an Optional, becomes the result. Otherwise, the result is empty.

You have just seen how to produce an alternative if no value is present. The other strategy for working with optional values is to consume the value only if it is present.

The ifPresent method accepts a function. If the optional value exists, it is passed to that function. Otherwise, nothing happens.

```
optionalValue.ifPresent(v -> Process v);
```

For example, if you want to add the value to a set if it is present, call

```
optionalValue.ifPresent(v -> results.add(v));
```

or simply

```
optionalValue.ifPresent(results::add);
```

If you want to take one action if the Optional has a value and another action if it doesn't, use ifPresentOrElse:

```
optionalValue.ifPresentOrElse(
    v -> Process v,
    () -> Do something else);
```

When using ifPresent to pass an optional value to a function, the function return value is lost. If you want to process the function result, use map instead:

```
Optional<Boolean> added = optionalValue.map(results::add);
```

Now added has one of three values: true or false wrapped into an Optional, if optionalValue was present, or an empty Optional otherwise.

 NOTE: This map method is the analog of the map method of the Stream interface that you have seen in Section 8.3, "The filter, map, and flatMap Methods" (page 263). Simply imagine an optional value as a stream of size zero or one. The result again has size zero or one, and in the latter case, the function has been applied.

8.7.2 How Not to Work with Optional Values

If you don't use Optional values correctly, you have no benefit over the "something or null" approach of the past.

The get method gets the wrapped element of an Optional value if it exists, or throws a NoSuchElementException if it doesn't. Therefore,

```
Optional<T> optionalValue = ...;
optionalValue.get().someMethod()
```

is no safer than

```
T value = ...;
value.someMethod();
```

The isPresent method reports whether an Optional<T> object has a value. But

```
if (optionalValue.isPresent()) optionalValue.get().someMethod();
```

is no easier than

```
if (value != null) value.someMethod();
```

8.7.3 Creating Optional Values

So far, we have discussed how to consume an Optional object someone else created. If you want to write a method that creates an Optional object, there are several static methods for that purpose, including Optional.of(result) and Optional.empty(). For example,

```
public static Optional<Double> inverse(Double x) {
    return x == 0 ? Optional.empty() : Optional.of(1 / x);
}
```

The ofNullable method is intended as a bridge from possibly null values to optional values. Optional.ofNullable(obj) returns Optional.of(obj) if obj is not null and Optional.empty() otherwise.

8.7.4 Composing Optional Value Functions with flatMap

Suppose you have a method f yielding an Optional<T>, and the target type T has a method g yielding an Optional<U>. If they were normal methods, you could compose them by calling s.f().g(). But that composition doesn't work since s.f() has type Optional<T>, not T. Instead, call

```
Optional<U> result = s.f().flatMap(T::g);
```

If s.f() is present, then g is applied to it. Otherwise, an empty Optional<U> is returned.

Clearly, you can repeat that process if you have more methods or lambdas that yield Optional values. You can then build a pipeline of steps, simply by chaining calls to flatMap, that will succeed only when all parts do.

For example, consider the safe inverse method of the preceding section. Suppose we also have a safe square root:

```
public static Optional<Double> squareRoot(Double x) {
    return x < 0 ? Optional.empty() : Optional.of(Math.sqrt(x));
}
```

Then you can compute the square root of the inverse as

```
Optional<Double> result = inverse(x).flatMap(MyMath::squareRoot);
```

or, if you prefer,

```
Optional<Double> result
    = Optional.of(-4.0).flatMap(Demo::inverse).flatMap(Demo::squareRoot);
```

If either the inverse method or the squareRoot returns Optional.empty(), the result is empty.

 NOTE: You have already seen a flatMap method in the Stream interface (see Section 8.3, "The filter, map, and flatMap Methods," page 263). That method was used to compose two methods that yield streams, by flattening out the resulting stream of streams. The Optional.flatMap method works in the same way if you interpret an optional value as having zero or one elements.

8.7.5 Turning an Optional Into a Stream

The stream method turns an Optional<T> into a Stream<T> with zero or one elements. Sure, why not, but why would you ever want that?

This becomes useful with methods that return an Optional result. Suppose you have a stream of user IDs and a method

```
Optional<User> lookup(String id)
```

How do you get a stream of users, skipping those IDs that are invalid?

Of course, you can filter out the invalid IDs and then apply get to the remaining ones:

```
Stream<String> ids = ...;
Stream<User> users = ids.map(Users::lookup)
    .filter(Optional::isPresent)
    .map(Optional::get);
```

But that uses the `isPresent` and `get` methods that we warned about. It is more elegant to call

```
Stream<User> users = ids.map(Users::lookup)
    .flatMap(Optional::stream);
```

Each call to `stream` returns a stream with 0 or 1 elements. The `flatMap` method combines them all. That means the nonexistent users are simply dropped.

 NOTE: In this section, we consider the happy scenario in which we have a method that returns an `Optional` value. These days, many methods return `null` when there is no valid result. Suppose `Users.classicLookup(id)` returns a `User` object or `null`, not an `Optional<User>`. Then you can of course filter out the `null` values:

```
Stream<User> users = ids.map(Users::classicLookup)
    .filter(Objects::nonNull);
```

But if you prefer the `flatMap` approach, you can use

```
Stream<User> users = ids.flatMap(
    id -> Stream.ofNullable(Users.classicLookup(id)));
```

or

```
Stream<User> users = ids.map(Users::classicLookup)
    .flatMap(Stream::ofNullable);
```

The call `Stream.ofNullable(obj)` yields an empty stream if `obj` is `null` or a stream just containing `obj` otherwise.

8.8 Collecting Results

When you are done with a stream, you will often want to look at the results. You can call the `iterator` method, which yields an old-fashioned iterator that you can use to visit the elements.

Alternatively, you can call the `forEach` method to apply a function to each element:

```
stream.forEach(System.out::println);
```

On a parallel stream, the `forEach` method traverses elements in arbitrary order. If you want to process them in stream order, call `forEachOrdered` instead. Of course, you might then give up some or all of the benefits of parallelism.

But more often than not, you will want to collect the result in a data structure. You can call `toArray` and get an array of the stream elements.

Since it is not possible to create a generic array at runtime, the expression `stream.toArray()` returns an `Object[]` array. If you want an array of the correct type, pass in the array constructor:

```
String[] result = stream.toArray(String[]::new);
    // stream.toArray() has type Object[]
```

For collecting stream elements to another target, there is a convenient `collect` method that takes an instance of the `Collector` interface. The `Collectors` class provides a large number of factory methods for common collectors. To collect a stream into a list or set, simply call

```
List<String> result = stream.collect(Collectors.toList());
```

or

```
Set<String> result = stream.collect(Collectors.toSet());
```

If you want to control which kind of set you get, use the following call instead:

```
TreeSet<String> result = stream.collect(Collectors.toCollection(TreeSet::new));
```

Suppose you want to collect all strings in a stream by concatenating them. You can call

```
String result = stream.collect(Collectors.joining());
```

If you want a delimiter between elements, pass it to the `joining` method:

```
String result = stream.collect(Collectors.joining(", "));
```

If your stream contains objects other than strings, you need to first convert them to strings, like this:

```
String result = stream.map(Object::toString).collect(Collectors.joining(", "));
```

If you want to reduce the stream results to a sum, count, average, maximum, or minimum, use one of the summarizing(Int|Long|Double) methods. These methods take a function that maps the stream objects to numbers and yield a result of type (Int|Long|Double)SummaryStatistics, simultaneously computing the sum, count, average, maximum, and minimum.

```
IntSummaryStatistics summary = stream.collect(
    Collectors.summarizingInt(String::length));
double averageWordLength = summary.getAverage();
double maxWordLength = summary.getMax();
```

8.9 Collecting into Maps

Suppose you have a Stream<Person> and want to collect the elements into a map so that later you can look up people by their ID. The Collectors.toMap method has two function arguments that produce the map's keys and values. For example,

```
Map<Integer, String> idToName = people.collect(
    Collectors.toMap(Person::getId, Person::getName));
```

In the common case when the values should be the actual elements, use Function.identity() for the second function.

```
Map<Integer, Person> idToPerson = people.collect(
    Collectors.toMap(Person::getId, Function.identity()));
```

If there is more than one element with the same key, there is a conflict, and the collector will throw an IllegalStateException. You can override that behavior by supplying a third function argument that resolves the conflict and determines the value for the key, given the existing and the new value. Your function could return the existing value, the new value, or a combination of them.

Here, we construct a map that contains, for each language in the available locales, as key its name in your default locale (such as "German"), and as value its localized name (such as "Deutsch").

```
Stream<Locale> locales = Stream.of(Locale.getAvailableLocales());
Map<String, String> languageNames = locales.collect(
    Collectors.toMap(
        Locale::getDisplayLanguage,
        loc -> loc.getDisplayLanguage(loc),
        (existingValue, newValue) -> existingValue));
```

We don't care that the same language might occur twice (for example, German in Germany and in Switzerland), so we just keep the first entry.

 NOTE: In this chapter, I use the Locale class as a source of an interesting data set. See Chapter 13 for more information about working with locales.

Now suppose we want to know all languages in a given country. Then we need a Map<String, Set<String>>. For example, the value for "Switzerland" is the set [French, German, Italian]. At first, we store a singleton set for each language. Whenever a new language is found for a given country, we form the union of the existing and the new set.

```
Map<String, Set<String>> countryLanguageSets = locales.collect(
    Collectors.toMap(
        Locale::getDisplayCountry,
        l -> Collections.singleton(l.getDisplayLanguage()),
        (a, b) -> { // Union of a and b
            Set<String> union = new HashSet<>(a);
            union.addAll(b);
            return union; }));
```

You will see a simpler way of obtaining this map in the next section.

If you want a `TreeMap`, supply the constructor as the fourth argument. You must provide a merge function. Here is one of the examples from the beginning of the section, now yielding a `TreeMap`:

```
Map<Integer, Person> idToPerson = people.collect(
    Collectors.toMap(
        Person::getId,
        Function.identity(),
        (existingValue, newValue) -> { throw new IllegalStateException(); },
        TreeMap::new));
```

NOTE: For each of the `toMap` methods, there is an equivalent `toConcurrentMap` method that yields a concurrent map. A single concurrent map is used in the parallel collection process. When used with a parallel stream, a shared map is more efficient than merging maps. Note that elements are no longer collected in stream order, but that doesn't usually make a difference.

8.10 Grouping and Partitioning

In the preceding section, you saw how to collect all languages in a given country. But the process was a bit tedious. You had to generate a singleton set for each map value and then specify how to merge the existing and new values. Forming groups of values with the same characteristic is very common, and the `groupingBy` method supports it directly.

Let's look at the problem of grouping locales by country. First, form this map:

```
Map<String, List<Locale>> countryToLocales = locales.collect(
    Collectors.groupingBy(Locale::getCountry));
```

The function `Locale::getCountry` is the *classifier function* of the grouping. You can now look up all locales for a given country code, for example

```
List<Locale> swissLocales = countryToLocales.get("CH");
    // Yields locales [it_CH, de_CH, fr_CH]
```

NOTE: A quick refresher on locales: Each locale has a language code (such as `en` for English) and a country code (such as `US` for the United States). The locale `en_US` describes English in the United States, and `en_IE` is English in Ireland. Some countries have multiple locales. For example, `ga_IE` is Gaelic in Ireland, and, as the preceding example shows, my JVM knows three locales in Switzerland.

When the classifier function is a predicate function (that is, a function returning a `boolean` value), the stream elements are partitioned into two lists: those where the function returns `true` and the complement. In this case, it is more efficient to use `partitioningBy` instead of `groupingBy`. For example, here we split all locales into those that use English and all others:

```
Map<Boolean, List<Locale>> englishAndOtherLocales = locales.collect(
    Collectors.partitioningBy(l -> l.getLanguage().equals("en")));
List<Locale> englishLocales = englishAndOtherLocales.get(true);
```

 NOTE: If you call the `groupingByConcurrent` method, you get a concurrent map that, when used with a parallel stream, is concurrently populated. This is entirely analogous to the `toConcurrentMap` method.

8.11 Downstream Collectors

The `groupingBy` method yields a map whose values are lists. If you want to process those lists in some way, supply a *downstream collector*. For example, if you want sets instead of lists, you can use the `Collectors.toSet` collector that you saw in the preceding section:

```
Map<String, Set<Locale>> countryToLocaleSet = locales.collect(
    groupingBy(Locale::getCountry, toSet()));
```

 NOTE: In this example, as well as the remaining examples of this section, I assume a static import of `java.util.stream.Collectors.*` to make the expressions easier to read.

Several collectors are provided for reducing grouped elements to numbers:

- `counting` produces a count of the collected elements. For example,

```
Map<String, Long> countryToLocaleCounts = locales.collect(
    groupingBy(Locale::getCountry, counting()));
```

counts how many locales there are for each country.

- summing(Int|Long|Double) takes a function argument, applies the function to the downstream elements, and produces their sum. For example,

```
Map<String, Integer> stateToCityPopulation = cities.collect(
    groupingBy(City::getState, summingInt(City::getPopulation)));
```

computes the sum of populations per state in a stream of cities.

- maxBy and minBy take a comparator and produce maximum and minimum of the downstream elements. For example,

```
Map<String, Optional<City>> stateToLargestCity = cities.collect(
    groupingBy(City::getState,
        maxBy(Comparator.comparing(City::getPopulation))));
```

produces the largest city per state.

The mapping collector applies a function to downstream results, and it requires yet another collector for processing its results. For example,

```
Map<String, Optional<String>> stateToLongestCityName = cities.collect(
    groupingBy(City::getState,
        mapping(City::getName,
            maxBy(Comparator.comparing(String::length)))));
```

Here, we group cities by state. Within each state, we produce the names of the cities and reduce by maximum length.

The mapping method also yields a nicer solution to a problem from the preceding section—gathering a set of all languages in a country.

```
Map<String, Set<String>> countryToLanguages = locales.collect(
    groupingBy(Locale::getDisplayCountry,
        mapping(Locale::getDisplayLanguage,
            toSet())));
```

There is a flatMapping method as well, for use with functions that return streams (see Exercise 8).

In the preceding section, I used toMap instead of groupingBy. In this form, you don't need to worry about combining the individual sets.

If the grouping or mapping function has return type int, long, or double, you can collect elements into a summary statistics object, as discussed in Section 8.8, "Collecting Results" (page 271). For example,

```
Map<String, IntSummaryStatistics> stateToCityPopulationSummary = cities.collect(
    groupingBy(City::getState,
        summarizingInt(City::getPopulation)));
```

Then you can get the sum, count, average, minimum, and maximum of the function values from the summary statistics objects of each group.

The `filtering` collector applies a filter to each group, for example:

```
Map<String, Set<City>> largeCitiesByState
    = cities.collect(
        groupingBy(City::getState,
            filtering(c -> c.getPopulation() > 500000,
                toSet())));  // States without large cities have empty sets
```

 NOTE: There are also three versions of a `reducing` method that apply general reductions, as described in the next section.

Composing collectors is powerful, but it can also lead to very convoluted expressions. The best use is with `groupingBy` or `partitioningBy` to process the "downstream" map values. Otherwise, simply apply methods such as `map`, `reduce`, `count`, `max`, or `min` directly on streams.

8.12 Reduction Operations

The `reduce` method is a general mechanism for computing a value from a stream. The simplest form takes a binary function and keeps applying it, starting with the first two elements. It's easy to explain this if the function is the sum:

```
List<Integer> values = ...;
Optional<Integer> sum = values.stream().reduce((x, y) -> x + y);
```

In this case, the `reduce` method computes $v_0 + v_1 + v_2 + \ldots$, where the v_i are the stream elements. The method returns an `Optional` because there is no valid result if the stream is empty.

 NOTE: In this case, you can write `reduce(Integer::sum)` instead of `reduce((x, y) -> x + y)`.

More generally, you can use any operation that combines a partial result x with the next value y to yield a new partial result.

Here is another way of looking at reductions. Given a reduction operation op, the reduction yields $v_0 \ op \ v_1 \ op \ v_2 \ op \ \ldots$, where $v_i \ op \ v_{i+1}$ denotes the function call $op(v_i, v_{i+1})$. There are many operations that might be useful in practice, such as sum, product, string concatenation, maximum and minimum, set union and intersection.

If you want to use reduction with parallel streams, the operation must be *associative*: It shouldn't matter in which order you combine the elements. In math notation, $(x\ op\ y)\ op\ z$ must be equal to $x\ op\ (y\ op\ z)$. An example of an operation that is not associative is subtraction. For example, $(6 - 3) - 2 \neq 6 - (3 - 2)$.

Often, there is an *identity e* such that $e\ op\ x = x$, and you can use that element as the start of the computation. For example, 0 is the identity for addition. Then call the second form of reduce:

```
List<Integer> values = ...;
Integer sum = values.stream().reduce(0, (x, y) -> x + y)
    // Computes 0 + v_0 + v_1 + v_2 + . . .
```

// Computes $0 + v_0 + v_1 + v_2 + \cdots$

The identity value is returned if the stream is empty, and you no longer need to deal with the Optional class.

Now suppose you have a stream of objects and want to form the sum of some property, such as all lengths in a stream of strings. You can't use the simple form of reduce. It requires a function (T, T) -> T, with the same types for the arguments and the result. But in this situation, you have two types: The stream elements have type String, and the accumulated result is an integer. There is a form of reduce that can deal with this situation.

First, you supply an "accumulator" function (total, word) -> total + word.length(). That function is called repeatedly, forming the cumulative total. But when the computation is parallelized, there will be multiple computations of this kind, and you need to combine their results. You supply a second function for that purpose. The complete call is

```
int result = words.reduce(0,
    (total, word) -> total + word.length(),
    (total1, total2) -> total1 + total2);
```

 NOTE: In practice, you probably won't use the reduce method a lot. It is usually easier to map to a stream of numbers and use one of its methods to compute sum, max, or min. (We discuss streams of numbers in Section 8.13, "Primitive Type Streams," page 279.) In this particular example, you could have called words.mapToInt(String::length).sum(), which is both simpler and more efficient since it doesn't involve boxing.

NOTE: There are times when `reduce` is not general enough. For example, suppose you want to collect the results in a `BitSet`. If the collection is parallelized, you can't put the elements directly into a single `BitSet` because a `BitSet` object is not threadsafe. For that reason, you can't use `reduce`. Each segment needs to start out with its own empty set, and `reduce` only lets you supply one identity value. Instead, use `collect`. It takes three arguments:

1. A *supplier* to make new instances of the target object, for example a constructor for a hash set

2. An *accumulator* that adds an element to the target, such as an `add` method

3. A *combiner* that merges two objects into one, such as `addAll`

Here is how the `collect` method works for a bit set:

```
BitSet result = stream.collect(BitSet::new, BitSet::set, BitSet::or);
```

8.13 Primitive Type Streams

So far, we have collected integers in a `Stream<Integer>`, even though it is clearly inefficient to wrap each integer into a wrapper object. The same is true for the other primitive types `double`, `float`, `long`, `short`, `char`, `byte`, and `boolean`. The stream library has specialized types `IntStream`, `LongStream`, and `DoubleStream` that store primitive values directly, without using wrappers. If you want to store `short`, `char`, `byte`, and `boolean`, use an `IntStream`, and for `float`, use a `DoubleStream`.

To create an `IntStream`, call the `IntStream.of` and `Arrays.stream` methods:

```
IntStream stream = IntStream.of(1, 1, 2, 3, 5);
stream = Arrays.stream(values, from, to); // values is an int[] array
```

As with object streams, you can also use the static `generate` and `iterate` methods. In addition, `IntStream` and `LongStream` have static methods `range` and `rangeClosed` that generate integer ranges with step size one:

```
IntStream zeroToNinetyNine = IntStream.range(0, 100); // Upper bound is excluded
IntStream zeroToHundred = IntStream.rangeClosed(0, 100); // Upper bound is included
```

The `CharSequence` interface has methods `codePoints` and `chars` that yield an `IntStream` of the Unicode codes of the characters or of the code units in the UTF-16 encoding. (See Chapter 1 for the sordid details.)

```
String sentence = "\uD835\uDD46 is the set of octonions.";
    // \uD835\uDD46 is the UTF-16 encoding of the letter 𝕆, unicode U+1D546

IntStream codes = sentence.codePoints();
    // The stream with hex values 1D546 20 69 73 20  . . .
```

When you have a stream of objects, you can transform it to a primitive type stream with the `mapToInt`, `mapToLong`, or `mapToDouble` methods. For example, if you have a stream of strings and want to process their lengths as integers, you might as well do it in an `IntStream`:

```
Stream<String> words = ...;
IntStream lengths = words.mapToInt(String::length);
```

To convert a primitive type stream to an object stream, use the `boxed` method:

```
Stream<Integer> integers = IntStream.range(0, 100).boxed();
```

Generally, the methods on primitive type streams are analogous to those on object streams. Here are the most notable differences:

- The `toArray` methods return primitive type arrays.

- Methods that yield an optional result return an `OptionalInt`, `OptionalLong`, or `OptionalDouble`. These classes are analogous to the `Optional` class, but they have methods `getAsInt`, `getAsLong`, and `getAsDouble` instead of the `get` method.

- There are methods `sum`, `average`, `max`, and `min` that return the sum, average, maximum, and minimum. These methods are not defined for object streams.

- The `summaryStatistics` method yields an object of type `IntSummaryStatistics`, `LongSummaryStatistics`, or `DoubleSummaryStatistics` that can simultaneously report the sum, count, average, maximum, and minimum of the stream.

 NOTE: The `Random` class has methods `ints`, `longs`, and `doubles` that return primitive type streams of random numbers.

8.14 Parallel Streams

Streams make it easy to parallelize bulk operations. The process is mostly automatic, but you need to follow a few rules. First of all, you must have a parallel stream. You can get a parallel stream from any collection with the `Collection.parallelStream()` method:

```
Stream<String> parallelWords = words.parallelStream();
```

Moreover, the `parallel` method converts any sequential stream into a parallel one.

```
Stream<String> parallelWords = Stream.of(wordArray).parallel();
```

As long as the stream is in parallel mode when the terminal method executes, all intermediate stream operations will be parallelized.

When stream operations run in parallel, the intent is that the same result is returned as if they had run serially. It is important that the operations are *stateless* and can be executed in an arbitrary order.

Here is an example of something you cannot do. Suppose you want to count all short words in a stream of strings:

```
int[] shortWords = new int[12];
words.parallelStream().forEach(
    s -> { if (s.length() < 12) shortWords[s.length()]++; });
        // Error—race condition!
System.out.println(Arrays.toString(shortWords));
```

This is very, very bad code. The function passed to `forEach` runs concurrently in multiple threads, each updating a shared array. As you will see in Chapter 10, that's a classic *race condition*. If you run this program multiple times, you are quite likely to get a different sequence of counts in each run—each of them wrong.

It is your responsibility to ensure that any functions you pass to parallel stream operations are safe to execute in parallel. The best way to do that is to stay away from mutable state. In this example, you can safely parallelize the computation if you group strings by length and count them.

```
Map<Integer, Long> shortWordCounts
    = words.parallelStream()
        .filter(s -> s.length() < 12)
        .collect(groupingBy(
            String::length,
            counting()));
```

By default, streams that arise from ordered collections (arrays and lists), from ranges, generators, and iterators, or from calling `Stream.sorted`, are *ordered*. Results are accumulated in the order of the original elements, and are entirely predictable. If you run the same operations twice, you will get exactly the same results.

Ordering does not preclude efficient parallelization. For example, when computing `stream.map(fun)`, the stream can be partitioned into *n* segments, each of which is concurrently processed. Then the results are reassembled in order.

Some operations can be more effectively parallelized when the ordering requirement is dropped. By calling the `Stream.unordered` method, you indicate that you are not interested in ordering. One operation that can benefit from this is `Stream.distinct`. On an ordered stream, `distinct` retains the first of all equal elements. That impedes parallelization—the thread processing a segment can't know which elements to discard until the preceding segment has been processed. If it is acceptable to retain *any* of the unique elements, all segments can be processed concurrently (using a shared set to track duplicates).

You can also speed up the `limit` method by dropping ordering. If you just want any n elements from a stream and you don't care which ones you get, call

```
Stream<String> sample = words.parallelStream().unordered().limit(n);
```

As discussed in Section 8.9, "Collecting into Maps" (page 273), merging maps is expensive. For that reason, the `Collectors.groupingByConcurrent` method uses a shared concurrent map. To benefit from parallelism, the order of the map values will not be the same as the stream order.

```
Map<Integer, List<String>> result = words.parallelStream().collect(
    Collectors.groupingByConcurrent(String::length));
    // Values aren't collected in stream order
```

Of course, you won't care if you use a downstream collector that is independent of the ordering, such as

```
Map<Integer, Long> wordCounts
    = words.parallelStream()
        .collect(
            groupingByConcurrent(
                String::length,
                counting()));
```

 NOTE: Don't turn all your streams into parallel streams with the hope of speeding up their operations. There is a substantial overhead to parallelization that will only pay off for very large data sets. Moreover, the thread pool that is used by parallel streams may perform poorly for blocking operations such as file I/O or network operations. Parallel streams work best with huge in-memory collections of data and computationally intensive processing.

CAUTION: It is very important that you don't modify the collection that is backing a stream while carrying out a stream operation (even if the modification is threadsafe). Remember that streams don't collect their data—that data is always in a separate collection. If you were to modify that collection, the outcome of the stream operations would be undefined. The JDK documentation refers to this requirement as *noninterference*. It applies both to sequential and parallel streams.

To be exact, since intermediate stream operations are lazy, it is possible to mutate the collection up to the point when the terminal operation executes. For example, the following, while certainly not recommended, will work:

```
List<String> wordList = ...;
Stream<String> words = wordList.stream();
wordList.add("END");
long n = words.distinct().count();
```

But this code is wrong:

```
Stream<String> words = wordList.stream();
words.forEach(s -> if (s.length() < 12) wordList.remove(s));
    // Error—interference
```

Exercises

1. Verify that asking for the first five long words does not call the `filter` method once the fifth long word has been found. Simply log each method call.

2. Measure the difference when counting long words with a `parallelStream` instead of a `stream`. Call `System.currentTimeMillis` before and after the call and print the difference. Switch to a larger document (such as *War and Peace*) if you have a fast computer.

3. Suppose you have an array `int[] values = { 1, 4, 9, 16 }`. What is `Stream.of(values)`? How do you get a stream of `int` instead?

4. Using `Stream.iterate`, make an infinite stream of random numbers—not by calling `Math.random` but by directly implementing a *linear congruential generator*. In such a generator, you start with $x_0 = seed$ and then produce $x_{n + 1} = (a \ x_n + c) \% m$, for appropriate values of a, c, and m. You should implement a method with parameters `a`, `c`, `m`, and `seed` that yields a `Stream<Long>`. Try out $a = 25214903917$, $c = 11$, and $m = 2^{48}$.

5. The `codePoints` method in Section 8.3, "The `filter`, `map`, and `flatMap` Methods" (page 263) was a bit clumsy, first filling an array list and then turning

it into a stream. Write a stream-based version instead, using the `IntStream.iterate` method to construct a finite stream of offsets, then extract the substrings.

6. Use the `String.codePoints` method to implement a method that tests whether a string is a word, consisting only of letters. (Hint: `Character.isAlphabetic`.) Using the same approach, implement a method that tests whether a string is a valid Java identifier.

7. Turning a file into a stream of tokens, list the first 100 tokens that are words in the sense of the preceding exercise. Read the file again and list the 10 most frequent words, ignoring letter case.

8. Find a realistic use for the `Collectors.flatMapping` method. Consider some class with a method yielding an `Optional`. Then group by some characteristic and, for each group, collect the nonempty optional values by using `flatMapping` and `Optional.stream`.

9. Read the words from /usr/share/dict/words (or a similar word list) into a stream and produce an array of all words containing five distinct vowels.

10. Given a finite stream of strings, find the average string length.

11. Given a finite stream of strings, find all strings of maximum length.

12. Your manager asks you to write a method `public static <T> boolean isFinite(Stream<T> stream)`. Why isn't that such a good idea? Go ahead and write it anyway.

13. Write a method `public static <T> Stream<T> zip(Stream<T> first, Stream<T> second)` that alternates elements from the streams `first` and `second` (or `null` if the stream whose turn it is runs out of elements).

14. Join all elements in a `Stream<ArrayList<T>>` to one `ArrayList<T>`. Show how to do this with each of the three forms of `reduce`.

15. Write a call to `reduce` that can be used to compute the average of a `Stream<Double>`. Why can't you simply compute the sum and divide by `count()`?

16. Find 500 prime numbers with 50 decimal digits, using a parallel stream of `BigInteger` and the `BigInter.isProbablePrime` method. Is it any faster than using a serial stream?

17. Find the 500 longest strings in *War and Peace* with a parallel stream. Is it any faster than using a serial stream?

18. How can you eliminate adjacent duplicates from a stream? Would your method work if the stream was parallel?

Processing
Input and Output

Topics in This Chapter

Chapter 9

In this chapter, you will learn how to work with files, directories, and web pages, and how to read and write data in binary and text format. You will also find a discussion of regular expressions, which can be useful for processing input. (I couldn't think of a better place to handle that topic, and apparently neither could the Java developers—when the regular expression API specification was proposed, it was attached to the specification request for "new I/O" features.) Finally, this chapter shows you the object serialization mechanism that lets you store objects as easily as you can store text or numeric data.

The key points of this chapter are:

1. An `InputStream` is a source of bytes, and an `OutputStream` is a destination for bytes.

2. A `Reader` reads characters, and a `Writer` writes them. Be sure to specify a character encoding.

3. The `Files` class has convenience methods for reading all bytes or lines of a file.

4. The `DataInput` and `DataOutput` interfaces have methods for writing numbers in binary format.

5. Use a `RandomAccessFile` or a memory-mapped file for random access.

6. A Path is an absolute or relative sequence of path components in a file system. Paths can be combined (or "resolved").

7. Use the methods of the Files class to copy, move, or delete files and to recursively walk through a directory tree.

8. To read or update a ZIP file, use a ZIP file system.

9. You can read the contents of a web page with the URL class. To read metadata or write data, use the URLConnection class.

10. With the Pattern and Matcher classes, you can find all matches of a regular expression in a string, as well as the captured groups for each match.

11. The serialization mechanism can save and restore any object implementing the Serializable interface, provided its instance variables are also serializable.

9.1 Input/Output Streams, Readers, and Writers

In the Java API, a source from which one can read bytes is called an *input stream*. The bytes can come from a file, a network connection, or an array in memory. (These streams are unrelated to the streams of Chapter 8.) Similarly, a destination for bytes is an *output stream*. In contrast, *readers* and *writers* consume and produce sequences of *characters*. In the following sections, you will learn how to read and write bytes and characters.

9.1.1 Obtaining Streams

The easiest way to obtain a stream from a file is with the static methods

```
InputStream in = Files.newInputStream(path);
OutputStream out = Files.newOutputStream(path);
```

Here, path is an instance of the Path class that is covered in Section 9.2.1, "Paths" (page 298). It describes a path in a file system.

If you have a URL, you can read its contents from the input stream returned by the openStream method of the URL class:

```
URL url = new URL("http://horstmann.com/index.html");
InputStream in = url.openStream();
```

Section 9.3, "HTTP Connections" (page 306) shows how to send data to a web server.

The ByteArrayInputStream class lets you read from an array of bytes.

```
byte[] bytes = ...;
InputStream in = new ByteArrayInputStream(bytes);
```

Conversely, to send output to a byte array, use a `ByteArrayOutputStream`:

```
ByteArrayOutputStream out = new ByteArrayOutputStream();
Write to out
byte[] bytes = out.toByteArray();
```

9.1.2 Reading Bytes

The `InputStream` class has a method to read a single byte:

```
InputStream in = ...;
int b = in.read();
```

This method either returns the byte as an integer between 0 and 255, or returns -1 if the end of input has been reached.

 CAUTION: The Java `byte` type has values between -128 and 127. You can cast the returned value into a `byte` *after* you have checked that it is not -1.

More commonly, you will want to read the bytes in bulk. The most convenient method is the `readAllBytes` method that simply reads all bytes from the stream into a byte array:

```
byte[] bytes = in.readAllBytes();
```

 TIP: If you want to read all bytes from a file, call the convenience method

```
byte[] bytes = Files.readAllBytes(path);
```

If you want to read some, but not all bytes, provide a byte array and call the `readNBytes` method:

```
byte[] bytes = new byte[len];
int bytesRead = in.readNBytes(bytes, offset, n);
```

The method reads until either `n` bytes are read or no further input is available, and returns the actual number of bytes read. If no input was available at all, the methods return -1.

 NOTE: There is also a `read(byte[], int, int)` method whose description seems exactly like `readNBytes`. The difference is that the `read` method only attempts to read the bytes and returns immediately with a lower count if it fails. The `readNBytes` method keeps calling `read` until all requested bytes have been obtained or `read` returns -1.

9.1.3 Writing Bytes

The write methods of an OutputStream can write individual bytes and byte arrays.

```
OutputStream out = ...;
int b = ...;
out.write(b);
byte[] bytes = ...;
out.write(bytes);
out.write(bytes, start, length);
```

When you are done writing a stream, you must *close* it in order to commit any buffered output. This is best done with a try-with-resources statement:

```
try (OutputStream out = ...) {
    out.write(bytes);
}
```

If you need to copy an input stream to an output stream, use the InputStream.transferTo method:

```
try (InputStream in = ...; OutputStream out = ...) {
    in.transferTo(out);
}
```

Both streams need to be closed after the call to transferTo. It is best to use a try-with-resources statement, as in the code example.

To write a file to an OutputStream, call

```
Files.copy(path, out);
```

Conversely, to save an InputStream to a file, call

```
Files.copy(in, path, StandardCopyOption.REPLACE_EXISTING);
```

9.1.4 Character Encodings

Input and output streams are for sequences of bytes, but in many cases you will work with text—that, is, sequences of characters. It then matters how characters are encoded into bytes.

Java uses the Unicode standard for characters. Each character or "code point" has a 21-bit integer number. There are different *character encodings*—methods for packaging those 21-bit numbers into bytes.

The most common encoding is UTF-8, which encodes each Unicode code point into a sequence of one to four bytes (see Table 9-1). UTF-8 has the advantage that the characters of the traditional ASCII character set, which contains all characters used in English, only take up one byte each.

Table 9-1 UTF-8 Encoding

Character Range	Encoding
0...7F	$0a_6a_5a_4a_3a_2a_1a_0$
80...7FF	$110a_{10}a_9a_8a_7a_6\ 10a_5a_4a_3a_2a_1a_0$
800...FFFF	$1110a_{15}a_{14}a_{13}a_{12}\ 10a_{11}a_{10}a_9a_8a_7a_6\ 10a_5a_4a_3a_2a_1a_0$
10000...10FFFF	$11110a_{20}a_{19}a_{18}\ 10a_{17}a_{16}a_{15}a_{14}a_{13}a_{12}\ 10a_{11}a_{10}a_9a_8a_7a_6\ 10a_5a_4a_3a_2a_1a_0$

Another common encoding is UTF-16, which encodes each Unicode code point into one or two 16-bit values (see Table 9-2). This is the encoding used in Java strings. Actually, there are two forms of UTF-16, called "big-endian" and "little-endian." Consider the 16-bit value 0x2122. In big-endian format, the more significant byte comes first: 0x21 followed by 0x22. In little-endian format, it is the other way around: 0x22 0x21. To indicate which of the two is used, a file can start with the "byte order mark," the 16-bit quantity 0xFEFF. A reader can use this value to determine the byte order and discard it.

Table 9-2 UTF-16 Encoding

Character Range	Encoding
0...FFFF	$a_{15}a_{14}a_{13}a_{12}a_{11}a_{10}a_9a_8a_7a_6a_5a_4a_3a_2a_1a_0$
10000...10FFFF	$110110b_{19}b_{18}b_{17}b_{16}a_{15}a_{14}a_{13}a_{12}a_{11}a_{10}\ 110111a_9a_8a_7a_6a_5a_4a_3a_2a_1a_0$ where $b_{19}b_{18}b_{17}b_{16} = a_{20}a_{19}a_{18}a_{17}a_{16} - 1$

CAUTION: Some programs, including Microsoft Notepad, add a byte order mark at the beginning of UTF-8 encoded files. Clearly, this is unnecessary since there are no byte ordering issues in UTF-8. But the Unicode standard allows it, and even suggests that it's a pretty good idea since it leaves little doubt about the encoding. It is supposed to be removed when reading a UTF-8 encoded file. Sadly, Java does not do that, and bug reports against this issue are closed as "will not fix." Your best bet is to strip out any leading \uFEFF that you find in your input.

In addition to the UTF encodings, there are partial encodings that cover a character range suitable for a given user population. For example, ISO 8859-1 is a one-byte code that includes accented characters used in Western European languages. Shift_JIS is a variable-length code for Japanese characters. A large number of these encodings are still in widespread use.

There is no reliable way to automatically detect the character encoding from a stream of bytes. Some API methods let you use the "default charset"—the character encoding that is preferred by the operating system of the computer. Is that the same encoding that is used by your source of bytes? These bytes may well originate from a different part of the world. Therefore, you should always explicitly specify the encoding. For example, when reading a web page, check the Content-Type header.

 NOTE: The platform encoding is returned by the static method Charset.defaultCharset. The static method Charset.availableCharsets returns all available Charset instances, as a map from canonical names to Charset objects.

 CAUTION: The Oracle implementation has a system property file.encoding for overriding the platform default. This is not an officially supported property, and it is not consistently followed by all parts of Oracle's implementation of the Java library. You should not set it.

The StandardCharsets class has static variables of type Charset for the character encodings that every Java virtual machine must support:

```
StandardCharsets.UTF_8
StandardCharsets.UTF_16
StandardCharsets.UTF_16BE
StandardCharsets.UTF_16LE
StandardCharsets.ISO_8859_1
StandardCharsets.US_ASCII
```

To obtain the Charset for another encoding, use the static forName method:

```
Charset shiftJIS = Charset.forName("Shift_JIS");
```

Use the Charset object when reading or writing text. For example, you can turn an array of bytes into a string as

```
String str = new String(bytes, StandardCharsets.UTF_8);
```

 TIP: Some methods allow you to specify a character encoding with a Charset object or a string. Choose the StandardCharsets constants, so you don't have to worry about the correct spelling. For example, new String(bytes, "UTF 8") is not acceptable and will cause a runtime error.

CAUTION: Some methods (such as the `String(byte[])` constructor) use the default platform encoding if you don't specify any; others (such as `Files.readAllLines`) use UTF-8.

9.1.5 Text Input

To read text input, use a `Reader`. You can obtain a `Reader` from any input stream with the `InputStreamReader` adapter:

```
InputStream inStream = ...;
Reader in = new InputStreamReader(inStream, charset);
```

If you want to process the input one UTF-16 code unit at a time, you can call the `read` method:

```
int ch = in.read();
```

The method returns a code unit between `0` and `65536`, or `-1` at the end of input.

That is not very convenient. Here are several alternatives.

With a short text file, you can read it into a string like this:

```
String content = new String(Files.readAllBytes(path), charset);
```

But if you want the file as a sequence of lines, call

```
List<String> lines = Files.readAllLines(path, charset);
```

Or better, process them lazily as a `Stream`:

```
try (Stream<String> lines = Files.lines(path, charset)) {
    ...
}
```

NOTE: If an `IOException` occurs as the stream fetches the lines, that exception is wrapped into an `UncheckedIOException` which is thrown out of the stream operation. (This subterfuge is necessary because stream operations are not declared to throw any checked exceptions.)

To read numbers or words from a file, use a `Scanner`, as you have seen in Chapter 1. For example,

```
Scanner in = new Scanner(path, "UTF-8");
while (in.hasNextDouble()) {
    double value = in.nextDouble();
    ...
}
```

TIP: To read alphabetic words, set the scanner's delimiter to a regular expression that is the complement of what you want to accept as a token. For example, after calling

```
in.useDelimiter("\\PL+");
```

the scanner reads in letters since any sequence of nonletters is a delimiter. See Section 9.4.1, "The Regular Expression Syntax" (page 310) for the regular expression syntax.

You can then obtain a stream of all words as

```
Stream<String> words = in.tokens();
```

If your input does not come from a file, wrap the `InputStream` into a `BufferedReader`:

```
try (BufferedReader reader
        = new BufferedReader(new InputStreamReader(url.openStream()))) {
    Stream<String> lines = reader.lines();
    ...
}
```

A `BufferedReader` reads input in chunks for efficiency. (Oddly, this is not an option for basic readers.) It has methods `readLine` to read a single line and `lines` to yield a stream of lines.

If a method asks for a `Reader` and you want it to read from a file, call `Files.newBufferedReader(path, charset)`.

9.1.6 Text Output

To write text, use a `Writer`. With the `write` method, you can write strings. You can turn any output stream into a `Writer`:

```
OutputStream outStream = ...;
Writer out = new OutputStreamWriter(outStream, charset);
out.write(str);
```

To get a writer for a file, use

```
Writer out = Files.newBufferedWriter(path, charset);
```

It is more convenient to use a `PrintWriter`, which has the `print`, `println`, and `printf` that you have always used with `System.out`. Using those methods, you can print numbers and use formatted output.

If you write to a file, construct a `PrintWriter` like this:

```
PrintWriter out = new PrintWriter(Files.newBufferedWriter(path, charset));
```

If you write to another stream, use

```
PrintWriter out = new PrintWriter(
    new OutputStreamWriter(outStream, charset));
```

NOTE: System.out is an instance of PrintStream, not PrintWriter. This is a relic from the earliest days of Java. However, the print, println, and printf methods work the same way for the PrintStream and PrintWriter classes, using a character encoding for turning characters into bytes.

If you already have the text to write in a string, call

```
String content = ...;
Files.write(path, content.getBytes(charset));
```

or

```
Files.write(path, lines, charset);
```

Here, lines can be a Collection<String>, or even more generally, an Iterable<? extends CharSequence>.

To append to a file, use

```
Files.write(path, content.getBytes(charset), StandardOpenOption.APPEND);
Files.write(path, lines, charset, StandardOpenOption.APPEND);
```

CAUTION: When writing text with a partial character set such as ISO 8859-1, any unmappable characters are silently changed to a "replacement"—in most cases, either the ? character or the Unicode replacement character U+FFFD.

Sometimes, a library method wants a Writer to write output. If you want to capture that output in a string, hand it a StringWriter. Or, if it wants a PrintWriter, wrap the StringWriter like this:

```
StringWriter writer = new StringWriter();
throwable.printStackTrace(new PrintWriter(writer));
String stackTrace = writer.toString();
```

9.1.7 Reading and Writing Binary Data

The DataInput interface declares the following methods for reading a number, a character, a boolean value, or a string in binary format:

```
byte readByte()
int readUnsignedByte()
char readChar()
short readShort()
int readUnsignedShort()
int readInt()
long readLong()
float readFloat()
double readDouble()
void readFully(byte[] b)
```

The DataOutput interface declares corresponding write methods.

 NOTE: These methods read and write numbers in big-endian format.

 CAUTION: There are also readUTF/writeUTF methods that use a "modified UTF-8" format. These methods are *not* compatible with regular UTF-8, and are only useful for JVM internals.

The advantage of binary I/O is that it is fixed width and efficient. For example, writeInt always writes an integer as a big-endian 4-byte binary quantity regardless of the number of digits. The space needed is the same for each value of a given type, which speeds up random access. Also, reading binary data is faster than parsing text. The main drawback is that the resulting files cannot be easily inspected in a text editor.

You can use the DataInputStream and DataOutputStream adapters with any stream. For example,

```
DataInput in = new DataInputStream(Files.newInputStream(path));
DataOutput out = new DataOutputStream(Files.newOutputStream(path));
```

9.1.8 Random-Access Files

The RandomAccessFile class lets you read or write data anywhere in a file. You can open a random-access file either for reading only or for both reading and writing; specify the option by using the string "r" (for read access) or "rw" (for read/write access) as the second argument in the constructor. For example,

```
RandomAccessFile file = new RandomAccessFile(path.toString(), "rw");
```

A random-access file has a *file pointer* that indicates the position of the next byte to be read or written. The seek method sets the file pointer to an arbitrary byte position within the file. The argument to seek is a long integer between zero and the length of the file (which you can obtain with the length method). The getFilePointer method returns the current position of the file pointer.

The RandomAccessFile class implements both the DataInput and DataOutput interfaces. To read and write numbers from a random-access file, use methods such as readInt/writeInt that you saw in the preceding section. For example,

```
int value = file.readInt();
file.seek(file.getFilePointer() - 4);
file.writeInt(value + 1);
```

9.1.9 Memory-Mapped Files

Memory-mapped files provide another, very efficient approach for random access that works well for very large files. However, the API for data access is completely different from that of input/output streams. First, get a *channel* to the file:

```
FileChannel channel = FileChannel.open(path,
    StandardOpenOption.READ, StandardOpenOption.WRITE)
```

Then, map an area of the file (or, if it is not too large, the entire file) into memory:

```
ByteBuffer buffer = channel.map(FileChannel.MapMode.READ_WRITE,
    0, channel.size());
```

Use methods get, getInt, getDouble, and so on to read values, and the equivalent put methods to write values.

```
int offset = ...;
int value = buffer.getInt(offset);
buffer.put(offset, value + 1);
```

At some point, and certainly when the channel is closed, these changes are written back to the file.

 NOTE: By default, the methods for reading and writing numbers use big-endian byte order. You can change the byte order with the command

```
buffer.order(ByteOrder.LITTLE_ENDIAN);
```

9.1.10 File Locking

When multiple simultaneously executing programs modify the same file, they need to communicate in some way, or the file can easily become damaged. File locks can solve this problem.

Suppose your application saves a configuration file with user preferences. If a user invokes two instances of the application, it could happen that both of them want to write the configuration file at the same time. In that situation, the first instance should lock the file. When the second instance finds the file locked, it can decide to wait until the file is unlocked or simply skip the writing process. To lock a file, call either the `lock` or `tryLock` methods of the `FileChannel` class.

```
FileChannel channel = FileChannel.open(path);
FileLock lock = channel.lock();
```

or

```
FileLock lock = channel.tryLock();
```

The first call blocks until the lock becomes available. The second call returns immediately, either with the lock or with `null` if the lock is not available. The file remains locked until the lock or the channel is closed. It is best to use a try-with-resources statement:

```
try (FileLock lock = channel.lock()) {
    ...
}
```

9.2 Paths, Files, and Directories

You have already seen `Path` objects for specifying file paths. In the following sections, you will see how to manipulate these objects and how to work with files and directories.

9.2.1 Paths

A `Path` is a sequence of directory names, optionally followed by a file name. The first component of a path may be a root component, such as / or C:\. The permissible root components depend on the file system. A path that starts with a root component is *absolute*. Otherwise, it is *relative*. For example, here we construct an absolute and a relative path. For the absolute path, we assume we are running on a Unix-like file system.

```
Path absolute = Paths.get("/", "home", "cay");
Path relative = Paths.get("myapp", "conf", "user.properties");
```

The static `Paths.get` method receives one or more strings, which it joins with the path separator of the default file system (/ for a Unix-like file system, \ for Windows). It then parses the result, throwing an `InvalidPathException` if the result is not a valid path in the given file system. The result is a `Path` object.

You can also provide a string with separators to the `Paths.get` method:

```
Path homeDirectory = Paths.get("/home/cay");
```

 NOTE: A `Path` object does not have to correspond to a file that actually exists. It is merely an abstract sequence of names. To create a file, first make a path, then call a method to create the corresponding file—see Section 9.2.2, "Creating Files and Directories" (page 300).

It is very common to combine or "resolve" paths. The call `p.resolve(q)` returns a path according to these rules:

- If `q` is absolute, then the result is `q`.
- Otherwise, the result is "`p` then `q`," according to the rules of the file system.

For example, suppose your application needs to find its configuration file relative to the home directory. Here is how you can combine the paths:

```
Path workPath = homeDirectory.resolve("myapp/work");
    // Same as homeDirectory.resolve(Paths.get("myapp/work"));
```

There is a convenience method `resolveSibling` that resolves against a path's parent, yielding a sibling path. For example, if `workPath` is /home/cay/myapp/work, the call

```
Path tempPath = workPath.resolveSibling("temp");
```

yields /home/cay/myapp/temp.

The opposite of `resolve` is `relativize`. The call `p.relativize(r)` yields the path `q` which, when resolved with `p`, yields `r`. For example,

```
Paths.get("/home/cay").relativize(Paths.get("/home/fred/myapp"))
```

yields ../fred/myapp, assuming we have a file system that uses .. to denote the parent directory.

The `normalize` method removes any redundant . and .. components (or whatever the file system may deem redundant). For example, normalizing the path /home/cay/../fred/./myapp yields /home/fred/myapp.

The `toAbsolutePath` method yields the absolute path of a given path. If the path is not already absolute, it is resolved against the "user directory"—that is, the directory from which the JVM was invoked. For example, if you launched a program from /home/cay/myapp, then `Paths.get("config").toAbsolutePath()` returns /home/cay/myapp/config.

The `Path` interface has methods for taking paths apart and combining them with other paths. This code sample shows some of the most useful ones:

```
Path p = Paths.get("/home", "cay", "myapp.properties");
Path parent = p.getParent(); // The path /home/cay
Path file = p.getFileName(); // The last element, myapp.properties
Path root = p.getRoot(); // The initial segment / (null for a relative path)
Path first = p.getName(0); // The first element
Path dir = p.subpath(1, p.getNameCount());
    // All but the first element, cay/myapp.properties
```

The Path interface extends the Iterable<Path> element, so you can iterate over the name components of a Path with an enhanced for loop:

```
for (Path component : path) {
    ...
}
```

 NOTE: Occasionally, you may need to interoperate with legacy APIs that use the File class instead of the Path interface. The Path interface has a toFile method, and the File class has a toPath method.

9.2.2 Creating Files and Directories

To create a new directory, call

```
Files.createDirectory(path);
```

All but the last component in the path must already exist. To create intermediate directories as well, use

```
Files.createDirectories(path);
```

You can create an empty file with

```
Files.createFile(path);
```

The call throws an exception if the file already exists. The checks for existence and the creation are atomic. If the file doesn't exist, it is created before anyone else has a chance to do the same.

The call Files.exists(path) checks whether the given file or directory exists. To test whether it is a directory or a "regular" file (that is, with data in it, not something like a directory or symbolic link), call the static methods isDirectory and isRegularFile of the Files class.

There are convenience methods for creating a temporary file or directory in a given or system-specific location.

```
Path tempFile = Files.createTempFile(dir, prefix, suffix);
Path tempFile = Files.createTempFile(prefix, suffix);
Path tempDir = Files.createTempDirectory(dir, prefix);
Path tempDir = Files.createTempDirectory(prefix);
```

Here, `dir` is a `Path`, and `prefix`/`suffix` are strings which may be null. For example, the call `Files.createTempFile(null, ".txt")` might return a path such as `/tmp/1234405522364837194.txt`.

9.2.3 Copying, Moving, and Deleting Files

To copy a file from one location to another, simply call

```
Files.copy(fromPath, toPath);
```

To move a file (that is, copy and delete the original), call

```
Files.move(fromPath, toPath);
```

You can also use this command to move an empty directory.

The copy or move will fail if the target exists. If you want to overwrite an existing target, use the `REPLACE_EXISTING` option. If you want to copy all file attributes, use the `COPY_ATTRIBUTES` option. You can supply both like this:

```
Files.copy(fromPath, toPath, StandardCopyOption.REPLACE_EXISTING,
    StandardCopyOption.COPY_ATTRIBUTES);
```

You can specify that a move should be atomic. Then you are assured that either the move completed successfully, or the source continues to be present. Use the `ATOMIC_MOVE` option:

```
Files.move(fromPath, toPath, StandardCopyOption.ATOMIC_MOVE);
```

See Table 9-3 for a summary of the options that are available for file operations.

Finally, to delete a file, simply call

```
Files.delete(path);
```

This method throws an exception if the file doesn't exist, so instead you may want to use

```
boolean deleted = Files.deleteIfExists(path);
```

The deletion methods can also be used to remove an empty directory.

Table 9-3 Standard Options for File Operations

Option	Description
StandardOpenOption; use with newBufferedWriter, newInputStream, newOutputStream, write	
READ	Open for reading
WRITE	Open for writing
APPEND	If opened for writing, append to the end of the file
TRUNCATE_EXISTING	If opened for writing, remove existing contents
CREATE_NEW	Create a new file and fail if it exists
CREATE	Atomically create a new file if it doesn't exist
DELETE_ON_CLOSE	Make a "best effort" to delete the file when it is closed
SPARSE	A hint to the file system that this file will be sparse
DSYNC|SYNC	Requires that each update to the file data|data and metadata be written synchronously to the storage device
StandardCopyOption; use with copy, move	
ATOMIC_MOVE	Move the file atomically
COPY_ATTRIBUTES	Copy the file attributes
REPLACE_EXISTING	Replace the target if it exists
LinkOption; use with all of the above methods and exists, isDirectory, isRegularFile	
NOFOLLOW_LINKS	Do not follow symbolic links
FileVisitOption; use with find, walk, walkFileTree	
FOLLOW_LINKS	Follow symbolic links

9.2.4 Visiting Directory Entries

The static Files.list method returns a Stream<Path> that reads the entries of a directory. The directory is read lazily, making it possible to efficiently process directories with huge numbers of entries.

Since reading a directory involves a system resource that needs to be closed, you should use a try-with-resources block:

```
try (Stream<Path> entries = Files.list(pathToDirectory)) {
    ...
}
```

The list method does not enter subdirectories. To process all descendants of a directory, use the Files.walk method instead.

```
try (Stream<Path> entries = Files.walk(pathToRoot)) {
    // Contains all descendants, visited in depth-first order
}
```

Here is a sample traversal of the unzipped src.zip tree:

```
java
java/nio
java/nio/DirectCharBufferU.java
java/nio/ByteBufferAsShortBufferRL.java
java/nio/MappedByteBuffer.java
...
java/nio/ByteBufferAsDoubleBufferB.java
java/nio/charset
java/nio/charset/CoderMalfunctionError.java
java/nio/charset/CharsetDecoder.java
java/nio/charset/UnsupportedCharsetException.java
java/nio/charset/spi
java/nio/charset/spi/CharsetProvider.java
java/nio/charset/StandardCharsets.java
java/nio/charset/Charset.java
...
java/nio/charset/CoderResult.java
java/nio/HeapFloatBufferR.java
...
```

As you can see, whenever the traversal yields a directory, it is entered before continuing with its siblings.

You can limit the depth of the tree that you want to visit by calling Files.walk(pathToRoot, depth). Both walk methods have a varargs parameter of type FileVisitOption..., but there is only one option you can supply: FOLLOW_LINKS to follow symbolic links.

 NOTE: If you filter the paths returned by walk and your filter criterion involves the file attributes stored with a directory, such as size, creation time, or type (file, directory, symbolic link), then use the find method instead of walk. Call that method with a predicate function that accepts a path and a BasicFileAttributes object. The only advantage is efficiency. Since the directory is being read anyway, the attributes are readily available.

This code fragment uses the `Files.walk` method to copy one directory to another:

```
Files.walk(source).forEach(p -> {
    try {
        Path q = target.resolve(source.relativize(p));
        if (Files.isDirectory(p))
            Files.createDirectory(q);
        else
            Files.copy(p, q);
    } catch (IOException ex) {
        throw new UncheckedIOException(ex);
    }
});
```

Unfortunately, you cannot easily use the `Files.walk` method to delete a tree of directories since you need to first visit the children before deleting the parent. In that case, use the `walkFileTree` method. It requires an instance of the `FileVisitor` interface. Here is when the file visitor gets notified:

1. Before a directory is processed:

   ```
   FileVisitResult preVisitDirectory(T dir, IOException ex)
   ```

2. When a file is encountered:

   ```
   FileVisitResult visitFile(T path, BasicFileAttributes attrs)
   ```

3. When an exception occurs in the `visitFile` method:

   ```
   FileVisitResult visitFileFailed(T path, IOException ex)
   ```

4. After a directory is processed:

   ```
   FileVisitResult postVisitDirectory(T dir, IOException ex)
   ```

In each case, the notification method returns one of the following results:

- Continue visiting the next file: `FileVisitResult.CONTINUE`
- Continue the walk, but without visiting the entries in this directory: `FileVisitResult.SKIP_SUBTREE`
- Continue the walk, but without visiting the siblings of this file: `FileVisitResult.SKIP_SIBLINGS`
- Terminate the walk: `FileVisitResult.TERMINATE`

If any of the methods throws an exception, the walk is also terminated, and that exception is thrown from the `walkFileTree` method.

The `SimpleFileVisitor` class implements this interface, continuing the iteration at each point and rethrowing any exceptions.

Here is how you can delete a directory tree:

```
Files.walkFileTree(root, new SimpleFileVisitor<Path>() {
    public FileVisitResult visitFile(Path file,
            BasicFileAttributes attrs) throws IOException {
        Files.delete(file);
        return FileVisitResult.CONTINUE;
    }
    public FileVisitResult postVisitDirectory(Path dir,
            IOException ex) throws IOException {
        if (ex != null) throw ex;
        Files.delete(dir);
        return FileVisitResult.CONTINUE;
    }
});
```

9.2.5 ZIP File Systems

The `Paths` class looks up paths in the default file system—the files on the user's local disk. You can have other file systems. One of the more useful ones is a ZIP file system. If `zipname` is the name of a ZIP file, then the call

```
FileSystem zipfs = FileSystems.newFileSystem(Paths.get(zipname), null);
```

establishes a file system that contains all files in the ZIP archive. It's an easy matter to copy a file out of that archive if you know its name:

```
Files.copy(zipfs.getPath(sourceName), targetPath);
```

Here, `zipfs.getPath` is the analog of `Paths.get` for an arbitrary file system.

To list all files in a ZIP archive, walk the file tree:

```
Files.walk(zipfs.getPath("/")).forEach(p -> {
    Process p
});
```

You have to work a bit harder to create a new ZIP file. Here is the magic incantation:

```
Path zipPath = Paths.get("myfile.zip");
URI uri = new URI("jar", zipPath.toUri().toString(), null);
    // Constructs the URI jar:file://myfile.zip
try (FileSystem zipfs = FileSystems.newFileSystem(uri,
        Collections.singletonMap("create", "true"))) {
    // To add files, copy them into the ZIP file system
    Files.copy(sourcePath, zipfs.getPath("/").resolve(targetPath));
}
```

 NOTE: There is an older API for working with ZIP archives, with classes `ZipInputStream` and `ZipOutputStream`, but it's not as easy to use as the one described in this section.

9.3 HTTP Connections

You can read from a URL by using the input stream returned from URL.getInputStream method. However, if you want additional information about a web resource, or if you want to write data, you need more control over the process than the URL class provides. The URLConnection class was designed before HTTP was the universal protocol of the Web. It provides support for a number of protocols, but its HTTP support is somewhat cumbersome. When the decision was made to support HTTP/2, it became clear that it would be best to provide a modern client interface instead of reworking the existing API. In Java 9, the HttpClient provides a more convenient API and HTTP/2 support. The API classes are located in the jdk.incubator.http package, to indicate that its API is likely to evolve as a result of user feedback before it is finalized in Java 10.

In the following sections, I provide a cookbook for using the HttpURLConnection class, and then give an overview of the API in the incubator.

9.3.1 The URLConnection and HttpURLConnection Classes

To use the URLConnection class, follow these steps:

1. Get an URLConnection object:

    ```
    URLConnection connection = url.openConnection();
    ```

    For an HTTP URL, the returned object is actually an instance of HttpURLConnection.

2. If desired, set request properties:

    ```
    connection.setRequestProperty("Accept-Charset", "UTF-8, ISO-8859-1");
    ```

    If a key has multiple values, separate them by commas.

3. To send data to the server, call

    ```
    connection.setDoOutput(true);
    try (OutputStream out = connection.getOutputStream()) {
        // Write to out
    }
    ```

4. If you want to read the response headers and you haven't called getOutputStream, call

    ```
    connection.connect();
    ```

Then query the header information:

```
Map<String, List<String>> headers = connection.getHeaderFields();
```

For each key, you get a list of values since there may be multiple header fields with the same key.

5. Read the response:

```
try (InputStream in = connection.getInputStream()) {
    // Read from in
}
```

A common use case is to post form data. The `URLConnection` class automatically sets the content type to `application/x-www-form-urlencoded` when writing data to a HTTP URL, but you need to encode the name/value pairs:

```
URL url = ...;
URLConnection connection = url.openConnection();
connection.setDoOutput(true);
try (Writer out = new OutputStreamWriter(
        connection.getOutputStream(), StandardCharsets.UTF_8)) {
    Map<String, String> postData = ...;
    boolean first = true;
    for (Map.Entry<String, String> entry : postData.entrySet()) {
        if (first) first = false;
        else out.write("&");
        out.write(URLEncoder.encode(entry.getKey(), "UTF-8"));
        out.write("=");
        out.write(URLEncoder.encode(entry.getValue(), "UTF-8"));
    }
}
try (InputStream in = connection.getInputStream()) {
    ...
}
```

9.3.2 The HTTP Client API

The HTTP client API whose incubator version is included in Java 9 provides another mechanism for connecting to a web server which is simpler than the `URLConnection` class with its rather fussy set of stages.

 NOTE: To use this feature, you need to run your program with the command-line option

```
--add-modules jdk.incubator.httpclient
```

An `HttpClient` can issue requests and receive responses. You get a client by calling

```
HttpClient client = HttpClient.newHttpClient();
```

Alternatively, if you need to configure the client, use a builder API like this:

```
HttpClient client = HttpClient.newBuilder()
    .followRedirects(HttpClient.Redirect.ALWAYS)
    .build();
```

That is, you get a builder, call methods to customize the item that is going to be built, and then call the `build` method to finalize the building process. This is a common pattern for constructing immutable objects.

Follow the same pattern for formulating requests. Here is a `GET` request:

```
HttpRequest request = HttpRequest.newBuilder()
    .uri(new URI("http://horstmann.com"))
    .GET()
    .build();
```

The URI is the "uniform resource identifier" which is, when using HTTP, the same as a URL. However, in Java, the `URL` class has methods for actually opening a connection to a URL, whereas the `URI` class is only concerned with the syntax (scheme, host, port, path, query, fragment, and so on).

When sending the request, you have to tell the client how to handle the response. If you just want the body as a string, send the request with a `HttpResponse.BodyHandler.asString()`, like this:

```
HttpResponse<String> response
    = client.send(request, HttpResponse.BodyHandler.asString());
```

The `HttpResponse` class is a template whose type denotes the type of the body. You get the response body string simply as

```
String bodyString = response.body();
```

There are other response body handlers that get the response as a byte array or a file. One can hope that eventually the JDK will support JSON and provide a JSON handler.

With a `POST` request, you similarly need a "body processor" that turns the request data into the data that is being posted. There are body processors for strings, byte arrays, and files. Again, one can hope that the library designers will wake up to the reality that most `POST` requests involve form data or JSON objects, and provide appropriate processors.

In the meantime, to send a form post, you need to URL-encode the request data, just like in the preceding section.

```
Map<String, String> postData = ...;
boolean first = true;
StringBuilder body = new StringBuilder();
for (Map.Entry<String, String> entry : postData.entrySet()) {
    if (first) first = false;
    else body.append("&");
    body.append(URLEncoder.encode(entry.getKey(), "UTF-8"));
    body.append("=");
    body.append(URLEncoder.encode(entry.getValue(), "UTF-8"));
}
HttpRequest request = HttpRequest.newBuilder()
    .uri(httpUrlString)
    .header("Content-Type", "application/x-www-form-urlencoded")
    .POST(HttpRequest.BodyProcessor.fromString(body.toString()))
    .build();
```

Note that, unlike with the URLConnection class, you need to specify the content type for forms.

Similarly, for posting JSON data, you specify the content type and provide a JSON string.

The HttpResponse object also yields the status code and the response headers.

```
int status = response.statusCode();
HttpHeaders responseHeaders = response.headers();
```

You can turn the HttpHeaders object into a map:

```
Map<String, List<String>> headerMap = responseHeaders.map();
```

The map values are lists since in HTTP, each key can have multiple values.

If you just want the value of a particular key, and you know that there won't be multiple values, call the firstValue method:

```
Optional<String> lastModified = headerMap.firstValue("Last-Modified");
```

You get the response value or an empty optional if none was supplied.

 TIP: To enable logging for the HttpClient, add this line to net.properties in your JDK:

```
jdk.httpclient.HttpClient.log=all
```

Instead of all, you can specify a comma-separated list of headers, requests, content, errors, ssl, trace, and frames, optionally followed by :control, :data, :window, or :all. Don't use any spaces.

Then set the logging level for the logger named jdk.httpclient.HttpClient to INFO, for example by adding this line to the logging.properties file in your JDK:

```
jdk.httpclient.HttpClient.level=INFO
```

9.4 Regular Expressions

Regular expressions specify string patterns. Use them whenever you need to locate strings that match a particular pattern. For example, suppose you want to find hyperlinks in an HTML file. You need to look for strings of the pattern <a href="...">. But wait—there may be extra spaces, or the URL may be enclosed in single quotes. Regular expressions give you a precise syntax for specifying what sequences of characters are legal matches.

In the following sections, you will see the regular expression syntax used by the Java API, and how to put regular expressions to work.

9.4.1 The Regular Expression Syntax

In a regular expression, a character denotes itself unless it is one of the reserved characters

   . * + ? { | ( ) [\ ^ $

For example, the regular expression Java only matches the string Java.

The symbol . matches any single character. For example, .a.a matches Java and data.

The * symbol indicates that the preceding constructs may be repeated 0 or more times; for a +, it is 1 or more times. A suffix of ? indicates that a construct is optional (0 or 1 times). For example, be+s? matches be, bee, and bees. You can specify other multiplicities with { } (see Table 9-4).

A | denotes an alternative: .(oo|ee)f matches beef or woof. Note the parentheses—without them, .oo|eef would be the alternative between .oo and eef. Parentheses are also used for grouping—see Section 9.4.4, "Groups" (page 316).

A *character class* is a set of character alternatives enclosed in brackets, such as [Jj], [0-9], [A-Za-z], or [^0-9]. Inside a character class, the - denotes a range (all characters whose Unicode values fall between the two bounds). However, a - that is the first or last character in a character class denotes itself. A ^ as the first character in a character class denotes the complement (all characters except those specified).

There are many *predefined character classes* such as \d (digits) or \p{Sc} (Unicode currency symbols). See Tables 9-4 and 9-5.

The characters ^ and $ match the beginning and end of input.

If you need to have a literal . * + ? { | ( ) [\ ^ $, precede it by a backslash. Inside a character class, you only need to escape [and \, provided you are careful about the positions of] - ^. For example, []^-] is a class containing all three of them.

Alternatively, surround a string with \Q and \E. For example, \(\\$0\.99\) and \Q($0.99)\E both match the string ($0.99).

 TIP: If you have a string that may contain some of the many special characters in the regular expression syntax, you can escape them all by calling Parse.quote(str). This simply surrounds the string with \Q and \E, but it takes care of the special case where str may contain \E.

Table 9-4 Regular Expression Syntax

Expression	Description	Example
Characters		
c, not one of . * + ? { | ( ) [\ ^ $	The character c	J
.	Any character except line terminators, or any character if the DOTALL flag is set	
\x{p}	The Unicode code point with hex code p	\x{1D546}
\uhhhh, \xhh, \0o, \0oo, \0ooo	The UTF-16 code unit with the given hex or octal value	\uFEFF
\a, \e, \f, \n, \r, \t	Alert (\x{7}), escape (\x{1B}), form feed (\x{B}), newline (\x{A}), carriage return (\x{D}), tab (\x{9})	\n
\cc, where c is in [A-Z] or one of @ [\ ] ^ _ ?	The control character corresponding to the character c	\cH is a backspace (\x{8})
\c, where c is not in [A-Za-z0-9]	The character c	\\
\Q ... \E	Everything between the start and the end of the quotation	\Q(...)\E matches the string (...)

(Continues)

Table 9-4 Regular Expression Syntax *(Continued)*

Expression	Description	Example
Character Classes		
$[C_1C_2...]$, where C_i are characters, ranges c-d, or character classes	Any of the characters represented by C_1, C_2, . . .	`[0-9+-]`
`[^...]`	Complement of a character class	`[^\d\s]`
`[...&&...]`	Intersection of character classes	`[\p{L}&&[^A-Za-z]]`
`\p{...}`, `\P{...}`	A predefined character class (see Table 9-5); its complement	`\p{L}` matches a Unicode letter, and so does `\pL`—you can omit braces around a single letter
`\d`, `\D`	Digits (`[0-9]`, or `\p{Digit}` when the `UNICODE_CHARACTER_CLASS` flag is set); the complement	`\d+` is a sequence of digits
`\w`, `\W`	Word characters (`[a-zA-Z0-9_]`, or Unicode word characters when the `UNICODE_CHARACTER_CLASS` flag is set); the complement	
`\s`, `\S`	Spaces (`[\n\r\t\f\x{B}]`, or `\p{IsWhite_Space}` when the `UNICODE_CHARACTER_CLASS` flag is set); the complement	`\s*,\s*` is a comma surrounded by optional white space
`\h`, `\v`, `\H`, `\V`	Horizontal whitespace, vertical whitespace, their complements	
Sequences and Alternatives		
XY	Any string from X, followed by any string from Y	`[1-9][0-9]*` is a positive number without leading zero
$X\|Y$	Any string from X or Y	`http|ftp`

(Continues)

Table 9-4 Regular Expression Syntax *(Continued)*

Expression	Description	Example
Grouping		
(*X*)	Captures the match of *X*	`'([^']*)'` captures the quoted text
n	The *n*th group	`(['"]).*\1` matches `'Fred'` or `"Fred"` but not `"Fred'`
(?<*name*>*X*)	Captures the match of *X* with the given name	`'(?<id>[A-Za-z0-9]+)'` captures the match with name `id`
\\k<*name*>	The group with the given name	`\k<id>` matches the group with name `id`
(?:*X*)	Use parentheses without capturing *X*	In `(?:http|ftp)://(.*)`, the match after `://` is `\1`
(?*f₁f₂*...:*X*), (?*f₁*...-*fₖ*...:*X*), with *fᵢ* in [`dimsuUx`]	Matches, but does not capture, *X* with the given flags on or off (after -)	`(?i:jpe?g)` is a case-insensitive match
Other (?...)	See the `Pattern` API documentation	
Quantifiers		
X?	Optional *X*	`\+?` is an optional + sign
X*, *X*+	0 or more *X*, 1 or more *X*	`[1-9][0-9]+` is an integer ≥ 10
X{*n*}, *X*{*n*,}, *X*{*m*,*n*}	*n* times *X*, at least *n* times *X*, between *m* and *n* times *X*	`[0-7]{1,3}` are one to three octal digits
Q?, where *Q* is a quantified expression	Reluctant quantifier, attempting the shortest match before trying longer matches	`.*(<.+?>).*` captures the shortest sequence enclosed in angle brackets
Q+, where *Q* is a quantified expression	Possessive quantifier, taking the longest match without backtracking	`'[^']*+'` matches strings enclosed in single quotes and fails quickly on strings without a closing quote
Boundary Matches		
^ $	Beginning, end of input (or beginning, end of line in multiline mode)	`^Java$` matches the input or line `Java`

(Continues)

Table 9-4 Regular Expression Syntax *(Continued)*

Expression	Description	Example
\A \Z \z	Beginning of input, end of input, absolute end of input (unchanged in multiline mode)	
\b \B	Word boundary, nonword boundary	\bJava\b matches the word Java
\R	A Unicode line break	
\G	The end of the previous match	

Table 9-5 Predefined Character Classes \p{...}

Name	Description
posixClass	*posixClass* is one of Lower, Upper, Alpha, Digit, Alnum, Punct, Graph, Print, Cntrl, XDigit, Space, Blank, ASCII, interpreted as POSIX or Unicode class, depending on the UNICODE_CHARACTER_CLASS flag
Is*Script*, sc=*Script*, script=*Script*	A script accepted by Character.UnicodeScript.forName
In*Block*, blk=*Block*, block=*Block*	A block accepted by Character.UnicodeBlock.forName
Category, In*Category*, gc=*Category*, general_category=*Category*	A one- or two-letter name for a Unicode general category
Is*Property*	*Property* is one of Alphabetic, Ideographic, Letter, Lowercase, Uppercase, Titlecase, Punctuation, Control, White_Space, Digit, Hex_Digit, Join_Control, Noncharacter_Code_Point, Assigned
java*Method*	Invokes the method Character.is*Method* (must not be deprecated)

9.4.2 Finding One Match

Generally, there are two ways to use a regular expression: Either you want to find out whether a string conforms to the expression, or you want to find all matches of a regular expressions in a string.

In the first case, simply use the static matches method:

```
String regex = "[+-]?\\d+";
CharSequence input = ...;
if (Pattern.matches(regex, input)) {
    ...
}
```

If you need to use the same regular expression many times, it is more efficient to compile it. Then, create a `Matcher` for each input:

```
Pattern pattern = Pattern.compile(regex);
Matcher matcher = pattern.matcher(input);
if (matcher.matches()) ...
```

If the match succeeds, you can retrieve the location of matched groups—see the following section.

If you want to match elements in a collection or stream, turn the pattern into a predicate:

```
Stream<String> strings = ...;
Stream<String> result = strings.filter(pattern.asPredicate());
```

The result contains all strings that match the regular expression.

9.4.3 Finding All Matches

In this section, we consider the other common use case for regular expressions—finding all matches in an input. Use this loop:

```
String input = ...;
Matcher matcher = pattern.matcher(input);
while (matcher.find()) {
    String match = matcher.group();
    int matchStart = matcher.start();
    int matchEnd = matcher.end();
    ...
}
```

In this way, you can process each match in turn. As shown in the code fragment, you can get the matched string as well as its position in the input string.

More elegantly, you can call the `results` method to get a `Stream<MatchResult>`. The `MatchResult` interface has methods `group`, `start`, and `end`, just like `Matcher`. (In fact, the `Matcher` class implements this interface.) Here is how you get a list of all matches:

```
List<String> matches = pattern.matcher(input)
    .results()
    .map(Matcher::group)
    .collect(Collectors.toList());
```

If you have the data in a file, then you can use the `Scanner.findAll` method to get a `Stream<MatchResult>`, without first having to read the contents into a string. You can pass a `Pattern` or a pattern string:

```
Scanner in = new Scanner(path, "UTF-8");
Stream<String> words = in.findAll("\\pL+")
    .map(MatchResult::group);
```

9.4.4 Groups

It is common to use groups for extracting components of a match. For example, suppose you have a line item in the invoice with item name, quantity, and unit price such as

```
Blackwell Toaster    USD29.95
```

Here is a regular expression with groups for each component:

```
(\p{Alnum}+(\s+\p{Alnum}+)*)\s+([A-Z]{3})([0-9.]*)
```

After matching, you can extract the *n*th group from the matcher as

```
String contents = matcher.group(n);
```

Groups are ordered by their opening parenthesis, starting at 1. (Group 0 is the entire input.) In this example, here is how to take the input apart:

```
Matcher matcher = pattern.matcher(input);
if (matcher.matches()) {
    item = matcher.group(1);
    currency = matcher.group(3);
    price = matcher.group(4);
}
```

We aren't interested in group 2; it only arose from the parentheses that were required for the repetition. For greater clarity, you can use a noncapturing group:

```
(\p{Alnum}+(?:\s+\p{Alnum}+)*)\s+([A-Z]{3})([0-9.]*)
```

Or, even better, capture by name:

```
(?<item>\p{Alnum}+(\s+\p{Alnum}+)*)\s+(?<currency>[A-Z]{3})(?<price>[0-9.]*)
```

Then, you can retrieve the items by name:

```
item = matcher.group("item");
```

With the `start` and `end` methods, you can get the group positions in the input:

```
int itemStart = matcher.start("item");
int itemEnd = matcher.end("item");
```

NOTE: Retrieving groups by name only works with a `Matcher`, not with a `MatchResult`.

 NOTE: When you have a group inside a repetition, such as `(\s+\p{Alnum}+)*` in the example above, it is not possible to get all of its matches. The `group` method only yields the last match, which is rarely useful. You need to capture the entire expression with another group.

9.4.5 Splitting along Delimiters

Sometimes, you want to break an input along matched delimiters and keep everything else. The `Pattern.split` method automates this task. You obtain an array of strings, with the delimiters removed:

```
String input = ...;
Pattern commas = Pattern.compile("\\s*,\\s*");
String[] tokens = commas.split(input);
    // "1, 2, 3" turns into ["1", "2", "3"]
```

If there are many tokens, you can fetch them lazily:

```
Stream<String> tokens = commas.splitAsStream(input);
```

If you don't care about precompiling the pattern or lazy fetching, you can just use the `String.split` method:

```
String[] tokens = input.split("\\s*,\\s*");
```

If the input is in a file, use a scanner:

```
Scanner in = new Scanner(path, "UTF-8");
in.useDelimiter("\\s*,\\s*");
Stream<String> tokens = in.tokens();
```

9.4.6 Replacing Matches

If you want to replace all matches of a regular expression with a string, call `replaceAll` on the matcher:

```
Matcher matcher = commas.matcher(input);
String result = matcher.replaceAll(",");
    // Normalizes the commas
```

Or, if you don't care about precompiling, use the `replaceAll` method of the `String` class.

```
String result = input.replaceAll("\\s*,\\s*", ",");
```

The replacement string can contain group numbers $n or names ${*name*}. They are replaced with the contents of the corresponding captured group.

```
String result = "3:45".replaceAll(
    "(\\d{1,2}):(?<minutes>\\d{2})",
    "$1 hours and ${minutes} minutes");
    // Sets result to "3 hours and 45 minutes"
```

You can use \ to escape $ and \ in the replacement string, or you can call the `Matcher.quoteReplacement` convenience method:

```
matcher.replaceAll(Matcher.quoteReplacement(str))
```

If you want to carry out a more complex operation than splicing in group matches, then you can provide a replacement function instead of a replacement string. The function accepts a `MatchResult` and yields a string. For example, here we replace all words with at least four letters with their uppercase version:

```
String result = Pattern.compile("\\pL{4,}")
    .matcher("Mary had a little lamb")
    .replaceAll(m -> m.group().toUpperCase());
    // Yields "MARY had a LITTLE LAMB"
```

The `replaceFirst` method replaces only the first occurrence of the pattern.

9.4.7 Flags

Several *flags* change the behavior of regular expressions. You can specify them when you compile the pattern:

```
Pattern pattern = Pattern.compile(regex,
    Pattern.CASE_INSENSITIVE | Pattern.UNICODE_CHARACTER_CLASS);
```

Or you can specify them inside the pattern:

```
String regex = "(?iU:expression)";
```

Here are the flags:

- `Pattern.CASE_INSENSITIVE` or i: Match characters independently of the letter case. By default, this flag takes only US ASCII characters into account.

- `Pattern.UNICODE_CASE` or u: When used in combination with CASE_INSENSITIVE, use Unicode letter case for matching.

- `Pattern.UNICODE_CHARACTER_CLASS` or U: Select Unicode character classes instead of POSIX. Implies `UNICODE_CASE`.

- `Pattern.MULTILINE` or m: Make ^ and $ match the beginning and end of a line, not the entire input.

- `Pattern.UNIX_LINES` or d: Only '\n' is a line terminator when matching ^ and $ in multiline mode.

- `Pattern.DOTALL` or s: Make the . symbol match all characters, including line terminators.

- `Pattern.COMMENTS` or x: Whitespace and comments (from # to the end of a line) are ignored.

- `Pattern.LITERAL`: The pattern is taking literally and must be matched exactly, except possibly for letter case.

- `Pattern.CANON_EQ`: Take canonical equivalence of Unicode characters into account. For example, u followed by ¨ (diaeresis) matches ü.

The last two flags cannot be specified inside a regular expression.

9.5 Serialization

In the following sections, you will learn about object serialization—a mechanism for turning an object into a bunch of bytes that can be shipped somewhere else or stored on disk, and for reconstituting the object from those bytes.

Serialization is an essential tool for distributed processing, where objects are shipped from one virtual machine to another. It is also used for fail-over and load balancing, when serialized objects can be moved to another server. If you work with server-side software, you will often need to enable serialization for classes. The following sections tell you how to do that.

9.5.1 The Serializable Interface

In order for an object to be serialized—that is, turned into a bunch of bytes—it must be an instance of a class that implements the `Serializable` interface. This is a marker interface with no methods, similar to the `Cloneable` interface that you saw in Chapter 4.

For example, to make `Employee` objects serializable, the class needs to be declared as

```
public class Employee implements Serializable {
    private String name;
    private double salary;
    ...
}
```

It is safe and appropriate to implement the `Serializable` interface if all instance variables have primitive or `enum` type, or refer to serializable objects. Many classes in the standard library are serializable. Arrays and the collection classes that you saw in Chapter 7 are serializable provided their elements are. More generally, all objects that you can reach from a serializable object need to be serializable.

In the case of the `Employee` class, and indeed with most classes, there is no problem. In the following sections, you will see what to do when a little extra help is needed.

To serialize objects, you need an `ObjectOutputStream`, which is constructed with another `OutputStream` that receives the actual bytes.

```
ObjectOutputStream out = new ObjectOutputStream(
    Files.newOutputStream(path));
```

Now call the `writeObject` method:

```
Employee peter = new Employee("Peter", 90000);
Employee paul = new Manager("Paul", 180000);
out.writeObject(peter);
out.writeObject(paul);
```

To read the objects back in, construct an `ObjectInputStream`:

```
ObjectInputStream in = new ObjectInputStream(
    Files.newInputStream(path));
```

Retrieve the objects in the same order in which they were written, using the `readObject` method.

```
Employee e1 = (Employee) in.readObject();
Employee e2 = (Employee) in.readObject();
```

When an object is written, the name of the class and the names and values of all instance variables are saved. If the value of an instance variable belongs to a primitive type, it is saved as binary data. If it is an object, it is again written with the `writeObject` method.

When an object is read in, the process is reversed. The class name and the names and values of the instance variables are read, and the object is reconstituted.

There is just one catch. Suppose there were two references to the same object. Let's say each employee has a reference to their boss:

```
Employee peter = new Employee("Peter", 90000);
Employee paul = new Manager("Barney", 105000);
Manager mary = new Manager("Mary", 180000);
peter.setBoss(mary);
paul.setBoss(mary);
out.writeObject(peter);
out.writeObject(paul);
```

When reading these two objects back in, both of them need to have the *same* boss, not two references to identical but distinct objects.

In order to achieve this, each object gets a *serial number* when it is saved. When you pass an object reference to writeObject, the ObjectOutputStream checks if the object reference was previously written. In that case, it just writes out the serial number and does not duplicate the contents of the object.

In the same way, an ObjectInputStream remembers all objects it has encountered. When reading in a reference to a repeated object, it simply yields a reference to the previously read object.

9.5.2 Transient Instance Variables

Certain instance variables should not be serialized—for example, database connections that are meaningless when an object is reconstituted. Also, when an object keeps a cache of values, it might be better to drop the cache and recompute it instead of storing it.

To prevent an instance variable from being serialized, simply tag it with the transient modifier. Also, mark instance variables as transient if they belong to nonserializable classes. Transient fields are always skipped when objects are serialized.

9.5.3 The readObject and writeObject Methods

In rare cases, you need to tweak the serialization mechanism. A serializable class can add any desired action to the default read and write behavior, by defining methods with the signature

```
private void readObject(ObjectInputStream in)
    throws IOException, ClassNotFoundException
private void writeObject(ObjectOutputStream out)
    throws IOException
```

Then, the object headers continue to be written as usual, but the instance variables fields are no longer automatically serialized. Instead, these methods are called.

Here is a typical example. The Point2D class in the JavaFX library is not serializable. Now, suppose you want to serialize a class LabeledPoint that stores a String and a Point2D. First, you need to mark the Point2D field as transient to avoid a NotSerializableException.

```
public class LabeledPoint implements Serializable {
    private String label;
    private transient Point2D point;
    ...
}
```

In the `writeObject` method, first write the nontransient `label` variable by calling the `defaultWriteObject` method. This is a special method of the `ObjectOutputStream` class that should only be called from within a `writeObject` method of a serializable class. Then, write the point coordinates using the `writeDouble` method from the `DataOutput` interface.

```
private void writeObject(ObjectOutputStream out)
      throws IOException {
   out.defaultWriteObject();
   out.writeDouble(point.getX());
   out.writeDouble(point.getY());
}
```

In the `readObject` method, reverse the process:

```
private void readObject(ObjectInputStream in)
      throws IOException, ClassNotFoundException {
   in.defaultReadObject();
   double x = in.readDouble();
   double y = in.readDouble();
   point = new Point2D(x, y);
}
```

The `readObject` and `writeObject` methods only need to read and write their own instance variables. They should not concern themselves with superclass data.

 NOTE: A class can define its own serialization format by implementing the `Externalizable` interface and providing methods

```
public void readExternal(ObjectInput in)
public void writeExternal(ObjectOutput out)
```

When reading an externalizable object, the object stream creates an object with the no-argument constructor and then calls the `readExternal` method. This can give better performance, but it is very rarely used.

9.5.4 The readResolve and writeReplace Methods

We take it for granted that objects can only be constructed with the constructor. However, a deserialized object is *not constructed*. Its instance variables are simply restored from an object stream.

This is a problem if the constructor enforces some condition. For example, a singleton object may be implemented so that the constructor can only be called once. Before Java had the `enum` construct, enumerated types were simulated by classes with a private constructor that was called once for each instance. As another example, database entities could be constructed so that they always come from a pool of managed instances.

These situations are exceedingly rare. Nowadays, the serialization of enum types is automatic. And you shouldn't implement your own mechanism for singletons. If you need a singleton, make an enumerated type with one instance that is, by convention, called INSTANCE.

```
public enum PersonDatabase {
    INSTANCE;

    public Person findById(int id) { ... }
    ...
}
```

Now let's suppose that you are in the rare situation where you want to control the identity of each deserialized instance. As an example, suppose a Person class wants to restore its instances from a database when deserializing. Then don't serialize the object itself but some proxy that can locate or construct the object. Provide a writeReplace method that returns the proxy object:

```
public class Person implements Serializable {
    private int id;
    // Other instance variables
    ...
    private Object writeReplace() {
        return new PersonProxy(id);
    }
}
```

When a Person object is serialized, none of its instance variables are saved. Instead, the writeReplace method is called and *its return value* is serialized and written to the stream.

The proxy class needs to implement a readResolve method that yields a Person:

```
public class PersonProxy implements Serializable {
    private int id;

    public PersonProxy(int id) {
        this.id = id;
    }

    public Object readResolve() {
        return PersonDatabase.INSTANCE.findById(id);
    }
}
```

When the readObject method finds a PersonProxy in an ObjectInputStream, it deserializes the proxy, calls its readResolve method, and returns the result.

9.5.5 Versioning

Serialization was intended for sending objects from one virtual machine to another, or for short-term persistence of state. If you use serialization for long-term persistence, or in any situation where classes can change between serialization and deserialization, you will need to consider what happens when your classes evolve. Can version 2 read the old data? Can the users who still use version 1 read the files produced by the new version?

The serialization mechanism supports a simple versioning scheme. When an object is serialized, both the name of the class and its serialVersionUID are written to the object stream. That unique identifier is assigned by the implementor, by defining an instance variable

```
private static final long serialVersionUID = 1L; // Version 1
```

When the class evolves in an incompatible way, the implementor should change the UID. Whenever a deserialized object has a nonmatching UID, the readObject method throws an InvalidClassException.

If the serialVersionUID matches, deserialization proceeds even if the implementation has changed. Each nontransient instance variable of the object to be read is set to the value in the serialized state, provided that the name and type match. All other instance variables are set to the default: null for object references, zero for numbers, and false for boolean values. Anything in the serialized state that doesn't exist in the object to be read is ignored.

Is that process safe? Only the implementor of the class can tell. If it is, then the implementor should give the new version of the class the same serialVersionUID as the old version.

If you don't assign a serialVersionUID, one is automatically generated by hashing a canonical description of the instance variables, methods, and supertypes. You can see the hash code with the serialver utility. The command

```
serialver ch09.sec05.Employee
```

displays

```
private static final long serialVersionUID = -4932578720821218323L;
```

When the class implementation changes, there is a very high probability that the hash code changes as well.

If you need to be able to read old version instances, and you are certain that is safe to do so, run serialver on the old version of your class and add the result to the new version.

NOTE: If you want to implement a more sophisticated versioning scheme, override the `readObject` method and call the `readFields` method instead of the `defaultReadObject` method. You get a description of all fields found in the stream, and you can do with them what you want.

Exercises

1. Write a utility method for copying all of an `InputStream` to an `OutputStream`, without using any temporary files. Provide another solution, without a loop, using operations from the `Files` class, using a temporary file.

2. Write a program that reads a text file and produces a file with the same name but extension `.toc`, containing an alphabetized list of all words in the input file together with a list of line numbers in which each word occurs. Assume that the file's encoding is UTF-8.

3. Write a program that reads a file containing text and, assuming that most words are English, guesses whether the encoding is ASCII, ISO 8859-1, UTF-8, or UTF-16, and if the latter, which byte ordering is used.

4. Using a `Scanner` is convenient, but it is a bit slower than using a `BufferedReader`. Read in a long file a line at a time, counting the number of input lines, with (a) a `Scanner` and `hasNextLine`/`nextLine`, (b) a `BufferedReader` and `readLine`, (c) a `BufferedReader` and `lines`. Which is the fastest? The most convenient?

5. When an encoder of a `Charset` with partial Unicode coverage can't encode a character, it replaces it with a default—usually, but not always, the encoding of `"?"`. Find all replacements of all available character sets that support encoding. Use the `newEncoder` method to get an encoder, and call its `replacement` method to get the replacement. For each unique result, report the canonical names of the charsets that use it.

6. The BMP file format for uncompressed image files is well documented and simple. Using random access, write a program that reflects each row of pixels in place, without writing a new file.

7. Look up the API documentation for the `MessageDigest` class and write a program that computes the SHA-512 digest of a file. Feed blocks of bytes to the `MessageDigest` object with the `update` method, then display the result of calling `digest`. Verify that your program produces the same result as the `sha512sum` utility.

8. Write a utility method for producing a ZIP file containing all files from a directory and its descendants.

9. Using the URLConnection class, read data from a password-protected web page with "basic" authentication. Concatenate the user name, a colon, and the password, and compute the Base64 encoding:

```
String input = username + ":" + password;
String encoding = Base64.getEncoder().encodeToString(
    input.getBytes(StandardCharsets.UTF_8));
```

Set the HTTP header Authorization to the value "Basic " + encoding. Then read and print the page contents.

10. Using a regular expression, extract all decimal integers (including negative ones) from a string into an ArrayList<Integer> (a) using find, and (b) using split. Note that a + or - that is not followed by a digit is a delimiter.

11. Using regular expressions, extract the directory path names (as an array of strings), the file name, and the file extension from an absolute or relative path such as /home/cay/myfile.txt.

12. Come up with a realistic use case for using group references in Matcher.replaceAll and implement it.

13. Implement a method that can produce a clone of any serializable object by serializing it into a byte array and deserializing it.

14. Implement a serializable class Point with instance variables for x and y. Write a program that serializes an array of Point objects to a file, and another that reads the file.

15. Continue the preceding exercise, but change the data representation of Point so that it stores the coordinates in an array. What happens when the new version tries to read a file generated by the old version? What happens when you fix up the serialVersionUID? Suppose your life depended upon making the new version compatible with the old. What could you do?

16. Which classes in the standard Java library implement Externalizable? Which of them use writeReplace/readResolve?

Concurrent Programming

Chapter 10

Java was one of the first mainstream programming languages with built-in support for concurrent programming. Early Java programmers were enthusiastic about how easy it was to load images in background threads or implement a web server that serves multiple requests concurrently. At the time, the focus was on keeping a processor busy while some tasks spend their time waiting for the network. Nowadays, most computers have multiple processors or cores, and programmers worry about keeping them all busy.

In this chapter, you will learn how to divide computations into concurrent tasks and how to execute them safely. My focus is on the needs of application programmers, not system programmers who write web servers or middleware.

For that reason, I arranged the information in this chapter so that I can, as much as possible, first show you the tools that you should be using in your work. I cover the low-level constructs later in the chapter. It is useful to know about these low-level details so that you get a feel for the costs of certain operations. But it is best to leave low-level thread programming to the experts. If you want to become one of them, I highly recommend the excellent book *Java Concurrency in Practice* by Brian Goetz et al. [Addison-Wesley, 2006].

The key points of this chapter are:

1. A `Runnable` describes a task that can be executed asynchronously but does not return a result.

2. An `ExecutorService` schedules tasks instances for execution.

3. A `Callable` describes a task that can be executed asynchronously and yields a result.

4. You can submit one or more `Callable` instances to an `ExecutorService` and combine the results when they are available.

5. When multiple threads operate on shared data without synchronization, the result is unpredictable.

6. Prefer using parallel algorithms and threadsafe data structures over programming with locks.

7. Parallel streams and array operations automatically and safely parallelize computations.

8. A `ConcurrentHashMap` is a threadsafe hash table that allows atomic update of entries.

9. You can use `AtomicLong` for a lock-free shared counter, or use `LongAdder` if contention is high.

10. A lock ensures that only one thread at a time executes a critical section.

11. An interruptible task should terminate when the interrupted flag is set or an `InterruptedException` occurs.

12. A long-running task should not block the user-interface thread of a program, but progress and final updates need to occur in the user-interface thread.

13. The `Process` class lets you execute a command in a separate process and interact with the input, output, and error streams.

10.1 Concurrent Tasks

When you design a concurrent program, you need to think about the tasks that can be run together. In the following sections, you will see how to execute tasks concurrently.

10.1.1 Running Tasks

In Java, the `Runnable` interface describes a task you want to run, perhaps concurrently with others.

```
public interface Runnable {
    void run();
}
```

Like all methods, the `run` method is executed in a *thread*. A thread is a mechanism for executing a sequence of instructions, usually provided by the operating system. Multiple threads run concurrently, by using separate processors or different time slices on the same processor.

If you want to execute a `Runnable` in a separate thread, you could spawn a thread just for this `Runnable`, and you will see how to do that in Section 10.8.1, "Starting a Thread" (page 363). But in practice, it doesn't usually make sense to have a one-to-one relationship between tasks and threads. When tasks are short-lived, you want to run many of them on the same thread, so you don't waste the time it takes to start a thread. When your tasks are computationally intensive, you just want one thread per processor instead of one thread per task, to avoid the overhead of switching among threads. You do not want to think of these issues when you design tasks, and therefore, it is best to separate tasks and task scheduling.

In the Java concurrency library, an *executor service* schedules and executes tasks, choosing the threads on which to run them.

```
Runnable task = () -> { ... };
ExecutorService executor = ...;
executor.execute(task);
```

The `Executors` class has factory methods for executor services with different scheduling policies. The call

```
exec = Executors.newCachedThreadPool();
```

yields an executor service optimized for programs with many tasks that are short lived or spend most of their time waiting. Each task is executed on an idle thread if possible, but a new thread is allocated if all threads are busy. There is no bound on the number of concurrent threads. Threads that are idle for an extended time are terminated.

The call

```
exec = Executors.newFixedThreadPool(nthreads);
```

yield a pool with a fixed number of threads. When you submit a task, it is queued up until a thread becomes available. This is a good choice to use for computationally intensive tasks, or to limit the resource consumption of a service. You can derive the number of threads from the number of available processors, which you obtain as

```
int processors = Runtime.getRuntime().availableProcessors();
```

Now go ahead and run the concurrency demo program in the book's companion code. It runs two tasks concurrently.

```
public static void main(String[] args) {
    Runnable hellos = () -> {
        for (int i = 1; i <= 1000; i++)
            System.out.println("Hello " + i);
    };
    Runnable goodbyes = () -> {
        for (int i = 1; i <= 1000; i++)
            System.out.println("Goodbye " + i);
    };

    ExecutorService executor = Executors.newCachedThreadPool();
    executor.execute(hellos);
    executor.execute(goodbyes);
}
```

Run the program a few times to see how the outputs are interleaved.

```
Goodbye 1
...
Goodbye 871
Goodbye 872
Hello 806
Goodbye 873
Goodbye 874
Goodbye 875
Goodbye 876
Goodbye 877
Goodbye 878
Goodbye 879
Goodbye 880
Goodbye 881
Hello 807
Goodbye 882
...
Hello 1000
```

 NOTE: You may note that the program waits a bit after the last printout. It terminates when the pooled threads have been idle for a while and the executor service terminates them.

 CAUTION: If concurrent tasks try to read or update a shared value, the result may be unpredictable. We will discuss this issue in detail in Section 10.3, "Thread Safety" (page 341). For now, we will assume that tasks do not share mutable data.

10.1.2 Futures

A `Runnable` carries out a task, but it doesn't yield a value. If you have a task that computes a result, use the `Callable<V>` interface instead. Its `call` method, unlike the `run` method of the `Runnable` interface, returns a value of type V:

```
public interface Callable<V> {
    V call() throws Exception;
}
```

As a bonus, the `call` method can throw arbitrary exceptions which can be relayed to the code that obtains the result.

To execute a `Callable`, submit it to an executor service:

```
ExecutorService executor = Executors.newFixedThreadPool();
Callable<V> task = ...;
Future<V> result = executor.submit(task);
```

When you submit the task, you get a *future*—an object that represents a computation whose result will be available at some future time. The `Future` interface has the following methods:

```
V get() throws InterruptedException, ExecutionException
V get(long timeout, TimeUnit unit)
    throws InterruptedException, ExecutionException, TimeoutException;
boolean cancel(boolean mayInterruptIfRunning)
boolean isCancelled()
boolean isDone()
```

The `get` method *blocks* until the result is available or until the timeout has been reached. That is, the thread containing the call does not progress until the method returns normally or throws an exception. If the `call` method yields a value, the `get` method returns that value. If the `call` method throws an exception, the `get` method throws an `ExecutionException` wrapping the thrown exception. If the timeout has been reached, the `get` method throws a `TimeoutException`.

The `cancel` method attempts to cancel the task. If the task isn't already running, it won't be scheduled. Otherwise, if `mayInterruptIfRunning` is `true`, the thread running the task is interrupted.

 NOTE: A task that wants to be interruptible must periodically check for interruption requests. This is required for any tasks that you'd like to cancel when some other subtask has succeeded. See Section 10.8.2, "Thread Interruption" (page 364) for more details on interruption.

A task may need to wait for the result of multiple subtasks. Instead of submitting each subtask separately, you can use the `invokeAll` method, passing a `Collection` of `Callable` instances.

For example, suppose you want to count how often a word occurs in a set of files. For each file, make a `Callable<Integer>` that returns the count for that file. Then submit them all to the executor. When all tasks have completed, you get a list of the futures (all of which are done), and you can total up the answers.

```
String word = ...;
Set<Path> paths = ...;
List<Callable<Long>> tasks = new ArrayList<>();
for (Path p : paths) tasks.add(
    () -> { return number of occurrences of word in p });
List<Future<Long>> results = executor.invokeAll(tasks);
    // This call blocks until all tasks have completed
long total = 0;
for (Future<Long> result : results) total += result.get();
```

There is also a variant of `invokeAll` with a timeout, which cancels all tasks that have not completed when the timeout is reached.

 NOTE: If it bothers you that the calling task blocks until all subtasks are done, you can use an `ExecutorCompletionService`. It returns the futures in the order of completion.

```
ExecutorCompletionService service
    = new ExecutorCompletionService(executor);
for (Callable<T> task : tasks) service.submit(task);
for (int i = 0; i < tasks.size(); i++) {
    Process service.take().get()
    Do something else
}
```

The `invokeAny` method is like `invokeAll`, but it returns as soon as any one of the submitted tasks has completed normally, without throwing an exception. It then returns the value of its `Future`. The other tasks are cancelled. This is useful for a search that can conclude as soon as a match has been found. This code snippet locates a file containing a given word:

```
String word = ...;
Set<Path> files = ...;
List<Callable<Path>> tasks = new ArrayList<>();
for (Path p : files) tasks.add(
    () -> { if (word occurs in p) return p; else throw ... });
Path found = executor.invokeAny(tasks);
```

As you can see, the ExecutorService does a lot of work for you. Not only does it map tasks to threads, but it also deals with task results, exceptions, and cancellation.

 NOTE: Java EE provides a ManagedExecutorService subclass that is suitable for concurrent tasks in a Java EE environment.

10.2 Asynchronous Computations

In the preceding section, our approach to concurrent computation was to break up a task and then wait until all pieces have completed. But waiting is not always a good idea. In the following sections, you will see how to implement wait-free or *asynchronous* computations.

10.2.1 Completable Futures

When you have a Future object, you need to call get to obtain the value, blocking until the value is available. The CompletableFuture class implements the Future interface, and it provides a second mechanism for obtaining the result. You register a *callback* that will be invoked (in some thread) with the result once it is available.

```
CompletableFuture<String> f = ...;
f.thenAccept((String s) -> Process the result s);
```

In this way, you can process the result, without blocking, as soon as it is available.

There are a few API methods that return CompletableFuture objects. For example, the HttpClient class can fetch a web page asynchronously:

```
HttpClient client = HttpClient.newHttpClient();
HttpRequest request = HttpRequest.newBuilder(new URI(urlString)).GET().build();
CompletableFuture<HttpResponse<String>> f = client.sendAsync(
    request, BodyHandler.asString());
```

To run a task asynchronously and obtain a CompletableFuture, you don't submit it directly to an executor service. Instead, you call the static method CompletableFuture.supplyAsync:

```
CompletableFuture<String> f = CompletableFuture.supplyAsync(
    () -> { String result; Compute the result; return result; },
    executor);
```

If you omit the executor, the task is run on a default executor (namely the executor returned by ForkJoinPool.commonPool()).

Note that the first argument of this method is a Supplier<T>, not a Callable<T>. Both interfaces describe functions with no arguments and a return value of type T, but a Supplier function cannot throw a checked exception.

A CompletableFuture can complete in two ways: either with a result, or with an uncaught exception. In order to handle both cases, use the whenComplete method. The supplied function is called with the result (or null if none) and the exception (or null if none).

```
f.whenComplete((s, t) -> {
    if (t == null) { Process the result s; }
    else { Process the Throwable t; }
});
```

The CompletableFuture is called completable because you can manually set a completion value. (In other concurrency libraries, such an object is called a *promise*). Of course, when you create a CompletableFuture with supplyAsync, the completion value is implicitly set when the task has finished. But setting the result explicitly gives you additional flexibility. For example, two tasks can work simultaneously on computing an answer:

```
CompletableFuture<Integer> f = new CompletableFuture<>();
executor.execute(() -> {
    int n = workHard(arg);
    f.complete(n);
});
executor.execute(() -> {
    int n = workSmart(arg);
    f.complete(n);
});
```

To instead complete a future with an exception, call

```
Throwable t = ...;
f.completeExceptionally(t);
```

 NOTE: It is safe to call complete or completeExceptionally on the same future in multiple threads. If the future is already completed, these calls have no effect.

The isDone method tells you whether a Future object has been completed (normally or with an exception). In the preceding example, the workHard and workSmart methods can use that information to stop working when the result has been determined by the other method.

CAUTION: Unlike a plain `Future`, the computation of a `CompletableFuture` is not interrupted when you invoke its `cancel` method. Canceling simply sets the `Future` object to be completed exceptionally, with a `CancellationException`. In general, this makes sense since a `CompletableFuture` may not have a single thread that is responsible for its completion. However, this restriction also applies to `CompletableFuture` instances returned by methods such as `supplyAsync`, which could in principle be interrupted. See Exercise 27 for a workaround.

10.2.2 Composing Completable Futures

Nonblocking calls are implemented through callbacks. The programmer registers a callback for the action that should occur after a task completes. Of course, if the next action is also asynchronous, the next action after that is in a different callback. Even though the programmer thinks in terms of "first do step 1, then step 2, then step 3," the program logic can become dispersed in "callback hell." It gets even worse when you have to add error handling. Suppose step 2 is "the user logs in." You may need to repeat that step since the user can mistype the credentials. Trying to implement such a control flow in a set of callbacks—or to understand it once it has been implemented—can be quite challenging.

The `CompletableFuture` class solves this problem by providing a mechanism for *composing* asynchronous tasks into a processing pipeline.

For example, suppose we want to extract all links from a web page in order to build a web crawler. Let's say we have a method

```
public void CompletableFuture<String> readPage(URI url)
```

that yields the text of a web page when it becomes available. If the method

```
public static List<URI> getLinks(String page)
```

yields the URIs in an HTML page, you can schedule it to be called when the page is available:

```
CompletableFuture<String> contents = readPage(url);
CompletableFuture<List<URI>> links = contents.thenApply(Parser::getLinks);
```

The `thenApply` method doesn't block either. It returns another future. When the first future has completed, its result is fed to the `getLinks` method, and the return value of that method becomes the final result.

With completable futures, you just specify what you want to have done and in which order. It won't all happen right away, of course, but what is important is that all the code is in one place.

Conceptually, CompletableFuture is a simple API, but there are many variants of methods for composing completable futures. Let us first look at those that deal with a single future (see Table 10-1). (For each method shown, there are also two Async variants that I don't show. One of them uses a shared ForkJoinPool, and the other has an Executor parameter.) In the table, I use a shorthand notation for the ponderous functional interfaces, writing T -> U instead of Function<? super T, U>. These aren't actual Java types, of course.

You have already seen the thenApply method. Suppose f is a function that receives values of type T and returns values of type U. The calls

```
CompletableFuture<U> future.thenApply(f);
CompletableFuture<U> future.thenApplyAsync(f);
```

return a future that applies the function f to the result of future when it is available. The second call runs f in yet another thread.

The thenCompose method, instead of taking a function mapping the type T to the type U, receives a function mapping T to CompletableFuture<U>. That sounds rather abstract, but it can be quite natural. Consider the action of reading a web page from a given URL. Instead of supplying a method

```
public String blockingReadPage(URI url)
```

it is more elegant to have that method return a future:

```
public CompletableFuture<String> readPage(URI url)
```

Now, suppose we have another method that gets the URL from user input, perhaps from a dialog that won't reveal the answer until the user has clicked the OK button. That, too, is an event in the future:

```
public CompletableFuture<URI> getURLInput(String prompt)
```

Here we have two functions T -> CompletableFuture<U> and U -> CompletableFuture<V>. Clearly, they compose to a function T -> CompletableFuture<V> if the second function is called when the first one has completed. That is exactly what thenCompose does.

In the preceding section, you saw the whenComplete method for handling exceptions. There is also a handle method that requires a function processing the result or exception and computing a new result. In many cases, it is simpler to call the exceptionally method instead:

```
CompletableFuture<String> contents = readPage(url)
    .exceptionally(t -> { Log t; return emptyPage; });
```

The supplied handler is only called if an exception occurred, and it produces a result to be used in the processing pipeline. If no exception occurred, the original result is used.

The methods in Table 10-1 with void result are normally used at the end of a processing pipeline.

Table 10-1 Adding an Action to a CompletableFuture<T> Object

Method	Parameter	Description
thenApply	T -> U	Apply a function to the result.
thenAccept	T -> void	Like thenApply, but with void result.
thenCompose	T -> CompletableFuture<U>	Invoke the function on the result and execute the returned future.
handle	(T, Throwable) -> U	Process the result or error and yield a new result.
whenComplete	(T, Throwable) -> void	Like handle, but with void result.
exceptionally	Throwable -> T	Turn the error into a default result.
thenRun	Runnable	Execute the Runnable with void result.

Now let us turn to methods that combine multiple futures (see Table 10-2).

The first three methods run a CompletableFuture<T> and a CompletableFuture<U> action concurrently and combine the results.

The next three methods run two CompletableFuture<T> actions concurrently. As soon as one of them finishes, its result is passed on, and the other result is ignored.

Finally, the static allOf and anyOf methods take a variable number of completable futures and yield a CompletableFuture<Void> that completes when all of them, or any one of them, completes. The allOf method does not yield a result. The anyOf method does *not* terminate the remaining tasks. Exercises 28 and 29 show useful improvements of these two methods.

 NOTE: Technically speaking, the methods in this section accept parameters of type CompletionStage, not CompletableFuture. The CompletionStage interface describes how to compose asynchronous computations, whereas the Future interface focuses on the result of a computation. A CompletableFuture is both a CompletionStage and a Future.

Table 10-2 Combining Multiple Composition Objects

Method	Parameters	Description
thenCombine	CompletableFuture<U>, (T, U) -> V	Execute both and combine the results with the given function.
thenAcceptBoth	CompletableFuture<U>, (T, U) -> void	Like thenCombine, but with void result.
runAfterBoth	CompletableFuture<?>, Runnable	Execute the runnable after both complete.
applyToEither	CompletableFuture<T>, T -> V	When a result is available from one or the other, pass it to the given function.
acceptEither	CompletableFuture<T>, T -> void	Like applyToEither, but with void result.
runAfterEither	CompletableFuture<?>, Runnable	Execute the runnable after one or the other completes.
static allOf	CompletableFuture<?>...	Complete with void result after all given futures complete.
static anyOf	CompletableFuture<?>...	Complete after any of the given futures completes and yield its result.

10.2.3 Long-Running Tasks in User-Interface Callbacks

One of the reasons to use threads is to make your programs more responsive. This is particularly important in an application with a user interface. When your program needs to do something time-consuming, you cannot do the work in the user-interface thread, or the user interface will freeze. Instead, fire up another worker thread.

For example, if you want to read a web page when the user clicks a button, don't do this:

```
Button read = new Button("Read");
read.setOnAction(event -> { // Bad—long-running action is executed on UI thread
    Scanner in = new Scanner(url.openStream());
    while (in.hasNextLine()) {
        String line = in.nextLine();
        ...
    }
});
```

Instead, do the work in a separate thread.

```
read.setOnAction(event -> { // Good—long-running action in separate thread
    Runnable task = () -> {
        Scanner in = new Scanner(url.openStream());
        while (in.hasNextLine()) {
            String line = in.nextLine();
            ...
        }
    }
    executor.execute(task);
});
```

However, you cannot directly update the user interface from the thread that executes the long-running task. User interfaces such as JavaFX, Swing, or Android are not threadsafe. You cannot manipulate user-interface elements from multiple threads, or they risk becoming corrupted. In fact, JavaFX and Android check for this, and throw an exception if you try to access the user interface from a thread other than the UI thread.

Therefore, you need to schedule any UI updates to happen on the UI thread. Each user-interface library provides some mechanism to schedule a Runnable for execution on the UI thread. For example, in JavaFX, you can use

```
Platform.runLater(() ->
    message.appendText(line + "\n"));
```

 NOTE: It is tedious to implement lengthy operations while giving users feedback on the progress, so user-interface libraries usually provide some kind of helper class for managing the details, such as SwingWorker in Swing and AsyncTask in Android. You specify actions for the long-running task (which is run on a separate thread), as well as progress updates and the final disposition (which are run on the UI thread).

The Task class in JavaFX takes a slightly different approach to progress updates. The class provides methods to update task properties (a message, completion percentage, and result value) in the long-running thread. You bind the properties to user-interface elements, which are then updated in the UI thread.

10.3 Thread Safety

Many programmers initially think that concurrent programming is pretty easy. You just divide your work into tasks, and that's it. What could possibly go wrong?

In the following sections, I show you what can go wrong, and give a high-level overview of what you can do about it.

10.3.1 Visibility

Even operations as simple as writing and reading a variable can be incredibly complicated with modern processors. Consider this example:

```
private static boolean done = false;

public static void main(String[] args) {
    Runnable hellos = () -> {
        for (int i = 1; i <= 1000; i++)
            System.out.println("Hello " + i);
        done = true;
    };
    Runnable goodbye = () -> {
        int i = 1;
        while (!done) i++;
        System.out.println("Goodbye " + i);
    };
    Executor executor = Executors.newCachedThreadPool();
    executor.execute(hellos);
    executor.execute(goodbye);
}
```

The first task prints "Hello" a thousand times, and then sets done to true. The second task waits for done to become true, and then prints "Goodbye" once, incrementing a counter while it is waiting for that happy moment.

You'd expect the output to be something like

```
Hello 1
...
Hello 1000
Goodbye 501249
```

When I run this program on my laptop, the program prints up to "Hello 1000" and never terminates. The effect of

```
done = true;
```

may not be *visible* to the thread running the second task.

Why wouldn't it be visible? Modern compilers, virtual machines, and processors perform many optimizations. These optimizations assume that the code is sequential unless explicitly told otherwise.

One optimization is caching of memory locations. We think of a memory location such as done as bits somewhere in the transistors of a RAM chip. But RAM chips are slow—many times slower than modern processors. Therefore, a processor tries to hold the data that it needs in registers or an onboard memory cache, and eventually writes changes back to memory. This caching is simply indispensable for processor performance. There are operations for synchronizing cached copies, but they have a significant performance cost and are only issued when requested.

Another optimization is instruction reordering. The compiler, the virtual machine, and the processor are allowed to change the order of instructions to speed up operations, provided it does not change the sequential semantics of the program.

For example, consider a computation

```
x = Something not involving y;
y = Something not involving x;
z = x + y;
```

The first two steps must occur before the third, but they can occur in either order. A processor can (and often will) run the first two steps concurrently, or swap the order if the inputs to the second step are more quickly available.

In our case, the loop

```
while (!done) i++;
```

can be reordered as

```
if (!done) while (true) i++;
```

since the loop body does not change the value of done.

By default, optimizations assume that there are no concurrent memory accesses. If there are, the virtual machine needs to know, so that it can then emit processor instructions that inhibit improper reorderings.

There are several ways of ensuring that an update to a variable is visible. Here is a summary:

1. The value of a final variable is visible after initialization.

2. The initial value of a static variable is visible after static initialization.

3. Changes to a volatile variable are visible.

4. Changes that happen before releasing a lock are visible to anyone acquiring the same lock (see Section 10.7.1, "Locks," page 357).

In our case, the problem goes away if you declare the shared variable done with the volatile modifier:

```
private static volatile boolean done;
```

Then the compiler generates instructions that cause the virtual machine to issue processor commands for cache synchronization. As a result, any change to done in one task becomes visible to the other tasks.

The volatile modifier happens to suffice to solve this particular problem. But as you will see in the next section, declaring shared variables as volatile is not a general solution.

 TIP: It is an excellent idea to declare any field that does not change after initialization as final. Then you never have to worry about its visibility.

10.3.2 Race Conditions

Suppose multiple concurrent tasks update a shared integer counter.

```
private static volatile int count = 0;
...
count++; // Task 1
...
count++; // Task 2
...
```

The variable has been declared as volatile, so the updates are visible. But that is not enough.

The update count++ actually means

```
register = count + 1;
count = register;
```

When these computations are interleaved, the wrong value can be stored back into the count variable. In the parlance of concurrency, we say that the increment operation is not *atomic*. Consider this scenario:

```
int count = 0; // Initial value
register₁ = count + 1; // Thread 1 computes count + 1
... // Thread 1 is preempted
register₂ = count + 1; // Thread 2 computes count + 1
count = register₂; // Thread 2 stores 1 in count
... // Thread 1 is running again
count = register₁; // Thread 1 stores 1 in count
```

Now count is 1, not 2. This kind of error is called a *race condition* because it depends on which thread wins the "race" for updating the shared variable.

Does this problem really happen? It certainly does. Run the demo program of the companion code. It has 100 threads, each incrementing the counter 1,000 times and printing the result.

```
for (int i = 1; i <= 100; i++) {
    int taskId = i;
    Runnable task = () -> {
        for (int k = 1; k <= 1000; k++)
            count++;
        System.out.println(taskId + ": " + count);
    };
    executor.execute(task);
}
```

The output usually starts harmlessly enough as something like

```
1: 1000
3: 2000
2: 3000
6: 4000
```

After a while, it looks a bit scary:

```
72: 58196
68: 59196
73: 61196
71: 60196
69: 62196
```

But that might just be because some threads were paused at inopportune moments. What matters is what happens with the task that finished last. Did it bring up the counter to 100,000?

I ran the program dozens of times on my multi-core laptop, and it fails every time. Years ago, when personal computers had a single CPU, race conditions were more difficult to observe, and programmers did not notice such dramatic failures often. But it doesn't matter whether a wrong value is computed within seconds or hours.

This example looks at the simple case of a shared counter in a toy program. Exercise 17 shows the same problem in a realistic example. But it's not just counters. Race conditions are a problem whenever shared variables are mutated. For example, when adding a value to the head of a queue, the insertion code might look like this:

```
Node n = new Node();
if (head == null) head = n;
else tail.next = n;
tail = n;
tail.value = newValue;
```

Lots of things can go wrong if this sequence of instructions is paused at an unfortunate time and another task gets control, accessing the queue while it is in an inconsistent state.

Work through Exercise 21 to get a feel for how a data structure can get corrupted by concurrent mutation.

We need to ensure that the entire sequence of operation is carried out together. Such an instruction sequence is called a *critical section*. You can use a *lock* to protect critical sections and make critical sequences of operation atomic. You will learn how to program with locks in Section 10.7.1, "Locks" (page 357).

While it is straightforward to use locks for protecting critical sections, locks are not a general solution for solving all concurrency problems. They are difficult to use properly, and it is easy to make mistakes that severely degrade performance or even cause "deadlock."

10.3.3 Strategies for Safe Concurrency

In languages such as C and C++, programmers need to manually allocate and deallocate memory. That sounds dangerous—and it is. Many programmers have spent countless miserable hours chasing memory allocation bugs. In Java, there is a garbage collector, and few Java programmers need to worry about memory management.

Unfortunately, there is no equivalent mechanism for shared data access in a concurrent program. The best you can do is to follow a set of guidelines to manage the inherent dangers.

A highly effective strategy is *confinement*. Just say no when it comes to sharing data among tasks. For example, when your tasks need to count something, give each of them a private counter instead of updating a shared counter. When the tasks are done, they can hand off their results to another task that combines them.

Another good strategy is *immutability*. It is safe to share immutable objects. For example, instead of adding results to a shared collection, a task can generate an immutable collection of results. Another task combines the results into another immutable data structure. The idea is simple, but there are a few things to watch out for—see Section 10.3.4, "Immutable Classes" (page 347).

The third strategy is *locking*. By granting only one task at a time access to a data structure, one can keep it from being damaged. In Section 10.5, "Threadsafe Data Structures" (page 350), you will see data structures provided by the Java concurrency library that are safe to use concurrently. Section 10.7.1, "Locks" (page 357) shows you how locking works, and how experts build these data structures.

Locking is error-prone, and it can be expensive since it reduces opportunities for concurrent execution. For example, if you have lots of tasks contributing results to a shared hash table, and the table is locked for each update, then that is a real bottleneck. If most tasks have to wait their turn, they aren't doing useful work. Sometimes it is possible to *partition* data so that different pieces can be accessed concurrently. Several data structures in the Java concurrency library use partitioning, as do the parallel algorithms in the streams library. Don't try this at home! It is really hard to get it right. Instead, use the data structures and algorithms from the Java library.

10.3.4 Immutable Classes

A class is immutable when its instances, once constructed, cannot change. It sounds at first as if you can't do much with them, but that isn't true. The ubiquitous `String` class is immutable, as are the classes in the date and time library (see Chapter 12). Each date instance is immutable, but you can obtain new dates, such as the one that comes a day after a given one.

Or consider a set for collecting results. You could use a mutable `HashSet` and update it like this:

```
results.addAll(newResults);
```

But that is clearly dangerous.

An immutable set always creates new sets. You would update the results somewhat like this:

```
results = results.union(newResults);
```

There is still mutation, but it is much easier to control what happens to one variable than to a hash set with many methods.

It is not difficult to implement immutable classes, but you should pay attention to these issues:

1. Don't change the object state after construction. Be sure to declare instance variables `final`. There is no reason not to, and you gain an important advantage: the virtual machine ensures that a `final` instance variable is visible after construction (Section 10.3.1, "Visibility," page 342).

2. Of course, none of the methods can be mutators. You should make them `final`, or better, declare the class `final`, so that mutators cannot be added in subclasses.

3. Don't leak state that can be mutated externally. None of your (non-`private`) methods can return a reference to any innards that could be used for mutation, such as an internal array or collection. When one of your

methods calls a method of another class, it must not pass any such references either, since the called method might otherwise use them for mutation. Instead, pass a copy.

4. Conversely, don't store any reference to a mutable object that the constructor receives. Instead, make a copy.

5. Don't let the this reference escape in a constructor. When you call another method, you know not to pass any internal references, but what about this? That's perfectly safe after construction, but if you reveal this in the constructor, someone could observe the object in an incomplete state. Also beware of constructors giving out inner class references that contain a hidden this reference. Naturally, these situations are quite rare.

10.4 Parallel Algorithms

Before starting to parallelize your computations, you should check if the Java library has done this for you. The stream library or the Arrays class may already do what you need.

10.4.1 Parallel Streams

The stream library can automatically parallelize operations on large data sets. For example, if coll is a large collection of strings, and you want to find how many of them start with the letter A, call

```
long result = coll.parallelStream().filter(s -> s.startsWith("A")).count();
```

The parallelStream method yields a parallel stream. The stream is broken up into segments. The filtering and counting is done on each segment, and the results are combined. You don't need to worry about the details.

 CAUTION: When you use parallel streams with lambdas (for example, as the argument to filter and map in the preceding examples), be sure to stay away from unsafe mutation of shared objects.

For parallel streams to work well, a number of conditions need to be fulfilled:

• There needs to be enough data. There is a substantial overhead for parallel streams that is only repaid for large data sets.

• The data should be in memory. It would be inefficient to have to wait for the data to arrive.

- The stream should be efficiently splittable into subregions. A stream backed by an array or a balanced binary tree works well, but a linked list or the result of Stream.iterate does not.

- The stream operations should do a substantial amount of work. If the total work load is not large, it does not make sense to pay for the cost of setting up the concurrent computation.

- The stream operations should not block.

In other words, don't turn all your streams into parallel streams. Use parallel streams only when you do a substantial amount of sustained computational work on data that is already in memory.

10.4.2 Parallel Array Operations

The Arrays class has a number of parallelized operations. Just as with the parallel stream operations of the preceding sections, the operations break the array into sections, work on them concurrently, and combine the results.

The static Arrays.parallelSetAll method fills an array with values computed by a function. The function receives the element index and computes the value at that location.

```
Arrays.parallelSetAll(values, i -> i % 10);
   // Fills values with 0 1 2 3 4 5 6 7 8 9 0 1 2 ...
```

Clearly, this operation benefits from being parallelized. There are versions for all primitive type arrays and for object arrays.

The parallelSort method can sort an array of primitive values or objects. For example,

```
Arrays.parallelSort(words, Comparator.comparing(String::length));
```

With all methods, you can supply the bounds of a range, such as

```
Arrays.parallelSort(values, values.length / 2, values.length); // Sort the upper half
```

 NOTE: At first glance, it seems a bit odd that these methods have parallel in their names—the user shouldn't care how the setting or sorting happens. However, the API designers wanted to make it clear that the operations are parallelized. That way, users are on notice to avoid generator or comparison functions with side effects.

Finally, there is a parallelPrefix that is rather specialized—Exercise 4 gives a simple example.

For other parallel operations on arrays, turn the arrays into parallel streams. For example, to compute the sum of a long array of integers, call

```
long sum = IntStream.of(values).parallel().sum();
```

10.5 Threadsafe Data Structures

If multiple threads concurrently modify a data structure, such as a queue or hash table, it is easy to damage the internals of the data structure. For example, one thread may begin to insert a new element. Suppose it is preempted in the middle of rerouting links, and another thread starts traversing the same location. The second thread may follow invalid links and create havoc, perhaps throwing exceptions or even getting trapped in an infinite loop.

As you will see in Section 10.7.1, "Locks" (page 357), you can use locks to ensure that only one thread can access the data structure at a given point in time, blocking any others. But you can do better than that. The collections in the `java.util.concurrent` package have been cleverly implemented so that multiple threads can access them without blocking each other, provided they access different parts.

 NOTE: These collections yield *weakly consistent* iterators. That means that the iterators present elements appearing at onset of iteration, but may or may not reflect some or all of the modifications that were made after they were constructed. However, such an iterator will not throw a `ConcurrentModificationException`.

In contrast, an iterator of a collection in the `java.util` package throws a `ConcurrentModificationException` when the collection has been modified after construction of the iterator.

10.5.1 Concurrent Hash Maps

A `ConcurrentHashMap` is, first of all, a hash map whose operations are threadsafe. No matter how many threads operate on the map at the same time, the internals are not corrupted. Of course, some threads may be temporarily blocked, but the map can efficiently support a large number of concurrent readers and a certain number of concurrent writers.

But that is not enough. Suppose we want to use a map to count how often certain features are observed. As an example, suppose multiple threads encounter words, and we want to count their frequencies. Obviously, the following code for updating a count is not threadsafe:

```
ConcurrentHashMap<String, Long> map = new ConcurrentHashMap<>();
...
Long oldValue = map.get(word);
Long newValue = oldValue == null ? 1 : oldValue + 1;
map.put(word, newValue); // Error—might not replace oldValue
```

Another thread might be updating the exact same count at the same time.

To update a value safely, use the `compute` method. It is called with a key and a function to compute the new value. That function receives the key and the associated value, or `null` if there is none, and computes the new value. For example, here is how we can update a count:

```
map.compute(word, (k, v) -> v == null ? 1 : v + 1);
```

The `compute` method is *atomic*—no other thread can mutate the map entry while the computation is in progress.

There are also variants `computeIfPresent` and `computeIfAbsent` that only compute a new value when there is already an old one, or when there isn't yet one.

Another atomic operation is `putIfAbsent`. A counter might be initialized as

```
map.putIfAbsent(word, 0L);
```

You often need to do something special when a key is added for the first time. The `merge` method makes this particularly convenient. It has a parameter for the initial value that is used when the key is not yet present. Otherwise, the function that you supplied is called, combining the existing value and the initial value. (Unlike `compute`, the function does not process the key.)

```
map.merge(word, 1L, (existingValue, newValue) -> existingValue + newValue);
```

or simply,

```
map.merge(word, 1L, Long::sum);
```

Of course, the functions passed to `compute` and `merge` should complete quickly, and they should not attempt to mutate the map.

NOTE: There are methods that atomically remove or replace an entry if it is currently equal to an existing one. Before the `compute` method was available, people would write code like this for incrementing a count:

```
do {
    oldValue = map.get(word);
    newValue = oldValue + 1;
} while (!map.replace(word, oldValue, newValue));
```

NOTE: There are several *bulk operations* for searching, transforming, or visiting a ConcurrentHashMap. They operate on a snapshot of the data and can safely execute even while other threads operate on the map. In the API documentation, look for the operations whose names start with search, reduce, and forEach. There are variants that operate on the keys, values, and entries. The reduce methods have specializations for int-, long-, and double-valued reduction functions.

10.5.2 Blocking Queues

One commonly used tool for coordinating work between tasks is a *blocking queue*. Producer tasks insert items into the queue, and consumer tasks retrieve them. The queue lets you safely hand over data from one task to another.

When you try to add an element and the queue is currently full, or you try to remove an element when the queue is empty, the operation blocks. In this way, the queue balances the workload. If the producer tasks run slower than the consumer tasks, the consumers block while waiting for the results. If the producers run faster, the queue fills up until the consumers catch up.

Table 10-3 shows the methods for blocking queues. The blocking queue methods fall into three categories that differ by the action they perform when the queue is full or empty. In addition to the blocking methods, there are methods that throw an exception when they don't succeed, and methods that return with a failure indicator instead of throwing an exception if they cannot carry out their tasks.

 NOTE: The poll and peek methods return null to indicate failure. Therefore, it is illegal to insert null values into these queues.

There are also variants of the offer and poll methods with a timeout. For example, the call

```
boolean success = q.offer(x, 100, TimeUnit.MILLISECONDS);
```

tries for 100 milliseconds to insert an element to the tail of the queue. If it succeeds, it returns true; otherwise, it returns false when it times out. Similarly, the call

```
Object head = q.poll(100, TimeUnit.MILLISECONDS)
```

Table 10-3 Blocking Queue Operations

Method	Normal Action	Error Action
put	Adds an element to the tail	Blocks if the queue is full
take	Removes and returns the head element	Blocks if the queue is empty
add	Adds an element to the tail	Throws an IllegalStateException if the queue is full
remove	Removes and returns the head element	Throws a NoSuchElementException if the queue is empty
element	Returns the head element	Throws a NoSuchElementException if the queue is empty
offer	Adds an element and returns true	Returns false if the queue is full
poll	Removes and returns the head element	Returns null if the queue is empty
peek	Returns the head element	Returns null if the queue is empty

tries for 100 milliseconds to remove the head of the queue. If it succeeds, it returns the head; otherwise, it returns null when it times out.

The java.util.concurrent package supplies several variations of blocking queues. A LinkedBlockingQueue is based on a linked list, and an ArrayBlockingQueue uses a circular array.

Exercise 11 shows how to use blocking queues for analyzing files in a directory. One thread walks the file tree and inserts files into a queue. Several threads remove the files and search them. In this application, it is likely that the producer quickly fills up the queue with files and blocks until the consumers can catch up.

A common challenge with such a design is stopping the consumers. A consumer cannot simply quit when the queue is empty. After all, the producer might not yet have started, or it may have fallen behind. If there is a single producer, it can add a "last item" indicator to the queue, similar to a dummy suitcase with a label "last bag" in a baggage claim belt.

10.5.3 Other Threadsafe Data Structures

Just like you can choose between hash maps and tree maps in the `java.util` package, there is a concurrent map that is based on comparing keys, called `ConcurrentSkipListMap`. Use it if you need to traverse the keys in sorted order, or if you need one of the added methods in the `NavigableMap` interface (see Chapter 7). Similarly, there is a `ConcurrentSkipListSet`.

The `CopyOnWriteArrayList` and `CopyOnWriteArraySet` are threadsafe collections in which all mutators make a copy of the underlying array. This arrangement is useful if the threads that iterate over the collection greatly outnumber the threads that mutate it. When you construct an iterator, it contains a reference to the current array. If the array is later mutated, the iterator still has the old array, but the collection's array is replaced. As a consequence, the older iterator has a consistent (but potentially outdated) view that it can access without any synchronization expense.

Suppose you want a large, threadsafe set instead of a map. There is no `ConcurrentHashSet` class, and you know better than trying to create your own. Of course, you can use a `ConcurrentHashMap` with bogus values, but that gives you a map, not a set, and you can't apply operations of the `Set` interface.

The static `newKeySet` method yields a `Set<K>` that is actually a wrapper around a `ConcurrentHashMap<K, Boolean>`. (All map values are `Boolean.TRUE`, but you don't actually care since you just use it as a set.)

```
Set<String> words = ConcurrentHashMap.newKeySet();
```

If you have an existing map, the `keySet` method yields the set of keys. That set is mutable. If you remove the set's elements, the keys (and their values) are removed from the map. But it doesn't make sense to add elements to the key set, because there would be no corresponding values to add. You can use a second `keySet` method, with a default value used when adding elements to the set:

```
Set<String> words = map.keySet(1L);
words.add("Java");
```

If `"Java"` wasn't already present in `words`, it now has a value of one.

10.6 Atomic Counters and Accumulators

If multiple threads update a shared counter, you need to make sure that this is done in a threadsafe way. There are a number of classes in the `java.util.concurrent.atomic` package that use safe and efficient machine-level instructions to guarantee atomicity of operations on integers, `long` and `boolean` values, object references, and arrays thereof. Using these classes correctly requires considerable expertise. However, atomic counters and accumulators are convenient for application-level programming.

For example, you can safely generate a sequence of numbers like this:

```
public static AtomicLong nextNumber = new AtomicLong();
// In some thread . . .
long id = nextNumber.incrementAndGet();
```

The `incrementAndGet` method atomically increments the `AtomicLong` and returns the post-increment value. That is, the operations of getting the value, adding 1, setting it, and producing the new value cannot be interrupted. It is guaranteed that the correct value is computed and returned, even if multiple threads access the same instance concurrently.

There are methods for atomically setting, adding, and subtracting values, but suppose you want to make a more complex update. One way is to use the `updateAndGet` method. For example, suppose you want to keep track of the largest value that is observed by different threads. The following won't work:

```
public static AtomicLong largest = new AtomicLong();
// In some thread . . .
largest.set(Math.max(largest.get(), observed)); // Error—race condition!
```

This update is not atomic. Instead, call `updateAndGet` with a lambda expression for updating the variable. In our example, we can call

```
largest.updateAndGet(x -> Math.max(x, observed));
```

or

```
largest.accumulateAndGet(observed, Math::max);
```

The `accumulateAndGet` method takes a binary operator that is used to combine the atomic value and the supplied argument.

There are also methods `getAndUpdate` and `getAndAccumulate` that return the old value.

 NOTE: These methods are also provided for the classes:

`AtomicInteger`	`AtomicLongFieldUpdater`
`AtomicIntegerArray`	`AtomicReference`
`AtomicIntegerFieldUpdater`	`AtomicReferenceArray`
`AtomicLongArray`	`AtomicReferenceFieldUpdater`

When you have a very large number of threads accessing the same atomic values, performance suffers because updates are carried out *optimistically*. That is, the operation computes a new value from a given old value, then does the replacement provided the old value is still the current one, or retries if it is not. Under heavy contention, updates require too many retries.

The classes LongAdder and LongAccumulator solve this problem for certain common updates. A LongAdder is composed of multiple variables whose collective sum is the current value. Multiple threads can update different summands, and new summands are automatically provided when the number of threads increases. This is efficient in the common situation where the value of the sum is not needed until after all work has been done. The performance improvement can be substantial—see Exercise 9.

If you anticipate high contention, you should simply use a LongAdder instead of an AtomicLong. The method names are slightly different. Call increment to increment a counter or add to add a quantity, and sum to retrieve the total.

```
final LongAdder count = new LongAdder();
for (...)
    executor.execute(() -> {
        while (...) {
            ...
            if (...) count.increment();
        }
    });
...
long total = count.sum();
```

 NOTE: Of course, the increment method does *not* return the old value. Doing that would undo the efficiency gain of splitting the sum into multiple summands.

The LongAccumulator generalizes this idea to an arbitrary accumulation operation. In the constructor, you provide the operation as well as its neutral element. To incorporate new values, call accumulate. Call get to obtain the current value.

```
LongAccumulator accumulator = new LongAccumulator(Long::sum, 0);
// In some tasks . . .
accumulator.accumulate(value);
// When all work is done
long sum = accumulator.get();
```

Internally, the accumulator has variables a_1, a_2, ..., a_n. Each variable is initialized with the neutral element (0 in our example).

When accumulate is called with value v, then one of them is atomically updated as $a_i = a_i \ op \ v$, where *op* is the accumulation operation written in infix form. In our example, a call to accumulate computes $a_i = a_i + v$ for some i.

The result of get is a_1 op a_2 op ... op a_n. In our example, that is the sum of the accumulators, $a_1 + a_2 + ... + a_n$.

If you choose a different operation, you can compute maximum or minimum (see Exercise 10). In general, the operation must be associative and commutative. That means that the final result must be independent of the order in which the intermediate values were combined.

There are also DoubleAdder and DoubleAccumulator that work in the same way, except with double values.

 TIP: If you use a hash map of LongAdder, you can use the following idiom to increment the adder for a key:

```
ConcurrentHashMap<String,LongAdder> counts = ...;
counts.computeIfAbsent(key, k -> new LongAdder()).increment();
```

When the count for key is incremented the first time, a new adder is set.

10.7 Locks and Conditions

Now you have seen several tools that application programmers can safely use for structuring concurrent applications. You may be curious how one would build a threadsafe counter or blocking queue. The following sections show you how it is done, so that you gain some understanding of the costs and complexities.

10.7.1 Locks

To avoid the corruption of shared variables, one needs to ensure that only one thread at a time can compute and set the new values. Code that must be executed in its entirety, without interruption, is called a *critical section*. One can use a *lock* to implement a critical section:

```
Lock countLock = new ReentrantLock(); // Shared among multiple threads
int count; // Shared among multiple threads
...
countLock.lock();
try {
    count++; // Critical section
} finally {
    countLock.unlock(); // Make sure the lock is unlocked
}
```

NOTE: In this section, I use the `ReentrantLock` class to explain how locking works. As you will see in the next section, there is no requirement to use explicit locks since there are "implicit" locks that are used by the `synchronized` keyword. But it is easier to understand what goes on under the hood by looking at explicit locks.

The first thread to execute the `lock` method locks the `countLock` object and then proceeds into the critical section. If another thread tries to call `lock` on the same object, it is blocked until the first thread executes the call to `unlock`. In this way, it is guaranteed that only one thread at a time can execute the critical section.

Note that, by placing the `unlock` method into a `finally` clause, the lock is released if any exception happens in the critical section. Otherwise, the lock would be permanently locked, and no other thread would be able to proceed past it. This would clearly be very bad. Of course, in this case, the critical section can't throw an exception since it only executes an integer increment. But it is a common idiom to use the `try`/`finally` statement anyway, in case more code gets added later.

At first glance, it seems simple enough to use locks for protecting critical sections. However, the devil is in the details. Experience has shown that many programmers have difficulty writing correct code with locks. They might use the wrong locks, or create situations that *deadlock* when no thread can make progress because all of them wait for a lock.

For that reason, application programmers should use locks as a matter of last resort. First try to avoid sharing, by using immutable data or handing off mutable data from one thread to another. If you must share, use prebuilt threadsafe structures such as a `ConcurrentHashMap` or a `LongAdder`. Still, it is useful to know about locks so you can understand how such data structures can be implemented.

10.7.2 The synchronized Keyword

In the preceding section, I showed you how to use a `ReentrantLock` to implement a critical section. You don't have to use an explicit lock because in Java, *every object* has an *intrinsic lock*. To understand intrinsic locks, however, it helps to have seen explicit locks first.

The `synchronized` keyword is used to lock the intrinsic lock. It can occur in two forms. You can lock a block:

```
synchronized (obj) {
    Critical section
}
```

This essentially means

```
obj.intrinsicLock.lock();
try {
    Critical section
} finally {
    obj.intrinsicLock.unlock();
}
```

An object does not actually have a field that is an intrinsic lock. The code is just meant to illustrate what goes on when you use the synchronized keyword.

You can also declare a method as synchronized. Then its body is locked on the receiver parameter this. That is,

```
public synchronized void method() {
    Body
}
```

is the equivalent of

```
public void method() {
    this.intrinsicLock.lock();
    try {
        Body
    } finally {
        this.intrinsicLock.unlock();
    }
}
```

For example, a counter can simply be declared as

```
public class Counter {
    private int value;
    public synchronized int increment() {
        value++;
        return value;
    }
}
```

By using the intrinsic lock of the Counter instance, there is no need to come up with an explicit lock.

As you can see, using the synchronized keyword yields code that is quite concise. Of course, to understand this code, you have to know that each object has an intrinsic lock.

NOTE: There is more to locks than atomicity. Locks also guarantee visibility. For example, consider the `done` variable that gave us so much grief in Section 10.3.1, "Visibility" (page 342). If you use a lock for both writing and reading the variable, then you are assured that the caller of `get` sees any update to the variable through a call by `set`.

```
public class Flag {
    private boolean done;
    public synchronized void set() { done = true; }
    public synchronized boolean get() { return done; }
}
```

Synchronized methods were inspired by the *monitor* concept that was pioneered by Per Brinch Hansen and Tony Hoare in the 1970s. A monitor is essentially a class in which all instance variables are private and all methods are protected by a private lock.

In Java, it is possible to have public instance variables and to mix synchronized and unsynchronized methods. More problematically, the intrinsic lock is publicly accessible.

Many programmers find this confusing. For example, Java 1.0 has a `Hashtable` class with synchronized methods for mutating the table. To safely iterate over such a table, you can acquire the lock like this:

```
synchronized (table) {
    for (K key : table.keySet()) ...
}
```

Here, `table` denotes both the hash table and the lock that its methods use. This is a common source of misunderstandings—see Exercise 22.

10.7.3 Waiting on Conditions

Consider a simple `Queue` class with methods for adding and removing objects. Synchronizing the methods ensures that these operations are atomic.

```
public class Queue {
    class Node { Object value; Node next; };
    private Node head;
    private Node tail;

    public synchronized void add(Object newValue) {
        Node n = new Node();
        if (head == null) head = n;
        else tail.next = n;
        tail = n;
```

```
        tail.value = newValue;
    }

    public synchronized Object remove() {
        if (head == null) return null;
        Node n = head;
        head = n.next;
        return n.value;
    }
}
```

Now suppose we want to turn the remove method into a method take that blocks if the queue is empty.

The check for emptiness must come inside the synchronized method because otherwise the inquiry would be meaningless—another thread might have emptied the queue in the meantime.

```
public synchronized Object take() {
    if (head == null) ... // Now what?
    Node n = head;
    head = n.next;
    return n.value;
}
```

But what should happen if the queue is empty? No other thread can add elements while the current thread holds the lock. This is where the wait method comes in.

If the take method finds that it cannot proceed, it calls the wait method:

```
public synchronized Object take() throws InterruptedException {
    while (head == null) wait();
    ...
}
```

The current thread is now deactivated and gives up the lock. This lets in another thread that can, we hope, add elements to the queue. This is called *waiting on a condition*.

Note that the wait method is a method of the Object class. It relates to the lock that is associated with the object.

There is an essential difference between a thread that is blocking to acquire a lock and a thread that has called wait. Once a thread calls the wait method, it enters a *wait set* for the object. The thread is not made runnable when the lock is available. Instead, it stays deactivated until another thread has called the notifyAll method on the same object.

When another thread has added an element, it should call that method:

```
public synchronized void add(Object newValue) {
    ...
    notifyAll();
}
```

The call to notifyAll reactivates all threads in the wait set. When the threads are removed from the wait set, they are again runnable and the scheduler will eventually activate them again. At that time, they will attempt to reacquire the lock. As one of them succeeds, it continues where it left off, returning from the call to wait.

At this time, the thread should test the condition again. There is no guarantee that the condition is now fulfilled—the notifyAll method merely signals to the waiting threads that it *may be* fulfilled at this time and that it is worth checking for the condition again. For that reason, the test is in a loop

```
while (head == null) wait();
```

A thread can only call wait, notifyAll, or notify on an object if it holds the lock on that object.

 CAUTION: Another method, notify, unblocks only a single thread from the wait set. That is more efficient than unblocking all threads, but there is a danger. If the chosen thread finds that it still cannot proceed, it becomes blocked again. If no other thread calls notify again, the program deadlocks.

 NOTE: When implementing data structures with blocking methods, the wait, notify, and notifyAll methods are appropriate. But they are not easy to use properly. Application programmers should never have a need to use these methods. Instead, use prebuilt data structures such as LinkedBlockingQueue or ConcurrentHashMap.

10.8 Threads

As we are nearing the end of this chapter, the time has finally come to talk about threads, the primitives that actually execute tasks. Normally, you are better off using executors that manage threads for you, but the following sections give you some background information about working directly with threads.

10.8.1 Starting a Thread

Here is how to run a thread in Java:

```
Runnable task = () -> { ... };
Thread thread = new Thread(task);
thread.start();
```

The static `sleep` method makes the current thread sleep for a given period, so that some other threads have a chance to do work.

```
Runnable task = () -> {
    ...
    Thread.sleep(millis);
    ...
}
```

If you want to wait for a thread to finish, call the `join` method:

```
thread.join(millis);
```

These two methods throw the checked `InterruptedException` that is discussed in the next section.

A thread ends when its `run` method returns, either normally or because an exception was thrown. In the latter case, the *uncaught exception handler* of the thread is invoked. When the thread is created, that handler is set to the uncaught exception handler of the thread group, which is ultimately the global handler (see Chapter 5). You can change the handler of a thread by calling the `setUncaughtExceptionHandler` method.

 NOTE: The initial release of Java defined a `stop` method that immediately terminates a thread, and a `suspend` method that blocks a thread until another thread calls `resume`. Both methods have since been deprecated.

The `stop` method is inherently unsafe. Suppose a thread is stopped in the middle of a critical section—for example, inserting an element into a queue. Then the queue is left in a partially updated state. However, the lock protecting the critical section is unlocked, and other threads can use the corrupted data structure. You should interrupt a thread when you want it to stop. The interrupted thread can then stop when it is safe to do so.

The `suspend` method is not as risky but still problematic. If a thread is suspended while it holds a lock, any other thread trying to acquire that lock blocks. If the resuming thread is among them, the program deadlocks.

10.8.2 Thread Interruption

Suppose that, for a given query, you are always satisfied with the first result. When the search for an answer is distributed over multiple tasks, you want to cancel all others as soon as the answer is obtained. In Java, task cancellation is *cooperative*.

Each thread has an *interrupted status* that indicates that someone would like to "interrupt" the thread. There is no precise definition of what interruption means, but most programmers use it to indicate a cancellation request.

A Runnable can check for this status, which is typically done in a loop:

```
Runnable task = () -> {
    while (more work to do) {
        if (Thread.currentThread().isInterrupted()) return;
        Do more work
    }
};
```

When the thread is interrupted, the run method simply ends.

 NOTE: There is also a static Thread.interrupted method which gets the interrupted status of the current thread, then clears it, and returns the old status.

Sometimes, a thread becomes temporarily inactive. That can happen if a thread waits for a value to be computed by another thread or for input/output, or if it goes to sleep to give other threads a chance.

If the thread is interrupted while it waits or sleeps, it is immediately reactivated—but in this case, the interrupted status is not set. Instead, an InterruptedException is thrown. This is a checked exception, and you must catch it inside the run method of a Runnable. The usual reaction to the exception is to end the run method:

```
Runnable task = () -> {
    try {
        while (more work to do) {
            Do more work
            Thread.sleep(millis);
        }
    }
    catch (InterruptedException ex) {
        // Do nothing
    }
};
```

When you catch the InterruptedException in this way, there is no need to check for the interrupted status. If the thread was interrupted outside the call to Thread.sleep, the status is set and the Thread.sleep method throws an InterruptedException as soon as it is called.

 TIP: The InterruptedException may seem pesky, but you should not just catch and hide it when you call a method such as sleep. If you can't do anything else, at least set the interrupted status:

```
try {
    Thread.sleep(millis);
} catch (InterruptedException ex) {
    Thread.currentThread().interrupt();
}
```

Or better, simply propagate the exception to a competent handler:

```
public void mySubTask() throws InterruptedException {
    ...
    Thread.sleep(millis);
    ...
}
```

10.8.3 Thread–Local Variables

Sometimes, you can avoid sharing by giving each thread its own instance, using the ThreadLocal helper class. For example, the NumberFormat class is not threadsafe. Suppose we have a static variable

```
public static final NumberFormat currencyFormat = NumberFormat.getCurrencyInstance();
```

If two threads execute an operation such as

```
String amountDue = currencyFormat.format(total);
```

then the result can be garbage since the internal data structures used by the NumberFormat instance can be corrupted by concurrent access. You could use a lock or provide a synchronized method to ensure atomic access to the shared NumberFormat variable. Alternatively, you could construct a local NumberFormat object whenever you need it, but that is also wasteful.

To construct one instance per thread, use the following code:

```
public static final ThreadLocal<NumberFormat> currencyFormat
    = ThreadLocal.withInitial(() -> NumberFormat.getCurrencyInstance());
```

To access the actual formatter, call

```
String amountDue = currencyFormat.get().format(total);
```

The first time you call get in a given thread, the lambda expression in the constructor is called to create the instance for the thread. From then on, the get method returns the instance belonging to the current thread.

10.8.4 Miscellaneous Thread Properties

The Thread class exposes a number of properties for threads, but most of them are more useful for students of certification exams than application programmers. This section briefly reviews them.

Threads can be collected in groups, and there are API methods to manage thread groups, such as interrupting all threads in a group. Nowadays, executors are the preferred mechanism for managing groups of tasks.

You can set *priorities* for threads, where high-priority threads are scheduled to run before lower-priority ones. Hopefully, priorities are honored by the virtual machine and the host platform, but the details are highly platform-dependent. Therefore, using priorities is fragile and not generally recommended.

Threads have *states*, and you can tell whether a thread is new, running, blocked on input/output, waiting, or terminated. When you use threads as an application programmer, you rarely have a reason to inquire about their states.

Threads have names, and you can change the name for debugging purposes. For example:

```
Thread.currentThread().setName("Bitcoin-miner-1");
```

When a thread terminates due to an uncaught exception, the exception is passed to the thread's *uncaught exception handler*. By default, its stack trace is dumped to System.err, but you can install your own handler (see Chapter 5).

A *daemon* is a thread that has no other role in life than to serve others. This is useful for threads that send timer ticks or clean up stale cache entries. When only daemon threads remain, the virtual machine exits.

To make a daemon thread, call thread.setDaemon(true) before starting the thread.

10.9 Processes

Up to now, you have seen how to execute Java code in separate threads within the same program. Sometimes, you need to execute another program. For this, use the ProcessBuilder and Process classes. The Process class executes a command in a separate operating system process and lets you interact with its standard input, output, and error streams. The `ProcessBuilder` class lets you configure a `Process` object.

 NOTE: The `ProcessBuilder` class is a more flexible replacement for the `Runtime.exec` calls.

10.9.1 Building a Process

Start the building process by specifying the command that you want to execute. You can supply a `List<String>` or simply the strings that make up the command.

```
ProcessBuilder builder = new ProcessBuilder("gcc", "myapp.c");
```

 CAUTION: The first string must be an executable command, not a shell builtin. For example, to run the `dir` command in Windows, you need to build a process with strings `"cmd.exe"`, `"/C"`, and `"dir"`.

Each process has a *working directory*, which is used to resolve relative directory names. By default, a process has the same working directory as the virtual machine, which is typically the directory from which you launched the `java` program. You can change it with the `directory` method:

```
builder = builder.directory(path.toFile());
```

 NOTE: Each of the methods for configuring a `ProcessBuilder` returns itself, so that you can chain commands. Ultimately, you will call

```
Process p = new ProcessBuilder(command).directory(file).start();
```

Next, you will want to specify what should happen to the standard input, output, and error streams of the process. By default, each of them is a pipe that you can access with

```
OutputStream processIn = p.getOutputStream();
InputStream processOut = p.getInputStream();
InputStream processErr = p.getErrorStream();
```

Note that the input stream of the process is an output stream in the JVM! You write to that stream, and whatever you write becomes the input of the process. Conversely, you read what the process writes to the output and error streams. For you, they are input streams.

You can specify that the input, output, and error streams of the new process should be the same as the JVM. If the user runs the JVM in a console, any user input is forwarded to the process, and the process output shows up in the console. Call

```
builder.inheritIO()
```

to make this setting for all three streams. If you only want to inherit some of the streams, pass the value

```
ProcessBuilder.Redirect.INHERIT
```

to the `redirectInput`, `redirectOutput`, or `redirectError` methods. For example,

```
builder.redirectOutput(ProcessBuilder.Redirect.INHERIT);
```

You can redirect the process streams to files by supplying `File` objects:

```
builder.redirectInput(inputFile)
    .redirectOutput(outputFile)
    .redirectError(errorFile)
```

The files for output and error are created or truncated when the process starts. To append to existing files, use

```
builder.redirectOutput(ProcessBuilder.Redirect.appendTo(outputFile));
```

It is often useful to merge the output and error streams, so you see the outputs and error messages in the sequence in which the process generates them. Call

```
builder.redirectErrorStream(true)
```

to activate the merging. If you do that, you can no longer call `redirectError` on the `ProcessBuilder` or `getErrorStream` on the `Process`.

Finally, you may want to modify the environment variables of the process. Here, the builder chain syntax breaks down. You need to get the builder's environment (which is initialized by the environment variables of the process running the JVM), then put or remove entries.

```
Map<String, String> env = builder.environment();
env.put("LANG", "fr_FR");
env.remove("JAVA_HOME");
Process p = builder.start();
```

10.9.2 Running a Process

After you have configured the builder, invoke its `start` method to start the process. If you configured the input, output, and error streams as pipes, you can now write to the input stream and read the output and error streams. For example,

```
Process process = new ProcessBuilder("/bin/ls", "-l")
    .directory(Paths.get("/tmp").toFile())
    .start();
try (Scanner in = new Scanner(process.getInputStream())) {
    while (in.hasNextLine())
        System.out.println(in.nextLine());
}
```

CAUTION: There is limited buffer space for the process streams. You should not flood the input, and you should read the output promptly. If there is a lot of input and output, you may need to produce and consume it in separate threads.

To wait for the process to finish, call

```
int result = process.waitFor();
```

or, if you don't want to wait indefinitely,

```
long delay = ...;
if (process.waitfor(delay, TimeUnit.SECONDS)) {
    int result = process.exitValue();
    ...
} else {
    process.destroyForcibly();
}
```

The first call to waitFor returns the exit value of the process (by convention, 0 for success or a nonzero error code). The second call returns true if the process didn't time out. Then you need to retrieve the exit value by calling the exitValue method.

Instead of waiting for the process to finish, you can just leave it running and occasionally call isAlive to see whether it is still alive. To kill the process, call destroy or destroyForcibly. The difference between these calls is platform-dependent. On Unix, the former terminates the process with SIGTERM, the latter with SIGKILL. (The supportsNormalTermination method returns true if the destroy method can terminate the process normally.)

Finally, you can receive an asynchronous notification when the process has completed. The call process.onExit() yields a CompletableFuture<Process> that you can use to schedule any action.

```
process.onExit().thenAccept(
    p -> System.out.println("Exit value: " + p.exitValue()));
```

10.9.3 Process Handles

To get more information about a process that your program started, or any other process that is currently running on your machine, use the `ProcessHandle` interface. You can obtain a `ProcessHandle` in four ways:

1. Given a `Process` object p, `p.toHandle()` yields its `ProcessHandle`.

2. Given a `long` operating system process ID, `ProcessHandle.of(id)` yields the handle of that process.

3. `ProcessHandle.current()` is the handle of the process that runs this Java virtual machine.

4. `ProcessHandle.allProcesses()` yields a `Stream<ProcessHandle>` of all operating system processes that are visible to the current process.

Given a process handle, you can get its process ID, its parent process, its children, and its descendants:

```
long pid = handle.pid();
Optional<ProcessHandle> parent = handle.parent();
Stream<ProcessHandle> children = handle.children();
Stream<ProcessHandle> descendants = handle.descendants();
```

 NOTE: The `Stream<ProcessHandle>` instances that are returned by the `allProcesses`, `children`, and `descendants` methods are just snapshots in time. Any of the processes in the stream may be terminated by the time you get around to seeing them, and other processes may have started that are not in the stream.

The `info` method yields a `ProcessHandle.Info` object with methods for obtaining information about the process.

```
Optional<String[]> arguments()
Optional<String> command()
Optional<String> commandLine()
Optional<String> startInstant()
Optional<String> totalCpuDuration()
Optional<String> user()
```

All of these methods return `Optional` values since it is possible that a particular operating system may not be able to report the information.

For monitoring or forcing process termination, the `ProcessHandle` interface has the same `isAlive`, `supportsNormalTermination`, `destroy`, `destroyForcibly`, and `onExit` methods as the `Process` class. However, there is no equivalent to the `waitFor` method.

Exercises

1. Using parallel streams, find all files in a directory that contain a given word. How do you find just the first one? Are the files actually searched concurrently?

2. How large does an array have to be for `Arrays.parallelSort` to be faster than `Arrays.sort` on your computer?

3. Implement a method yielding a task that reads through all words in a file, trying to find a given word. The task should finish immediately (with a debug message) when it is interrupted. For all files in a directory, schedule one task for each file. Interrupt all others when one of them has succeeded.

4. One parallel operation not discussed in Section 10.4.2, "Parallel Array Operations" (page 349) is the `parallelPrefix` method that replaces each array element with the accumulation of the prefix for a given associative operation. Huh? Here is an example. Consider the array [1, 2, 3, 4, ...] and the × operation. After executing `Arrays.parallelPrefix(values, (x, y) -> x * y)`, the array contains

    [1, 1 × 2, 1 × 2 × 3, 1 × 2 × 3 × 4, ...]

    Perhaps surprisingly, this computation can be parallelized. First, join neighboring elements, as indicated here:

    [1, 1 × 2, 3, 3 × 4, 5, 5 × 6, 7, 7 × 8]

    The gray values are left alone. Clearly, one can make this computation concurrently in separate regions of the array. In the next step, update the indicated elements by multiplying them with elements that are one or two positions below:

    [1, 1 × 2, 1 × 2 × 3, 1 × 2 × 3 × 4, 5, 5 × 6, 5 × 6 × 7, 5 × 6 × 7 × 8]

    This can again be done concurrently. After $\log(n)$ steps, the process is complete. This is a win over the straightforward linear computation if sufficient processors are available.

    In this exercise, you will use the `parallelPrefix` method to parallelize the computation of Fibonacci numbers. We use the fact that the nth Fibonacci number is the top left coefficient of F^n, where $F = \begin{pmatrix} 1 & 1 \\ 1 & 0 \end{pmatrix}$. Make an array filled with 2×2 matrices. Define a `Matrix` class with a multiplication method, use `parallelSetAll` to make an array of matrices, and use `parallelPrefix` to multiply them.

5. Produce an example that demonstrates escaping of `this` in a constructor of an immutable class (see Section 10.3.3, "Strategies for Safe Concurrency," page 346). Try to come up with something convincing and scary. If you use an event listener (as many examples on the Web do), it should listen for something interesting, which isn't easy for an immutable class.

6. Write an application in which multiple threads read all words from a collection of files. Use a `ConcurrentHashMap<String, Set<File>>` to track in which files each word occurs. Use the `merge` method to update the map.

7. Repeat the preceding exercise, but use `computeIfAbsent` instead. What is the advantage of this approach?

8. In a `ConcurrentHashMap<String, Long>`, find the key with maximum value (breaking ties arbitrarily). Hint: `reduceEntries`.

9. Generate 1,000 threads, each of which increments a counter 100,000 times. Compare the performance of using `AtomicLong` versus `LongAdder`.

10. Use a `LongAccumulator` to compute the maximum or minimum of the accumulated elements.

11. Use a blocking queue for processing files in a directory. One thread walks the file tree and inserts files into a queue. Several threads remove the files and search each one for a given keyword, printing out any matches. When the producer is done, it should put a dummy file into the queue.

12. Repeat the preceding exercise, but instead have each consumer compile a map of words and their frequencies that are inserted into a second queue. A final thread merges the dictionaries and prints the ten most common words. Why don't you need to use a `ConcurrentHashMap`?

13. Repeat the preceding exercise, making a `Callable<Map<String, Integer>>` for each file and using an appropriate executor service. Merge the results when all are available. Why don't you need to use a `ConcurrentHashMap`?

14. Use an `ExecutorCompletionService` instead and merge the results as soon as they become available.

15. Repeat the preceding exercise, using a global `ConcurrentHashMap` for collecting the word frequencies.

16. Repeat the preceding exercise, using parallel streams. None of the stream operations should have any side effects.

17. Write a program that walks a directory tree and generates a thread for each file. In the threads, count the number of words in the files and, without using locks, update a shared counter that is declared as

```
public static long count = 0;
```

Run the program multiple times. What happens? Why?

18. Fix the program of the preceding exercise with using a lock.

19. Fix the program of the preceding exercise with using a LongAdder.

20. Consider this stack implementation:
    ```
    public class Stack {
        class Node { Object value; Node next; };
        private Node top;

        public void push(Object newValue) {
            Node n = new Node();
            n.value = newValue;
            n.next = top;
            top = n;
        }

        public Object pop() {
            if (top == null) return null;
            Node n = top;
            top = n.next;
            return n.value;
        }
    }
    ```
    Describe two different ways in which the data structure can fail to contain the correct elements.

21. Consider this queue implementation:
    ```
    public class Queue {
        class Node { Object value; Node next; };
        private Node head;
        private Node tail;

        public void add(Object newValue) {
            Node n = new Node();
            if (head == null) head = n;
            else tail.next = n;
            tail = n;
            tail.value = newValue;
        }

        public Object remove() {
            if (head == null) return null;
            Node n = head;
            head = n.next;
            return n.value;
        }
    }
    ```

Describe two different ways in which the data structure can fail to contain the correct elements.

22. What is wrong with this code snippet?

```java
public class Stack {
    private Object myLock = "LOCK";

    public void push(Object newValue) {
        synchronized (myLock) {
            ...
        }
    }
    ...
}
```

23. What is wrong with this code snippet?

```java
public class Stack {
    public void push(Object newValue) {
        synchronized (new ReentrantLock()) {
            ...
        }
    }
    ...
}
```

24. What is wrong with this code snippet?

```java
public class Stack {
    private Object[] values = new Object[10];
    private int size;

    public void push(Object newValue) {
        synchronized (values) {
            if (size == values.length)
                values = Arrays.copyOf(values, 2 * size);
            values[size] = newValue;
            size++;
        }
    }
    ...
}
```

25. Write a program that asks the user for a URL, reads the web page at that URL, and displays all the links. Use a CompletableFuture for each step. Don't call get.

26. Write a method

```java
public static <T> CompletableFuture<T> repeat(
    Supplier<T> action, Predicate<T> until)
```

that asynchronously repeats the action until it produces a value that is accepted by the until function, which should also run asynchronously. Test with a function that reads a java.net.PasswordAuthentication from the console, and a function that simulates a validity check by sleeping for a second and then checking that the password is "secret". Hint: Use recursion.

27. Implement a static method CompletableFuture<T> <T> supplyAsync(Supplier<T> action, Executor exec) that returns an instance of a subclass of CompletableFuture<T> whose cancel method can interrupt the thread that executes the action method, provided the task is running. In a Runnable, capture the current thread, then call action.get(), and complete the CompletableFuture with the result or exception.

28. The method

    ```
    static CompletableFuture<Void> CompletableFuture.allOf(CompletableFuture<?>... cfs)
    ```

    does not yield the results of the arguments, which makes it a bit cumbersome to use. Implement a method that combines completable futures of the same type:

    ```
    static <T> CompletableFuture<List<T>> allOf(List<CompletableFuture<T>> cfs)
    ```

    Note that this method has a List parameter since you cannot have variable arguments of a generic type.

29. The method

    ```
    static CompletableFuture<Object>
        CompletableFuture.anyOf(CompletableFuture<?>... cfs)
    ```

    returns as soon as any of the arguments completes, normally *or exceptionally*. This is markedly different from ExecutorService.invokeAny which keeps going until one of the tasks completes successfully and prevents the method from being used for a concurrent search. Implement a method

    ```
    static CompletableFuture<T> anyOf(List<Supplier<T>> actions, Executor exec)
    ```

    that yields the first actual result, or a NoSuchElementException if all actions completed with exceptions.

Annotations

Topics in This Chapter

Chapter

Annotations are tags that you insert into your source code so that some tool can process them. The tools can operate on the source level, or they can process class files into which the compiler has placed annotations.

Annotations do not change the way your programs are compiled. The Java compiler generates the same virtual machine instructions with or without the annotations.

To benefit from annotations, you need to select a processing tool and use annotations that your processing tool understands, before you can apply that tool to your code.

There is a wide range of uses for annotations. For example, JUnit uses annotations to mark methods that execute tests and to specify how the tests should be run. The Java Persistence Architecture uses annotations to define mappings between classes and database tables, so that objects can be persisted automatically without the developer having to write SQL queries.

In this chapter, you will learn the details of the annotation syntax, how to define your own annotations, and how to write annotation processors that work at the source level or at runtime.

The key points of this chapter are:

1. You can annotate declarations just as you use modifiers such as `public` or `static`.

2. You can also annotate types that appear in declarations, casts, `instanceof` checks, or method references.

3. An annotation starts with a @ symbol and may contain key/value pairs called elements.

4. Annotation values must be compile-time constants: primitive types, `enum` constants, `Class` literals, other annotations, or arrays thereof.

5. An item can have repeating annotations or annotations of different types.

6. To define an annotation, specify an annotation interface whose methods correspond to the annotation elements.

7. The Java library defines over a dozen annotations, and annotations are extensively used in the Java Enterprise Edition.

8. To process annotations in a running Java program, you can use reflection and query the reflected items for annotations.

9. Annotation processors process source files during compilation, using the Java language model API to locate annotated items.

11.1 Using Annotations

Here is an example of a simple annotation:

```
public class CacheTest {
    ...
    @Test public void checkRandomInsertions()
}
```

The annotation `@Test` annotates the `checkRandomInsertions` method. In Java, an annotation is used like a modifier (such as `public` or `static`). The name of each annotation is preceded by an @ symbol.

By itself, the `@Test` annotation does not do anything. It needs a tool to be useful. For example, the JUnit 4 testing tool (available at `http://junit.org`) calls all methods that are labeled `@Test` when testing a class. Another tool might remove all test methods from a class file so they are not shipped with the program after it has been tested.

11.1.1 Annotation Elements

Annotations can have key/value pairs called *elements*, such as

```
@Test(timeout=10000)
```

The names and types of the permissible elements are defined by each annotation (see Section 11.2, "Defining Annotations," page 383). The elements can be processed by the tools that read the annotations.

An annotation element is one of the following:

- A primitive type value
- A String
- A Class object
- An instance of an enum
- An annotation
- An array of the preceding (but not an array of arrays)

For example,

```
@BugReport(showStopper=true,
    assignedTo="Harry",
    testCase=CacheTest.class,
    status=BugReport.Status.CONFIRMED)
```

 CAUTION: An annotation element can never have the value null.

Elements can have default values. For example, the timeout element of the JUnit @Test annotation has default 0L. Therefore, the annotation @Test is equivalent to @Test(timeout=0L).

If the element name is value, and that is the only element you specify, you can omit value=. For example, @SuppressWarnings("unchecked") is the same as @SuppressWarnings(value="unchecked").

If an element value is an array, enclose its components in braces:

```
@BugReport(reportedBy={"Harry", "Fred"})
```

You can omit the braces if the array has a single component:

```
@BugReport(reportedBy="Harry") // Same as {"Harry"}
```

An annotation element can be another annotation:

```
@BugReport(ref=@Reference(id=11235811), ...)
```

 NOTE: Since annotations are processed by the compiler, all element values must be compile-time constants.

11.1.2 Multiple and Repeated Annotations

An item can have multiple annotations:

```
@Test
@BugReport(showStopper=true, reportedBy="Joe")
public void checkRandomInsertions()
```

If the author of an annotation declared it to be repeatable, you can repeat the same annotation multiple times:

```
@BugReport(showStopper=true, reportedBy="Joe")
@BugReport(reportedBy={"Harry", "Carl"})
public void checkRandomInsertions()
```

11.1.3 Annotating Declarations

So far, you have seen annotations applied to method declarations. There are many other places where annotations can occur. They fall into two categories: *declarations* and *type uses*. Declaration annotations can appear at the declarations of

- Classes (including `enum`) and interfaces (including annotation interfaces)
- Methods
- Constructors
- Instance variables (including `enum` constants)
- Local variables (including those declared in `for` and try-with-resources statements)
- Parameter variables and `catch` clause parameters
- Type parameters
- Packages

For classes and interfaces, put the annotations before the `class` or `interface` keyword:

```
@Entity public class User { ... }
```

For variables, put them before the type:

```
@SuppressWarnings("unchecked") List<User> users = ...;
public User getUser(@Param("id") String userId)
```

A type parameter in a generic class or method can be annotated like this:

```
public class Cache<@Immutable V> { ... }
```

A package is annotated in a file `package-info.java` that contains only the package statement preceded by annotations.

```
/**
    Package-level Javadoc
*/
@GPL(version="3")
package com.horstmann.corejava;
import org.gnu.GPL;
```

Note that the `import` statement for the annotation comes *after* the `package` declaration.

> **NOTE:** Annotations for local variables and packages are discarded when a class is compiled. Therefore, they can only be processed at the source level.

11.1.4 Annotating Type Uses

A declaration annotation provides some information about the item being declared. For example, in the declaration

```
public User getUser(@NonNull String userId)
```

it is asserted that the `userId` parameter is not `null`.

> **NOTE:** The `@NonNull` annotation is a part of the Checker Framework (`http://types.cs.washington.edu/checker-framework`). With that framework, you can include assertions in your program, such that a parameter is non-`null` or that a `String` contains a regular expression. A static analysis tool then checks whether the assertions are valid in a given body of source code.

Now suppose we have a parameter of type `List<String>`, and we want to express that all of the strings are non-`null`. That is where type use annotations come in. Place the annotation before the type argument: `List<@NonNull String>`

Type use annotations can appear in the following places:

- With generic type arguments: `List<@NonNull String>`, `Comparator.<@NonNull String> reverseOrder()`.

- In any position of an array: `@NonNull String[][] words` (`words[i][j]` is not `null`), `String @NonNull [][] words` (`words` is not `null`), `String[] @NonNull [] words` (`words[i]` is not `null`).

- With superclasses and implemented interfaces: `class Warning extends @Localized Message`.

- With constructor invocations: `new @Localized String(...)`.

- With nested types: `Map.@Localized Entry`.

- With casts and `instanceof` checks: `(@Localized String) text`, `if (text instanceof @Localized String)`. (The annotations are only for use by external tools. They have no effect on the behavior of a cast or an `instanceof` check.)

- With exception specifications: `public String read() throws @Localized IOException`.

- With wildcards and type bounds: `List<@Localized ? extends Message>`, `List<? extends @Localized Message>`.

- With method and constructor references: `@Localized Message::getText`.

There are a few type positions that cannot be annotated:

```
@NonNull String.class // Error—cannot annotate class literal
import java.lang.@NonNull String; // Error—cannot annotate import
```

You can place annotations before or after other modifiers such as `private` and `static`. It is customary (but not required) to put type use annotations after other modifiers, and declaration annotations before other modifiers. For example,

```
private @NonNull String text; // Annotates the type use
@Id private String userId; // Annotates the variable
```

> **NOTE:** As you will see in Section 11.2, "Defining Annotations" (page 383), an annotation author needs to specify where a particular annotation can appear. If an annotation is permissible both for a variable and a type use, and it is used in a variable declaration, then both the variable and the type use are annotated. For example, consider
>
> ```
> public User getUser(@NonNull String userId)
> ```
>
> if `@NonNull` can apply both to parameters and to type uses, the `userId` parameter is annotated, and the parameter type is `@NonNull String`.

11.1.5 Making Receivers Explicit

Suppose you want to annotate parameters that are not being mutated by a method.

```
public class Point {
    public boolean equals(@ReadOnly Object other) { ... }
}
```

Then a tool that processes this annotation would, upon seeing a call

```
p.equals(q)
```

reason that `q` has not been changed.

But what about p?

When the method is called, the receiver variable this is bound to p, but this is never declared, so you cannot annotate it.

Actually, you can declare it, with a rarely used syntax variant, just so that you can add an annotation:

```
public class Point {
    public boolean equals(@ReadOnly Point this, @ReadOnly Object other) { ... }
}
```

The first parameter is called the *receiver parameter*. It must be named this. Its type is the class that is being constructed.

 NOTE: You can provide a receiver parameter only for methods, not for constructors. Conceptually, the this reference in a constructor is not an object of the given type until the constructor has completed. Instead, an annotation placed on the constructor describes a property of the constructed object.

A different hidden parameter is passed to the constructor of an inner class, namely the reference to the enclosing class object. You can make this parameter explicit as well:

```
static class Sequence {
    private int from;
    private int to;

    class Iterator implements java.util.Iterator<Integer> {
        private int current;

        public Iterator(@ReadOnly Sequence Sequence.this) {
            this.current = Sequence.this.from;
        }
        ...
    }
    ...
}
```

The parameter must be named just like when you refer to it, *EnclosingClass*.this, and its type is the enclosing class.

11.2 Defining Annotations

Each annotation must be declared by an *annotation interface*, with the @interface syntax. The methods of the interface correspond to the elements of the annotation. For example, the JUnit Test annotation is defined by the following interface:

```
@Target(ElementType.METHOD)
@Retention(RetentionPolicy.RUNTIME)
public @interface Test {
    long timeout();
    ...
}
```

The @interface declaration creates an actual Java interface. Tools that process annotations receive objects that implement the annotation interface. When the JUnit test runner tool gets an object that implements Test, it simply invokes the timeout method to retrieve the timeout element of a particular Test annotation.

The element declarations in the annotation interface are actually method declarations. The methods of an annotation interface can have no parameters and no throws clauses, and they cannot be generic.

The @Target and @Retention annotations are *meta-annotations*. They annotate the Test annotation, indicating the places where the annotation can occur and where it can be accessed.

The value of the @Target meta-annotation is an array of ElementType objects, specifying the items to which the annotation can apply. You can specify any number of element types, enclosed in braces. For example,

```
@Target({ElementType.TYPE, ElementType.METHOD})
public @interface BugReport
```

Table 11-1 shows all possible targets. The compiler checks that you use an annotation only where permitted. For example, if you apply @BugReport to a variable, a compile-time error results.

 NOTE: An annotation without an @Target restriction can be used with any declarations but not with type parameters and type uses. (These were the only possible targets in the first Java release that supported annotations.)

The @Retention meta-annotation specifies where the annotation can be accessed. There are three choices.

1. RetentionPolicy.SOURCE: The annotation is available to source processors, but it is not included in class files.

2. RetentionPolicy.CLASS: The annotation is included in class files, but the virtual machine does not load them. This is the default.

Table 11-1 Element Types for the @Target Annotation

Element Type	Annotation Applies To
ANNOTATION_TYPE	Annotation type declarations
PACKAGE	Packages
TYPE	Classes (including enum) and interfaces (including annotation types)
METHOD	Methods
CONSTRUCTOR	Constructors
FIELD	Instance variables (including enum constants)
PARAMETER	Method or constructor parameters
LOCAL_VARIABLE	Local variables
TYPE_PARAMETER	Type parameters
TYPE_USE	Uses of a type

3. RetentionPolicy.RUNTIME: The annotation is available at runtime and can be accessed through the reflection API.

You will see examples of all three scenarios later in this chapter.

There are several other meta-annotations—see Section 11.3, "Standard Annotations" (page 386) for a complete list.

To specify a default value for an element, add a default clause after the method defining the element. For example,

```
public @interface Test {
    long timeout() default 0L;
    ...
}
```

This example shows how to denote a default of an empty array and a default for an annotation:

```
public @interface BugReport {
    String[] reportedBy() default {};
        // Defaults to empty array
    Reference ref() default @Reference(id=0);
        // Default for an annotation
    ...
}
```

> **CAUTION:** Defaults are not stored with the annotation; instead, they are dynamically computed. If you change a default and recompile the annotation class, all annotated elements will use the new default, even in class files that have been compiled before the default changed.

You cannot extend annotation interfaces, and you never supply classes that implement annotation interfaces. Instead, source processing tools and the virtual machine generate proxy classes and objects when needed.

11.3 Standard Annotations

The Java API defines a number of annotation interfaces in the `java.lang`, `java.lang.annotation`, and `javax.annotation` packages. Four of them are meta-annotations that describe the behavior of annotation interfaces. The others are regular annotations that you use to annotate items in your source code. Table 11-2 shows these annotations. I will discuss them in detail in the following two sections.

Table 11–2 The Standard Annotations

Annotation Interface	Applicable To	Purpose
Override	Methods	Checks that this method overrides a superclass method.
Deprecated	All declarations	Marks item as deprecated.
SuppressWarnings	All declarations except packages	Suppresses warnings of a given type.
SafeVarargs	Methods and constructors	Asserts that the varargs parameter is safe to use.
FunctionalInterface	Interfaces	Marks an interface as functional (with a single abstract method).
PostConstruct PreDestroy	Methods	The method should be invoked immediately after construction or before removal of an injected object.
Resource	Classes and interfaces, methods, fields	On a class or interface, marks it as a resource to be used elsewhere. On a method or field, marks it for dependency injection.

(Continues)

Table 11–2 The Standard Annotations *(Continued)*

Annotation Interface	Applicable To	Purpose
Resources	Classes and interfaces	Specifies an array of resources.
Generated	All declarations	Marks an item as source code that has been generated by a tool.
Target	Annotations	Specifies the locations to which this annotation can be applied.
Retention	Annotations	Specifies where this annotation can be used.
Documented	Annotations	Specifies that this annotation should be included in the documentation of annotated items.
Inherited	Annotations	Specifies that this annotation is inherited by subclasses.
Repeatable	Annotations	Specifies that this annotation can be applied multiple times to the same item.

11.3.1 Annotations for Compilation

The @Deprecated annotation can be attached to any items whose use is no longer encouraged. The compiler will warn when you use a deprecated item. This annotation has the same role as the @deprecated Javadoc tag. However, the annotation persists until runtime.

 NOTE: The jdeprscan utility which is part of the JDK can scan a set of JAR files for deprecated elements.

The @Override makes the compiler check that the annotated method really overrides a method from the superclass. For example, if you declare

```
public class Point {
    @Override public boolean equals(Point other) { ... }
    ...
}
```

then the compiler will report an error—this equals method does not override the equals method of the Object class because that method has a parameter of type Object, not Point.

The@SuppressWarnings annotation tells the compiler to suppress warnings of a particular type, for example,

```
@SuppressWarnings("unchecked") T[] result
    = (T[]) Array.newInstance(cl, n);
```

The @SafeVarargs annotation asserts that a method does not corrupt its varargs parameter (see Chapter 6).

The @Generated annotation is intended for use by code generator tools. Any generated source code can be annotated to differentiate it from programmer-provided code. For example, a code editor can hide the generated code, or a code generator can remove older versions of generated code. Each annotation must contain a unique identifier for the code generator. A date string (in ISO 8601 format) and a comment string are optional. For example,

```
@Generated(value="com.horstmann.generator",
    date="2015-01-04T12:08:56.235-0700");
```

You have seen the FunctionalInterface annotation in Chapter 3. It is used to annotate conversion targets for lambda expressions, such as

```
@FunctionalInterface
public interface IntFunction<R> {
    R apply(int value);
}
```

If you later add another abstract method, the compiler will generate an error.

Of course, you should only add this annotation to interfaces that describe functions. There are other interfaces with a single abstract method (such as AutoCloseable) that are not conceptually functions.

11.3.2 Annotations for Managing Resources

The @PostConstruct and @PreDestroy annotations are used in environments that control the lifecycle of objects, such as web containers and application servers. Methods tagged with these annotations should be invoked immediately after an object has been constructed or immediately before it is being removed.

The @Resource annotation is intended for resource injection. For example, consider a web application that accesses a database. Of course, the database access information should not be hardwired into the web application. Instead, the web container has some user interface for setting connection parameters and a JNDI name for a data source. In the web application, you can reference the data source like this:

```
@Resource(name="jdbc/employeedb")
private DataSource source;
```

When an object containing this instance variable is constructed, the container "injects" a reference to the data source—that is, sets the instance variable to a `DataSource` object that is configured with the name `"jdbc/employeedb"`.

11.3.3 Meta-Annotations

You have already seen the `@Target` and `@Retention` meta-annotations in Section 11.2, "Defining Annotations" (page 383).

The `@Documented` meta-annotation gives a hint to documentation tools such as Javadoc. Documented annotations should be treated just like other modifiers (such as `private` or `static`) for documentation purposes. In contrast, other annotations should not be included in the documentation.

For example, the `@SuppressWarnings` annotation is not documented. If a method or field has that annotation, it is an implementation detail that is of no interest to the Javadoc reader. On the other hand, the `@FunctionalInterface` annotation is documented since it is useful for the programmer to know that the interface is intended to describe a function. Figure 11-1 shows the documentation.

The `@Inherited` meta-annotation applies only to annotations for classes. When a class has an inherited annotation, then all of its subclasses automatically have the same annotation. This makes it easy to create annotations that work similar to marker interfaces (such as the `Serializable` interface).

Suppose you define an inherited annotation `@Persistent` to indicate that objects of a class can be saved in a database. Then the subclasses of persistent classes are automatically annotated as persistent.

```
@Inherited @interface Persistent { }

@Persistent class Employee { ... }
class Manager extends Employee { ... } // Also @Persistent
```

The `@Repeatable` meta-annotation makes it possible to apply the same annotation multiple times. For example, suppose the `@TestCase` annotation is repeatable. Then it can be used like this:

```
@TestCase(params="4", expected="24")
@TestCase(params="0", expected="1")
public static long factorial(int n) { ... }
```

For historical reasons, the implementor of a repeatable annotation needs to provide a *container annotation* that holds the repeated annotations in an array.

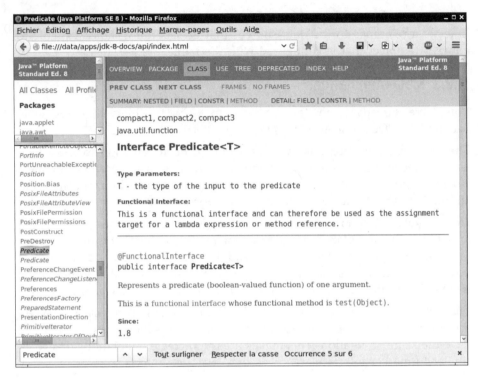

Figure 11-1 A documented annotation

Here is how to define the @TestCase annotation and its container:

```
@Repeatable(TestCases.class)
@interface TestCase {
    String params();
    String expected();
}

@interface TestCases {
    TestCase[] value();
}
```

Whenever the user supplies two or more @TestCase annotations, they are automatically wrapped into a @TestCases annotation. This complicates processing of the annotation, as you will see in the next section.

11.4 Processing Annotations at Runtime

So far, you have seen how to add annotations to source files and how to define annotation types. Now the time has come to see what good can come out of that.

In this section, I show you a simple example of processing an annotation at runtime using the reflection API that you have already seen in Chapter 4. Suppose we want to reduce the tedium of implementing toString methods. Of course, one can write a generic toString method using reflection that simply includes all instance variable names and values. But suppose we want to customize that process. We may not want to include all instance variables, or we may want to skip class and variable names. For example, for the Point class we may prefer [5,10] instead of Point[x=5,y=10]. Of course, any number of other enhancements would be plausible, but let's keep it simple. The point is to demonstrate what an annotation processor can do.

Annotate all classes that you want to benefit from this service with the @ToString annotation. In addition, all instance variables that should be included need to be annotated as well. The annotation is defined like this:

```java
@Target({ElementType.FIELD, ElementType.TYPE})
@Retention(RetentionPolicy.RUNTIME)
public @interface ToString {
    boolean includeName() default true;
}
```

Here are annotated Point and Rectangle classes:

```java
@ToString(includeName=false)
public class Point {
    @ToString(includeName=false) private int x;
    @ToString(includeName=false) private int y;
    ...
}

@ToString
public class Rectangle {
    @ToString(includeName=false) private Point topLeft;
    @ToString private int width;
    @ToString private int height;
    ...
}
```

The intent is for a rectangle to be represented as string as `Rectangle[[5, 10], width=20,height=30]`.

At runtime, we cannot modify the implementation of the `toString` method for a given class. Instead, let us provide a method that can format any object, discovering and using the `ToString` annotations if they are present.

The key are the methods

```
T getAnnotation(Class<T>)
T getDeclaredAnnotation(Class<T>)
T[] getAnnotationsByType(Class<T>)
T[] getDeclaredAnnotationsByType(Class<T>)
Annotation[] getAnnotations()
Annotation[] getDeclaredAnnotations()
```

of the `AnnotatedElement` interface. The reflection classes `Class`, `Field`, `Parameter`, `Method`, `Constructor`, and `Package` implement that interface.

As with other reflection methods, the methods with `Declared` in their name yield annotations in the class itself, whereas the others include inherited ones. In the context of annotations, this means that the annotation is `@Inherited` and applied to a superclass.

If an annotation is not repeatable, call `getAnnotation` to locate it. For example:

```
Class cl = obj.getClass();
ToString ts = cl.getAnnotation(ToString.class);
if (ts != null && ts.includeName()) ...
```

Note that you pass the class object for the annotation (here, `ToString.class`) and you get back an object of some proxy class that implements the `ToString` interface. You can then invoke the interface methods to get the values of the annotation elements. If the annotation is not present, the `getAnnotation` method returns `null`.

It gets a bit messy if an annotation is repeatable. If you call `getAnnotation` to look up a repeatable annotation, and the annotation was actually repeated, then you also get `null`. That is because the repeated annotations were wrapped inside the container annotation.

In this case, you should call `getAnnotationsByType`. That call "looks through" the container and gives you an array of the repeated annotations. If there was just one annotation, you get it in an array of length 1. With this method, you don't have to worry about the container annotation.

The `getAnnotations` method gets all annotations (of any type) with which an item is annotated, with repeated annotations wrapped into containers.

Here is the implementation of the annotation-aware toString method:

```java
public class ToStrings {
    public static String toString(Object obj) {
        if (obj == null) return "null";
        Class<?> cl = obj.getClass();
        ToString ts = cl.getAnnotation(ToString.class);
        if (ts == null) return obj.toString();
        StringBuilder result = new StringBuilder();
        if (ts.includeName()) result.append(cl.getName());
        result.append("[");
        boolean first = true;
        for (Field f : cl.getDeclaredFields()) {
            ts = f.getAnnotation(ToString.class);
            if (ts != null) {
                if (first) first = false; else result.append(",");
                f.setAccessible(true);

                if (ts.includeName()) {
                    result.append(f.getName());
                    result.append("=");
                }
                try {
                    result.append(ToStrings.toString(f.get(obj)));
                } catch (ReflectiveOperationException ex) {
                    ex.printStackTrace();
                }
            }
        }
        result.append("]");
        return result.toString();
    }
}
```

When a class is annotated with ToString, the method iterates over its fields and prints the ones that are also annotated. If the includeName element is true, then the class or field name is included in the string.

Note that the method calls itself recursively. Whenever an object belongs to a class that isn't annotated, its regular toString method is used and the recursion stops.

This is a simple but typical use of the runtime annotation API. Look up classes, fields, and so on, using reflection; call getAnnotation or getAnnotationsByType on the potentially annotated elements to retrieve the annotations; then, invoke the methods of the annotation interfaces to obtain the element values.

11.5 Source-Level Annotation Processing

In the preceding section, you saw how to analyze annotations in a running program. Another use for annotation is the automatic processing of source files to produce more source code, configuration files, scripts, or whatever else one might want to generate.

To show you the mechanics, I will repeat the example of generating toString methods. However, this time, let's generate them in Java source. Then the methods will get compiled with the rest of the program, and they will run at full speed instead of using reflection.

11.5.1 Annotation Processors

Annotation processing is integrated into the Java compiler. During compilation, you can *invoke annotation processors* by running

```
javac -processor ProcessorClassName₁,ProcessorClassName₂,... sourceFiles
```

The compiler locates the annotations of the source files. Each annotation processor is executed in turn and given the annotations in which it expressed an interest. If an annotation processor creates a new source file, the process is repeated. Once a processing round yields no further source files, all source files are compiled.

 NOTE: An annotation processor can only generate new source files. It cannot modify an existing source file.

An annotation processor implements the Processor interface, generally by extending the AbstractProcessor class. You need to specify which annotations your processor supports. In our case:

```
@SupportedAnnotationTypes("com.horstmann.annotations.ToString")
@SupportedSourceVersion(SourceVersion.RELEASE_8)
public class ToStringAnnotationProcessor extends AbstractProcessor {
    @Override
    public boolean process(Set<? extends TypeElement> annotations,
            RoundEnvironment currentRound) {
        ...
    }
}
```

A processor can claim specific annotation types, wildcards such as "com.horstmann.*" (all annotations in the com.horstmann package or any subpackage), or even "*" (all annotations).

The process method is called once for each round, with the set of all annotations that were found in any files during this round, and a RoundEnvironment reference that contains information about the current processing round.

11.5.2 The Language Model API

You use the *language model* API for analyzing source-level annotations. Unlike the reflection API, which presents the virtual machine representation of classes and methods, the language model API lets you analyze a Java program according to the rules of the Java language.

The compiler produces a tree whose nodes are instances of classes that implement the javax.lang.model.element.Element interface and its subinterfaces, TypeElement, VariableElement, ExecutableElement, and so on. These are the compile-time analogs to the Class, Field/Parameter, Method/Constructor reflection classes.

I do not want to cover the API in detail, but here are the highlights that you need to know for processing annotations.

- The RoundEnvironment gives you a set of all elements annotated with a particular annotation, by calling the method

  ```
  Set<? extends Element> getElementsAnnotatedWith(Class<? extends Annotation> a)
  Set<? extends Element> getElementsAnnotatedWithAny(
      Set<Class<? extends Annotation>> annotations)
      // Useful for repeated annotations
  ```

- The source-level equivalent of the AnnotateElement interface is AnnotatedConstruct. You use the methods

  ```
  A getAnnotation(Class<A> annotationType)
  A[] getAnnotationsByType(Class<A> annotationType)
  ```

  to get the annotation or repeated annotations for a given annotation class.

- A TypeElement represents a class or interface. The getEnclosedElements method yields a list of its fields and methods.

- Calling getSimpleName on an Element or getQualifiedName on a TypeElement yields a Name object that can be converted to a string with toString.

11.5.3 Using Annotations to Generate Source Code

Let us return to our task of automatically generating toString methods. We can't put these methods into the original classes—annotation processors can only produce new classes, not modify existing ones.

Therefore, we'll add all methods into a utility class `ToStrings`:

```
public class ToStrings {
    public static String toString(Point obj) {
        Generated code
    }
    public static String toString(Rectangle obj) {
        Generated code
    }
    ...
    public static String toString(Object obj) {
        return Objects.toString(obj);
    }
}
```

Since we don't want to use reflection, we annotate accessor methods, not fields:

```
@ToString
public class Rectangle {
    ...
    @ToString(includeName=false) public Point getTopLeft() { return topLeft; }
    @ToString public int getWidth() { return width; }
    @ToString public int getHeight() { return height; }
}
```

The annotation processor should then generate the following source code:

```
public static String toString(Rectangle obj) {
    StringBuilder result = new StringBuilder();
    result.append("Rectangle");
    result.append("[");
    result.append(toString(obj.getTopLeft()));
    result.append(",");
    result.append("width=");
    result.append(toString(obj.getWidth()));
    result.append(",");
    result.append("height=");
    result.append(toString(obj.getHeight()));
    result.append("]");
    return result.toString();
}
```

The "boilerplate" code is in gray. Here is an outline of the method that produces the `toString` method for a class with given `TypeElement`:

```
private void writeToStringMethod(PrintWriter out, TypeElement te) {
    String className = te.getQualifiedName().toString();
    Print method header and declaration of string builder
    ToString ann = te.getAnnotation(ToString.class);
    if (ann.includeName()) Print code to add class name
    for (Element c : te.getEnclosedElements()) {
        ann = c.getAnnotation(ToString.class);
        if (ann != null) {
            if (ann.includeName()) Print code to add field name
            Print code to append toString(obj.methodName())
        }
    }
    Print code to return string
}
```

And here is an outline of the `process` method of the annotation processor. It creates a source file for the helper class and writes the class header and one method for each annotated class.

```
public boolean process(Set<? extends TypeElement> annotations,
        RoundEnvironment currentRound) {
    if (annotations.size() == 0) return true;
    try {
        JavaFileObject sourceFile = processingEnv.getFiler().createSourceFile(
            "com.horstmann.annotations.ToStrings");
        try (PrintWriter out = new PrintWriter(sourceFile.openWriter())) {
            Print code for package and class
            for (Element e : currentRound.getElementsAnnotatedWith(ToString.class)) {
                if (e instanceof TypeElement) {
                    TypeElement te = (TypeElement) e;
                    writeToStringMethod(out, te);
                }
            }
            Print code for toString(Object)
        } catch (IOException ex) {
            processingEnv.getMessager().printMessage(
                Kind.ERROR, ex.getMessage());
        }
    }
    return true;
}
```

For the tedious details, check the book's companion code.

Note that the `process` method is called in subsequent rounds with an empty list of annotations. It then returns immediately so it doesn't create the source file twice.

TIP: To see the rounds, run the `javac` command with the `-XprintRounds` flag:

```
Round 1:
  input files: {ch11.sec05.Point, ch11.sec05.Rectangle,
    ch11.sec05.SourceLevelAnnotationDemo}
  annotations: [com.horstmann.annotations.ToString]
  last round: false
Round 2:
  input files: {com.horstmann.annotations.ToStrings}
  annotations: []
  last round: false
Round 3:
  input files: {}
  annotations: []
  last round: true
```

This example demonstrates how tools can harvest source file annotations to produce other files. The generated files don't have to be source files. Annotation processors may choose to generate XML descriptors, property files, shell scripts, HTML documentation, and so on.

 NOTE: You have now seen how to process annotations in source files and in a running program. A third possibility is to process annotations in class files, usually on the fly when loading them into the virtual machine. You need a tool such as ASM (`http://asm.ow2.org`) to locate and evaluate the annotations, and rewrite the byte codes.

Exercises

1. Describe how `Object.clone` could be modified to use a `@Cloneable` annotation instead of the `Cloneable` marker interface.

2. If annotations had existed in early versions of Java, then the `Serializable` interface would surely have been an annotation. Implement a `@Serializable` annotation. Choose a text or binary format for persistence. Provide classes for streams or readers/writers that persist the state of objects by saving and restoring all fields that are primitive values or themselves serializable. Don't worry about cyclic references for now.

3. Repeat the preceding assignment, but do worry about cyclic references.

4. Add a `@Transient` annotation to your serialization mechanism that acts like the `transient` modifier.

5. Define an annotation @Todo that contains a message describing whatever it is that needs to be done. Define an annotation processor that produces a reminder list from a source file. Include a description of the annotated item and the todo message.

6. Turn the annotation of the preceding exercise into a repeating annotation.

7. If annotations had existed in early versions of Java, they might have taken the role of Javadoc. Define annotations @Param, @Return, and so on, and produce a basic HTML document from them with an annotation processor.

8. Implement the @TestCase annotation, generating a source file whose name is the name of the class in which the annotation occurs, followed by Test. For example, if MyMath.java contains

```
@TestCase(params="4", expected="24")
@TestCase(params="0", expected="1")
public static long factorial(int n) { ... }
```

then generate a file MyMathTest.java with statements

```
assert(MyMath.factorial(4) == 24);
assert(MyMath.factorial(0) == 1);
```

You may assume that the test methods are static, and that params contains a comma-separated list of parameters of the correct type.

9. Implement the @TestCase annotation as a runtime annotation and provide a tool that checks it. Again, assume that the test methods are static and restrict yourself to a reasonable set of parameter and return types that can be described by strings in the annotation elements.

10. Implement a processor for the @Resource annotation that accepts an object of some class and looks for fields of type String annotated with @Resource(name="URL"). Then load the URL and "inject" the string variable with that content, using reflection.

The Date and Time API

Chapter 12

Time flies like an arrow, and we can easily set a starting point and count forwards and backwards in seconds. So why is it so hard to deal with time? The problem is humans. All would be easy if we could just tell each other: "Meet me at 1371409200, and don't be late!" But we want time to relate to daylight and the seasons. That's where things get complicated. Java 1.0 had a Date class that was, in hindsight, naïve, and had most of its methods deprecated in Java 1.1 when a Calendar class was introduced. Its API wasn't stellar, its instances were mutable, and it didn't deal with issues such as leap seconds. The third time is a charm, and the java.time API introduced in Java 8 has remedied the flaws of the past and should serve us for quite some time. In this chapter, you will learn what makes time computations so vexing, and how the Date and Time API solves these issues.

The key points of this chapter are:

1. All java.time objects are immutable.

2. An Instant is a point on the time line (similar to a Date).

3. In Java time, each day has exactly 86,400 seconds (that is, no leap seconds).

4. A Duration is the difference between two instants.

5. LocalDateTime has no time zone information.

6. `TemporalAdjuster` methods handle common calendar computations, such as finding the first Tuesday of a month.

7. `ZonedDateTime` is a point in time in a given time zone (similar to `GregorianCalendar`).

8. Use a `Period`, not a `Duration`, when advancing zoned time, in order to account for daylight savings time changes.

9. Use `DateTimeFormatter` to format and parse dates and times.

12.1 The Time Line

Historically, the fundamental time unit—the second—was derived from Earth's rotation around its axis. There are 24 hours or 24 × 60 × 60 = 86400 seconds in a full revolution, so it seems just a question of astronomical measurements to precisely define a second. Unfortunately, Earth wobbles slightly, and a more precise definition was needed. In 1967, a new precise definition of a second, matching the historical definition, was derived from an intrinsic property of atoms of caesium-133. Since then, a network of atomic clocks keeps the official time.

Ever so often, the official time keepers synchronize the absolute time with the rotation of Earth. At first, the official seconds were slightly adjusted, but starting in 1972, "leap seconds" were occasionally inserted. (In theory, a second might need to be removed once in a while, but that has not yet happened.) There is talk of changing the system again. Clearly, leap seconds are a pain, and many computer systems instead use "smoothing" where time is artificially slowed down or sped up just before the leap second, keeping 86,400 seconds per day. This works because the local time on a computer isn't all that precise, and computers are used to synchronizing themselves with an external time service.

The Java Date and Time API specification requires that Java uses a time scale that:

• Has 86,400 seconds per day

• Exactly matches the official time at noon each day

• Closely matches it elsewhere, in a precisely defined way

That gives Java the flexibility to adjust to future changes in the official time.

In Java, an `Instant` represents a point on the time line. An origin, called the *epoch*, is arbitrarily set at midnight of January 1, 1970 at the prime meridian that passes through the Greenwich Royal Observatory in London. This is the same convention used in the Unix/POSIX time. Starting from that origin, time is measured in 86,400 seconds per day, forwards and backwards, to nanosecond precision. The Instant values go back as far as a billion years (Instant.MIN). That's not quite enough to express the age of the Universe (around 13.5 billion years), but it should be enough for all practical purposes. After all, a billion years ago, the Earth was covered in ice and populated by micro-scopic ancestors of today's plants and animals. The largest value, Instant.MAX, is December 31 of the year 1,000,000,000.

The static method call Instant.now() gives the current instant. You can compare two instants with the equals and compareTo methods in the usual way, so you can use instants as timestamps.

To find out the difference between two instants, use the static method Duration.between. For example, here is how you can measure the running time of an algorithm:

```
Instant start = Instant.now();
runAlgorithm();
Instant end = Instant.now();
Duration timeElapsed = Duration.between(start, end);
long millis = timeElapsed.toMillis();
```

A Duration is the amount of time between two instants. You can get the length of a Duration in conventional units by calling toNanos, toMillis, toSeconds, toMinutes, toHours, or toDays.

Conversely, you can obtain a duration with one of the static methods ofNanos, ofMillis, ofSeconds, ofMinutes, ofHours, ofDays:

```
Duration oneWeek = Duration.ofDays(7);
long secondsPerWeek = oneWeek.toSeconds();
```

Durations require more than a long value for their internal storage. The number of seconds is stored in a long, and the number of nanoseconds in an additional int. If you want to make computations to nanosecond accuracy, and you actually need the entire range of a Duration, you can use one of the methods in Table 12-1. Otherwise, you can just call toNanos and do your calculations with long values.

 NOTE: It takes almost 300 years of nanoseconds to overflow a long.

For example, if you want to check whether an algorithm is at least ten times faster than another, you can compute

```
Duration timeElapsed2 = Duration.between(start2, end2);
boolean overTenTimesFaster
   = timeElapsed.multipliedBy(10).minus(timeElapsed2).isNegative();
   // Or timeElapsed.toNanos() * 10 < timeElapsed2.toNanos()
```

 NOTE: The `Instant` and `Duration` classes are immutable, and all methods, such as `multipliedBy` or `minus`, return a new instance.

Table 12-1 Arithmetic Operations for Time Instants and Durations

Method	Description
plus, minus	Adds a duration to, or subtracts a duration from, this `Instant` or `Duration`.
plusNanos, plusMillis, plusSeconds, plusMinutes, plusHours, plusDays	Adds a number of the given time units to this `Instant` or `Duration`.
minusNanos, minusMillis, minusSeconds, minusMinutes, minusHours, minusDays	Subtracts a number of the given time units from this `Instant` or `Duration`.
multipliedBy, dividedBy, negated	Returns a duration obtained by multiplying or dividing this `Duration` by a given `long`, or by −1, or a `long` obtained by dividing two durations. Note that you can scale only durations, not instants.
isZero, isNegative	Checks whether this `Duration` is zero or negative.

12.2 Local Dates

Now let us turn from absolute time to human time. There are two kinds of human time in the Java API, *local date/time* and *zoned time*. Local date/time has a date and/or time of day, but no associated time zone information. An example of a local date is June 14, 1903 (the day on which Alonzo Church, inventor of the lambda calculus, was born). Since that date has neither a time of day nor time zone information, it does not correspond to a precise instant of time. In contrast, July 16, 1969, 09:32:00 EDT (the launch of Apollo 11) is a zoned date/time, representing a precise instant on the time line.

There are many calculations where time zones are not required, and in some cases they can even be a hindrance. Suppose you schedule a meeting every week at 10:00. If you add 7 days (that is, 7 × 24 × 60 × 60 seconds) to the last zoned time, and you happen to cross the daylight savings time boundary, the meeting will be an hour too early or too late!

For that reason, the API designers recommend that you do not use zoned time unless you really want to represent absolute time instances. Birthdays, holidays, schedule times, and so on are usually best represented as local dates or times.

A LocalDate is a date with a year, month, and day of the month. To construct one, you can use the now or of static methods:

```
LocalDate today = LocalDate.now(); // Today's date
LocalDate alonzosBirthday = LocalDate.of(1903, 6, 14);
alonzosBirthday = LocalDate.of(1903, Month.JUNE, 14);
    // Uses the Month enumeration
```

Unlike the irregular conventions in Unix and java.util.Date, where months are zero-based and years are counted from 1900, you supply the usual numbers for the month of year. Alternatively, you can use the Month enumeration.

Table 12-2 shows the most useful methods for working with LocalDate objects.

For example, *Programmer's Day* is the 256th day of the year. Here is how you can easily compute it:

```
LocalDate programmersDay = LocalDate.of(2014, 1, 1).plusDays(255);
    // September 13, but in a leap year it would be September 12
```

Recall that the difference between two time instants is a Duration. The equivalent for local dates is a Period, which expresses a number of elapsed years, months, or days. You can call birthday.plus(Period.ofYears(1)) to get the birthday next year. Of course, you can also just call birthday.plusYears(1). But birthday.plus(Duration.ofDays(365)) won't produce the correct result in a leap year.

The until method yields the difference between two local dates. For example,

```
independenceDay.until(christmas)
```

yields a period of 5 months and 21 days. That is actually not terribly useful because the number of days per month varies. To find the number of days, use

```
independenceDay.until(christmas, ChronoUnit.DAYS) // 174 days
```

Table 12-2 LocalDate Methods

Method	Description
now, of, ofInstant	These static methods construct a LocalDate from the current time, from the given year, month, and day, or from an Instant and ZoneId.
plusDays, plusWeeks, plusMonths, plusYears	Adds a number of days, weeks, months, or years to this LocalDate.
minusDays, minusWeeks, minusMonths, minusYears	Subtracts a number of days, weeks, months, or years from this LocalDate.
datesUntil	Yields a Stream<LocalDate> of all dates between this one and the given date.
plus, minus	Adds or subtracts a Duration or Period.
withDayOfMonth, withDayOfYear, withMonth, withYear	Returns a new LocalDate with the day of month, day of year, month, or year changed to the given value.
getDayOfMonth	Gets the day of the month (between 1 and 31).
getDayOfYear	Gets the day of the year (between 1 and 366).
getDayOfWeek	Gets the day of the week, returning a value of the DayOfWeek enumeration.
getMonth, getMonthValue	Gets the month as a value of the Month enumeration, or as a number between 1 and 12.
getYear	Gets the year, between −999,999,999 and 999,999,999.
until	Gets the Period, or the number of the given ChronoUnits, between two dates.
toEpochSecond	Given a LocalTime and ZoneOffset, yields the number of seconds from the epoch to the specified point in time.
isBefore, isAfter	Compares this LocalDate with another.
isLeapYear	Returns true if the year is a leap year—that is, if it is divisible by 4 but not by 100, or divisible by 400. The algorithm is applied for all past years, even though that is historically inaccurate. (Leap years were invented in the year −46, and the rules involving divisibility by 100 and 400 were introduced in the Gregorian calendar reform of 1582. The reform took over 300 years to become universal.)

CAUTION: Some methods in Table 12-2 could potentially create nonexistent dates. For example, adding one month to January 31 should not yield February 31. Instead of throwing an exception, these methods return the last valid day of the month. For example,

```
LocalDate.of(2016, 1, 31).plusMonths(1)
```

and

```
LocalDate.of(2016, 3, 31).minusMonths(1)
```

yield February 29, 2016.

The `datesUntil` method yields a stream of `LocalDate` objects between a start and an end date:

```
Stream<LocalDate> allDaysInMay2018
    = LocalDate.of(2018,5,1).datesUntil(LocalDate.of(2018,6,1));
Stream<LocalDate> allMondaysIn2018
    = LocalDate.of(2018,1,1).datesUntil(LocalDate.of(2019,1,1), Period.ofDays(7));
```

The `getDayOfWeek` yields the weekday, as a value of the `DayOfWeek` enumeration. `DayOfWeek.MONDAY` has the numerical value 1, and `DayOfWeek.SUNDAY` has the value 7. For example,

```
LocalDate.of(1900, 1, 1).getDayOfWeek().getValue()
```

yields 1. The `DayOfWeek` enumeration has convenience methods `plus` and `minus` to compute weekdays modulo 7. For example, `DayOfWeek.SATURDAY.plus(3)` yields `DayOfWeek.TUESDAY`.

 NOTE: The weekend days actually come at the end of the week. This is different from `java.util.Calendar` where Sunday has value 1 and Saturday value 7.

In addition to `LocalDate`, there are also classes `MonthDay`, `YearMonth`, and `Year` to describe partial dates. For example, December 25 (with the year unspecified) can be represented as a `MonthDay`.

12.3 Date Adjusters

For scheduling applications, you often need to compute dates such as "the first Tuesday of every month." The `TemporalAdjusters` class provides a number of static methods for common adjustments. You pass the result of an adjustment method to the `with` method. For example, the first Tuesday of a month can be computed like this:

```
LocalDate firstTuesday = LocalDate.of(year, month, 1).with(
   TemporalAdjusters.nextOrSame(DayOfWeek.TUESDAY));
```

As always, the `with` method returns a new `LocalDate` object without modifying the original. Table 12-3 shows the available adjusters.

Table 12-3 Date Adjusters in the `TemporalAdjusters` Class

Method	Description
`next(weekday)`, `previous(weekday)`	Next or previous date that falls on the given `weekday`
`nextOrSame(weekday)`, `previousOrSame(weekday)`	Next or previous date that falls on the given `weekday`, starting from the given date
`dayOfWeekInMonth(n, weekday)`	The nth `weekday` in the month
`lastInMonth(weekday)`	The last `weekday` in the month
`firstDayOfMonth()`, `firstDayOfNextMonth()`, `firstDayOfNextYear()`, `lastDayOfMonth()`, `lastDayOfPreviousMonth()`, `lastDayOfYear()`	The date described in the method name

You can also make your own adjuster by implementing the `TemporalAdjuster` interface. Here is an adjuster for computing the next weekday:

```
TemporalAdjuster NEXT_WORKDAY = w -> {
   LocalDate result = (LocalDate) w;
   do {
      result = result.plusDays(1);
   } while (result.getDayOfWeek().getValue() >= 6);
   return result;
};

LocalDate backToWork = today.with(NEXT_WORKDAY);
```

Note that the parameter of the lambda expression has type `Temporal`, and it must be cast to `LocalDate`. You can avoid this cast with the `ofDateAdjuster` method that expects a `UnaryOperator<LocalDate>`. Here we specify the adjuster as a lambda expression.

```
TemporalAdjuster NEXT_WORKDAY = TemporalAdjusters.ofDateAdjuster(w -> {
   LocalDate result = w; // No cast
   do {
      result = result.plusDays(1);
   } while (result.getDayOfWeek().getValue() >= 6);
   return result;
});
```

12.4 Local Time

A LocalTime represents a time of day, such as 15:30:00. You can create an instance with the now or of methods:

```
LocalTime rightNow = LocalTime.now();
LocalTime bedtime = LocalTime.of(22, 30); // or LocalTime.of(22, 30, 0)
```

Table 12-4 shows common operations with local times. The plus and minus operations wrap around a 24-hour day. For example,

```
LocalTime wakeup = bedtime.plusHours(8); // wakeup is 6:30:00
```

 NOTE: LocalTime doesn't concern itself with AM/PM. That silliness is left to a formatter—see Section 12.6, "Formatting and Parsing" (page 413).

Table 12-4 LocalTime Methods

Method	Description
now, of, ofInstant	These static methods construct a LocalTime from the current time, from the given hours, minutes, and, optionally, seconds and nanoseconds, or from an Instant and ZoneId.
plusHours, plusMinutes, plusSeconds, plusNanos	Adds a number of hours, minutes, seconds, or nanoseconds to this LocalTime.
minusHours, minusMinutes, minusSeconds, minusNanos	Subtracts a number of hours, minutes, seconds, or nanoseconds from this LocalTime.
plus, minus	Adds or subtracts a Duration.
withHour, withMinute, withSecond, withNano	Returns a new LocalTime with the hour, minute, second, or nanosecond changed to the given value.
getHour, getMinute, getSecond, getNano	Gets the hour, minute, second, or nanosecond of this LocalTime.
toSecondOfDay, toNanoOfDay	Returns the number of seconds or nanoseconds between midnight and this LocalTime.
toEpochSecond	Given a LocalDate and ZoneOffset, yields the number of seconds from the epoch to the specified point in time.
isBefore, isAfter	Compares this LocalTime with another.

There is a LocalDateTime class representing a date and time. That class is suitable for storing points in time in a fixed time zone—for example, for a schedule of classes or events. However, if you need to make calculations that span the daylight savings time, or if you need to deal with users in different time zones, you should use the ZonedDateTime class that we discuss next.

12.5 Zoned Time

Time zones, perhaps because they are an entirely human creation, are even messier than the complications caused by the Earth's irregular rotation. In a rational world, we'd all follow the clock in Greenwich, and some of us would eat our lunch at 02:00, others at 22:00. Our stomachs would figure it out. This is actually done in China, which spans four conventional time zones. Elsewhere, we have time zones with irregular and shifting boundaries and, to make matters worse, the daylight savings time.

As capricious as the time zones may appear to the enlightened, they are a fact of life. When you implement a calendar application, it needs to work for people who fly from one country to another. When you have a conference call at 10:00 in New York, but happen to be in Berlin, you expect to be alerted at the correct local time.

The Internet Assigned Numbers Authority (IANA) keeps a database of all known time zones around the world (https://www.iana.org/time-zones), which is updated several times per year. The bulk of the updates deals with the changing rules for daylight savings time. Java uses the IANA database.

Each time zone has an ID, such as America/New_York or Europe/Berlin. To find out all available time zones, call ZoneId.getAvailableIds. At the time of this writing, there were almost 600 IDs.

Given a time zone ID, the static method ZoneId.of(id) yields a ZoneId object. You can use that object to turn a LocalDateTime object into a ZonedDateTime object by calling local.atZone(zoneId), or you can construct a ZonedDateTime by calling the static method ZonedDateTime.of(year, month, day, hour, minute, second, nano, zoneId). For example,

```
ZonedDateTime apollo11launch = ZonedDateTime.of(1969, 7, 16, 9, 32, 0, 0,
   ZoneId.of("America/New_York"));
   // 1969-07-16T09:32-04:00[America/New_York]
```

This is a specific instant in time. Call apollo11launch.toInstant to get the Instant. Conversely, if you have an instant in time, call instant.atZone(ZoneId.of("UTC")) to get the ZonedDateTime at the Greenwich Royal Observatory, or use another ZoneId to get it elsewhere on the planet.

NOTE: UTC stands for "Coordinated Universal Time," and the acronym is a compromise between the aforementioned English and the French "Temps Universel Coordiné," having the distinction of being incorrect in either language. UTC is the time at the Greenwich Royal Observatory, without daylight savings time.

Many of the methods of ZonedDateTime are the same as those of LocalDateTime (see Table 12-5). Most are straightforward, but daylight savings time introduces some complications.

Table 12–5 ZonedDateTime Methods

Method	Description
now, of, ofInstant	These static methods construct a ZonedDateTime from the current time, or from a year, month, day, hour, minute, second, nanosecond (or a LocalDate and LocalTime), and ZoneId, or from an Instant and ZoneId.
plusDays, plusWeeks, plusMonths, plusYears, plusHours, plusMinutes, plusSeconds, plusNanos	Adds a number of temporal units to this ZonedDateTime.
minusDays, minusWeeks, minusMonths, minusYears, minusHours, minusMinutes, minusSeconds, minusNanos	Subtracts a number of temporal units from this LocalDate.
plus, minus	Adds or subtracts a Duration or Period.
withDayOfMonth, withDayOfYear, withMonth, withYear, withHour, withMinute, withSecond, withNano	Returns a new ZonedDateTime, with one temporal unit changed to the given value.
withZoneSameInstant, withZoneSameLocal	Returns a new ZonedDateTime in the given time zone, either representing the same instant or the same local time.
getDayOfMonth	Gets the day of the month (between 1 and 31).
getDayOfYear	Gets the day of the year (between 1 and 366).
getDayOfWeek	Gets the day of the week, returning a value of the DayOfWeek enumeration.

(Continues)

Table 12-5 ZonedDateTime Methods *(Continued)*

Method	Description
getMonth, getMonthValue	Gets the month as a value of the Month enumeration, or as a number between 1 and 12.
getYear	Gets the year, between −999,999,999 and 999,999,999.
getHour, getMinute, getSecond, getNano	Gets the hour, minute, second, or nanosecond of this ZonedDateTime.
getOffset	Gets the offset from UTC, as a ZoneOffset instance. Offsets can vary from −12:00 to +14:00. Some time zones have fractional offsets. Offsets change with daylight savings time.
toLocalDate, toLocalTime, toInstant	Yields the local date or local time, or the corresponding instant.
isBefore, isAfter	Compares this ZonedDateTime with another.

When daylight savings time starts, clocks advance by an hour. What happens when you construct a time that falls into the skipped hour? For example, in 2013, Central Europe switched to daylight savings time on March 31 at 2:00. If you try to construct nonexistent time March 31 2:30, you actually get 3:30.

```
ZonedDateTime skipped = ZonedDateTime.of(
    LocalDate.of(2013, 3, 31),
    LocalTime.of(2, 30),
    ZoneId.of("Europe/Berlin"));
    // Constructs March 31 3:30
```

Conversely, when daylight time ends, clocks are set back by an hour, and there are two instants with the same local time! When you construct a time within that span, you get the earlier of the two.

```
ZonedDateTime ambiguous = ZonedDateTime.of(
    LocalDate.of(2013, 10, 27), // End of daylight savings time
    LocalTime.of(2, 30),
    ZoneId.of("Europe/Berlin"));
    // 2013-10-27T02:30+02:00[Europe/Berlin]
ZonedDateTime anHourLater = ambiguous.plusHours(1);
    // 2013-10-27T02:30+01:00[Europe/Berlin]
```

An hour later, the time has the same hours and minutes, but the zone offset has changed.

You also need to pay attention when adjusting a date across daylight savings time boundaries. For example, if you set a meeting for next week, don't add a duration of seven days:

```
ZonedDateTime nextMeeting = meeting.plus(Duration.ofDays(7));
   // Caution! Won't work with daylight savings time
```

Instead, use the `Period` class.

```
ZonedDateTime nextMeeting = meeting.plus(Period.ofDays(7)); // OK
```

 CAUTION: There is also an `OffsetDateTime` class that represents times with an offset from UTC, but without time zone rules. That class is intended for specialized applications that specifically require the absence of those rules, such as certain network protocols. For human time, use `ZonedDateTime`.

12.6 Formatting and Parsing

The `DateTimeFormatter` class provides three kinds of formatters to print a date/time value:

- Predefined standard formatters (see Table 12-6)
- Locale-specific formatters
- Formatters with custom patterns

To use one of the standard formatters, simply call its `format` method:

```
String formatted = DateTimeFormatter.ISO_DATE_TIME.format(apollo11launch);
   // 1969-07-16T09:32:00-05:00[America/New_York]
```

The standard formatters are mostly intended for machine-readable timestamps. To present dates and times to human readers, use a locale-specific formatter. There are four styles, `SHORT`, `MEDIUM`, `LONG`, and `FULL`, for both date and time—see Table 12-7.

The static methods `ofLocalizedDate`, `ofLocalizedTime`, and `ofLocalizedDateTime` create such a formatter. For example:

```
DateTimeFormatter formatter = DateTimeFormatter.ofLocalizedDateTime(FormatStyle.LONG);
String formatted = formatter.format(apollo11launch);
   // July 16, 1969 9:32:00 AM EDT
```

These methods use the default locale. To change to a different locale, simply use the `withLocale` method.

```
formatted = formatter.withLocale(Locale.FRENCH).format(apollo11launch);
   // 16 juillet 1969 09:32:00 EDT
```

Table 12-6 Predefined Formatters

Formatter	Description	Example
BASIC_ISO_DATE	Year, month, day, zone offset without separators	19690716-0500
ISO_LOCAL_DATE, ISO_LOCAL_TIME, ISO_LOCAL_DATE_TIME	Separators -, :, T	1969-07-16, 09:32:00, 1969-07-16T09:32:00
ISO_OFFSET_DATE, ISO_OFFSET_TIME, ISO_OFFSET_DATE_TIME	Like ISO_LOCAL_*XXX*, but with zone offset	1969-07-16-05:00, 09:32:00-05:00, 1969-07-16T09:32:00-05:00
ISO_ZONED_DATE_TIME	With zone offset and zone ID	1969-07-16T09:32:00-05:00[America/New_York]
ISO_INSTANT	In UTC, denoted by the Z zone ID	1969-07-16T14:32:00Z
ISO_DATE, ISO_TIME, ISO_DATE_TIME	Like ISO_OFFSET_DATE, ISO_OFFSET_TIME, and ISO_ZONED_DATE_TIME, but the zone information is optional	1969-07-16-05:00, 09:32:00-05:00, 1969-07-16T09:32:00-05:00[America/New_York]
ISO_ORDINAL_DATE	The year and day of year, for LocalDate	1969-197
ISO_WEEK_DATE	The year, week, and day of week, for LocalDate	1969-W29-3
RFC_1123_DATE_TIME	The standard for email timestamps, codified in RFC 822 and updated to four digits for the year in RFC 1123	Wed, 16 Jul 1969 09:32:00 -0500

Table 12-7 Date and Time Formatting Styles

Style	Date	Time
SHORT	7/16/69	9:32 AM
MEDIUM	Jul 16, 1969	9:32:00 AM
LONG	July 16, 1969	9:32:00 AM EDT
FULL	Wednesday, July 16, 1969	9:32:00 AM EDT

The `DayOfWeek` and `Month` enumerations have methods `getDisplayName` for giving the names of weekdays and months in different locales and formats.

```
for (DayOfWeek w : DayOfWeek.values())
    System.out.print(w.getDisplayName(TextStyle.SHORT, Locale.ENGLISH) + " ");
    // Prints Mon Tue Wed Thu Fri Sat Sun
```

See Chapter 13 for more information about locales.

NOTE: The `java.time.format.DateTimeFormatter` class is intended as a replacement for `java.util.DateFormat`. If you need an instance of the latter for backwards compatibility, call `formatter.toFormat()`.

Finally, you can roll your own date format by specifying a pattern. For example,

```
formatter = DateTimeFormatter.ofPattern("E yyyy-MM-dd HH:mm");
```

formats a date in the form `Wed 1969-07-16 09:32`. Each letter denotes a different time field, and the number of times the letter is repeated selects a particular format, according to rules that are arcane and seem to have organically grown over time. Table 12-8 shows the most useful pattern elements.

To parse a date/time value from a string, use one of the static `parse` methods. For example,

```
LocalDate churchsBirthday = LocalDate.parse("1903-06-14");
ZonedDateTime apollo11launch
    = ZonedDateTime.parse("1969-07-16 03:32:00-0400",
        DateTimeFormatter.ofPattern("yyyy-MM-dd HH:mm:ssxx"));
```

The first call uses the standard `ISO_LOCAL_DATE` formatter, the second one a custom formatter.

Table 12-8 Commonly Used Formatting Symbols for Date/Time Formats

ChronoField or Purpose	Examples
ERA	G: AD, GGGG: Anno Domini, GGGGG: A
YEAR_OF_ERA	yy: 69, yyyy: 1969
MONTH_OF_YEAR	M: 7, MM: 07, MMM: Jul, MMMM: July, MMMMM: J
DAY_OF_MONTH	d: 6, dd: 06
DAY_OF_WEEK	e: 3, E: Wed, EEEE: Wednesday, EEEEE: W
HOUR_OF_DAY	H: 9, HH: 09
CLOCK_HOUR_OF_AM_PM	K: 9, KK: 09
AMPM_OF_DAY	a: AM
MINUTE_OF_HOUR	mm: 02
SECOND_OF_MINUTE	ss: 00
NANO_OF_SECOND	nnnnnn: 000000
Time zone ID	VV: America/New_York
Time zone name	z: EDT, zzzz: Eastern Daylight Time
Zone offset	x: -04, xx: -0400, xxx: -04:00, XXX: same, but use Z for zero
Localized zone offset	O: GMT-4, OOOO: GMT-04:00

12.7 Interoperating with Legacy Code

The Java Date and Time API must interoperate with existing classes, in particular, the ubiquitous java.util.Date, java.util.GregorianCalendar, and java.sql.Date/Time/Timestamp.

The Instant class is a close analog to java.util.Date. In Java 8, that class has two added methods: the toInstant method that converts a Date to an Instant, and the static from method that converts in the other direction.

Similarly, ZonedDateTime is a close analog to java.util.GregorianCalendar, and that class has gained conversion methods in Java 8. The toZonedDateTime method converts a GregorianCalendar to a ZonedDateTime, and the static from method does the opposite conversion.

Another set of conversions is available for the date and time classes in the java.sql package. You can also pass a DateTimeFormatter to legacy code that uses java.text.Format. Table 12-9 summarizes these conversions.

Table 12-9 Conversions between java.time Classes and Legacy Classes

Classes	To Legacy Class	From Legacy Class
Instant ↔ java.util.Date	Date.from(instant)	date.toInstant()
ZonedDateTime ↔ java.util.GregorianCalendar	GregorianCalendar.from(zonedDateTime)	cal.toZonedDateTime()
Instant ↔ java.sql.Timestamp	TimeStamp.from(instant)	timestamp.toInstant()
LocalDateTime ↔ java.sql.Timestamp	Timestamp.valueOf(localDateTime)	timeStamp.toLocalDateTime()
LocalDate ↔ java.sql.Date	Date.valueOf(localDate)	date.toLocalDate()
LocalTime ↔ java.sql.Time	Time.valueOf(localTime)	time.toLocalTime()
DateTimeFormatter → java.text.DateFormat	formatter.toFormat()	None
java.util.TimeZone → ZoneId	Timezone.getTimeZone(id)	timeZone.toZoneId()
java.nio.file.attribute.FileTime → Instant	FileTime.from(instant)	fileTime.toInstant()

Exercises

1. Compute Programmer's Day without using plusDays.
2. What happens when you add one year to LocalDate.of(2000, 2, 29)? Four years? Four times one year?
3. Implement a method next that takes a Predicate<LocalDate> and returns an adjuster yielding the next date fulfilling the predicate. For example,

   ```
   today.with(next(w -> getDayOfWeek().getValue() < 6))
   ```

   computes the next workday.

4. Write an equivalent of the Unix cal program that displays a calendar for a month. For example, java Cal 3 2013 should display

    ```
              1  2  3
     4  5  6  7  8  9 10
    11 12 13 14 15 16 17
    18 19 20 21 22 23 24
    25 26 27 28 29 30 31
    ```

    indicating that March 1 is a Friday. (Show the weekend at the end of the week.)

5. Write a program that prints how many days you have been alive.

6. List all Friday the 13th in the twentieth century.

7. Implement a TimeInterval class that represents an interval of time, suitable for calendar events (such as a meeting on a given date from 10:00 to 11:00). Provide a method to check whether two intervals overlap.

8. Obtain the offsets of today's date in all supported time zones for the current time instant, turning ZoneId.getAvailableZoneIds into a stream and using stream operations.

9. Again using stream operations, find all time zones whose offsets aren't full hours.

10. Your flight from Los Angeles to Frankfurt leaves at 3:05 pm local time and takes 10 hours and 50 minutes. When does it arrive? Write a program that can handle calculations like this.

11. Your return flight leaves Frankfurt at 14:05 and arrives in Los Angeles at 16:40. How long is the flight? Write a program that can handle calculations like this.

12. Write a program that solves the problem described at the beginning of Section 12.5, "Zoned Time" (page 410). Read a set of appointments in different time zones and alert the user which ones are due within the next hour in local time.

Internationalization

Topics in This Chapter

Chapter 13

There's a big world out there, and hopefully many of its inhabitants will be interested in your software. Some programmers believe that all they need to do to internationalize their application is to support Unicode and translate the messages in the user interface. However, as you will see, there is a lot more to internationalizing programs. Dates, times, currencies, even numbers are formatted differently in different parts of the world. In this chapter, you will learn how to use the internationalization features of Java so that your programs present and accept information in a way that makes sense to your users, wherever they may be.

At the end of this chapter, you will find a brief overview of the Java Preferences API for storing user preferences.

The key points of this chapter are:

1. Translating an application for international users requires more than translating messages. In particular, formatting for numbers and dates varies widely across the world.

2. A locale describes language and formatting preferences for a population of users.

3. The `NumberFormat` and `DateTimeFormat` classes handle locale-aware formatting of numbers, currencies, dates, and times.

4. The `MessageFormat` class can format message strings with placeholders, each of which can have its own format.

5. Use the `Collator` class for locale-dependent sorting of strings.

6. The `ResourceBundle` class manages localized strings and objects for multiple locales.

7. The `Preferences` class can be used for storing user preferences in a platform-independent way.

13.1 Locales

When you look at an application that is adapted to an international market, the most obvious difference is the language. But there are many more subtle differences; for example, numbers are formatted quite differently in English and in German. The number

```
123,456.78
```

should be displayed as

```
123.456,78
```

for a German user—that is, the roles of the decimal point and the decimal comma separator are reversed. There are similar variations in the display of dates. In the United States, dates are displayed as month/day/year; Germany uses the more sensible order of day/month/year, whereas in China, the usage is year/month/day. Thus, the American date

```
3/22/61
```

should be presented as

```
22.03.1961
```

to a German user. If the month names are written out explicitly, then the difference in languages becomes even more apparent. The English

```
March 22, 1961
```

should be presented as

```
22. März 1961
```

in German, or

```
1961年3月22日
```

in Chinese.

A *locale* specifies the language and location of a user, which allows formatters to take user preferences into account. The following sections show you how to specify a locale and how to control the locale settings of a Java program.

13.1.1 Specifying a Locale

A locale consists of up to five components:

1. A language, specified by two or three lowercase letters, such as en (English), de (German), or zh (Chinese). Table 13-1 shows common codes.

2. Optionally, a script, specified by four letters with an initial uppercase, such as Latn (Latin), Cyrl (Cyrillic), or Hant (traditional Chinese characters). This can be useful because some languages, such as Serbian, are written in Latin or Cyrillic, and some Chinese readers prefer the traditional over the simplified characters.

3. Optionally, a country or region, specified by two uppercase letters or three digits, such as US (United States) or CH (Switzerland). Table 13-2 shows common codes.

4. Optionally, a *variant*.

5. Optionally, an extension. Extensions describe local preferences for calendars (such as the Japanese calendar), numbers (Thai instead of Western digits), and so on. The Unicode standard specifies some of these extensions. Extensions start with u- and a two-letter code specifying whether the extension deals with the calendar (ca), numbers (nu), and so on. For example, the extension u-nu-thai denotes the use of Thai numerals. Other extensions are entirely arbitrary and start with x-, such as x-java.

 NOTE: Variants are rarely used nowadays. There used to be a "Nynorsk" variant of Norwegian, but it is now expressed with a different language code, nn. What used to be variants for the Japanese imperial calendar and Thai numerals are now expressed as extensions.

Rules for locales are formulated in the "Best Current Practices" memo BCP 47 of the Internet Engineering Task Force (http://tools.ietf.org/html/bcp47). You can find a more accessible summary at www.w3.org/International/articles/language-tags.

Table 13-1 Common Language Codes

Language	Code	Language	Code
Chinese	zh	Japanese	ja
Danish	da	Korean	ko
Dutch	du	Norwegian	no
English	en	Portugese	pt
French	fr	Spanish	es
Finnish	fi	Swedish	sv
Italian	it	Turkish	tr

Table 13-2 Common Country Codes

Country	Code	Country	Code
Austria	AT	Japan	JP
Belgium	BE	Korea	KR
Canada	CA	The Netherlands	NL
China	CN	Norway	NO
Denmark	DK	Portugal	PT
Finland	FI	Spain	ES
Germany	DE	Sweden	SE
Great Britain	GB	Switzerland	CH
Greece	GR	Taiwan	TW
Ireland	IE	Turkey	TR
Italy	IT	United States	US

 NOTE: The codes for languages and countries seem a bit random because some of them are derived from local languages. German in German is Deutsch, Chinese in Chinese is zhongwen; hence de and zh. And Switzerland is CH, deriving from the latin term *Confoederatio Helvetica* for the Swiss confederation.

Locales are described by tags—hyphenated strings of locale elements such as en-US.

In Germany, you would use a locale de-DE. Switzerland has four official languages (German, French, Italian, and Rhaeto-Romance). A German speaker in Switzerland would want to use a locale de-CH. This locale uses the rules for the German language, but currency values are expressed in Swiss francs, not euros.

If you only specify the language, say, de, then the locale cannot be used for country-specific issues such as currencies.

You can construct a Locale object from a tag string like this:

```
Locale usEnglish = Locale.forLanguageTag("en-US");
```

The toLanguageTag method yields the language tag for a given locale. For example, Locale.US.toLanguageTag() is the string "en-US".

For your convenience, there are predefined locale objects for various countries:

```
Locale.CANADA
Locale.CANADA_FRENCH
Locale.CHINA
Locale.FRANCE
Locale.GERMANY
Locale.ITALY
Locale.JAPAN
Locale.KOREA
Locale.PRC
Locale.TAIWAN
Locale.UK
Locale.US
```

A number of predefined locales specify just a language without a location:

```
Locale.CHINESE
Locale.ENGLISH
Locale.FRENCH
Locale.GERMAN
Locale.ITALIAN
Locale.JAPANESE
Locale.KOREAN
Locale.SIMPLIFIED_CHINESE
Locale.TRADITIONAL_CHINESE
```

Finally, the static getAvailableLocales method returns an array of all locales known to the virtual machine.

 NOTE: You can get all language codes as Locale.getISOLanguages() and all country codes as Locale.getISOCountries().

13.1.2 The Default Locale

The static `getDefault` method of the `Locale` class initially gets the default locale as stored by the local operating system.

Some operating systems allow the user to specify different locales for displayed messages and for formatting. For example, a French speaker living in the United States can have French menus but currency values in dollar.

To obtain these preferences, call

```
Locale displayLocale = Locale.getDefault(Locale.Category.DISPLAY);
Locale formatLocale = Locale.getDefault(Locale.Category.FORMAT);
```

 NOTE: In Unix, you can specify separate locales for numbers, currencies, and dates, by setting the `LC_NUMERIC`, `LC_MONETARY`, and `LC_TIME` environment variables. Java does not pay attention to these settings.

 TIP: For testing, you might want to switch the default locale of your program. Supply the language and region properties when you launch your program. For example, here we set the default locale to German (Switzerland):

```
java -Duser.language=de -Duser.country=CH MainClass
```

You can also change the script and variant, and you can have separate settings for the display and format locales, for example, `-Duser.script.display=Hant`.

You can change the default locale of the virtual machine by calling one of

```
Locale.setDefault(newLocale);
Locale.setDefault(category, newLocale);
```

The first call changes the locales returned by `Locale.getDefault()` and `Locale.getDefault(category)` for all categories.

13.1.3 Display Names

Suppose you want to allow a user to choose among a set of locales. You don't want to display cryptic tag strings; the `getDisplayName` method returns a string describing the locale in a form that can be presented to a user, such as

```
German (Switzerland)
```

Actually, there is a problem here. The display name is issued in the default locale. That might not be appropriate. If your user already selected German as the preferred language, you probably want to present the string in German. You can do just that by giving the German locale as a parameter. The code

```
Locale loc = Locale.forLanguageTag("de-CH");
System.out.println(loc.getDisplayName(Locale.GERMAN));
```

prints

```
Deutsch (Schweiz)
```

This example shows why you need `Locale` objects. You feed them to locale-aware methods that produce text to be presented to users in different locations. You will see many examples in the following sections.

 CAUTION: Even such mundane operations as turning a string into lowercase or uppercase can be locale-specific. For example, in the Turkish locale, the lowercase of the letter I is a dotless ı. Programs that tried to normalize strings by storing them in lowercase have mysteriously failed for Turkish customers. It is a good idea to always use the variants of `toUpperCase` and `toLowerCase` that take a `Locale` argument. For example, try out:

```
String cmd = "QUIT".toLowerCase(Locale.forLanguageTag("tr"));
    // "quıt" with a dotless ı
```

Of course, in Turkey, where `Locale.getDefault()` yields just that locale, `"QUIT".toLowerCase()` is not the same as `"quit"`.

If you want to normalize English language strings to lowercase, you should pass an English locale to the `toLowerCase` method.

 NOTE: You can explicitly set the locale for input and output operations.

- When reading numbers from a `Scanner`, you can set its locale with the `useLocale` method.

- The `String.format` and `PrintWriter.printf` methods optionally take a `Locale` argument.

13.2 Number Formats

The `NumberFormat` class in the `java.text` package provides three factory methods for formatters that can format and parse numbers: `getNumberInstance`, `getCurrencyInstance`, and `getPercentInstance`. For example, here is how you can format a currency value in German:

```
Locale loc = Locale.GERMANY;
NumberFormat formatter = NumberFormat.getCurrencyInstance(loc);
double amt = 123456.78;
String result = formatter.format(amt);
```

The result is

```
123.456,78€
```

Note that the currency symbol is € and that it is placed at the end of the string. Also, note the reversal of decimal points and decimal commas.

Conversely, to read in a number that was entered or stored with the conventions of a certain locale, use the parse method:

```
String input = ...;
NumberFormat formatter = NumberFormat.getNumberInstance();
   // Get the number formatter for default format locale
Number parsed = formatter.parse(input);
double x = parsed.doubleValue();
```

The return type of parse is the abstract type Number. The returned object is either a Double or a Long wrapper object, depending on whether the parsed number was a floating-point number. If you don't care about the distinction, you can simply use the doubleValue method of the Number class to retrieve the wrapped number.

If the text for the number is not in the correct form, the method throws a ParseException. For example, leading whitespace in the string is not allowed. (Call trim to remove it.) However, any characters that follow the number in the string are simply ignored, and no exception is thrown.

13.3 Currencies

To format a currency value, you can use the NumberFormat.getCurrencyInstance method. However, that method is not very flexible—it returns a formatter for a single currency. Suppose you prepare an invoice for an American customer in which some amounts are in dollars and others are in euros. You can't just use two formatters

```
NumberFormat dollarFormatter = NumberFormat.getCurrencyInstance(Locale.US);
NumberFormat euroFormatter = NumberFormat.getCurrencyInstance(Locale.GERMANY);
```

Your invoice would look very strange, with some values formatted like $100,000 and others like 100.000€. (Note that the euro value uses a decimal point, not a comma.)

Instead, use the Currency class to control the currency used by the formatters. You can get a Currency object by passing a currency identifier to the static

`Currency.getInstance` method. Table 13-3 lists common identifiers. The static method `Currency.getAvailableCurrencies` yields a `Set<Currency>` with the currencies known to the virtual machine.

Once you have a `Currency` object, call the `setCurrency` method for the formatter. Here is how to format euro amounts for your American customer:

```
NumberFormat formatter = NumberFormat.getCurrencyInstance(Locale.US);
formatter.setCurrency(Currency.getInstance("EUR"));
System.out.println(formatter.format(euros));
```

If you need to display localized names or symbols of currencies, call

```
getDisplayName()
getSymbol()
```

These methods return strings in the default display locale. You can also provide an explicit locale parameter.

Table 13–3 Common Currency Identifiers

Currency	Identifier	Currency	Identifier
U. S. Dollar	USD	Chinese Renminbi (Yuan)	CNY
Euro	EUR	Indian Rupee	INR
British Pound	GBP	Russian Ruble	RUB
Japanese Yen	JPY	Swiss Francs	CHF

13.4 Date and Time Formatting

When formatting date and time, there are four locale-dependent issues:

1. The names of months and weekdays should be presented in the local language.
2. There will be local preferences for the order of year, month, and day.
3. The Gregorian calendar might not be the local preference for expressing dates.
4. The time zone of the location must be taken into account.

Use the `DateTimeFormatter` from the `java.time.format` package, and not the legacy `java.util.DateFormat`. Decide whether you need the date, time, or both. Pick one of four formats—see Table 13-4. If you format date and time, you can pick them separately.

Table 13-4 Locale-Specific Formatting Styles

Style	Date	Time
SHORT	7/16/69	9:32 AM
MEDIUM	Jul 16, 1969	9:32:00 AM
LONG	July 16, 1969	9:32:00 AM EDT
FULL	Wednesday, July 16, 1969	9:32:00 AM EDT

Then get a formatter:

```
FormatStyle style = ...; // One of FormatStyle.SHORT, FormatStyle.MEDIUM, . . .
DateTimeFormatter dateFormatter = DateTimeFormatter.ofLocalizedDate(style);
DateTimeFormatter timeFormatter = DateTimeFormatter.ofLocalizedTime(style);
DateTimeFormatter dateTimeFormatter = DateTimeFormatter.ofLocalizedDateTime(style);
   // or DateTimeFormatter.ofLocalizedDateTime(style1, style2)
```

These formatters use the current format locale. To use a different locale, use the withLocale method:

```
DateTimeFormatter dateFormatter
   = DateTimeFormatter.ofLocalizedDate(style).withLocale(locale);
```

Now you can format a LocalDate, LocalDateTime, LocalTime, or ZonedDateTime:

```
ZonedDateTime appointment = ...;
String formatted = formatter.format(appointment);
```

To parse a string, use one of the static parse methods of LocalDate, LocalDateTime, LocalTime, or ZonedDateTime.

```
LocalTime time = LocalTime.parse("9:32 AM", formatter);
```

If the string cannot be successfully parsed, a DateTimeParseException is thrown.

 CAUTION: These methods are not suitable for parsing human input, at least not without preprocessing. For example, the short time formatter for the United States will parse "9:32 AM" but not "9:32AM" or "9:32 am".

 CAUTION: Date formatters parse nonexistent dates, such as November 31, and adjust them to the last date in the given month.

Sometimes, you need to display just the names of weekdays and months, for example, in a calendar application. Call the getDisplayName method of the DayOfWeek and Month enumerations.

```
for (Month m : Month.values())
    System.out.println(m.getDisplayName(textStyle, locale) + " ");
```

Table 13-5 shows the text styles. The STANDALONE versions are for display outside a formatted date. For example, in Finnish, January is "tammikuuta" inside a date, but "tammikuu" standalone.

 NOTE: The first day of the week can be Saturday, Sunday, or Monday, depending on the locale. You can obtain it like this:

```
DayOfWeek first = WeekFields.of(locale).getFirstDayOfWeek();
```

Table 13-5 Values of the `java.time.format.TextStyle` Enumeration

Style	Example
FULL / FULL_STANDALONE	January
SHORT / SHORT_STANDALONE	Jan
NARROW / NARROW_STANDALONE	J

13.5 Collation and Normalization

Most programmers know how to compare strings with the compareTo method of the String class. Unfortunately, when interacting with human users, this method is not very useful. The compareTo method uses the values of the UTF-16 encoding of the string, which leads to absurd results, even in English. For example, the following five strings are ordered according to the compareTo method:

```
Athens
Zulu
able
zebra
Ångström
```

For dictionary ordering, you would want to consider upper case and lower case equivalent, and accents should not be significant. To an English speaker, the sample list of words should be ordered as

```
able
Ångström
Athens
zebra
Zulu
```

However, that order would not be acceptable to a Swedish user. In Swedish, the letter Å is different from the letter A, and it is collated *after* the letter Z! That is, a Swedish user would want the words to be sorted as

```
able
Athens
zebra
Zulu
Ångström
```

To obtain a locale-sensitive comparator, call the static `Collator.getInstance` method:

```
Collator coll = Collator.getInstance(locale);
words.sort(coll);
    // Collator implements Comparator<Object>
```

There are a couple of advanced settings for collators. You can set a collator's *strength* to adjust how selective it should be. Character differences are classified as primary, secondary, or tertiary. For example, in English, the difference between e and f is considered primary, the difference between e and é is secondary, and between e and E is tertiary.

For example, when processing city names, you may not care about the differences between

```
San José
San Jose
SAN JOSE
```

In that case, configure the collator by calling

```
coll.setStrength(Collator.PRIMARY);
```

A more technical setting is the *decomposition mode* which deals with the fact that a character or sequence of characters can sometimes be described in more than one way in Unicode. For example, an é (U+00E9) can also be expressed as a plain e (U+0065) followed by a ´ (combining acute accent U+0301). You probably don't care about that difference, and by default, it is not significant. If you do care, you need to configure the collator as follows:

```
coll.setStrength(Collator.IDENTICAL);
coll.setDecomposition(Collator.NO_DECOMPOSITION);
```

Conversely, if you want to be very lenient and consider the trademark symbol ™ (U+2122) the same as the character combination TM, then set the decomposition mode to `Collator.FULL_DECOMPOSITION`.

You might want to convert strings into normalized forms even when you don't do collation—for example, for persistent storage or communication with another program. The Unicode standard defines four normalization forms (C,

D, KC, and KD)—see www.unicode.org/unicode/reports/tr15/tr15-23.html. In the normalization form C, accented characters are always composed. For example, a sequence of e and a combining acute accent ´ is combined into a single character é. In form D, accented characters are always decomposed into their base letters and combining accents: é is turned into e followed by ´. Forms KC and KD also decompose characters such as the trademark symbol ™. The W3C recommends that you use normalization form C for transferring data over the Internet.

The static normalize method of the java.text.Normalizer class carries out the normalization process. For example,

```
String city = "San Jose\u0301";
String normalized = Normalizer.normalize(city, Normalizer.Form.NFC);
```

13.6 Message Formatting

When you internationalize a program, you often have messages with variable parts. The static format method of the MessageFormat class takes a template string with placeholders, followed by the placeholder values, like this:

```
String template = "{0} has {1} messages";
String message = MessageFormat.format(template, "Pierre", 42);
```

Of course, instead of hardcoding the template, you should look up a locale-specific one, such as "Il y a {1} messages pour {0}" in French. You will see how to do that in Section 13.7, "Resource Bundles" (page 435).

Note that the ordering of the placeholders may differ among languages. In English, the message is "Pierre has 42 messages", but in French, it is "Il y a 42 messages pour Pierre". The placeholder {0} is the first argument after the template in the call to format, {1} is the next argument, and so on.

You can format numbers as currency amounts by adding a suffix number,currency to the placeholder, like this:

```
template="Your current total is {0,number,currency}."
```

In the United States, a value of 1023.95 is be formatted as $1,023.95. The same value is displayed as 1.023,95€ in Germany, using the local currency symbol and decimal separator convention.

The number indicator can be followed by currency, integer, percent, or a number format pattern of the DecimalFormat class, such as $,##0.

You can format values of the legacy java.util.Date class with an indicator date or time, followed by the format short, medium, long, or full, or a format pattern of the SimpleDateFormat such as yyyy-MM-dd.

Note that you need to convert java.time values; for example,

```
String message = MessageFormat("It is now {0,time,short}.", Date.from(Instant.now()));
```

Finally, a choice formatter lets you generate messages such as

```
No files copied
1 file copied
42 files copied
```

depending on the placeholder value.

A choice format is a sequence of pairs, each containing a lower limit and a format string. The limit and format string are separated by a # character, and the pairs are separated by | characters.

```
String template = "{0,choice,0#No files|1#1 file|2#{0} files} copied";
```

Note that {0} occurs twice in the template. When the message format applies the choice format to the {0} placeholder and the value is 42, the choice format returns "{0} files". That string is then formatted again, and the result is spliced into the message.

NOTE: The design of the choice format is a bit muddleheaded. If you have three format strings, you need *two* limits to separate them. (In general, you need one fewer limit than you have format strings.) The MessageFormat class actually ignores the first limit!

Use the < symbol instead of # to denote that a choice should be selected if the lower bound is strictly less than the value. You can also use the ≤ symbol (U+2264) as a synonym for #, and specify a lower bound of -∞ (a minus sign followed by U+221E) for the first value. This makes the format string easier to read:

```
-∞<No files|0<1 file|2≤{0} files
```

CAUTION: Any text in single quotes ' ... ' is included literally. For example, '{0}' is not a placeholder but the literal string {0}. If the template has single quotes, you must *double them*.

```
String template = "<a href=''{0}''>{1}</a>";
```

The static MessageFormat.format method uses the current format locale to format the values. To format with an arbitrary locale, you have to work a bit harder because there is no "varargs" method that you can use. You need to place the values to be formatted into an Object[] array, like this:

```
MessageFormat mf = new MessageFormat(template, locale);
String message = mf.format(new Object[] { arg1, arg2, ... });
```

13.7 Resource Bundles

When localizing an application, it is best to separate the program from the message strings, button labels, and other texts that need to be translated. In Java, you can place them into *resource bundles*. Then, you can give these bundles to a translator who can edit them without having to touch the source code of the program.

 NOTE: Chapter 4 describes a concept of JAR file resources, whereby data files, sounds, and images can be placed in a JAR file. The `getResource` method of the class `Class` finds the file, opens it, and returns a URL to the resource. That is a useful mechanism for bundling files with a program, but it has no locale support.

13.7.1 Organizing Resource Bundles

When localizing an application, you produce a set of resource bundles. Each bundle is either a property file or a special class, with entries for a particular locale or set of matching locales.

In this section, I only discuss property files since they are much more common than resource classes. A property file is a text file with extension .properties that contains key/value pairs. For example, a file messages_de_DE.properties might contain

```
computeButton=Rechnen
cancelButton=Abbrechen
defaultPaperSize=A4
```

You need to use a specific naming convention for the files that make up these bundles. For example, resources specific to Germany go into a file *bundleName_de_DE*, whereas those shared by all German-speaking countries go into *bundleName_de*. For a given combination of language, script, and country, the following *candidates* are considered:

bundleName_language_script_country
bundleName_language_script
bundleName_language_country
bundleName_language

If *bundleName* contains periods, then the file must be placed in a matching subdirectory. For example, files for the bundle `com.mycompany.messages` are `com/mycompany/messages_de_DE.properties`, and so on.

To load a bundle, call

```
ResourceBundle res = ResourceBundle.getBundle(bundleName);
```

for the default locale, or

```
ResourceBundle bundle = ResourceBundle.getBundle(bundleName, locale);
```

for the given locale.

> **CAUTION:** The first `getBundle` method does *not* use the default display locale, but the overall default locale. If you look up a resource for the user interface, be sure to pass `Locale.getDefault(Locale.Category.DISPLAY)` as the locale.

To look up a string, call the `getString` method with the key.

```
String computeButtonLabel = bundle.getString("computeButton");
```

The rules for loading bundle files are a bit complex and involve two phases. In the first phase, a matching bundle is located. This involves up to three steps.

1. First, all candidate combinations of bundle name, language, script, country, and variant are attempted, in the order given above, until a match is found. For example, if the target locale is `de-DE` and there is no `messages_de_DE.properties` but there is `messages_de.properties`, that becomes the matching bundle.

2. If there is no match, the process is repeated with the default locale. For example, if a German bundle is requested but there is none, and the default locale is `en-US`, then `messages_en_US.properties` is accepted as a match.

3. If there is no match with the default locale either, then the bundle with no suffixes (for example, `messages.properties`) is a match. If that is not present either, the search fails.

> **NOTE:** There are special rules for variants, Chinese simplified and traditional scripts, and Norwegian languages. See the Javadoc for `ResourceBundle.Control` for details.

In the second phase, the *parents* of the matching bundle are located. The parents are those in the candidate list below the matching bundle, and

the bundle without suffixes. For example, the parents of messages_de_DE.properties
are messages_de.properties and messages.properties.

The getString method looks for keys in the matching bundle and its parents.

 NOTE: If the matching bundle was found in the first phase, then its
parents are never taken from the default locale.

 NOTE: In the past, property files were limited to using the ASCII
character set. All non-ASCII characters had to be encoded using the
\u*xxxx* encoding, like this:

```
prefs=Pr\u00E9fer\u00E9nces
```

Nowadays, property files are assumed to be in UTF-8, and you can
simply write the localized string in the file:

```
prefs=Préférences
```

13.7.2 Bundle Classes

To provide resources that are not strings, define classes that extend the
ResourceBundle class. Use a naming convention similar to that of property
resources, for example

```
com.mycompany.MyAppResources_en_US
com.mycompany.MyAppResources_de
com.mycompany.MyAppResources
```

To implement a resource bundle class, you can extend the ListResourceBundle
class. Place all your resources into an array of key/value pairs and return it
in the getContents method. For example,

```
package com.mycompany;
public class MyAppResources_de extends ListResourceBundle {
    public Object[][] getContents() {
        return new Object[][] {
            { "backgroundColor", Color.BLACK },
            { "defaultPaperSize", new double[] { 210, 297 } }
        };
    }
}
```

To get objects out of such a resource bundle, call the getObject method:

```
ResourceBundle bundle
    = ResourceBundle.getBundle("com.mycompany.MyAppResources", locale);
Color backgroundColor = (Color) bundle.getObject("backgroundColor");
double[] paperSize = (double[]) bundle.getObject("defaultPaperSize");
```

CAUTION: The ResourceBundle.getBundle method gives preference to classes over property files when it finds both a class and a property file with the same bundle name.

13.8 Character Encodings

The fact that Java uses Unicode doesn't mean that all your problems with character encodings have gone away. Fortunately, you don't have to worry about the encoding of String objects. Any string you receive, be it a command-line argument, console input, or input from a GUI text field, will be a UTF-16 encoded string that contains the text provided by the user.

When you display a string, the virtual machine encodes it for the local platform. There are two potential problems. It could happen that a display font does not have a glyph for a particular Unicode character. In a Java GUI, such characters are displayed as hollow boxes. For console output, if the console uses a character encoding that cannot represent all output characters, missing characters are displayed as ?. Users can correct these issues by installing appropriate fonts or by switching the console to UTF-8.

The situation gets more complex when your program reads plain text files produced by users. Simple-minded text editors often produce files in the local platform encoding. You can obtain that encoding by calling

```
Charset platformEncoding = Charset.defaultCharset();
```

This is a reasonable guess for the user's preferred character encoding, but you should allow your users to override it.

If you want to offer a choice of character encodings, you can obtain localized names as

```
String displayName = encoding.displayName(locale);
    // Yields names such as UTF-8, ISO-8859-6, or GB18030
```

Unfortunately, these names aren't really suitable for end users who would want to have choices between Unicode, Arabic, Chinese Simplified, and so on.

 TIP: Java source files are also text files. Assuming you are not the only programmer on a project, don't store source files in the platform encoding. You could represent any non-ASCII characters in code or comments with \u*xxxx* escapes, but that is tedious. Instead, set your text editor to use UTF-8. Either set your console preference to UTF-8, or compile with

```
javac -encoding UTF-8 *.java
```

13.9 Preferences

I close this chapter with an API that is tangentially related to internationalization—the storage of user preferences (which might include the preferred locale).

Of course, you can store preferences in a property file that you load on program startup. However, there is no standard convention for naming and placing configuration files, which increases the likelihood of conflicts as users install multiple Java applications.

Some operating systems have a central repository for configuration information. The best-known example is the registry in Microsoft Windows. The Preferences class, which is the standard mechanism in Java for storing user preferences, uses the registry on Windows. On Linux, the information is stored in the local file system instead. The specific repository implementation is transparent to the programmer using the Preferences class.

The Preferences repository holds a tree of nodes. Each node in the repository has a table of key/value pairs. Values can be numbers, boolean values, strings, or byte arrays.

 NOTE: No provision is made for storing arbitrary objects. You are, of course, free to store a serialized object as a byte array if you aren't worried about using serialization for long-term storage.

Paths to nodes look like /com/mycompany/myapp. As with package names, you can avoid name clashes by starting the paths with reversed domain names.

There are two parallel trees. Each program user has one tree. An additional tree, called the system tree, is available for settings that are common to all users. The Preferences class uses the operating system notion of the "current user" for accessing the appropriate user tree. To access a node in the tree, start with the user or system root:

```
Preferences root = Preferences.userRoot();
```

or

```
Preferences root = Preferences.systemRoot();
```

Then access nodes through their path names:

```
Preferences node = root.node("/com/mycompany/myapp");
```

Alternatively, provide a Class object to the static userNodeForPackage or systemNodeForPackage method, and the node path is derived from the package name of the class.

```
Preferences node = Preferences.userNodeForPackage(obj.getClass());
```

Once you have a node, you can access the key/value table. Retrieve a string with

```
String preferredLocale = node.get("locale", "");
```

For other types, use one of these methods:

```
String get(String key, String defval)
int getInt(String key, int defval)
long getLong(String key, long defval)
float getFloat(String key, float defval)
double getDouble(String key, double defval)
boolean getBoolean(String key, boolean defval)
byte[] getByteArray(String key, byte[] defval)
```

You must specify a default value when reading the information, in case the repository data is not available.

Conversely, you can write data to the repository with put methods such as

```
void put(String key, String value)
void putInt(String key, int value)
```

and so on.

To remove an entry from a node, call

```
void remove(String key)
```

Call node.removeNode() to remove the entire node and its children.

You can enumerate all keys stored in a node, and all child paths of a node, with the methods

```
String[] keys()
String[] childrenNames()
```

 NOTE: There is no way to find out the type of the value of a particular key.

You can export the preferences of a subtree by calling the method

```
void exportSubtree(OutputStream out)
```

on the root node of the subtree.

The data is saved in XML format. You can import it into another repository by calling

```
InputStream in = Files.newInputStream(path);
Preferences.importPreferences(in);
```

Exercises

1. Write a program that demonstrates the date and time formatting styles in France, China, and Thailand (with Thai digits).

2. Which of the locales in your JVM don't use Western digits for formatting numbers?

3. Which of the locales in your JVM use the same date convention (month/day/year) as the United States?

4. Write a program that prints the names of all languages of locales in your JVM in all available languages. Collate them and suppress duplicates.

5. Repeat the preceding exercise for currency names.

6. Write a program that lists all currencies that have different symbols in at least two locales.

7. Write a program that lists the display and standalone month names in all locales in which they differ, excepting those where the standalone names consist of digits.

8. Write a program that lists all Unicode characters that are expanded to two or more ASCII characters in normalization form KC or KD.

9. Take one of your programs and internationalize all messages, using resource bundles in at least two languages.

10. Provide a mechanism for showing available character encodings with a human-readable description, like in your web browser. The language names should be localized. (Use the translations for locale languages.)

11. Provide a class for locale-dependent display of paper sizes, using the preferred dimensional unit and default paper size in the given locale. (Everyone on the planet, with the exception of the United States and Canada, uses ISO 216 paper sizes. Only three countries in the world have not yet officially adopted the metric system: Liberia, Myanmar (Burma), and the United States.)

Compiling and Scripting

Topics in This Chapter

Chapter 14

In this chapter, you will learn how to use the compiler API to compile Java code from inside of your application. You will also see how to run programs written in other languages from your Java programs, using the scripting API. This is particularly useful if you want to give your users the ability to enhance your program with scripts.

The key points of this chapter are:

1. With the compiler API, you can generate Java code on the fly and compile it.

2. The scripting API lets Java program interoperate with a number of scripting languages.

3. The JDK includes Nashorn, a JavaScript interpreter with good performance and fidelity to the JavaScript standard.

4. Nashorn offers a convenient syntax for working with Java lists and maps, as well as JavaBeans properties.

5. Nashorn supports lambda expressions and a limited mechanism for extending Java classes and implementing Java interfaces.

6. Nashorn has support for writing shell scripts in JavaScript.

14.1 The Compiler API

There are quite a few tools that need to compile Java code. Obviously, development environments and programs that teach Java programming are among them, as well as testing and build automation tools. Another example is the processing of JavaServer Pages—web pages with embedded Java statements.

14.1.1 Invoking the Compiler

It is very easy to invoke the compiler. Here is a sample call:

```
JavaCompiler compiler = ToolProvider.getSystemJavaCompiler();
OutputStream outStream = ...;
OutputStream errStream = ...;
int result = compiler.run(null, outStream, errStream,
    "-sourcepath", "src", "Test.java");
```

A result value of 0 indicates successful compilation.

The compiler sends output and error messages to the provided streams. You can set these parameters to null, in which case System.out and System.err are used. The first parameter of the run method is an input stream. As the compiler takes no console input, you can always leave it as null. (The run method is inherited from a generic Tool interface, which allows for tools that read input.)

The remaining parameters of the run method are the arguments that you would pass to javac if you invoked it on the command line. These can be options or file names.

14.1.2 Launching a Compilation Task

You can have more control over the compilation process with a CompilationTask object. This can be useful if you want to supply source from string, capture class files in memory, or process the error and warning messages.

To obtain a CompilationTask, start with a compiler object as in the preceding section. Then call

```
JavaCompiler.CompilationTask task = compiler.getTask(
    errorWriter, // Uses System.err if null
    fileManager, // Uses the standard file manager if null
    diagnostics, // Uses System.err if null
    options, // null if no options
    classes, // For annotation processing; null if none
    sources);
```

The last three arguments are `Iterable` instances. For example, a sequence of options might be specified as

```
Iterable<String> options = List.of("-d", "bin");
```

The `sources` parameter is an `Iterable` of `JavaFileObject` instances. If you want to compile disk files, get a `StandardJavaFileManager` and call its `getJavaFileObjects` method:

```
StandardJavaFileManager fileManager
    = compiler.getStandardFileManager(null, null, null);
Iterable<JavaFileObject> sources
    = fileManager.getJavaFileObjectsFromFiles("File1.java", "File2.java");
JavaCompiler.CompilationTask task
    = compiler.getTask(null, null, null, options, null, sources);
```

 NOTE: The `classes` parameter is only used for annotation processing. In that case, you also need to call `task.processors(annotationProcessors)` with a list of `Processor` objects. See Chapter 11 for an example of annotation processing.

The `getTask` method returns the task object but does not yet start the compilation process. The `CompilationTask` class extends `Callable<Boolean>`. You can pass it to an `ExecutorService` for concurrent execution, or you can just make a synchronous call:

```
Boolean success = task.call();
```

14.1.3 Reading Source Files from Memory

If you generate source code on the fly, you can have it compiled from memory, without having to save files to disk. Use this class to hold the code:

```
public class StringSource extends SimpleJavaFileObject {
    private String code;

    StringSource(String name, String code) {
        super(URI.create("string:///" + name.replace('.','/') + ".java"), Kind.SOURCE);
        this.code = code;
    }

    public CharSequence getCharContent(boolean ignoreEncodingErrors) {
        return code;
    }
}
```

Then generate the code for your classes and give the compiler a list of `StringSource` objects.

```
String pointCode = ...;
String rectangleCode = ...;
List<StringSource> sources = List.of(
    new StringSource("Point", pointCode),
    new StringSource("Rectangle", rectangleCode));
task = compiler.getTask(null, null, null, null, null, sources);
```

14.1.4 Writing Byte Codes to Memory

If you compile classes on the fly, there is no need to save the class files to
disk. You can save them to memory and load them right away.

First, here is a class for holding the bytes:

```
public class ByteArrayClass extends SimpleJavaFileObject {
    private ByteArrayOutputStream out;

    ByteArrayClass(String name) {
        super(URI.create("bytes:///" + name.replace('.','/') + ".class"), Kind.CLASS);
    }

    public byte[] getCode() {
        return out.toByteArray();
    }

    public OutputStream openOutputStream() throws IOException {
        out = new ByteArrayOutputStream();
        return out;
    }
}
```

Next, you need to configure the file manager to use these classes for output:

```
List<ByteArrayClass> classes = new ArrayList<>();
StandardJavaFileManager stdFileManager
    = compiler.getStandardFileManager(null, null, null);
JavaFileManager fileManager
    = new ForwardingJavaFileManager<JavaFileManager>(stdFileManager) {
        public JavaFileObject getJavaFileForOutput(Location location,
            String className, Kind kind, FileObject sibling)
                throws IOException {
            if (kind == Kind.CLASS) {
                ByteArrayClass outfile = new ByteArrayClass(className);
                classes.add(outfile);
                return outfile;
            } else
                return super.getJavaFileForOutput(
                    location, className, kind, sibling);
        }
    };
```

To load the classes, you need a class loader (see Chapter 4):

```
public class ByteArrayClassLoader extends ClassLoader {
    private Iterable<ByteArrayClass> classes;

    public ByteArrayClassLoader(Iterable<ByteArrayClass> classes) {
        this.classes = classes;
    }

    @Override public Class<?> findClass(String name) throws ClassNotFoundException {
        for (ByteArrayClass cl : classes) {
            if (cl.getName().equals("/" + name.replace('.','/') + ".class")) {
                byte[] bytes = cl.getCode();
                return defineClass(name, bytes, 0, bytes.length);
            }
        }
        throw new ClassNotFoundException(name);
    }
}
```

After compilation has finished, call the `Class.forName` method with that class loader:

```
ByteArrayClassLoader loader = new ByteArrayClassLoader(classes);
Class<?> cl = Class.forName("Rectangle", true, loader);
```

14.1.5 Capturing Diagnostics

To listen to error messages, install a `DiagnosticListener`. The listener receives a `Diagnostic` object whenever the compiler reports a warning or error message. The `DiagnosticCollector` class implements this interface. It simply collects all diagnostics so that you can iterate through them after the compilation is complete.

```
DiagnosticCollector<JavaFileObject> collector = new DiagnosticCollector<>();
compiler.getTask(null, fileManager, collector, null, null, sources).call();
for (Diagnostic<? extends JavaFileObject> d : collector.getDiagnostics()) {
    System.out.println(d);
}
```

A `Diagnostic` object contains information about the problem location (including file name, line number, and column number) as well as a human-readable description.

You can also install a `DiagnosticListener` to the standard file manager, in case you want to trap messages about missing files:

```
StandardJavaFileManager fileManager
    = compiler.getStandardFileManager(diagnostics, null, null);
```

14.2 The Scripting API

A scripting language is a language that avoids the usual edit/compile/link/run cycle by interpreting the program text at runtime. This encourages experimentation. Also, scripting languages tend to be less complex, which makes them suitable as extension languages for expert users of your programs.

The scripting API lets you combine the advantages of scripting and traditional languages. It enables you to invoke scripts written in JavaScript, Groovy, Ruby, and even exotic languages such as Scheme and Haskell, from a Java program. In the following sections, you will see how to select an engine for a particular language, how to execute scripts, and how to take advantage of advanced features that some scripting engines offer.

14.2.1 Getting a Scripting Engine

A scripting engine is a library that can execute scripts in a particular language. When the virtual machine starts, it discovers the available scripting engines. To enumerate them, construct a `ScriptEngineManager` and invoke the `getEngineFactories` method.

Usually, you know which engine you need, and you can simply request it by name. For example:

```
ScriptEngineManager manager = new ScriptEngineManager();
ScriptEngine engine = manager.getEngineByName("nashorn");
```

The Java Development Kit contains a JavaScript engine called "Nashorn" described in Section 14.3, "The Nashorn Scripting Engine" (page 452). You can add more languages by providing the necessary JAR files on the class path. There is no longer an official list of languages with Java scripting integration. Just use your favorite search engine to find "JSR 223 support" for your favorite language.

Once you have an engine, you can call a script simply by invoking

```
Object result = engine.eval(scriptString);
```

You can also read a script from a `Reader`:

```
Object result = engine.eval(Files.newBufferedReader(path, charset));
```

You can invoke multiple scripts on the same engine. If one script defines variables, functions, or classes, most scripting engines retain the definitions for later use. For example,

```
engine.eval("n = 1728");
Object result = engine.eval("n + 1");
```

will return 1729.

 NOTE: To find out whether it is safe to concurrently execute scripts in multiple threads, call `engine.getFactory().getParameter("THREADING")`. The returned value is one of the following:

- `null`: Concurrent execution is not safe.

- `"MULTITHREADED"`: Concurrent execution is safe. Effects from one thread might be visible from another thread.

- `"THREAD-ISOLATED"`: In addition, different variable bindings are maintained for each thread.

- `"STATELESS"`: In addition, scripts do not alter variable bindings.

14.2.2 Bindings

A *binding* consists of a name and an associated Java object. For example, consider these statements:

```
engine.put("k", 1728);
Object result = engine.eval("k + 1");
```

Conversely, you can retrieve variables that were bound by scripting statements:

```
engine.eval("n = 1728");
Object result = engine.get("n");
```

These bindings live in the *engine scope*. In addition, there is a global scope. Any bindings that you add to the `ScriptEngineManager` are visible to all engines.

Instead of adding bindings to the engine or global scope, you can collect them in an object of type `Bindings` and pass it to the `eval` method:

```
Bindings scope = engine.createBindings();
scope.put("k", 1728);
Object result = engine.eval("k + 1", scope);
```

This is useful if a set of bindings should not persist for future calls to the `eval` method.

14.2.3 Redirecting Input and Output

You can redirect the standard input and output of a script by calling the `setReader` and `setWriter` methods of the script context. For example,

```
StringWriter writer = new StringWriter();
engine.getContext().setWriter(writer);
engine.eval("print('Hello')");
String result = writer.toString();
```

Any output written with the JavaScript `print` function is sent to `writer`.

The `setReader` and `setWriter` methods only affect the scripting engine's standard input and output sources. For example, if you execute the JavaScript code

```
print('Hello');
java.lang.System.out.println('World');
```

only the first output is redirected.

NOTE: The Nashorn engine does not have the notion of a standard input source. Calling `setReader` has no effect.

NOTE: In JavaScript, semicolons at the end of a line are optional. Many JavaScript programmers put them in anyway, but in this chapter, I omit them so you can more easily distinguish between Java and JavaScript code snippets.

For the same reason, I use '...', not "...", for JavaScript strings whenever possible.

14.2.4 Calling Scripting Functions and Methods

With some scripting engines, you can invoke a function in the scripting language without evaluating the code for the invocation as a script. This is useful if you allow users to implement a service in a scripting language of their choice, so that you can call it from Java.

The scripting engines that offer this functionality (among them Nashorn) implement the `Invocable` interface. To call a function, call the `invokeFunction` method with the function name, followed by the arguments:

```
// Define greet function in JavaScript
engine.eval("function greet(how, whom) { return how + ', ' + whom + '!' }");

// Call the function with arguments "Hello", "World"
result = ((Invocable) engine).invokeFunction(
    "greet", "Hello", "World");
```

If the scripting language is object-oriented, call `invokeMethod`:

```
// Define Greeter class in JavaScript
engine.eval("function Greeter(how) { this.how = how }");
engine.eval("Greeter.prototype.welcome = "
   + " function(whom) { return this.how + ', ' + whom + '!' }");
// Construct an instance
Object yo = engine.eval("new Greeter('Yo')");

// Call the welcome method on the instance
result = ((Invocable) engine).invokeMethod(yo, "welcome", "World");
```

 NOTE: For more information on how to define classes in JavaScript, see *JavaScript—The Good Parts* by Douglas Crockford (O'Reilly, 2008).

 NOTE: If the script engine does not implement the `Invocable` interface, you might still be able to call a method in a language-independent way. The `getMethodCallSyntax` method of the `ScriptEngineFactory` class produces a string that you can pass to the `eval` method.

You can go a step further and ask the scripting engine to implement a Java interface. Then you can call scripting functions and methods with the Java method call syntax.

The details depend on the scripting engine, but typically you need to supply a function for each method of the interface. For example, consider a Java interface

```
public interface Greeter {
    String welcome(String whom);
}
```

If you define a global function with the same name in Nashorn, you can call it through this interface.

```
// Define welcome function in JavaScript
engine.eval("function welcome(whom) { return 'Hello, ' + whom + '!' }");
// Get a Java object and call a Java method
Greeter g = ((Invocable) engine).getInterface(Greeter.class);
result = g.welcome("World");
```

In an object-oriented scripting language, you can access a script class through a matching Java interface. For example, here is how to call an object of the JavaScript `Greeter` class with Java syntax:

```
Greeter g = ((Invocable) engine).getInterface(yo, Greeter.class);
result = g.welcome("World");
```

See Exercise 2 for a more useful example.

14.2.5 Compiling a Script

Some scripting engines can compile scripting code into an intermediate form for efficient execution. Those engines implement the `Compilable` interface. The following example shows how to compile and evaluate code contained in a script file:

```
if (engine implements Compilable) {
    Reader reader = Files.newBufferedReader(path, charset);
    CompiledScript script = ((Compilable) engine).compile(reader);
    script.eval();
}
```

Of course, it only makes sense to compile a script if it does a lot of work or if you need to execute it frequently.

14.3 The Nashorn Scripting Engine

The Java Development Kit ships with a JavaScript engine called Nashorn, which is very fast and highly compliant with version 5.1 of the ECMAScript standard for JavaScript. (An ECMAScript 6.0 implementation is in progress.) You can use Nashorn like any other script engine, but it also has special features for interoperating with Java.

 NOTE: Nashorn is the German word for rhinoceros—literally, nose-horn, an allusion to a well-regarded JavaScript book that has a rhino on the cover. (You get extra karma for pronouncing it nas-horn, not na-shorn.)

14.3.1 Running Nashorn from the Command Line

The Java Development Kit ships with a command-line tool called `jjs` that is similar to the `jshell` tool, except that it is a shell for JavaScript. Simply launch it and issue JavaScript commands.

```
$ jjs
jjs> 'Hello, World'
Hello, World
```

The JavaScript shell provides a "read-eval-print" loop, or REPL. Whenever you enter an expression, its value is printed.

```
jjs> 'Hello, World!'.length
13
```

You can define functions and call them:

```
jjs> function factorial(n) { return n <= 1 ? 1 : n * factorial(n - 1) }
function factorial(n) { return n <= 1 ? 1 : n * factorial(n - 1) }
jjs> factorial(10)
3628800
```

 TIP: When writing more complex functions, it is a good idea to put the JavaScript code into a file and load it into `jjs` with the `load` command:

```
load('functions.js')
```

You can call Java methods:

```
var url = new java.net.URL('http://horstmann.com')
var input = new java.util.Scanner(url.openStream())
input.useDelimiter('$')
var contents = input.next()
```

Now, when you type `contents`, you see the contents of the web page.

Look how refreshing this is. You didn't have to worry about exceptions. You can make experiments dynamically. I wasn't quite sure whether I could read the entire contents by setting the delimiter to $, but I tried it out and it worked. And I didn't have to write `public static void main`. I didn't have to compile a thing. I didn't have to make a project in my IDE. The REPL is an easy way to explore an API. It is a bit odd that one drives Java from JavaScript, but it is also convenient. Note how I didn't have to define the types for the `input` and `contents` variables.

 TIP: The JavaScript REPL would be even more refreshing if it supported command-line editing. On Linux/Unix/Mac OS, you can install `rlwrap` and run `rlwrap jjs`. Then you can press the ↑ key to get the previous commands, and you can edit them. Alternatively, you can run `jjs` inside Emacs. Don't worry—this won't hurt a bit. Start Emacs and hit M-x (that is, Alt+x or Esc x) `shell` Enter, then type `jjs`. Type expressions as usual. Use M-p and M-n to recall the previous or next line, and the left and right arrow keys to move within a line. Edit a command, then press Enter to see it executed.

14.3.2 Invoking Getters, Setters, and Overloaded Methods

When you have Java objects in a Nashorn program, you can invoke methods on them. For example, suppose you get an instance of the Java class `NumberFormat`:

```
var fmt = java.text.NumberFormat.getPercentInstance()
```

Of course, you can call a method on it:

```
fmt.setMinimumFractionDigits(2)
```

But in the case of a property getter or setter, you can do better than that, using the property access syntax:

```
fmt.minimumFractionDigits = 2
```

If the expression `fmt.minimumFractionDigits` occurs to the left of the = operator, it is translated to an invocation of the `setMinimumFractionDigits` method. Otherwise it turns into a call `fmt.getMinimumFractionDigits()`.

You can even use the JavaScript bracket notation to access properties:

```
fmt['minimumFractionDigits'] = 2
```

Note that the argument of the [] operator is a string. In this context, it's not useful, but you can call `fmt[str]` with a string variable and thereby access arbitrary properties.

JavaScript has no concept of method overloading. There can be only one method with a given name, and it can have any number of parameters of any type. Nashorn attempts to pick the correct Java method by looking at the number and types of the parameters.

In almost all cases, there is only one Java method that matches the supplied parameters. If there is not, you can manually pick the correct method with the following rather strange syntax:

```
list['remove(Object)'](1)
```

Here, we specify the `remove(Object)` method that removes the Integer object 1 from the list. (There is also a `remove(int)` method that removes the object at position 1.)

14.3.3 Constructing Java Objects

When you want to construct objects in JavaScript (as opposed to having them handed to you from the scripting engine), you need to know how to access Java packages. There are two mechanisms.

There are global objects java, javax, javafx, com, org, and edu that yield package and class objects via the dot notation. For example,

```
var javaNetPackage = java.net // A JavaPackage object
var URL = java.net.URL // A JavaClass object
```

If you need to access a package that does not start with one of the above identifiers, you can find it in the Package object, such as `Package.ch.cern`.

Alternatively, call the `Java.type` function:

```
var URL = Java.type('java.net.URL')
```

This is a bit faster than java.net.URL, and you get better error checking. (If you make a spelling error such as java.net.Url, Nashorn will think it is a package.) But if you want speed and good error handling, you probably shouldn't be using a scripting language in the first place, so I will stick with the shorter form.

 NOTE: The Nashorn documentation suggests that class objects should be defined at the top of a script file, just like you place imports at the top of a Java file:

```
var URL = Java.type('java.net.URL')
var JMath = Java.type('java.lang.Math')
    // Avoids conflict with JavaScript Math object
```

Once you have a class object, you can call static methods:

```
JMath.floorMod(-3, 10)
```

To construct an object, pass the class object to the JavaScript new operator. Pass any constructor parameters in the usual way:

```
var URL = java.net.URL
var url = new URL('http://horstmann.com')
```

If you aren't concerned about efficiency, you can also call

```
var url = new java.net.URL('http://horstmann.com')
```

 CAUTION: If you use Java.type with new, you need an extra set of parentheses:

```
var url = new (Java.type('java.net.URL'))('http://horstmann.com')
```

If you need to specify an inner class, you can do so with the dot notation:

```
var entry = new java.util.AbstractMap.SimpleEntry('hello', 42)
```

Alternatively, if you use Java.type, add a $ like the JVM does:

```
var Entry = Java.type('java.util.AbstractMap$SimpleEntry')
```

14.3.4 Strings in JavaScript and Java

Strings in Nashorn are, of course, JavaScript objects. For example, consider the call

```
'Hello'.slice(-2) // Yields 'lo'
```

Here, we call the JavaScript method slice. There is no such method in Java. But the call

```
'Hello'.compareTo('World')
```

also works, even though in JavaScript there is no compareTo method. (You just use the < operator.)

In this case, the JavaScript string is converted to a Java string. In general, a JavaScript string is converted to a Java string whenever it is passed to a Java method.

Also note that *any* JavaScript object is converted to a string when it is passed to a Java method with a String parameter. Consider

```
var path = java.nio.file.Paths.get(/home/)
    // A JavaScript RegExp is converted to a Java String!
```

Here, /home/ is a regular expression. The Paths.get method wants a String, and it gets one, even though it makes no sense in this situation. One shouldn't blame Nashorn for this. It follows the general JavaScript behavior to turn anything into a string when a string is expected. The same conversion happens for numbers and Boolean values. For example, 'Hello'.slice('-2') is perfectly valid. The string '-2' is silently converted to the number −2. It is features like this one that make programming in a dynamically typed language such an exciting adventure.

14.3.5 Numbers

JavaScript has no explicit support for integers. Its Number type is the same as the Java double type. When a number is passed to Java code that expects an int or long, any fractional part is silently removed. For example, 'Hello'.slice(-2.99) is the same as 'Hello'.slice(-2).

For efficiency, Nashorn keeps computations as integers when possible, but that difference is generally transparent. Here is one situation when it is not:

```
var price = 10
java.lang.String.format('Price: %.2f', price)
    // Error: f format not valid for java.lang.Integer
```

The value of price happens to be an integer, and it is assigned to an Object since the format method has an Object... varargs parameter. Therefore, Nashorn produces a java.lang.Integer. That causes the format method to fail because the f format is intended for floating-point numbers. In this case, you can force conversion to java.lang.Double by calling the Number function:

```
java.lang.String.format('Unit price: %.2f', Number(price))
```

14.3.6 Working with Arrays

To construct a Java array, first make a class object:

```
var intArray = Java.type('int[]')
var StringArray = Java.type('java.lang.String[]')
```

Then call the `new` operator and supply the length of the array:

```
var numbers = new intArray(10) // A primitive int[] array
var names = new StringArray(10) // An array of String references
```

Then use the bracket notation in the usual way:

```
numbers[0] = 42
print(numbers[0])
```

You get the length of the array as `numbers.length`. To iterate through all values of the `names` array, use

```
for each (var elem in names)
    Do something with elem
```

This is the equivalent of the enhanced `for` loop in Java. If you need the index values, use the following loop instead:

```
for (var i in names)
    Do something with i and names[i]
```

 CAUTION: Even though this loop looks just like the enhanced `for` loop in Java, it visits the index values. JavaScript arrays can be sparse. Suppose you initialize a JavaScript array as

```
var names = []
names[0] = 'Fred'
names[2] = 'Barney'
```

Then the loop `for (var i in names) print(i)` prints `0` and `2`.

Java and JavaScript arrays are quite different. When you supply a JavaScript array where a Java array is expected, Nashorn will carry out the conversion. But sometimes, you need to help it along. Given a JavaScript array, use the `Java.to` method to obtain the equivalent Java array:

```
var javaNames = Java.to(names, StringArray) // An array of type String[]
```

Conversely, use `Java.from` to turn a Java array into a JavaScript array:

```
var jsNumbers = Java.from(numbers)
jsNumbers[-1] = 42
```

You need to use `Java.to` to resolve overload ambiguities. For example,

```
java.util.Arrays.toString([1, 2, 3])
```

is ambiguous since Nashorn can't decide whether to convert to an `int[]` or `Object[]` array. In that situation, call

```
java.util.Arrays.toString(Java.to([1, 2, 3], Java.type('int[]')))
```

or simply

```
java.util.Arrays.toString(Java.to([1, 2, 3], 'int[]'))
```

14.3.7 Lists and Maps

Nashorn provides "syntactic sugar" for Java lists and maps. You can use the bracket operator with any Java `List` to invoke the `get` and `set` methods:

```
var names = java.util.List.of('Fred', 'Wilma', 'Barney')
var first = names[0]
names[0] = 'Duke'
```

The bracket operator also works for Java maps:

```
var scores = new java.util.HashMap
scores['Fred'] = 10 // Calls scores.put('Fred', 10)
```

To visit all elements in the map, you can use the JavaScript `for each` loop:

```
for (var key in scores) ...
for each (var value in scores) ...
```

If you want to process keys and values together, simply iterate over the entry set:

```
for each (var e in scores.entrySet())
    Process e.key and e.value
```

 NOTE: The `for each` loop works for any Java class that implements the `Iterable` interface.

14.3.8 Lambdas

JavaScript has anonymous functions, such as

```
var square = function(x) { return x * x }
    // The right-hand side is an anonymous function
var result = square(2)
    // The () operator invokes the function
```

Syntactically, such an anonymous function is very similar to a Java lambda expression. Instead of an arrow after the parameter list, you have the keyword `function`.

You can use an anonymous function as a functional interface argument of a Java method, just like you could use a lambda expression in Java. For example,

```
java.util.Arrays.sort(words,
    function(s, t) { return s.length - t.length })
    // Sorts the array by increasing length
```

If you turn on ECMAScript 6 syntax by starting `jjs` with the `--language=es6` option, you can use the "arrow function" syntax:

```
java.util.Arrays.sort(words, (s, t) => s.length - t.length);
```

This looks just like a Java lambda expression, except that JavaScript uses a "fat arrow" `=>` where Java uses the `->` symbol.

14.3.9 Extending Java Classes and Implementing Java Interfaces

To extend a Java class, or to implement a Java interface, use the `Java.extend` function. Supply the class object of the superclass or interface and a JavaScript object with the methods that you want to override or implement.

For example, here is an iterator that produces an infinite sequence of random numbers. We override two methods, `next` and `hasNext`. For each method, we provide an implementation as an anonymous JavaScript function:

```
var RandomIterator = Java.extend(java.util.Iterator, {
    next: function() Math.random(),
    hasNext: function() true
}) // RandomIterator is a class object
var iter = new RandomIterator() // Use it to construct an instance
```

 NOTE: When calling `Java.extend`, you can specify any number of superinterfaces as well as a superclass. Place all class objects before the object with the implemented methods.

Another Nashorn syntax extension lets you define anonymous subclasses of interfaces or abstract classes. When `new` *JavaClassObject* is followed by a JavaScript object, an object of the extended class is returned. For example,

```
var iter = new java.util.Iterator {
    next: function() Math.random(),
    hasNext: function() true
}
```

If the supertype is abstract and has only one abstract method, you don't even have to name the method. Instead, pass the function as if it were a constructor parameter:

```
var task = new java.lang.Runnable(function() { print('Hello') })
    // task is an object of an anonymous class implementing Runnable
```

CAUTION: When extending a *concrete* class, you cannot use this constructor syntax. For example,

```
new java.lang.Thread(function() { print('Hello') })
```

calls a `Thread` constructor, in this case the constructor `Thread(Runnable)`. The call to `new` returns an object of class `Thread`, not of a subclass of `Thread`.

If you want instance variables in your subclass, add them to the JavaScript object. For example, here is an iterator that produces ten random numbers:

```
var iter = new java.util.Iterator {
    count: 10,
    next: function() { this.count--; return Math.random() },
    hasNext: function() this.count > 0
}
```

Note that the JavaScript methods `next` and `hasNext` refer to the instance variable as `this.count`.

It is possible to invoke a superclass method when overriding a method, but it is quite finicky. The call `Java.super(obj)` yields an object on which you can invoke the superclass method of the class to which `obj` belongs, but you must have that object available. Here is a way to achieve that:

```
var arr = new (Java.extend(java.util.ArrayList)) {
    add: function(x) {
        print('Adding ' + x);
        return Java.super(arr).add(x)
    }
}
```

When you call `arr.add('Fred')`, a message is printed before the value is added to the array list. Note that the call `Java.super(arr)` requires the `arr` variable, which is being set to the value returned by `new`. Calling `Java.super(this)` does not work—that only gets the JavaScript object that defines the method, not the Java proxy. The `Java.super` mechanism is only useful for defining individual objects, not subclasses.

 NOTE: Instead of calling `Java.super(arr).add(x)`, you can also use the syntax `arr.super$add(x)`.

14.3.10 Exceptions

When a Java method throws an exception, you can catch it in JavaScript in the usual way:

```
try {
    var first = list.get(0)
    ...
} catch (e) {
    if (e instanceof java.lang.IndexOutOfBoundsException)
        print('list is empty')
}
```

Note that there is only one `catch` clause, unlike in Java where you can catch expressions by type. That, too, is in the spirit of dynamic languages where all type inquiry happens at runtime.

14.4 Shell Scripting with Nashorn

If you need to automate a repetitive task on your computer, chances are that you have put the commands in a *shell script*—a script that replays a set of OS-level commands. I have a directory `~/bin` filled with dozens of shell scripts: to upload files to my website, my blog, my photo storage, and to my publisher's FTP site; to convert images to blog size; to bulk-email my students; to back up my computer at two o'clock in the morning.

For me, these are bash scripts, but in the olden days when I used Windows they were batch files. So what is wrong with that? The problem comes once you have a need for branches and loops. For some reason, most implementors of command shells are terrible at programming language design. The way variables, branches, loops, and functions are implemented in bash is simply awful, and the batch language in Windows is even worse. I have a few bash scripts that started out modest but have over time accreted so much cruft that they are unmanageable. This is a common problem.

Why not just write these scripts in Java? Java is quite verbose. If you call external commands via `Runtime.exec`, you need to manage standard input/output/error streams. The Nashorn designers want you to consider JavaScript as an alternative. The syntax is comparatively lightweight, and Nashorn offers some conveniences that are specifically geared towards shell programmers.

14.4.1 Executing Shell Commands

To use the scripting extensions in Nashorn, run

```
jjs -scripting
```

Now you can execute shell commands by including them in backquotes, for example

```
`ls -al`
```

The standard output and standard error streams of the last command are captured in $OUT and $ERR. The exit code of the command is in $EXIT. (By convention, an exit code of zero means success, and nonzero codes describe error conditions.)

You can also capture the standard output by assigning the result of the backquoted command to a variable:

```
var output = `ls -al`
```

You can use the familiar < and > operators to redirect standard input and output:

```
`sort < /etc/group`
`ls -al > /tmp/dir.txt`
```

Use the | operator to pipe the output of one command into the input of another:

```
`ls -al | sort`
```

Use semicolons to separate commands:

```
`cd /usr/bin ; ls -al`
```

14.4.2 String Interpolation

In shell scripts, expressions inside ${...} are evaluated within doubly quoted and backquoted strings. This is called "string interpolation." For example,

```
var cmd = "javac -classpath ${classpath} ${mainclass}.java"
$EXEC(cmd)
```

or simply

```
`javac -classpath ${classpath} ${mainclass}.java`
```

injects the contents of the variables classpath and mainclass into the command.

You can use arbitrary expressions inside the ${...}:

```
var message = "The current time is ${java.time.Instant.now()}"
    // Sets message to a string such as The current time is 2013-10-12T21:48:58.545Z
```

As with the bash shell, string interpolation does not work inside singly quoted strings.

```
var message = 'The current time is ${java.time.Instant.now()}'
    // Sets message to The current time is ${java.time.Instant.now()}
```

Strings are also interpolated in "here documents"—inline documents in a script. These inline documents are useful when a command reads multiple lines from standard input and the script author doesn't want to put the input in a separate file. As an example, here is how you can feed commands to the GlassFish administration tool:

```
name='myapp'
dir='/opt/apps/myapp'
$EXEC("asadmin", <<END)
start-domain
start-database
deploy ${name} ${dir}
exit
END
```

The `<<END` construct means: "Insert the string that starts on the next line and is terminated by the line `END`." (Instead of `END`, you can use any identifier that doesn't appear inside the string.)

Note that the name and location of the application are interpolated.

String interpolation and here documents are only available in scripting mode.

14.4.3 Script Inputs

You can supply command-line arguments to a script. Since it is possible to include multiple script files on the `jjs` command line, you need to separate the script files and arguments with a `--`:

```
jjs script1.js script2.js -- arg1 arg2 arg3
```

In the script file, you receive the command-line arguments in the `arguments` array:

```
var deployCommand = "deploy ${arguments[0]} ${arguments[1]}"
```

You can use `$ARG` instead of `arguments`. If you use that variable with string interpolation, you need two dollar signs:

```
var deployCommand = "deploy ${$ARG[0]} ${$ARG[1]}"
```

In your script, you can obtain the shell's environment variables through the `$ENV` object:

```
var javaHome = $ENV.JAVA_HOME
```

In scripting mode, you can prompt the user for input with the readLine function:

```
var username = readLine('Username: ')
```

Finally, to exit a script, use the exit function. You can supply an optional exit code.

```
if (username.length == 0) exit(1)
```

The first line of a script can be a "shebang," the symbols #! followed by the location of the script interpreter. For example,

```
#!/opt/java/bin/jjs
```

On Linux/Unix/Mac OS X, you can make the script file executable, add the script directory to the PATH, and then simply run it as script.js.

When a script starts with a shebang, scripting mode is automatically activated.

 CAUTION: When you use a shebang in a script with command-line arguments, script users need to supply dashes before the arguments:

```
script.js -- arg1 arg2 arg3
```

Exercises

1. In the JavaServer Pages technology, a web page is a mixture of HTML and Java, for example:

```
<ul>
<% for (int i = 10; i >= 0; i--) { %>
    <li><%= i %></li>
<% } %>
<p>Liftoff!</p>
```

Everything outside <%...%> and <%=...%> is printed as is. Code inside is evaluated. If the starting delimiter is <%=, the result is added to the printout.

Implement a program that reads such a page, turns it into a Java method, executes it, and yields the resulting page.

2. From a Java program, call the JavaScript JSON.parse method to turn a JSON-formatted string into a JavaScript object, then turn it back into a string.

Do this (a) with eval, (b) with invokeMethod, (c) by a Java method call through the interface

```
public interface JSON {
    Object parse(String str);
    String stringify(Object obj);
}
```

3. Is compiling worthwhile with Nashorn? Write a JavaScript program that sorts an array the dumb way, trying all permutations until it is sorted. Compare the running time of the compiled and interpreted version. Here is a JavaScript function for computing the next permutation:

```
function nextPermutation(a) {
    // Find the largest nonincreasing suffix starting at a[i]
    var i = a.length - 1
    while (i > 0 && a[i - 1] >= a[i]) i--
    if (i > 0) {
        // Swap a[i - 1] with the rightmost a[k] > a[i - 1]
        // Note that a[i] > a[i - 1]
        var k = a.length - 1
        while (a[k] <= a[i - 1]) k--
        swap(a, i - 1, k)
    } // Otherwise, the suffix is the entire array

    // Reverse the suffix
    var j = a.length - 1
    while (i < j) { swap(a, i, j); i++; j-- }
}
```

4. Find a Scheme implementation that is compatible with the Java Scripting API. Write a factorial function in Scheme and call it from Java.

5. Pick some part of the Java API that you want to explore—for example, the ZonedDateTime class. Run some experiments in jjs: construct objects, call methods, and observe the returned values. Did you find it easier than writing test programs in Java?

6. Run jjs and, using the stream library, interactively work out a solution for the following problem: Print all unique long words (> 12 characters) from a file in sorted order. First read the words, then filter the long words, and so on. How does this interactive approach compare to your usual workflow?

7. Run jjs. Call

```
var b = new java.math.BigInteger('12345678900987654321')
```

Then display b (simply by typing b and Enter). What do you get? What is the value of b.mod(java.math.BigInteger.TEN)? Why is b displayed so strangely? How can you display the actual value of b?

8. At the end of Section 14.3.9, "Extending Java Classes and Implementing Java Interfaces" (page 459), you saw how to extend ArrayList so that every call to add is logged. But that only worked for a single object. Write a JavaScript function that is a factory for such objects, so that you can generate any number of logging array lists.

9. Write a script that makes a JAR file containing all class files in the sub-directories of a given directory. Derive the JAR file name from the last component of the directory name. Use the JAVA_HOME environment variable to locate the jar executable.

10. Write a script that prints the values of all environment variables.

11. Write a script nextYear.js that obtains the age of the user and then prints Next year, you will be ..., adding 1 to the input. The age can be specified on the command line or in the AGE environment variable. If neither are present, prompt the user.

The Java Platform Module System

Topics in This Chapter

Chapter 15

An important characteristic of object-oriented programming is encapsulation. A class declaration consists of a public interface and a private implementation. A class can evolve by changing the implementation without affecting its users. A module system provides the same benefits for programming in the large. A module can make classes and packages selectively available so that its evolution can be controlled.

Several existing Java module systems rely on class loaders to isolate classes. However, Java 9 introduces a new system, called the Java Platform Module System, that is supported by the Java compiler and virtual machine. It was designed to modularize the large code base of the Java platform. You can, if you choose, use this system to modularize your own applications.

Whether or not you use Java platform modules in your own applications, you may be impacted by the modularized Java platform. This chapter shows you how to declare and use Java platform modules. You will also learn how to migrate your applications to work with the modularized Java platform and third-party modules.

The key points of this chapter are:

1. The Java Platform Module System was designed to modularize the Java platform.

2. You can use the Java Platform Module System to modularize applications and libraries.

3. A module is a collection of packages.

4. The properties of a module are defined in `module-info.java`.

5. A module declares on which other modules it depends.

6. A module provides encapsulation. Accessible packages must be explicitly exported.

7. A module may allow reflective access to private features by opening a package or the entire module.

8. The module system provides support for the `ServiceLoader` facility.

9. A modular JAR is a JAR with a `module-info.class` file that is placed on the module path.

10. By placing a regular JAR on the module path, it becomes an automatic module that exports and opens all of its packages.

11. All packages on the class path form the unnamed module.

12. To migrate existing applications, you may need to override access restrictions with command-line options.

13. The `jdeps` tool analyzes the dependencies of a given set of JAR files. The `jlink` tool produces an application with minimal dependencies.

15.1 The Module Concept

In object-oriented programming, the fundamental building block is the class. Classes provide encapsulation. Private features can only be accessed by code that has explicit permission, namely the methods of the class. This makes it possible to reason about access. If a private variable has changed, you can produce a set of all possible culprits. If you need to modify the private representation, you know which methods are affected.

In Java, packages provide the next larger organizational grouping. A package is a collection of classes. Packages also provide a level of encapsulation. Any feature with package access (neither public nor private) is accessible only from methods in the same package.

However, in large systems, this level of access control is not enough. Any public feature (that is, a feature that is accessible outside a package) is accessible everywhere. Suppose you want to modify or drop a rarely used feature. Once it is public, there is no way to reason about the impact of that change.

This is the situation that the Java platform designers faced. Over twenty years, the JDK grows by leaps and bounds, but clearly some features are essentially obsolete. Everyone's favorite example is CORBA. When is the last time you used it? Yet, the `org.omg.corba` package is shipped with every JDK. As it happens, it would not be too difficult to put all of CORBA into a JAR file so that it can be used by those few who still need it.

What about `java.awt`? It shouldn't be required in a server-side application, right? Except that the class `java.awt.DataFlavor` is used in the implementation of SOAP, an XML-based web services protocol.

The Java platform designers, faced with a giant hairball of code, decided that they needed a structuring mechanism that provides more control. They looked at existing module systems (such as OSGi) and found them unsuitable for their problem. Instead, they designed a new system, called the *Java Platform Module System*, that is now a part of the Java language and virtual machine. That system has been used successfully to modularize the Java API, and you can, if you so choose, use it with your own applications.

A Java platform module consists of:

• A collection of packages

• Optionally, resource files and other files such as native libraries

• A list of the accessible packages in the module

• A list of all modules on which this module depends

The Java platform enforces encapsulation and dependencies, both at compile time and in the virtual machine.

Why should you consider using the Java Platform Module System for your own programs instead of following the traditional approach of using JAR files on the class path? There are two advantages.

1. Strong encapsulation: You can control which of your packages are accessible, and you don't have to worry about maintaining code that you didn't intend for public consumption.

2. Reliable configuration: You avoid common class path problems such as duplicate or missing classes.

There are some issues that the Java Platform Module System does not address, such as versioning of modules. There is no support for specifying which version of a module is required, or for using multiple versions of a module in the same program. These can be desirable features, but you must use mechanisms other than the Java Platform Module System if you need them.

15.2 Naming Modules

A module is a collection of packages. The package names in the module need not be related. For example, the module java.sql contains packages java.sql, javax.sql, and javax.transaction.xa. Also, as you can see from this example, it is perfectly acceptable for the module name to be the same as a package name.

Just like a package name, a module name is made up of letters, digits, underscores, and periods. Also, just as with package names, there is no hierarchical relationship between modules. If you had a module com.horstmann and another module com.horstmann.corejava, they would be unrelated, as far as the module system is concerned.

When creating a module for use by others, it is important that its name is globally unique. It is expected that most module names will follow the "reverse domain name" convention, just like package names.

The easiest approach is to name a module after the top-level package that the module provides. For example, the SLF4J logging façade has a module org.slf4j with packages org.slf4j, org.slf4j.spi, org.slf4j.event, and org.slf4j.helpers.

This convention prevents package name conflicts in modules. Any given package can only be placed in one module. If your module names are unique and your package names start with the module name, then your package names will also be unique.

You can use shorter module names for modules that are not meant to be used by other programmers, such as a module containing an application program. Just to show that it can be done, I will do the same in this chapter. Modules with what could plausibly be library code will have names such as com.horstmann.greet, and modules containing programs (with a class that has a main method) will have catchy names such as ch15.sec03.

 NOTE: You only use module names in module declarations. In the source files for your Java classes, you never refer to module names. Instead, you use package names in the same way that they have always been used.

15.3 The Modular "Hello, World!" Program

Let us put the traditional "Hello, World!" program into a module. First we need to put the class into a package—the "unnamed package" cannot be contained in a module. Here it is:

```
package com.horstmann.hello;

public class HelloWorld {
    public static void main(String[] args) {
        System.out.println("Hello, Modular World!");
    }
}
```

So far, nothing has changed. To make a module `ch15.sec03` containing this package, you need to add a module declaration. You place it in a file named `module-info.java`, located in the base directory (that is, the same directory that contains the `com` directory). By convention, the name of the base directory is the same as the module name.

```
ch15.sec03/
 └ module-info.java
   com/
    └ horstmann/
       └ hello/
          └ HelloWorld.java
```

The `module-info.java` file contains the module declaration:

```
module ch15.sec03 {
}
```

This module declaration is empty because the module has nothing to offer to anyone, nor does it need anything.

Now you compile as usual:

```
javac ch15.sec03/module-info.java ch15.sec03/com/horstmann/hello/HelloWorld.java
```

The `module-info.java` file doesn't look like a Java source file, and of course there can't be a class with the name `module-info`, since class names cannot contain hyphens. The `module` keyword, as well as keywords `requires`, `exports`, and so on, that you will see in the following sections, are "restricted keywords" that have a special meaning only in module declarations. The file is compiled into a class file `module-info.class` that contains the module definition in binary form.

To run this program as a modular application, you specify the *module path*, which is similar to the class path, but it contains modules. You also specify the main class in the format *modulename/classname*:

```
java --module-path ch15.sec03 --module ch15.sec03/com.horstmann.hello.HelloWorld
```

Instead of `--module-path` and `--module`, you can use the single-letter options `-p` and `-m`:

```
java -p ch15.sec03 -m ch15.sec03/com.horstmann.hello.HelloWorld
```

Either way, the "Hello, Modular World!" greeting will appear, demonstrating that you have successfully modularized your first application.

> **NOTE:** When you compile this module, you get two warnings:
>
> ```
> warning: [module] module name component sec03 should avoid terminal digits
> warning: [module] module name component ch15 should avoid terminal digits
> ```
>
> These warnings are intended to discourage programmers from adding version numbers to module names. You can ignore them, or suppress them with an annotation:
>
> ```
> @SuppressWarnings("module")
> module ch15.sec03 {
> }
> ```
>
> In this one respect, the module declaration is just like a class declaration: You can annotate it. (The annotation type must have target ElementType.MODULE.)

15.4 Requiring Modules

Let us make a new module ch15.sec04 in which a program uses a JOptionPane to show the "Hello, Modular World!" message:

```
package com.horstmann.hello;

import javax.swing.JOptionPane;

public class HelloWorld {
    public static void main(String[] args) {
        JOptionPane.showMessageDialog(null, "Hello, Modular World!");
    }
}
```

Now compilation fails with this message:

```
error: package javax.swing is not visible
  (package javax.swing is declared in module java.desktop,
    but module ch15.sec04 does not read it)
```

The JDK has been modularized, and the javax.swing package is now contained in the java.desktop module. Our module needs to declare that it relies on that module:

```
module ch15.sec04 {
    requires java.desktop;
}
```

It is a design goal of the module system that modules are explicit about their requirements, so that the virtual machine can ensure that all requirements are fulfilled before starting a program.

In the preceding section, the need for explicit requireents did not arise because we only used the java.lang package. This package is included in the java.base module which is required by default.

Note that our ch15.sec04 module lists only its own module requirements. It requires the java.desktop module so that it can use the javax.swing package. The java.desktop module itself declares that it requires three other modules, namely java.datatransfer, java.prefs, and java.xml.

Figure 15-1 shows the *module graph* whose nodes are modules. The edges of the graph (that is, the arrows joining nodes) are either declared requirements or the implied requirement on java.base when none is declared.

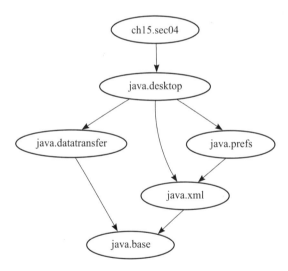

Figure 15-1 The module graph of the Swing "Hello, Modular World!" application

You cannot have cycles in the module graph. That is, a module cannot directly or indirectly require itself.

A module does not automatically pass on access rights to other modules. In our example, the java.desktop module declares that it requires java.prefs, and the java.prefs module declares that it requires java.xml. That does not give java.desktop the right to use packages from the java.xml module. It needs to explicitly declare that requirement. In mathematical terms, the requires relationship is not "transitive." Generally, this behavior is desirable because it makes requirements explicit, but as you will see in Section 15.10, "Transitive and Static Requirements" (page 487), you can relax it in some cases.

 NOTE: The error message at the beginning of this section stated that our ch15.sec04 module did not "read" the java.desktop module. In the parlance of the Java Platform Module System, module *M* *reads* module *N* in the following cases:

1. *M* requires *N*.

2. *M* requires a module that transitively requires *N* (see Section 15.10, "Transitive and Static Requirements," page 487).

3. *N* is *M* or java.base.

15.5 Exporting Packages

In the preceding section, you saw that a module must require another module if it wants to use its packages. However, that does not automatically make all packages in the required module available. A module states which of its packages are accessible, using the exports keyword. For example, here is a part of the module declaration for the java.xml module:

```
module java.xml {
    exports javax.xml;
    exports javax.xml.catalog;
    exports javax.xml.datatype;
    exports javax.xml.namespace;
    exports javax.xml.parsers;
    ...
}
```

This module makes many packages available, but hides others (such as jdk.xml.internal) by not exporting them.

When a package is exported, its public and protected classes and interfaces, and their public and protected members, are accessible outside the module. (As always, protected types and members are accessible only in subclasses.)

However, a package that is not exported is not accessible outside its own module. This is quite different from Java before modules. In the past, you were able to use public classes from any package, even if it was not part of the public API. For example, it was commonly recommended to use classes such as sun.misc.BASE64Encoder or com.sun.rowset.CachedRowSetImpl when the public API did not provide the appropriate functionality.

Nowadays, you can no longer access unexported packages from the Java platform API since all of them are contained inside modules. As a result, some programs will no longer run with Java 9. Of course, nobody ever committed to keeping non-public APIs available, so this should not come as a shock.

Let us put exports to use in a simple situation. We will prepare a module com.horstmann.greet that exports a package, also called com.horstmann.greet, following the convention that a module that provides code for others should be named after the top-level package inside it. There is also a package com.horstmann.greet.internal that we don't export.

A public Greeter interface is in the first package.

```
package com.horstmann.greet;

public interface Greeter {
    static Greeter newInstance() {
        return new com.horstmann.greet.internal.GreeterImpl();
    }

    String greet(String subject);
}
```

The second package has a class that implements the interface. The class is public since it is accessed in the first package.

```
package com.horstmann.greet.internal;

import com.horstmann.greet.Greeter;

public class GreeterImpl implements Greeter {
    public String greet(String subject) {
        return "Hello, " + subject + "!";
    }
}
```

The com.horstmann.greet module contains both packages but only exports the first:

```
module com.horstmann.greet {
    exports com.horstmann.greet;
}
```

The second package is inaccessible outside the module.

We put our application into a second module, which will require the first module:

```
module ch15.sec05 {
    requires com.horstmann.greet;
}
```

NOTE: The `exports` statement is followed by a package name, whereas `requires` is followed by a module name.

Our application now uses a `Greeter` to obtain a greeting:

```
package com.horstmann.hello;

import com.horstmann.greet.Greeter;

public class HelloWorld {
    public static void main(String[] args) {
        Greeter greeter = Greeter.newInstance();
        System.out.println(greeter.greet("Modular World"));
    }
}
```

Here is the source file structure for these two modules:

```
com.horstmann.greet
├ module-info.java
└ com
  └ horstmann
    └ greet
      ├ Greeter.java
      └ internal
        └ GreeterImpl.java
ch15.sec05
├ module-info.java
└ com
  └ horstmann
    └ hello
      └ HelloWorld.java
```

To build this application, first compile the `com.horstmann.greet` module:

```
javac com.horstmann.greet/module-info.java \
    com.horstmann.greet/com/horstmann/greet/Greeter.java \
    com.horstmann.greet/com/horstmann/greet/internal/GreeterImpl.java
```

Then compile the application module with the first module on the module path:

```
javac -p com.horstmann.greet ch15.sec05/module-info.java \
    ch15.sec05/com/horstmann/hello/HelloWorld.java
```

Finally, run the program with both modules on the module path:

```
java -p ch15.sec05:com.horstmann.greet \
    -m ch15.sec05/com.horstmann.hello.HelloWorld
```

You have now seen the requires and exports statements that form the backbone of the Java Platform Module System. As you can see, the module system is conceptually simple. Modules specify what modules they need, and which packages they offer to other modules. Section 15.11, "Qualified Exporting and Opening" (page 489) shows a minor variation of the exports statement.

 CAUTION: A module does not provide a scope. You cannot have two packages with the same name in different modules. This is true even for hidden packages (that is, packages that are not exported.)

15.6 Modules and Reflective Access

In the preceding section, you saw that the module system enforces encapsulation. A module can only access explicitly exported packages from another module. In the past, it was always possible to overcome pesky access restrictions by using reflection. As you have seen in Chapter 4, reflection can access private members of any class.

However, in the modular world, that is no longer true. If a class is inside a module, reflective access to non-public members will fail. Specifically, recall how we accessed private fields:

```
Field f = obj.getClass().getDeclaredField("salary");
f.setAccessible(true);
double value = f.getDouble(obj);
f.setDouble(obj, value * 1.1);
```

The call f.setAccessible(true) succeeds unless a security manager disallows private field access. However, it is not common to run Java applications with security managers, and there are many libraries that use reflective access. Typical examples are object-relational mappers such as JPA that automatically persist objects in databases.

If you use such a library, and you also want to use modules, you have to be careful. To demonstrate this issue, I will use JAXB instead of JPA. (JPA isn't a part of Java SE, but JAXB is, at least for now—its module is deprecated). JAXB can turn arbitrary objects into XML, and conversely turn XML back into objects. You use annotations to direct the process. Here is a trivial class that illustrates the mechanism:

```
package com.horstmann.places;

import javax.xml.bind.annotation.XmlElement;
import javax.xml.bind.annotation.XmlRootElement;

@XmlRootElement
public class Country {
    @XmlElement private String name;
    @XmlElement private double area;

    public Country() {}

    public Country(String name, double area) {
        this.name = name;
        this.area = area;
    }
    // ...
}
```

The @XmlRootElement annotation indicates that objects of this class can be formatted (or "marshalled") into XML, and the @XmlElement annotation is applied to
the fields that should be included in the generated XML.

Here is a short program that demonstrates how to convert an object into XML:

```
package com.horstmann.places;

import javax.xml.bind.JAXBContext;
import javax.xml.bind.JAXBException;
import javax.xml.bind.Marshaller;

public class Demo {
    public static void main(String[] args) throws JAXBException {
        Country belgium = new Country("Belgium", 30510);
        JAXBContext context = JAXBContext.newInstance(Country.class);
        Marshaller m = context.createMarshaller();
        m.setProperty(Marshaller.JAXB_FORMATTED_OUTPUT, true);
        m.marshal(belgium, System.out);
    }
}
```

When you run the program, it prints

```
<country>
    <name>Belgium</name>
    <area>30510.0</area>
</country>
```

As you can see, there is nothing that the programmer needs to do to make this happen. Through reflection, the JAXB library determines the names and values of the fields. (There are numerous ways to tweak the XML that is generated, but those details are not important here. I just use JAXB as an example of a library that uses reflection.)

Now let us put the `Country` and `Demo` classes inside a module. When you do that, the `Demo` program will fail with an exception:

```
Exception in thread "main" java.lang.reflect.InaccessibleObjectException:
    Unable to make field
private java.lang.String com.horstmann.places.Country.name accessible:
module ch15.sec06 does not "opens com.horstmann.places" to module java.xml.bind
```

Of course, in pristine theory, it is wrong to violate encapsulation and poke around in the private members of an object. But mechanisms such as XML binding or object-relational mapping are so common that the module system must accommodate them.

Using the `opens` keyword, a module can *open* a package, which enables runtime access to all types and members in the given package, allowing access of private members through reflection. Here is what our module has to do:

```
module ch15.sec06 {
    requires java.xml.bind;
    opens com.horstmann.places;
}
```

With this change, JAXB will work correctly.

A module can be declared as `open`, such as

```
open module ch15.sec06 {
    requires java.xml.bind;
}
```

An open module grants runtime access to all of its packages, as if all packages had been declared with `exports` and `opens`. However, only explicitly exported packages are accessible at compile time. Open modules combine the compile-time safety of the module system with the classic permissive runtime behavior.

Recall from Section 4.4.2, "Loading Resources" (page 162) that JAR files can contain, in addition to class files and a manifest, *file resources* which can be loaded with the method `Class.getResourceAsStream`, and now also with `Module.getResourceAsStream`. If a resource is stored in a directory that matches a package in a module, then the package must be opened to the caller. Resources in other directories, as well as the class files and manifest, can be read by anyone.

NOTE: It is possible that future libraries will use *variable handles* instead of reflection for reading and writing fields. A VarHandle is similar to a Field. You can use it to read or write a specific field of any instance of a specific class. However, to obtain a VarHandle, the library code needs a Lookup object:

```
public Object getFieldValue(Object obj, String fieldName, Lookup lookup)
        throws NoSuchFieldException, IllegalAccessException {
    Class<?> cl = obj.getClass();
    Field field = cl.getDeclaredField(fieldName);
    VarHandle handle = MethodHandles.privateLookupIn(cl, lookup)
        .unreflectVarHandle(field);
    return handle.get(obj);
}
```

This works provided the Lookup object is generated in the module that has the permission to access the field. Some method in the module simply calls MethodHandles.lookup(), which yields an object encapsulating the access rights of the caller. In this way, one module can give permission for accessing private members to another module. The practical issue is how those permissions can be given with a minimum of hassle.

15.7 Modular JARs

So far, we have simply compiled modules into the directory tree of the source code. Clearly, that is not satisfactory for deployment. Instead, a module can be deployed by placing all its classes in a JAR file, with a module-info.class in the root. Such a JAR file is called a *modular* JAR.

To create a modular JAR file, you use the jar tool in the usual way. If you have multiple packages, it is best to compile with the -d option which places class files into a separate directory. The directory is created if it doesn't already exists. Then use the -C option of the jar command to change to that directory when collecting files.

```
javac -d modules/com.horstmann.greet `find com.horstmann.greet -name *.java`
jar -cvf com.horstmann.greet.jar -C modules/com.horstmann.greet .
```

If you use a build tool such as Maven, Ant, or Gradle, just keep building your JAR file as you always do. As long as module-info.class is included, you get a modular JAR.

Then you can include the modular JAR in the module path, and the module will be loaded.

 CAUTION: In the past, the classes of a package were sometimes distributed over multiple JAR files. (Such a package is called a "split package.") This was probably never a good idea, and it is not possible with modules.

As with regular JAR files, you can specify a main class in a modular JAR:

```
javac -p com.horstmann.greet.jar -d modules/ch15.sec05 `find ch15.sec05 -name *.java`
jar -c -v -f ch15.sec05.jar -e com.horstmann.hello.HelloWorld -C modules/ch15.sec05 .
```

When you launch the program, you specify the module containing the main class:

```
java -p com.horstmann.greet.jar:ch15.sec05.jar -m ch15.sec05
```

When creating a JAR file, you can optionally specify a version number. Use the --module-version parameter, and also add @ and the version number to the JAR file name:

```
jar -c -v -f com.horstmann.greet@1.0.jar --module-version 1.0 -C com.horstmann.greet .
```

As already discussed, the version number is not used by the Java Platform Module System for resolving modules, but it can be queried by other tools and frameworks.

 NOTE: You can find out the version number through the reflection API. In our example:

```
Optional<String> version
    = Greeter.class.getModule().getDescriptor().rawVersion();
```

yields an Optional containing the version string "1.0".

 NOTE: The module equivalent to a class loader is a *layer*. The Java Platform Module System loads the JDK modules and application modules into the *boot layer*. A program can load other modules, using the layer API (which is not covered in this book). Such a program may choose to take module versions into account. Is is expected that developers of programs such as Java EE application servers make use of the layer API to provide support for modules.

TIP: If you want to load a module into JShell, include the JAR on the module path and use the `--add-modules` option:

```
jshell --module-path com.horstmann.greet@1.0.jar \
    --add-modules com.horstmann.greet
```

15.8 Automatic Modules and the Unnamed Module

You now know to put the Java Platform Module System to use. If you start with a brand-new project in which you write all the code yourself, you can design modules, declare module dependencies, and package your application into modular JAR files.

However, that is an extremely uncommon scenario. Almost all projects rely on third-party libraries. Of course, you can wait until the providers of all libraries have turned them into modules, and then modularize your own code.

But what if you don't want to wait? The Java Platform Module System provides two mechanisms for crossing the chasm that separates today's pre-modular world and fully modular applications: automatic modules and the unnamed module.

For migration purposes, you can turn any JAR file into a module, simply by placing it onto a directory in the module path instead of the class path. A JAR without a `module-info.class` on the module path is called an *automatic module*. An automatic module has the following properties:

1. The module implicitly has a `requires` clause for all other modules.

2. All of its packages are exported and opened.

3. If there is an entry with key `Automatic-Module-Name` in the JAR file manifest `META-INF/MANIFEST.MF`, the value becomes the module name.

4. Otherwise the module name is obtained from the JAR file name, dropping any trailing version number and replacing sequences of non-alphanumeric characters with a dot.

The first two rules imply that the packages in the automatic module act as if they were on the class path. The reason for using the module path is for the benefit of other modules, allowing them to express dependencies on this module.

Suppose, for example, that you are implementing a module that processes CSV files and uses the Apache Commons CSV library. You would like to express in your `module-info.java` file that your module depends on Apache Commons CSV.

If you add commons-csv-1.4.jar onto the module path, then your modules can reference the module. Its name is commons.csv since the trailing version number -1.4 is removed and the non-alphanumeric character - is replaced by a dot.

This name might be an acceptable module name because Commons CSV is well known and it is unlikely that someone else will try to use the same name for a different module. But it would be better if the maintainers of this JAR file could quickly agree to reserve a reverse DNS name, preferably the top-level package name org.apache.commons.csv as the module name. They just need to add a line

```
Automatic-Module-Name: org.apache.commons.csv
```

to the META-INF/MANIFEST.MF file inside the JAR. Eventually, hopefully, they will turn the JAR file into a true module by adding module-info.java with the reserved module name, and every other module that refers to the CSV module with that name will just continue to work.

 NOTE: The migration plan to modules is a great social experiment, and nobody knows whether it will end well. Before you put third-party JARs on the module path, check whether they are modular, and if not, whether their manifest has a module name. If not, you can still turn the JAR into an automatic module, but be prepared to update the module name later.

Any class that is not on the module path is part of an *unnamed module*. Technically, there may be more than one unnamed module, but all of them together act as if they were a single module, which is called *the* unnamed module. As with automatic modules, the unnamed module can access all other modules, and all of its packages are exported and opened.

However, *no named module* can access the unnamed module. Therefore, migration to the Java Platform Module System is necessarily a bottom-up process. The Java platform itself is modularized. Next, you modularize libraries, either by using automatic modules or by turning them into true modules. Once all libraries used by your application are modularized, you can turn the code of your application into a module.

15.9 Command–Line Flags for Migration

Even if your programs do not use modules, you cannot escape the modular world when running with Java 9 and beyond. Even if the application code resides on the class path in an unnamed module and all packages are exported and opened, it interacts with the Java platform, which is modularized.

In Java 9, the default behavior is to permit illegal module access but to display a warning on the console for the first instance of each offense. In a future version of Java, the default behavior will change, and illegal access with be denied. In order to give you time to prepare for that change, you should test your applications with the --illegal-access flag. There are four possible settings:

1. --illegal-access=permit is the Java 9 default behavior, printing a message for the first instance of illegal access.

2. --illegal-access=warn prints a message for each illegal access.

3. --illegal-access=debug prints a message and stack trace for each illegal access.

4. --illegal-access=deny is the future default behavior, denying all illegal access.

Now is the time to test with --illegal-access=deny so that you can be ready when that behavior becomes the default.

Consider an application that uses an internal API that is no longer accessible, such as com.sun.rowset.CachedRowSetImpl. The best remedy is to change the implementation. (As of Java 7, you can get a cached row set from a RowSetProvider.) But suppose you don't have access to the source code.

In that case, start the application with the --add-exports flag. Specify the module and the package that you want to export, and the module to which you want to export the package, which in our case is the unnamed module.

```
java --illegal-access=deny --add-exports java.sql.rowset/com.sun.rowset=ALL_UNNAMED \
    -jar MyApp.jar
```

Now suppose your application uses reflection to access private fields or methods. Reflection inside the unnamed module is OK, but it is no longer possible to reflectively access non-public members of the Java platform classes. For example, some libraries that dynamically generate Java classes call the protected ClassLoader.defineClass method through reflection. If an application uses such a library, add the flag

```
--add-opens java.base/java.lang=ALL-UNNAMED
```

A small number of modules in the Java SE platform are not in the java.se aggregator module, and they are not accessible by default. These are the modules java.activation, java.corba, java.transaction, java.xml.bind, java.xml.ws, java.xml.ws.annotation, which contain packages that are a part of the Java EE specification. Java EE application servers include these packages. They would not start up under Java 9 if there were conflicting packages in the Java platform.

You can use these modules from a modular application simply by requiring them in the module descriptor. But if an application is not modularized and you need one of them, you have to add it explicitly. Use the `--add-module` flag when compiling and running the program:

```
java --illegal-access=deny --add-module java.xml.bind -jar MyProg.java
```

 NOTE: The `java.activation`, `java.corba`, `java.transaction`, `java.xml.bind`, `java.xml.ws`, and `java.xml.ws.annotation` modules are deprecated in Java 9 and may be removed from the Java SE platform in a future version.

When adding all those command-line options to get a legacy app to work, you may well end up with the command line from hell. To better manage a multitude of options, you can put options in one or more files which you specify with an @ prefix. For example,

```
java @options1 @options2 -jar MyProg.java
```

where the files `options1` and `options2` contain options for the `java` command.

There are a few syntax rules for the options files:

- Separate options with spaces, tabs, or newlines.
- Use double quotes around arguments that include spaces, such as `"Program Files"`.
- A line ending in a \ is merged with the next line.
- Backslashes must be escaped, such as `C:\\Users\\Fred`.
- Comment lines start with #.

15.10 Transitive and Static Requirements

In Section 15.4, "Requiring Modules" (page 474), you have seen the basic form of the `requires` statement. In this section, you will see two variants that are occasionally useful.

In some situation, it can be tedious for a user of a given module to declare all required modules. Consider for example the `javafx.controls` module that contains JavaFX user interface elements such as buttons. The `javafx.controls` requires the `javafx.base` module, and everyone using `javafx.controls` will also need `javafx.base`. (You wouldn't be able to do much with a user interface control such as a `Button` if you didn't have packages from the `javafx.base` module available.) For that reason, the `javafx.controls` module declares the requirement with the `transitive` modifier:

```
module javafx.controls {
    requires transitive javafx.base;
    ...
}
```

Any module that declares a requirement on `javafx.controls` now automatically requires `javafx.base`.

 NOTE: Some programmers recommend that you should always use `requires transitive` when a package from another module is used in the public API. But that is not a rule of the Java language. Consider for example, the `java.sql` module:

```
module java.sql {
    requires transitive java.logging;
    ...
}
```

There is a single use of a package from the `java.logging` module in the entire `java.sql` API, namely the `java.sql.Driver.parentLogger` method that returns a `java.util.logging.Logger`. It would have been perfectly acceptable to not declare this module requirement as transitive. Then those modules, and only those, who actually use that method would need to declare that they require `java.logging`.

One compelling use of the `requires transitive` statement is an *aggregator* module—a module with no packages and only transitive requirements. One such module is the `java.se` module, declared like this:

```
module java.se {
    requires transitive java.compiler;
    requires transitive java.datatransfer;
    requires transitive java.desktop;
    . . .
    requires transitive java.sql;
    requires transitive java.sql.rowset;
    requires transitive java.xml;
    requires transitive java.xml.crypto;
}
```

A programmer who isn't interested in fine-grained module dependencies can simply require `java.se` and get all modules of the Java SE platform.

Finally, there is an uncommon `requires static` variant that states that a module must be present at compile time but is optional at runtime. There are two use cases:

1. To access an annotation that is processed at compile time and declared in a different module.

2. To use a class in a different module if it is available, and otherwise do something else, such as:

```
try {
    new oracle.jdbc.driver.OracleDriver();
    ...
} catch (NoClassDefFoundError er) {
    // Do something else
}
```

15.11 Qualified Exporting and Opening

In this section, you will see a variant of the exports and opens statement that narrows their scope to a specified set of modules. For example, the javafx.base module contains a statement

```
exports com.sun.javafx.collections to
    javafx.controls, javafx.graphics, javafx.fxml, javafx.swing;
```

Such a statement is called a *qualified export*. The listed modules can access the package, but other modules cannot.

Excessive use of qualified exports can indicate a poor modular structure. Nevertheless, they can arise when modularizing an existing code base. Here, the Java platform designers distributed the code for JavaFX into multiple modules, which is a good idea because not all JavaFX applications need FXML or Swing interoperability. However, the JavaFX implementors liberally used internal classes such as com.sun.javafx.collections.ListListenerHelper in their code. In a greenfield project, one can instead design a more robust public API.

Similarly, you can restrict the opens statement to specific modules. For example, in Section 15.6, "Modules and Reflective Access" (page 479) we could have used a qualified opens statement, like this:

```
module ch15.sec06 {
    requires java.xml.bind;
    opens com.horstmann.places to java.xml.bind;
}
```

Now the com.horstmann.places package is only opened to the java.xml.bind module.

Admittedly, it seems rather brittle to put a dependency on a particular persistence mechanism into the module descriptor. Instead, you could place all classes that need to be persisted into a separate package and open up that package to all modules, so that any persistence mechanism can access it.

15.12 Service Loading

The ServiceLoader class (see Section 4.4.5, "Service Loaders," page 166) provides a lightweight mechanism for matching up service interfaces with implementations. The Java Platform Module System makes it easier to use this mechanism.

Here is a quick reminder of service loading. A service has an interface and one or more possible implementations. Here is a simple example of a simple interface:

```
public interface GreeterService {
    String greet(String subject);
    Locale getLocale();
}
```

One or more modules provide implementations, such as

```
public class FrenchGreeter implements GreeterService {
    public String greet(String subject) { return "Bonjour " + subject; }
    public Locale getLocale() { return Locale.FRENCH; }
}
```

The service consumer must pick an implementation among all offered implementations, based on whatever criteria it deems appropriate.

```
ServiceLoader<GreeterService> greeterLoader = ServiceLoader.load(GreeterService.class);
GreeterService chosenGreeter;
for (GreeterService greeter : greeterLoader) {
    if (...) {
        chosenGreeter = greeter;
    }
}
```

In the past, implementations were offered by placing text files into the META-INF/services directory of the JAR file containing the implementation classes. The module system provides a better approach. Instead of text files, you add statements to the module descriptors.

A module providing an implementation of a service adds a provides statement that lists the service interface (which may be defined in any module) and the implementing class (which must be a part of this module). Here is an example from the jdk.security.auth module:

```
module jdk.security.auth {
    ...
    provides javax.security.auth.spi.LoginModule with
        com.sun.security.auth.module.Krb5LoginModule,
        com.sun.security.auth.module.UnixLoginModule,
        com.sun.security.auth.module.JndiLoginModule,
        com.sun.security.auth.module.KeyStoreLoginModule,
        com.sun.security.auth.module.LdapLoginModule,
        com.sun.security.auth.module.NTLoginModule;
}
```

This is the equivalent of the META-INF/services file.

The consuming modules contain a uses statement.

```
module java.base {
    ...
    uses javax.security.auth.spi.LoginModule;
}
```

When code in a consuming module calls ServiceLoader.load(*serviceInterface*.class), the matching provider classes will be loaded, even though they may not be in accessible packages.

15.13 Tools for Working with Modules

The jdeps tool analyzes the dependencies of a given set of JAR files. Suppose, for example, you want to modularize JUnit 4. Run

```
jdeps -s junit-4.12.jar hamcrest-core-1.3.jar
```

The -s flag generates a summary output:

```
hamcrest-core-1.3.jar -> java.base
junit-4.12.jar -> hamcrest-core-1.3.jar
junit-4.12.jar -> java.base
junit-4.12.jar -> java.management
```

That tells you the module graph:

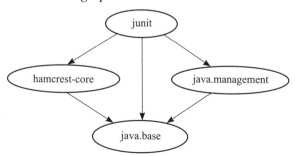

If you omit the -s flag, you get the module summary followed by a mapping from packages to required packages and modules. If you add the -v flag, the listing maps classes to required packages and modules.

The --generate-module-info option produces module-info files for each analyzed module:

```
jdeps --generate-module-info /tmp/junit junit-4.12.jar hamcrest-core-1.3.jar
```

 NOTE: There is also an option to generate graphical output in the "dot" language for describing graphs. Assuming you have the dot tool installed, run these commands:

```
jdeps -s -dotoutput /tmp/junit junit-4.12.jar hamcrest-core-1.3.jar
dot -Tpng /tmp/junit/summary.dot > /tmp/junit/summary.png
```

Then you get this summary.png image:

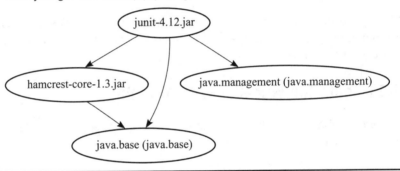

You use the jlink tool to produce an application that executes without a separate Java runtime. The resulting image is much smaller than the entire JDK. You specify the modules that you want to have included and an output directory.

```
jlink --module-path com.horstmann.greet.jar:ch15.sec05.jar:$JAVA_HOME/jmods \
    --add-modules ch15.sec05 --output /tmp/hello
```

The output directory has a subdirectory bin with a java executable. If you run

```
bin/java -m ch15.sec05
```

the main method of the module's main class is invoked.

The point of jlink is that it bundles up the minimal set of modules that is required to run the application. You can list them all:

```
bin/java --list-modules
```

In this example, the output is

```
ch15.sec05
com.horstmann.greet
java.base@9
```

All modules are included in a *runtime image* file lib/modules. On my computer, that file is 23MB, whereas the runtime image of all JDK modules take up 181MB. The entire application takes up 45MB, less than 10% of the JDK which is 486MB.

This can be the basis of a useful tool for packaging an application. You would still need to produce file sets for multiple platforms and launch scripts for the application.

 NOTE: You can inspect the runtime image with the jimage command. However, the format is internal to the JVM, and runtime images are not meant to be generated or used by other tools.

Finally, the jmod tool builds and inspects the module files that are included with the JDK. When you look into the jmods directory inside the JDK, you will find a file with extension jmod for each module. There is no longer a rt.jar file.

Like JAR files, these files contain class files. In addition, they can hold native code libraries, commands, header files, configuration files, and legal notices. The JMOD files use the ZIP format. You can inspect their contents with any ZIP tool.

Unlike JAR files, JMOD files are only useful for linking; that is, for producing runtime images. There is no need for you to produce JMOD files unless you also want to bundle binary files such as native code libraries with your modules.

 NOTE: Since the rt.jar and tools.jar files are no longer included with Java 9, you need to update any references to them. For example, if you referred to tools.jar in a security policy file, change it to a reference to the module:

```
grant codeBase "jrt:/jdk.compiler" {
    permission java.security.AllPermission;
};
```

The jrt: syntax denotes the Java runtime file.

Exercises

1. The "restricted keywords" `module`, `exports`, `requires`, `uses`, `to`, and so on, have specific meanings in module declarations. Can you use them as names for classes? Packages? Modules? In particular, can you make a module called `module`? Try creating a context where you can produce declarations such as the following:

   ```
   requires requires;
   exports exports;
   opens to to opens;
   ```

   How about a module `transitive`? Can you require it?

2. Try accessing `GreeterImpl` in the program in Section 15.5, "Exporting Packages" (page 476) from the `HelloWorld` class. What happens? Is it a compile-time or a runtime error?

3. In the program in Section 15.5, "Exporting Packages" (page 476), use `java.util.logging.Level` to make a `Greeter` return an empty string when the level is less than `Level.INFO`. What is the effect on the module descriptors?

4. What happens if you put the Apache CSV JAR onto the class path as an unnamed module and try accessing its packages from a module? What should you do instead?

5. Develop an example that demonstrates a compelling use for a `requires transitive` dependency on a module such as `java.sql`, `java.xml`, or `java.desktop`.

6. Develop examples for the two uses cases of `requires static`. Would you ever want to have `requires transitive static`?

7. In the program in Section 15.12, "Service Loading" (page 490), what happens if the `provides` or `uses` statements are omitted? Why aren't these compile-time errors?

8. In the program in Section 15.12, "Service Loading" (page 490), use a service provider factory; that is, a class with a public static method `provider()` that returns the service object.

9. Reorganize the program in Section 15.7, "Modular JARs" (page 482) so that the service interface and implementation are defined in separate modules.

10. Download the open source JFreeChart program and use `jdeps` to analyze the dependencies of the demo program and the JAR files in the `lib` subdirectory.

11. Turn the demo program of JFreeChart into a module and the JAR files in the lib subdirectory into automatic modules.

12. Run jlink to get a runtime image of the JFreeChart demo program.

13. Try running a Java 8 version of the JavaFX SceneBuilder program under Java 9. What command-line flags do you need to start it? How did you find out?

Index

Register Your Product at informit.com/register

Access additional benefits and **save 35%** on your next purchase

- Automatically receive a coupon for 35% off your next purchase, valid for 30 days. Look for your code in your InformIT cart or the Manage Codes section of your account page.
- Download available product updates.
- Access bonus material if available.
- Check the box to hear from us and receive exclusive offers on new editions and related products.

InformIT.com—The Trusted Technology Learning Source

InformIT is the online home of information technology brands at Pearson, the world's foremost education company. At InformIT.com, you can:

- Shop our books, eBooks, software, and video training
- Take advantage of our special offers and promotions (informit.com/promotions)
- Sign up for special offers and content newsletter (informit.com/newsletters)
- Access thousands of free chapters and video lessons

Connect with InformIT—Visit informit.com/community

the trusted technology learning source

Addison-Wesley · Adobe Press · Cisco Press · Microsoft Press · Pearson IT Certification · Prentice Hall · Que · Sams · Peachpit Press

 Pearson